TEN STEPS TO ADVANCING COLLEGE READING SKILLS

TEN STEPS TO ADVANCING COLLEGE READING SKILLS

SECOND EDITION

JOHN LANGAN

ATLANTIC COMMUNITY COLLEGE

TOWNSEND PRESS   Marlton, NJ 08053

Books in the Townsend Press Reading Series:

GROUNDWORK FOR COLLEGE READING
KEYS TO BETTER COLLEGE READING
TEN STEPS TO BUILDING COLLEGE READING SKILLS, FORM A
TEN STEPS TO BUILDING COLLEGE READING SKILLS, FORM B
TEN STEPS TO IMPROVING COLLEGE READING SKILLS
IMPROVING READING COMPREHENSION SKILLS
TEN STEPS TO ADVANCING COLLEGE READING SKILLS

Books in the Townsend Press Vocabulary Series:

GROUNDWORK FOR A BETTER VOCABULARY
BUILDING VOCABULARY SKILLS
IMPROVING VOCABULARY SKILLS
ADVANCING VOCABULARY SKILLS
BUILDING VOCABULARY SKILLS, SHORT VERSION
IMPROVING VOCABULARY SKILLS, SHORT VERSION
ADVANCING VOCABULARY SKILLS, SHORT VERSION

Supplements Available for Most Books:

Instructor's Edition
Instructor's Manual, Test Bank and Computer Guide
Set of Computer Disks (Apple, IBM, or Macintosh)

Send book orders and requests for desk copies or supplements to:

Townsend Press
1038 Industrial Drive
Berlin, NJ 08009

For even faster service, call us at our toll-free number:

1-800-772-6410

Or FAX your request to:
1-609-753-0649

ISBN 0-944210-56-2

Contents

PART III
Ten Reading Selections   369

Note: A reading selection concludes each of the ten chapters in Part I. Here are the titles and page numbers of these ten selections:

Preface to the Instructor

We all know that many students entering college today do not have the reading skills needed to do effective work in their courses. A related problem, apparent even in class discussions, is that students often lack the skills required to think in a clear and logical way.

The purpose of TEN STEPS TO ADVANCING COLLEGE READING SKILLS, Second Edition, is to develop effective reading *and* clear thinking. To do so, Part I presents a sequence of ten reading skills that are widely recognized as essential for basic and advanced comprehension. The first five skills concern the more literal levels of comprehension:

- Using vocabulary in context
- Recognizing main ideas
- Identifying supporting details
- Understanding transitions
- Understanding patterns of organization.

The next skill, summarizing and outlining, involves two processes that are a vital part of effective reading, study, thinking, and writing. The remaining four skills cover the more advanced, critical levels of comprehension:

- Distinguishing facts from opinions
- Making inferences
- Identifying purpose and tone
- Evaluating arguments.

In every chapter in Part I, the key aspects of a skill are explained and illustrated clearly and simply. Explanations are accompanied by a series of practices, and each chapter ends with three review tests. The last review test includes a reading selection, so that students can apply the skill just learned to real-world reading materials, including newspaper and magazine articles and textbook selections. Together, the ten chapters provide students with the skills needed for basic and more advanced reading comprehension.

Part II is made up of six mastery tests for each of the ten skills, as well as six combined skills tests. The tests progress in difficulty, providing students with the additional practice and challenge they may need for the solid learning of each skill. While designed for quick grading, the tests also ensure that students must think carefully before answering each question.

Part III consists of ten additional readings that will help improve both reading and thinking skills. Each reading is followed by *Basic Skill Questions* and *Advanced Skill Questions* so students can practice all of the ten skills presented in Part I and reinforced in Part II. In addition, an *Outlining, Mapping, or Summarizing* activity after each reading helps students think carefully about the basic content and organization of a selection. Finally, *Discussion Questions* provide teachers with an opportunity to engage students in a variety of reading skills and to deepen their understanding of a selection.

Important Features of the Book

• **Focus on the basics.** The book seeks to explain in an extremely clear, step-by-step way the essential elements of each skill. Many examples are provided to ensure that students understand each point. In general, the focus is on *teaching* the skills—not just on explaining them and not just on testing them.

• **Frequent practice and feedback.** In the belief that it is largely through abundant practice and careful feedback that progress is made, this book includes numerous activities. Students can get immediate feedback on the practice exercises in Part I by turning to the limited answer key at the back. The answers to the review tests in Part I, the mastery tests in Part II, and the readings in Part III are in the Instructor's Edition as well as in the Instructor's Manual.

The limited answer key increases the active role that students take in their own learning. They are likely to use the answer key in an honest and positive way if they know they may be tested on the many activities and selections for which answers are not provided. (Answers not in the book can be easily copied from the Instructor's Manual and passed out at the teacher's discretion.)

• **High interest level.** Dull and unvaried readings and exercises work against learning. Students need to experience genuine interest and enjoyment in what they read. Teachers as well should be able to take pleasure in the selections, for their own good feeling can carry over favorably into class work. The readings in the book, then, have been chosen not only for the appropriateness of their reading level but also for their compelling content. They should engage teachers and students alike.

• **Ease of use.** The straightforward sequence in each chapter—from explanation to example to practice to review test—helps make the skills easy to teach. The book's organization into three distinct parts also makes for ease of use. Within a single class, for instance, teachers can work on a new skill in Part I, review skills with one or more mastery tests in Part II, and provide variety by having students read one of the selections in Part III. The limited answer key at the back of the text also makes for versatility: it means that the teacher can assign some chapters for self-teaching. Finally, the mastery and combined skills tests—each on its own tear-out page—make it a simple matter for teachers to test and evaluate student progress.

• **Integration of skills.** Students do more than learn the skills individually in Parts I and II. They also learn to apply the skills together through the reading selections that close the chapters in Part I, through the combined-skills tests in Part II, and through the readings in Part III. They become effective readers and thinkers through a good deal of practice in applying a combination of skills.

• **Thinking activities.** Thinking activities in the form of summarizing, outlining, and mapping (using a map, or diagram, to organize material in a highly visual way) are a distinctive feature of the book. While educators agree that such organizational abilities are important, they are all too seldom taught. From a practical standpoint, it is almost impossible for a teacher to respond individually to entire collections of class outlines or summaries. This book seeks, then, to create activities that truly involve students in summarizing and outlining—in other words, that truly make students *think*—and yet that enable a teacher to give feedback. Again, it is through continued practice *and* feedback on challenging material that a student becomes a more effective reader and thinker.

• **Supplementary materials.** The three helpful supplements listed below are available at no charge to instructors using the text. Any or all can be obtained quickly by writing or calling Townsend Press (Pavilions at Greentree—408, Marlton, New Jersey 08053; 800-772-6410).

1   An *Instructor's Edition*—chances are you are holding it in your hand—is identical to the student book except that it also provides both of the following: 1) hints for teachers (see the front of the book); and 2) answers to all the practices and tests.

2   A combined *Instructor's Manual, Test Bank, and Computer Guide* consists of the following:

   a   Suggestions for teaching the course, a model syllabus, readability levels, a complete answer key, and writing activities for each reading selection.

   b   Four additional mastery tests for each of the ten skills, and four additional combined skills tests—all on letter-sized sheets so they can be copied easily for use with students.

    c A computer guide that reproduces the two additional mastery tests for each skill that are on the computer disks available with the book.

3   A *set of computer disks* (in Apple, IBM, and Macintosh formats) that contain two additional mastery tests for each of the ten skill chapters in the book. The disks are self-booting and contain a number of other user- and instructor-friendly features: brief explanations of answers, a sound option, frequent mention of the user's first name, a running score at the bottom of the screen, and a record-keeping score file.

    Since the disk tests are reproduced in the *Computer Guide*, teachers can readily decide just how to use the materials without having to work through each test on the computer. And teachers without a computer lab can copy these tests for use in class as additional mastery tests.

• **One of a sequence of books.** This is the advanced text in a series that includes two other books. TEN STEPS TO BUILDING COLLEGE READING SKILLS is the basic book in the series, and TEN STEPS TO IMPROVING COLLEGE READING SKILLS is an intermediate text.

The BUILDING book is a lower-level book suited for a first college reading course. The IMPROVING book is appropriate for the core developmental reading course offered at most colleges. The ADVANCING book is a slightly higher developmental text than the IMPROVING book. It can be used as the core book for a more advanced class, as a sequel to the intermediate book, or as a second-semester alternative to it.

A companion set of vocabulary books, listed on page iv, has been designed to go with the TEN STEPS books. Recommended to accompany this book is ADVANCING VOCABULARY SKILLS or ADVANCING VOCABULARY SKILLS, SHORT VERSION.

Together, the books and their full range of supplements form a sequence that should be ideal for any college reading program.

To summarize, then, TEN STEPS TO ADVANCING COLLEGE READING SKILLS, Second Edition, provides ten key reading skills to help developmental college students become independent readers and thinkers. Through an appealing collection of readings and a carefully designed series of activities and tests, students receive extensive guided practice in the skills. The result is an integrated approach to learning that will, by the end of a course, produce better readers and stronger thinkers.

Changes in the Second Edition

I am grateful for helpful ideas from many teachers who have either written or spoken to me at conferences about the book over the last couple of years. Based on their suggestions and my own classroom use of the text, I have made some major changes:

- *More progression in the mastery tests from easier to more difficult material.* Students are given a greater challenge, especially with the fifth and sixth tests, which usually feature textbook excerpts.

- *Integration of the individual comprehension skills with the reading selections.* A reading selection now follows each chapter in Part I, so students can immediately apply the skill they have learned to an actual reading. As students move from one chapter to the next, they both apply the new skill learned and review the skills covered in earlier chapters.

- *More tests and practice materials.* There are now six mastery tests instead of five, and there are twenty reading selections, compared to seventeen in the first edition. Completely new are brief content tests for each of the ten skills chapters in Part I; these tests begin the final review test in each chapter. Also new are six combined skills tests—short reading passages followed by questions on a variety of skills. The passages and tests approximate those in typical standardized reading tests. These combination tests will help prepare students for such standardized tests, which are often a requirement at the end of a semester.

- *Many revisions and additions throughout the text.* Most notably, the chapter on summarizing and outlining is new to the book, having replaced a chapter on bias and propaganda. Propaganda is now covered in one of the ten reading selections in Part III. And bias has been moved to a spot where it more logically belongs, in the fact and opinion chapter.

  Users of the first edition will also note that a second color is now used to make the content more readable and visually appealing. They will see that ten of the readings are new and include more material from textbooks; that maps as well as outlines now dramatize the patterns of organization; that the first half of the argument chapter is completely new; and that there have been changes of some kind on virtually every page of the text.

- *An* Instructor's Edition *of the book.* In the special teacher's version of the book, users now have at their fingertips the answers to all of the tests and practices. And starting on the inside front cover of the text is a series of teaching hints that may be of help—especially for people teaching a reading course or using this book for the first time.

Acknowledgments

Thanks to the exceptional design skills of Janet M. Goldstein, the book enjoys a remarkably clear and "user-friendly" format. I owe appreciation as well to others who helped along the way: Dot Carroll, Amy Fisher, Elaine J. Lessig, and Beth Johnson Ruth. I value especially the exceptional editorial role played by Carole Mohr, who has worked closely with me for many months on every page of the book. Thanks to her many insights into the nature of each skill and her unfailing sensitivity to the needs of students, the text is significantly better than it would have been otherwise. It has been a special pleasure to work with colleagues who aspire toward excellence. With them, I have been able to create a much better book than I could have managed on my own.

John Langan

How to Become a Better Reader and Thinker

The chances are you are not as good a reader as you should be to do well in college. If so, it's not surprising. You live in a culture where people watch on the average of *over seven hours of television every day!!!* All that passive viewing does not allow much time for reading. Reading is a skill that must be actively practiced. The simple fact is that people who do not read very often are not likely to be strong readers.

- How much TV do you guess you watch on an average day? _____

Another reason besides TV for not reading much is that you may have a lot of responsibilities. You may be going to school and working at the same time, and you may have a lot of family duties as well. Given a hectic schedule, you're not going to have much time to read. When you have free time, you're exhausted, and it's easier to turn on the TV than to open up a book.

- Do you do any regular reading (for example, a daily newspaper, weekly

  magazines, occasional novels)? _____

- When are you most likely to do your reading? _____

A third reason for not reading is that our public school system may have soured you on it. One government study after another has said that our schools have not done a good job of turning people on to the rewards of reading. If you had to read a lot of uninteresting and irrelevant material in grade and high school, you may have decided (mistakenly) that reading in general is not for you.

- Do you think that school made you dislike reading, rather than enjoy it?

Here are three final questions to ask yourself.

- Do you feel that perhaps you don't need a reading course, since you "already know how to read"? _____

- If you had a choice, would you be taking a reading course? (It's OK to be honest.) _____

- Do you think that a bit of speed reading may be all you need? _____

Chances are that you don't need to read *faster* as much as you need to read *smarter.* And it's a safe bet that if you don't read much, you can benefit enormously from the reading course in which you are using this book.

One goal of the book is to help you become a better reader. You will learn and practice ten key reading comprehension skills. As a result, you'll be able to better read and understand the many materials in your other college courses. The skills in this book have direct and practical value: they can help you perform better and more quickly—giving you an edge for success—in all of your college work.

The book is also concerned with helping you become a stronger thinker, a person able not just to understand what is read but to analyze and evaluate it as well. In fact, reading and thinking are closely related skills, and practice in thoughtful reading will also strengthen your ability to think clearly and logically. To find out just how the book will help you achieve these goals, read the next several pages and do the brief activities as well. The activities are easily completed and will give you a quick, helpful overview of the book.

HOW THE BOOK IS ORGANIZED

The book is organized into three parts:

Part I: Ten Steps to Advancing College Reading Skills (Pages 7–234)

To help you become a more effective reader and thinker, this book presents a series of ten key reading skills. They are listed in the table of contents on page v. Turn to that page to fill in the skills missing below:

1   Vocabulary in Context

2   _____

3   Supporting Details

4   _____

5   Patterns of Organization

6   Summarizing and Outlining

7   Fact and Opinion

8   _____

9   Purpose and Tone

10 _____

Each chapter is developed in the same way. First of all, clear explanations and examples help you *understand* each skill. Practices then give you the "hands-on" experience needed to *review* the skill.

- How many practices are there for the second skill, "Main Ideas" (pages 25–50)? _____

Closing each chapter are three review tests.

- On which pages are the first two review tests for "Main Ideas"? _____

The third review test always consists of two parts: a review of the chapter and a reading selection that gives you a chance both to practice the skill learned in the chapter and to review skills learned in earlier chapters.

- How many questions are asked about the "Main Ideas" chapter (page 45)?

  _____

- What is the title of the reading on page 46? _____

  _____

Part II: Mastery Tests (Pages 235–368)

This part of the book provides mastery tests for each of the ten skills in Part I.

- Look through pages 235–368. How many mastery tests are there for each skill? _____

The test pages are perforated and can be torn out and given to your instructor. There is a scorebox for each test so you can track your progress. Your score can also be entered in the "Reading Performance Chart" at the back of the book.

- Exactly where is this chart located? _____

Part III: Ten Reading Selections (Pages 369–478)

The ten reading selections that make up Part III are followed by activities that give you practice in all of the skills studied in Parts I and II. Turn to the table of contents on page vi and answer the following question:

· Which selection is probably about the conflict in Vietnam? _____

_____

Each reading begins in the same way. Look, for example, at "Writing Effectively in Business," which starts on page 371. What are the headings of the two sections that come before the reading itself?

· _____

· _____

Note that the vocabulary words in "Words to Watch" are followed by the numbers of the paragraphs in which the words appear. Now look at the first reading, "Writing Effectively in Business" (pages 371–375), and explain how each vocabulary word is marked in the reading itself:

· _____

Activities Following Each Reading Selection

After each selection, there are four kinds of activities to improve your reading and thinking skills. Look at those following "Writing Effectively in Business" (pages 375–380). Note that the first activity consists of **basic skill questions**. The second consists of *(fill in the missing words)* _____.
The third activity involves **outlining, mapping,** or **summarizing**. The fourth consists of *(fill in the missing words)* _____.

· Look at the **basic skill questions** for "Writing Effectively in Business" on pages 375–377. You'll see that there are ten questions covering five basic skills. Note that there are always one to three questions for each skill. The questions give you a chance to practice the skills you learned in Part I and strengthened in Part II. How many questions deal with the skill of understanding transitions? _____

· Look at the **advanced skill questions** on pages 377-378. Again, there are ten questions, covering the five more advanced skills. How many questions here deal with making inferences? _____

· The third activity is always **outlining, mapping,** or **summarizing**. Any one of these will sharpen your ability to get to the heart of a piece and to think logically and clearly about what you read. What kind of activity is provided for the reading titled "A & P" on page 414? _____

Note that a **map**, or diagram, is a highly visual way of organizing material. Like an outline, it shows at a glance the main parts of a selection.

- Write down how many **discussion questions** there are for "Writing Effectively in Business" (page 380)—and for every other reading: _____. The questions provide a chance for you to deepen your understanding of each selection.

HELPFUL FEATURES OF THE BOOK

1   The book centers on *what you really need to know* to become a better reader and thinker. It presents ten key comprehension skills, and it explains the most important points about each skill.

2   The book gives you *lots of practice*. We seldom learn a skill only by hearing or reading about it; we make it part of us by repeated practice. There are, then, numerous activities in the text. They are not "busy work," but carefully designed materials that should help you truly learn each skill.

Notice that after you learn each skill in Part I, you read a selection in Review Test 3 that enables you to apply that skill. And as you move from one skill to the next, you continue to practice and reinforce the ones already learned.

3   The selections throughout the book are *lively and appealing*. Dull and unvaried readings work against learning, so subjects have been carefully chosen for their high interest level. Almost all of the selections here are excellent examples of how what we read can capture our attention. For example, take a look at the textbook selection, "Personal Relationships in the Not-So-Good Old Days," on page 84. It is full of surprising details about times past when one's friends counted for more than one's family.

4   The readings include twelve *selections from college textbooks*. Therefore, you are practicing on materials very much like the ones in your other courses. Doing so will increase your chances of transferring what you learn in your reading class to your other college subjects.

HOW TO USE THE BOOK

1   A good way to proceed is to read and reread the explanations and examples in a given chapter in Part I until you feel you understand the ideas presented. Then carefully work through the practices. As you finish each one, check your answers with the "Limited Answer Key" that starts on page 479.

For your own sake, don't just copy in the answers without trying to do the practices! The only way to learn a skill is to practice it first and *then* use the answer key to give yourself feedback. Also, take whatever time is needed to figure out just why you got some answers wrong. By using the answer key to help teach yourself the skills, you will prepare yourself for the review tests at the end of each chapter as well as for the mastery tests and the reading selection tests in the book. Your instructor can supply you with answers to those tests.

If you have trouble catching on to a particular skill, stick with it. In time, you will learn each one.

2   Read the selections with the intent of simply enjoying them. There will be time afterwards for rereading each selection and using it to develop your comprehension skills.

3   Keep track of your progress. In the "Reading Performance Chart" on the inside back cover, enter your scores for the mastery tests in Part II. In addition, fill in the "Check Your Performance" chart at the end of each reading in Part III. These scores can also be entered on the inside-back-cover chart, giving you a good view of your overall performance as you work through the book.

In summary, TEN STEPS TO ADVANCING COLLEGE READING SKILLS has been designed to interest and benefit you as much as possible. Its format is straightforward, its explanations are clear, its readings are appealing, and its many practices will help you learn through doing. *It is a book that has been created to reward effort*, and if you provide that effort, you will make yourself a better reader and a stronger thinker. I wish you success.

John Langan

Part I

TEN STEPS TO ADVANCING COLLEGE READING SKILLS

1

Vocabulary in Context

If you were asked to define the words *candid, quelled,* and *inundated,* you might have some difficulty. On the other hand, if you saw these words in the sentences below, chances are you could come up with fairly accurate definitions. To illustrate, see if you can define the words in *italics* in the three sentences below. Circle the letter of the meaning you think is correct in each case.

Since you want a *candid* opinion of your new pants, I honestly think they are too tight.

Candid means
a. complimentary   b. straightforward and honest   c. creative

The kindergarten teacher *quelled* the racket in her classroom by promising that she'd finish the funny story she had started yesterday.

Quelled means
a. taught   b. recorded   c. quieted

The town was *inundated* with water when the river overflowed during the storm.

Inundated means
a. flooded   b. sprinkled   c. blessed

In the sentences above, the *context*—the words surrounding the unfamiliar word—provides clues to each word's meaning. You may have guessed from the context that a *candid* opinion is a straightforward and honest one, that *quelled* means "quieted," and that *inundated* means "flooded."

Using context clues to understand the meaning of unfamiliar words will help you in several ways:

- It will save you time when reading. You will not have to stop to look up words in the dictionary. (Of course, you won't always be able to understand a word from its context, so you should always have a dictionary nearby as you read.)

- After you figure out the meaning of the same word more than once through its context, it may become a part of your working vocabulary. You will therefore add to your vocabulary simply by reading thoughtfully.

- You will get a good sense of how a word is actually used, including its shades of meaning.

TYPES OF CONTEXT CLUES

There are four common types of context clues:

1   Examples

2   Synonyms

3   Antonyms

4   General Sense of the Sentence or Passage

In the following sections, you will read about and practice using each type. The practices will sharpen your skills in recognizing and using context clues. They will also help you add new words to your vocabulary.

1   Examples

If you are given *examples* that relate to an unknown word, you can often figure out its meaning. To understand how this type of clue works, read the sentences below. An *italicized* word in each sentence is followed by examples that serve as context clues for that word. These examples, which are in **boldfaced** type, will help you figure out the meaning of each word. Circle the letter of each meaning you think is correct.

Note that examples are often introduced with such signal words and phrases as *including* and *such as*.

1.   There was obviously *animosity* between Carmen and Jack—they **glared at each other** and **refused to stay in the same room together**.

Animosity means

a. space   b. nothing   c. ill will

2. The neighborhood is so *affluent* that there are **Olympic-sized swimming pools, tennis courts**, and **luxury cars** on most properties.

   Affluent means
   a. wealthy　　　　　　　b. crowded　　　　　　　c. far away

3. The children had only two *options* after school—either **study at school until their mother picked them up** or **walk the four miles home**.

   Options means
   a. ways to get somewhere　　b. choices　　　　　　c. classes

   In the first sentence, the examples of Carmen and Jack's behavior toward each other suggest that *animosity* means "ill will." In the second sentence, the examples— pools, tennis courts, and luxury cars—show that *affluent* means "wealthy." Finally, the examples in sentence three indicate that *options* means "choices."

➤ Practice 1

In each of the sentences below, underline the examples of the italicized word. Then circle the letter of the meaning of the word in italics.

1. The mayor introduced various *stringent* financial measures, including cutting the police force in half and reducing the pay of all city employees.

   Stringent means
   a. minor　　　　　　　　b. strict　　　　　　　c. expensive

2. My grandmother loves gardening, so her garage is filled with such *implements* as spades, hoes, and rakes.

   Implements means
   a. tools　　　　　　　　b. junk　　　　　　　c. boxes

3. Under the new contract, *stipends* for top employees, including wages and transportation allowances, were increased by 10 percent.

   Stipends means
   a. bonuses　　　　　　　b. payments　　　　　c. charges

4. As they moved westward, early pioneers faced many *adversities,* including unknown routes and loneliness.

   Adversities means
   a. criminals　　　　　　b. decisions　　　　　c. hardships

5. Large crowds, skyscrapers, and subways are characteristic of an *urban* environment.

   Urban means
   a. country　　　　　　　b. central　　　　　　c. city

2   Synonyms

Context clues are often found in the form of *synonyms*: words that mean the same as the unknown word. Synonyms may be purposely included by an author to help readers understand a less familiar word. In such cases, the synonyms are usually set off by special punctuation within the sentence, such as commas, dashes, or parentheses; and they may be introduced by *or* ("Nuptials, or weddings, . . .") and *that is* ("Our work was arduous, that is, difficult . . ."). A synonym may also appear anywhere in a sentence as a restatement of the meaning of the unknown word.

In each of the following sentences, the word to be defined is italicized. Underline the synonym for the italicized word in each sentence.

1.   Gaining the help of a *mentor,* that is, a wise and trusted adviser, is helpful when beginning a new job.

2.   Kim had *fortified* the walls of her sand castle with aluminum cans, but that hadn't strengthened them enough to resist the incoming tide.

3.   The five-year-old girl must have an *innate* musical talent; playing piano that well at her age requires an inborn gift.

(*Hint*: In sentences 2 and 3, a synonym of the italicized word is used later in the sentence to restate the word's meaning.)

You should have underlined "a wise and trusted adviser" as a synonym for *mentor,* "strengthened" as a synonym for *fortified*, and "inborn" as a synonym for *innate*. (Remember, by the way, that you can turn to your dictionary whenever you want to learn to pronounce an unfamiliar word.)

➤ *Practice 2*

Each sentence below includes a word or phrase that is a synonym of the italicized word. Underline the synonym of the italicized word in each case.

1.   I swore not to reveal Anita's secret, but then I did *divulge* it to Ted.

2.   The children tried to *divert*, or distract, the cat until the baby bird could fly to safety.

3.   The trappers left *explicit* directions to their cabin in the mountains. Without those clear directions, we might never have made it there.

4.   "This is a *poignant* book, as it is filled with touching stories of the author's days in a small Southern town," wrote the reviewer.

5.   Stan was convicted of several *felonies;* as a result of being involved in such serious crimes, he was given a sentence of twenty years.

3 Antonyms

Antonyms—words and phrases that mean the opposite of a word—are also useful as context clues. Antonyms are often signaled by words and phrases such as *however, but, yet, on the other hand,* and *in contrast.*

In the sentences below, underline the words that mean the *opposite* of the italicized words; then circle the letter of the meaning of each word in italics.

1. *Novices* at bowling throw more gutter balls than people who are experienced at the game.

   Novices means
   a. experts   b. beginners   c. players

2. The teacher would have achieved better results if she had been as quick to *commend* students for their successes as she was to criticize them for their failures.

   Commend means
   a. blame   b. grade   c. praise

3. Most of my friends' mothers seemed ordinary; mine, however, did such *bizarre* things as speaking to strangers in the supermarket and spraying the dead tree in front of our house green.

   Bizarre means
   a. odd   b. easy   c. dangerous

In the first sentence, *novices* is the opposite of "people who are experienced"; *novices* thus means "beginners." In the second sentence, the opposite of *commend* is "criticize"; *commend* means "praise." Last, *bizarre* is the opposite of "ordinary"; *bizarre* means "odd."

➤ *Practice 3*

Each sentence below includes a word or phrase that is an antonym of the italicized word. Underline the antonym of the italicized word in each case. Then, based on each clue, circle the letter of the meaning of the word in italics.

1. Those who were in agreement with the mayor's tax proposal were in the majority, but there were also some outspoken *dissidents*.

   Definition of *dissidents*:
   a. those in the majority   b. supporters   c. people who disagree

2. It was always hard to know what Uncle Harold was really thinking—was his enthusiasm for the trip *feigned* or genuine?

   Feigned means
   a. secret   b. pretended   c. formal

3. My piano teacher's criticism was always *profuse,* but her praise was scarce.

    Profuse means
    a. loud   b. well-founded   c. plentiful

4. Roberto's mother was *lenient* when he took some money from her dresser drawer, but when he stole candy from the local drugstore, her punishment was harsh.

    Lenient means
    a. not strict in punishing   b. tough   c. complimentary

5. Mom thinks it's *futile* to try to talk Dad into exercising, but I think it could be useful to show him statistics that tell how beneficial exercise is.

    Futile means
    a. unlikely   b. useless   c. sentimental

4   General Sense of the Sentence or Passage

Sometimes it takes a bit more detective work to puzzle out the meaning of an unfamiliar word. In such cases, you must draw conclusions based on the information given. Asking yourself questions about the passage may help you make a fairly accurate guess about the meaning of the unfamiliar word.

Each of the sentences below is followed by a question. Think about the answer to each question, and then circle the letter of the meaning you think is correct.

1. Several times Lucy told the *anecdote* about her winning the hog-calling contest.
    (What would we call the telling of an event?)

    Anecdote means
    a. sermon   b. short story   c. question

2. One argument against capital punishment is that if an innocent person is executed, the mistake cannot be *rectified.*
    (What cannot be done about a mistake as final as an execution?)

    Rectified means
    a. remembered   b. predicted   c. corrected

3. It took two days for volunteers to *extricate* the little girl from the bottom of the well.
    (How would volunteers try to help the trapped girl?)

    Extricate means
    a. free   b. delay   c. remember

The first sentence provides enough evidence for you to guess that *anecdote* means "short story." *Rectified* in the second sentence means "corrected." And *to extricate* means "to free." (You may not hit on the exact dictionary definition of a word by using context clues, but you will often be accurate enough to make good sense of what you are reading.)

➤ Practice 4

Try to answer the question that follows each item below. Then, making a logical guess based on your answer, circle the letter of the meaning you think is correct.

1. My three-year-old likes to fight for her *autonomy* by saying, "I can do it myself."
   (What is being sought with the statement "I can do it myself"?)

   Autonomy means
   a. sister   b. independence   c. toys

2. The puppy had such a *tenacious* grip on my sneakers that I finally decided to wear my loafers instead.
   (What kind of grip would make the speaker choose other footwear?)

   Tenacious means
   a. short   b. firm   c. loose

3. Emily's signature, *embellished* with loops and swirls, was easy to recognize.
   (What do loops and swirls do to the signature?)

   Embellished means
   a. hidden   b. decorated   c. made plain

4. Athletes from all over the world *convened* in Barcelona, Spain, in order to compete in the 1992 Summer Olympic Games.
   (What would the athletes do first before actually competing in the Olympic Games?)

   Convened means
   a. gathered   b. left   c. remembered

5. Hector thought his mother's suggestion to use peanut butter to remove the gum from his hair was *ludicrous*—but it worked!
   (What is a likely first opinion of Hector's mother's suggestion?)

   Ludicrous means
   a. practical   b. delicious   c. ridiculous

A NOTE ON TEXTBOOK DEFINITIONS

You don't always have to use context clues or the dictionary to find definitions. Very often, textbook authors provide definitions of important terms. They usually follow a definition with one or more examples to ensure that you understand the word being defined. Here is a short textbook passage that includes a definition and example:

> People do not always satisfy their needs directly; sometimes they use a substitute object. Such use of a substitute is known as **displacement**. This is the process that takes place, for instance, when you control your impulse to yell at your boss and then go home and yell at the first member of your family who is unlucky enough to cross your path.

Textbook authors, then, often do more than provide context clues: they define a word and provide examples as well. When they take the time to define and illustrate a word, you should assume that the material is important enough to learn.

More about textbook definitions and examples appears on page 105 of the "Patterns of Organization" chapter.

➤ *Review Test 1*

A. Using context clues for help, circle the letter of the best meaning for each word in italics.

1. The dean was *adamant*: "Make up your gym classes or don't graduate, and no arguments."

    a. vague   c. firm
    b. friendly   d. confused

2. There were many things about the library that made it *conducive* to study, including good lighting, quiet, and nearby reference books.

    a. harmful   c. unattractive
    b. cold   d. helpful

3. After the funeral, the widow's friends were very *solicitous*—they came to see her each day and took turns calling every evening to be sure she was all right.

    a. bold   c. annoyed
    b. concerned   d. careless

4. As the six members of the President's staff were charged with various crimes, the public's confidence in the government *eroded;* and once the public trust wears down, it is difficult to rebuild.

   a. deteriorated
   b. healed
   c. grew
   d. repeated

5. Imagine my *chagrin* when I looked in the mirror right after giving a report in front of class—and discovered that on my chin was some of the blueberry pie I had eaten for lunch.

   a. embarrassment
   b. encouragement
   c. pleasure
   d. hatred

B. Using context clues for help, write the definition for each word in italics. Choose from the definitions in the box below. Each definition will be used once.

sociable	by chance	belittling
continuous	backslide	

6. When people are stressed, they often *regress.* My little brother, for example, started to suck his thumb when he first went to camp.

   Definition of *regress* ___b_____

7. Little Amanda hid shyly behind her mother when she met new people, yet her twin brother Adam was very *gregarious.*

   Definition of *gregarious* ___s_____

8. During the argument, the angry woman called her husband such *derogatory* names as "idiot" and "fool."

   Definition of *derogatory* ___be_____

9. The noise in the nursery school classroom was *incessant;* the crying, laughing, and yelling never stopped for a second.

   Definition of *incessant* ___con_____

10. Did you plan to meet your brother for lunch, or was your meeting at the restaurant *fortuitous?*

    Definition of *fortuitous* ___by chance_____

➤ *Review Test 2*

A. Five words are italicized in the two paragraphs below. Write the definition for each italicized word, choosing from the definitions in the box. (Four definitions will be left over.)

weakening	dust	suggest
rock fragments	negatively	narrow
wisely	disbelief	despair

Divorce, death, and demands on family members' time can isolate senior citizens, producing deep loneliness which then *adversely* affects their health. Increasingly, doctors are recommending that lonely older Americans acquire pets to help halt their slide into despair, which is *debilitating* physically as well as mentally. Dogs, cats, parakeets, and other sociable pets can provide seniors with companionship. And caring for their dependent pets gives senior citizens an appreciated and needed feeling—an important preventive to *despondency*. Both pets and their owners win in this relationship.

1. Definition of *adversely:* _____

2. Definition of *debilitating:* _____

3. Definition of *despondency:* _____

Every day almost twenty tons of interplanetary *debris,* including pebbles and boulders the size of cars, come raining down through the atmosphere. In 1988 an asteroid one-half mile in diameter just missed Earth by a matter of six hours, rocketing through space at 44,000 miles per hour only twice the distance from the moon. Eighty years earlier a comet the size of an office building exploded above Siberia, leveling trees for over 750 square miles. Similar incidents this century have inspired nervous scientists to *propose* shooting a rocket armed with nuclear weapons at incoming asteroids to jolt them off course. If the idea that these relatively small bodies that revolve around the sun are really something to fear seems unbelievable, remember that over 1500 asteroids, some the size of mountains, cross and recross Earth's orbit every day.

4. Definition of *debris:* _____

5. Definition of *propose*: _____

B. Use context clues to figure out the meaning of the italicized word in each of the following sentences, and write your definition in the space provided.

6. The lawyer tried to confuse the jury by bringing in many facts that weren't *pertinent* to the case.

Definition of *pertinent:* _____

7. The physician could only *conjecture* about the cause of the bad bruise on the unconscious man's head.

    Definition of *conjecture:* _____

8. Freshman are often *naive* about college at first, but by their second semester they are usually quite sophisticated in the ways of their new school.

    Definition of *naive:* _____

9. We firmly believed that Uncle Albert would be found innocent in court, so we were delighted but not surprised when the jury *exonerated* him.

    Definition of *exonerate:* _____

10. Cosmetic manufacturers often claim that their products can *rejuvenate* the skin, but very few creams have been proven to make skin look younger.

    Definition of *rejuvenate:* _____

➤ *Review Test 3*

A. To review what you've learned in this chapter, answer each of the following questions.

1. Often, a reader can figure out the meaning of a new word without using the dictionary—by paying attention to the word's ___Context___.

2. One type of clue that helps readers figure out the meaning of a new word is the general sense of a ___sentence or passage___.

3. In the sentence below, which type of context clue is used for the italicized word?

    a. example   b. antonym   c. synonym

    In addition to getting a jail sentence, some criminals are required to pay *restitution.* One thief had to pay an elderly woman both the money he stole from her and several thousand dollars for her injuries.

4. In the sentence below, which type of context clue is used for the italicized word?

    a. example   b. antonym   c. synonym

    Many students are simply *passive* during lectures, but it is more productive to be active, taking notes and asking yourself questions about what is being said.

5. Often when textbook authors introduce a new word, they provide you with a ___def.___ and follow it with ___ex.___ that help make the meaning of the word clear.

B. Does most of the conversation in your household come from the television set? In the following article, Robert Mayer suggests an alternative. Here is a chance to apply the skill of understanding vocabulary in context to a full-length selection. After reading the selection, answer the vocabulary questions that follow.

Words to Watch

Following are some words in the reading that do not have strong context support. Each word is followed by the number of the paragraph in which it appears and its meaning there.

> *slack* (2): loose
> *byword* (5): slogan
> *byproduct* (7): side effect
> *pompous* (14): given an exaggerated importance
> *drivel* (14): nonsense

THE QUIET HOUR

Robert Mayer

What would you consider an ideal family evening? Call me a romantic, but that question calls up in my mind pictures of parents and children lingering around the dinner table to cozily discuss the day's events; munching popcorn from a common bowl as they engage in the friendly competition of a board game; or perhaps strolling through their neighborhood on an early summer evening, stopping to chat with friends in their yards. 1

Let me tell you what "an ideal family evening" does not conjure up for me: the image of a silent group of people—the intimate word "family" seems hardly to apply— bathed in the faint blue light of a television screen that barely illuminates their glazed eyes and slack° jaws. 2

Yet we all know that such a scenario is the typical one. I would like to suggest a different scenario. I propose that for sixty to ninety minutes each evening, right after the early-evening news, all television broadcasting in the United States be prohibited by law. Let us pause for a moment while the howls of protest subside. 3

Now let us take a serious, reasonable look at what the results might be if such a proposal were adopted. 4

New Explorations

Without the distraction of the tube, families might sit around together after dinner and actually talk to one another. It is a byword° in current psychology that many of our emotional problems—everything, in fact, from the generation gap to the soaring divorce rate to some forms of mental illness—are caused at least in part by failure to communicate. We do not tell each other what is bothering us. Resentments build. The 5 result is an emotional explosion of one kind or another. By using the quiet family hour to discuss our problems, we might get to know each other better, and to like each other better.

On evenings when such talk is unnecessary, families could rediscover more active pastimes. Freed from the chain of the tube, forced to find their own diversions, they might take a ride together to watch the sunset. Or they might take a walk together (remember feet?) and explore the neighborhood with fresh, innocent eyes. 6

Pros and Cons

With time to kill and no TV to slay it for them, children and adults alike might rediscover reading. There is more entertainment and intellectual nourishment in a decent book than in a month of typical TV programming. Educators report that the generation growing up under television can barely write an English sentence, even at the college level. Writing is often learned from reading. A more literate new generation could be a major byproduct° of the quiet hour. 7

A different form of reading might also be dug up from the past: reading aloud. Few pastimes bring a family closer together than gathering around and listening to Mother or Father read a good story. 8

It has been forty years since my mother read to me, a chapter a night, from *Tom Sawyer*. After four decades, the white-washing of the fence, Tom and Becky in the cave, Tom at his own funeral remain more vivid in my mind than any show I have ever seen on TV. 9

When the quiet hour ends, the networks might even be forced to come up with better shows in order to lure us back from our newly discovered diversions. 10

Now let us look at the other side of the proposal. What are the negatives? 11

At a time when "big government" is becoming a major political bugaboo, a television-free hour created by law would be attacked as further intrusion by the government on people's lives. But that would not be the case. Television stations already must be federally licensed. A simple regulation making TV licenses invalid for sixty to ninety minutes each evening would hardly be a major violation of individual freedom. 12

It will be argued that every television set ever made has an "off" knob; that any family that wants to sit down and talk, or go for a drive, or listen to music, or read a book need only switch off the set, without interfering with the freedom of others to watch. That is a strong, valid argument—in theory. But in practice, it doesn't hold up. Twenty-five years of saturation television have shown us the hypnotic lure of the tube. Television viewing tends to expand to fill the available time. What's more, what is this "freedom to watch" of which we would be deprived? It is the freedom to watch three or four quiz shows and mediocre sitcoms. That's all. In practice, the quiet hour would not limit our freedom; it would expand it. It would revitalize a whole range of activities that have wasted away in the consuming glare of the tube. 13

A Radical Notion?

Economically, the quiet hour would produce screams of outrage from the networks, which would lose an hour or so of prime-time advertising revenues; and from 14 the sponsors, who would have that much less opportunity to peddle us deodorants and hemorrhoid preparations while we are trying to digest our dinners. But given the vast sums the networks waste on such pompous° drivel° as almost any of the TV "mini-series," I'm sure they could make do. The real question is, how long are we going to keep passively selling our own and our children's souls to keep Madison Avenue on Easy Street?

At first glance, the notion of a TV-less hour seems radical. What will parents do   15
without the electronic baby-sitter? How will we spend the quiet? But it is not radical at all. It has been only about thirty-five years since television came to dominate American free time. Those of us 45 and older can remember television-free childhoods, spent partly with radio—which at least involved the listener's imagination—but also with reading, learning, talking, playing games, inventing new diversions, creating fantasylands.

It wasn't that difficult. Honest.   16

The truth is, we had a ball.   17

Vocabulary Questions

Use context clues to help you decide on the best definition for each italicized word. Then circle the letter of each of your answers.

1. The word *lingering* in "an ideal family evening . . . calls up in my mind pictures of parents and children lingering around the dinner table to cozily discuss the day's events" (paragraph 1) means
   a. rushing.
   b. leaving.
   c. staying.
   d. arguing.

2. The words *conjure up* in "an ideal family evening . . . calls up in my mind pictures of parents and children lingering around the dinner table. . . . Let me tell you what 'an ideal family evening' does not conjure up for me: the image of a silent group of people . . . bathed in the faint blue light of a television screen" (paragraph 2) mean
   a. provide help.
   b. question.
   c. bring to mind.
   d. break.

3. The word *scenario* in "a silent group of people . . . bathed in the faint blue light of a television screen that barely illuminates their glazed eyes and slack jaws . . . such a scenario is the typical one" (paragraph 3) means
   a. imagined scene.
   b. television show.
   c. light.
   d. achievement.

4. The word *subside* in "I propose that for sixty to ninety minutes each evening
. . . all television broadcasting in the United States be prohibited by law. Let us
pause for a moment while the howls of protest subside" (paragraph 3) means
   a. investigate.
   b. persuade.
   c. inform.
   d. quiet down.

5. The word *distraction* in "Without the distraction of the tube, families might
sit around together after dinner and actually talk to one another" (paragraph
5) means
   a. cost.
   b. attention-grabbing.
   c. principle.
   d. dislike.

6. The word *diversions* in "forced to find their own diversions, they might take
a ride together to watch the sunset. Or they might take a walk together
(remember feet?) and explore the neighborhood" (paragraph 6) means
   a. facts.
   b. stories.
   c. pastimes.
   d. friends.

7. The word *slay* in "With time to kill and no TV to slay it for them, children
and adults alike might rediscover reading" (paragraph 7) means
   a. build up.
   b. forget.
   c. rediscover.
   d. kill.

8. The word *literate* in "children and adults alike might rediscover reading. . . .
Writing is often learned from reading. A more literate new generation could
be a major byproduct of the quiet hour" (paragraph 7) means
   a. able to read and write.
   b. active outdoors.
   c. having a close family.
   d. being understanding of others.

9. The word *revitalize* in "the quiet hour . . . would revitalize a whole range of
activities that have wasted away in the consuming glare of the tube"
(paragraph 13) means
   a. bury.
   b. bring new life to.
   c. cleverly invent.
   d. follow.

10. The word *radical* in "At first glance, the notion of a TV-less hour seems radical. What will parents do without the electronic baby-sitter? . . . But it is not radical at all. It has been only about thirty-five years since television came to dominate American free time" (paragraph 15) means
    a. secure.
    b. extreme.
    c. useful.
    d. old-fashioned.

2

Main Ideas

More than any other skill, recognizing main ideas leads to good reading comprehension. The basic question you should ask about any selection that you read is, "What is the main point the author is trying to make?" To begin to better understand how to find an author's main point, read the following paragraph and the explanation that follows it.

> Does watching violence on television make people more prone to violence themselves? Clearly, TV violence does affect people in negative ways. One study showed that people who watch a great deal of television are especially fearful and suspicious of others. They try to protect themselves from the outside world with extra locks on the doors, guard dogs, and guns. That same study also showed that heavy TV watchers become less upset about real-life violence than non-TV watchers. It seems that the constant violence they see on TV makes them less sensitive to the real thing. Another study, of a group of children, found that TV violence increases aggressive behavior. Children who watched violent shows were more willing to hurt another child in games where they are given a choice between helping or hurting. They were also more likely to select toy weapons over other kinds of playthings.

To discover the main point, it is often useful first to determine what topic is being discussed. In the above paragraph, for example, the topic is "violence on television"; the main idea about the topic is that "TV violence does affect people in negative ways." The rest of the paragraph then supports that idea by detailing the negative ways.

The purpose of this and the following chapter is to give you a solid sense of the two key parts in any communication:

- the *main idea*—the main point of any communication;
- the *supporting details*—the specific ideas that explain and support the main idea.

In relation to the supporting details, the main idea is *general*. In the above paragraph, for instance, the main point is the general statement "TV violence does affect people in negative ways." The supporting details are all of the more specific ideas naming and illustrating those weaknesses.

AN OVERVIEW: TOPIC, MAIN IDEA, SUPPORTING DETAILS

To fully understand any selection that you read, you must find the main idea and its supporting details. One way to find the main idea is to use a two-step process:

1 Find the topic.
2 Then find the writer's primary point about that topic. You will now have the main idea.

Any selection that you read will be about a particular topic. The *topic* is a selection's general subject. The topic of a paragraph, for example, might be "Children Today."

Topic: Children Today

In contrast, the *main idea* is the writer's primary point *about* the subject. The main idea of the paragraph on children might be that children today face special challenges in growing up.

Topic: Children Today
Main idea: Children today face special challenges in growing up.

The rest of the paragraph—the supporting details—might be a few sentences that give examples of the special challenges. Think about children you know or have heard about. What special challenges do they face? Write down in the spaces below two examples of challenges faced by today's children.

Topic: Children Today
Main idea: Children today face special challenges in growing up.
Supporting details:

_____

_____

Compare what you have written with challenges faced by some children I know. In one case, a young elementary school girl comes home every day after school to an empty house. She has no brothers or sisters, and her parents work in a nearby big city. They don't get home until about six-thirty in the evening. They can't afford a babysitter. Because they don't want their daughter in any danger, they insist that she stay indoors at home after school. Thus the girl spends a large percentage of her time alone, indoors, and often in front of a television set. Another family I know lives in the inner city. They are a wholesome family. Yet their children are exposed to drug dealers and gang violence almost every day on their way to and from school.

I could easily write a paragraph about children. The topic would be children today, the main idea would be that they face special challenges in growing up, and the evidence would be supporting details such as the ones provided above. My paragraph would be typical of paragraphs in general: it would have a topic, a main idea about the topic, and details that develop the main idea.

Note that in longer selections made up of many paragraphs, such as articles or textbook chapters, there is an overall main idea called the *central point* or *thesis*. There may also be a number of intermediate and smaller main ideas within a long selection.

This chapter focuses on finding the main idea in a paragraph, and the next chapter focuses on identifying supporting details. Once you can identify main ideas and details on the level of the paragraph, you can begin to identify them as well in the longer selections that are included in this book.

MORE ON USING THE TOPIC TO FIND THE MAIN IDEA

Remember that the *topic* is the subject of a selection. It is a general term that can usually be expressed in a few words. Textbooks typically give the overall topic of each chapter in the title of the chapter; they also provide many topics and subtopics in boldface headings within the chapter. Most magazine and journal articles, as well, give you the topic in the title of the piece.

To find the topic of a selection for which there is no title, ask the simple question, "Who or what is the selection about?" Ask this question as you read carefully the paragraph that follows. Then write, on the line below, what you think the topic is.

Topic: _____

Flextime, or flexibility of working hours, has become popular in recent years. Many companies have found that flextime has several advantages. The most obvious advantage is less absenteeism. When employees can choose working hours that meet their needs, they are less likely to take time off. Another advantage is more efficient use of the physical plant. The additional hours that a company is "open for business" could mean higher productivity and greater profits. Finally, giving employees a choice of working hours permits them more control over their work environment, leading to increased job satisfaction and less turnover.

The first sentence suggests that the topic of this paragraph is flextime. And as you read the paragraph, you see that everything has to do with that topic. Thus your first impression in this case was correct—the topic *is* flextime. Once you have the topic, your next step is to ask, "What is the author's primary point about the topic?" The answer will be the main idea of the paragraph. Read the flextime paragraph again, and then write down in the space below the author's main point about flextime:

Main idea: _____

At first the main idea about the topic, flextime, may seem to be that it has become popular in recent years. But as we read on, we see that the paragraph discusses some reasons for that popularity—that is, the advantages of flextime to companies. Since the main idea is a general idea that summarizes what an entire paragraph is about, the main idea in this case is that flextime has several advantages for companies.

The main idea is thus an "umbrella" statement under which the other material in the paragraph fits. In the case of the paragraph about flextime, the other material is in the form of specific advantages that back up the main idea. The parts of the paragraph can be shown as follows:

Topic: Flextime

Main idea: Flextime offers several advantages to companies.

Supporting details:

1. Flextime results in less absenteeism.

2. Flextime allows for more efficient use of the physical plant.

3. Flextime leads to increased job satisfaction and thus less worker turnover.

The following activities will sharpen your sense of the difference between the topic of a selection and the main idea of that selection.

➤ *Practice 1*

Circle the letter of the correct topic of each paragraph. (To find the topic, remember to ask yourself, "Who or what is the paragraph about?") Then circle the letter of the main idea—the author's main point about the topic.

1. Some wedding customs of other times and cultures were notably dramatic. For example, in ancient Rome, grooms carried their brides over the threshold. Before they did, however, they smeared the doorposts with fat and wrapped them in wool to banish evil spirits. In old Mexico, bridal couples shaved their heads to show that they had set aside childish ideas and welcomed the responsibilities of marriage. And, in 18th-century England, the groom's mother broke a loaf of bread over the bride's head as the bride entered her new home. This, they believed, ensured future happiness for the married couple.

Topic:

a. Other Cultures

b. Customs in Old Mexico and 18th-Century England

c. Our Own Wedding Customs

d. Wedding Customs of Other Times and Cultures

Main idea:

a. Our own wedding customs are colorful.

b. Customs of old Mexico and 18th-century England were dramatic.

c. Some wedding customs of other times and cultures were quite dramatic.

d. Other cultures and other times had some unusually dramatic customs.

2. Smoking has been proven dangerous to people's health, yet many continue to smoke for various reasons. For young people, smoking often represents maturity and individuality. Many smoke as a way to reduce tension. In addition, the regular smoker becomes addicted psychologically and physically to the nicotine in cigarettes.

Topic:

a. Health

b. Smoking

c. Addiction

d. Nicotine

Main idea:

a. Smoking has been proven dangerous to people's health in various ways.

b. Regular smokers become addicted to nicotine.

c. Although smoking is dangerous, people continue doing it for various reasons.

d. Nicotine is what smokers become addicted to, both psychologically and physically.

3. Five years after his earthquake experience, one man claims that even the rocking of a boat is fearful for him. A young woman who survived an earthquake several years ago says that every loud noise she hears now makes her dive for cover. And another person who experienced an earthquake tells how he always plans an escape route every time he enters a building. Apparently, experiencing an earthquake can affect a person's sense of security for a long time.

Topic:

a. A Sense of Security

b. Frightening Experiences

c. Experiencing an Earthquake

d. Loud Noises

Main idea:

a. Experiencing an earthquake can affect one's sense of security for a long time.

b. Frightening experiences of all types can influence people long after the events have occurred.

    c. Loud noises make one person who experienced an earthquake dive for cover.

    d. There are various types of frightening experiences, including earthquakes.

4.   Small talk is a useful way to find out what interests we share with the other person. It serves other purposes as well. It provides a way to "audition" the other person—to help us decide whether a relationship is worth pursuing. Small talk is a safe way to ease into a relationship. Finally, small talk does provide some kind of link to others; it's often better than being alone.

Topic:

a. Auditioning Others   c. Relationships

b. Small Talk   d. Conversations

Main idea:

a. Small talk is a safe way to ease into a relationship.

b. Very few people enjoy being alone.

c. Small talk serves a number of purposes.

d. Small talk is often considered unimportant.

THE TOPIC SENTENCE

In a paragraph, authors often give readers the main idea in a single sentence called the *topic sentence*. For example, look again at the paragraph on TV violence:

> Does watching violence on television make people more prone to violence themselves? Clearly, TV violence does affect people in negative ways. One study showed that people who watch a great deal of television are especially fearful and suspicious of others. They try to protect themselves from the outside world with extra locks on the doors, guard dogs, and guns. That same study also showed that heavy TV watchers become less upset about real-life violence than non-TV watchers. It seems that the constant violence they see on TV makes them less sensitive to the real thing. Another study, of a group of children, found that TV violence increases aggressive behavior. Children who watched violent shows were more willing to hurt another child in games where they are given a choice between helping or hurting. They were also more likely to select toy weapons over other kinds of playthings.

As we have already seen, the topic of this paragraph is "TV violence," and the primary point about TV violence is that it "does affect people in negative ways." Both the topic and the point about the topic are expressed in the second sentence, which is therefore the topic sentence. All the sentences that follow provide details about the negative ways in which people are affected by TV violence. The parts of the paragraph can be shown as follows:

Topic: TV violence

Main idea (expressed in the topic sentence): TV violence does affect people in negative ways.

Supporting details:

1. Heavy TV watchers are especially fearful and suscipious.

2. Heavy TV watchers are less upset about real-life violence.

3. Children watching violent shows increase aggressive behavior.

Now read the paragraph below and try to find the topic sentence, the sentence that states its main idea. Test a statement that you think is the main idea by asking, "Is this statement supported by all or most of the other material in the paragraph?" Write the number of the sentence you choose in the space provided. Then read the explanation that follows.

Topic sentence: _____

1For most Americans, work is more than merely a means to food, shelter, and physical warmth. 2When people work, they gain a contributing place in society. 3The fact that they receive pay for their work indicates that what they do is needed by other people, and that they are a necessary part of the social fabric. 4Work is also a major social mechanism for providing people with personal and social identities. 5Much of who individuals are, to themselves and others, is interwoven with how they earn their livelihood. 6In the United States, it is a blunt and ruthlessly public fact that to do nothing is to be nothing and to do little is to be little. 7Work is commonly seen as the measure of an individual.

After thinking about the paragraph, you may have decided that the first sentence is the topic sentence. If so, you should have checked yourself by asking, "Does the other material in the paragraph support the idea that work is more than food, shelter, and physical warmth?" In fact, the rest of the paragraph does discuss two other values of work: it provides a contributing place in society as well as personal and social identities. By asking and answering a basic question, you have made it clear that the first sentence is indeed the topic sentence.

The important hint given above for finding the topic sentence and main idea is worth repeating: *Always test what you think is the main idea by asking the question, "Is this statement supported by all or most of the other material in the paragraph?"*

➤ *Practice 2*

This exercise will give you more practice in distinguishing between a topic (the general subject), a main idea (the primary point being made about the subject), and the specific ideas that support and develop the main idea. Each of the following groups includes one topic, one main idea (topic sentence), and two supporting details. In the space provided, label each item with one of the following:

> *T*   (for *Topic*)
> *MI*   (for *Main Idea*, expressed in a topic sentence)
> *SD*   (for *Supporting Detail*)

Group 1

_SD_ a. Instead of stepping into a snapping device, the mouse enters a plastic box with a small hole at each end.

_MI_ b. A new type of mousetrap provides greater safety for children and pets.

_SD_ c. The poison is in a block form that won't crumble or fall out of its tray.

_T_ d. A new type of mousetrap.

Group 2

_MI_ a. Shopping at a catalogue store isn't as satisfying for us as going to a regular department store.

_SD_ b. We don't get to look at the merchandise before buying it.

_T_ c. Shopping at a catalogue store.

_SD_ d. The catalogue salesclerks don't seem to know much about the products they sell.

Group 3

_SD_ a. In later adulthood, we begin to come to terms with our own mortality.

_T_ b. Stages of human development.

_SD_ c. Adolescence is typically a time of identity crisis.

_MI_ d. According to psychologists, we pass through various stages of human development throughout our lives.

Group 4

____T____ a. Food coupons for the homeless.

____MI____ b. Food coupons are redeemed for food, not drugs or alcohol, thereby reducing a city's drug abuse problem.

____SO____ c. Food coupons bring the homeless into city-run kitchens, from where they can be referred to other needed social services.

____SO____ d. Cities should make food coupons for the homeless available for purchase.

LOCATIONS OF THE TOPIC SENTENCE

In one of the paragraphs considered in this chapter, the topic sentence was the first sentence of the paragraph: "For most Americans, work is more than merely a means to food, shelter, and physical warmth." That is a common pattern, but not the only one. Topic sentences may also appear within the paragraph. For example, the topic sentence of the flextime paragraph is the second sentence: "Many companies have found that flextime has several advantages." Topic sentences may also appear at the very end of a paragraph. Or they may even appear twice—at the beginning and the end.

Within a Paragraph

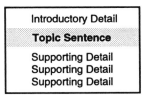

When the topic sentence appears somewhere *within* a paragraph, it is preceded by one or more introductory sentences that may relate the main idea to the previous paragraph, arouse the reader's interest, give background for the main idea, or provide support for the as yet unstated main idea. Here is an example of a paragraph in which the topic sentence is somewhere in the middle. Try to find it, and then write its number in the space provided. Then read the explanation that follows.

Topic sentence: _____

[1]A television ad for a new sports car showed scenes of beautiful open country. [2]The car never appeared in the ad at all. [3]An ad for a hotel chain showed a romantic couple in bed together. [4]They are obviously on vacation and having a leisurely, romantic, sexy morning. [5]As these ads suggest, advertisers often try to sell products by associating them with certain images rather than with strictly realistic details about the products. [6]In the sports car ad, for example, the image is freedom and adventure. [7]An ad of a freeway traffic jam might be more honest and realistic—but it would not sell very many cars. [8]Nor does the hotel's ad show us its usual customer—a tired business person crawling out of bed to get ready for an early-morning meeting in a strange city.

If you thought the fifth sentence gives the main idea, you were correct. The first four sentences introduce the topic and provide specific examples of the main idea. The fifth sentence then gives the writer's main idea, which is that advertisers often try to sell their products by associating them with appealing images rather than with realistic details. The rest of the paragraph continues to develop that idea.

End of a Paragraph

```
┌─────────────────────────────┐
│     Supporting Detail       │
│     Supporting Detail       │
│     Supporting Detail       │
│     Supporting Detail       │
│ ▒▒▒▒▒▒Topic Sentence▒▒▒▒▒▒ │
└─────────────────────────────┘
```

When the topic sentence is at the end of a paragraph, the previous sentences build up to the main idea. Here is an example of a paragraph in which the topic sentence comes last.

A study at one prison showed that owning a pet can change a hardened prison inmate into a more caring person. Another study discovered that senior citizens, both those living alone and those in nursing homes, became more interested in life when they were given pets to care for. Even emotionally disturbed children have been observed to smile and react with interest if there is a cuddly kitten or puppy to hold. **Animals, then, can be a means of therapy for many kinds of individuals.**

Beginning and End of a Paragraph

Topic Sentence
Supporting Detail
Supporting Detail
Supporting Detail
Topic Sentence

Even though paragraphs have only one main idea, they may include two topic sentences, with each providing the main idea in different words. In such cases, the topic sentences are often at the beginning and the end. In these cases, the author has chosen to introduce the main idea at the start of the paragraph and then emphasize it by restating it in other words at the end. Such is the case in the following paragraph.

> **We are on our way to becoming a cashless, checkless society, a trend that began with the credit card.** Now some banks are offering "debit cards" instead of credit cards. The costs of purchases made with these cards are deducted from the holder's bank account instead of being added to a monthly bill. And checking accounts, which are mainly used for paying bills, are going electronic. Now some people can make computer transactions over their pushbutton phones to pay bills by transferring money from their account to the account of whomever they owe. **Soon we may be able to conduct most of our business without signing a check or actually seeing the money we earn and spend.**

Note that the main idea of the first sentence of this paragraph—that "we are on our way to becoming a cashless, checkless society"—is restated in other words in the final sentence.

➤ *Practice 3*

The topic sentences of the following paragraphs appear at different locations. Identify each topic sentence by filling in its sentence number in the space provided. In the one case where the paragraph has a topic sentence at both the beginning and the end, write in both sentence numbers.

A. ¹When you were younger, your mother cautioned you not to act like an animal. ²What Mother obviously didn't realize is that much of the rest of the world holds animals in such high regard that they use animals' names for their organizations and products. ³For instance, many professional sports teams, such as the Tigers and Rams, have chosen animal names to suggest power. ⁴Also, cars are given names to make consumers associate them with speed and grace. [5]Examples are the Jaguar, the Cougar, and the Bobcat. [6]Even our political parties have adopted animals to represent them.

Topic sentence(s): _____

B.   [1]Americans express a remarkably high agreement that pornography should be restricted. [2]An overwhelming 91 percent of all Americans think that the law should limit or forbid its distribution—48 percent favoring laws that forbid the distribution of pornography to persons under eighteen, and another 43 percent favoring laws that would keep pornography from people no matter what their age. [3]Females feel even more strongly about this matter than do males, with a full 50 percent wanting to entirely forbid the distribution of pornography.

Topic sentence(s): _____

C.   [1]I'm a dedicated saver. [2]My mother always said that if my pile of junk got any higher, the people in the apartment upstairs would have to move. [3]My husband says that just because our house has an attic, it doesn't mean that I can't throw anything out. [4]We do own a trash can, too. [5]But how can I throw something out when I might need it some day? [6]You never know when a Styrofoam meat tray, empty yogurt container, or old magazine might be needed. [7]Of course, I also have to save my old clothes—the four different sizes I'll need when I finally go on a diet to lose thirty pounds. [8]And I couldn't possibly part with my children's art work, baby clothes, and zoo rings. [9]Yes, I'm a saver and proud of it.

Topic sentence(s): _____

D.   [1]The essence of many perfumes comes from the oils in the petals of fresh flowers, such as the rose, carnation, and orange blossom. [2]However, fragrances can also come from the leaves of plants, including lavender, peppermint, and geranium leaves. [3]In addition, the oils of cinnamon and balsam are derived from bark, while the oil of cedar comes from its wood. [4]The fragrance of ginger and sassafras comes from roots, whereas that of orange, lemon, and nutmeg comes from fruits and seeds. [5]Clearly, we derive fragrances for perfumes from various parts of plants.

Topic sentence(s): _____

Topic Sentences That Cover More Than One Paragraph

At times you will find that a topic sentence does double duty—it provides the main idea for more than one paragraph. This occurs when an author considers the development of the main idea to be too lengthy for one paragraph. He or she then breaks up the material into one or more added paragraphs to make it easier to read.

See if you can find and write down the number of the topic sentence for the two paragraphs below. Then read the explanation that follows.

Topic sentence: _____

¹There's no need to spend hundreds of dollars to join a health club to keep in shape—you can get a satisfying workout at home using just a chair and a broomstick. ²The chair, for example, can be used for pushups. ³Stand about three feet behind it with your feet spaced six to eight inches apart. ⁴Hold onto the chair back, and let yourself down slowly, elbows pointing out, until your chest touches the back of the chair. ⁵Then push up again.

⁶The broomstick can be used for waistline and back exercises. ⁷For instance, sit on the floor with back straight and legs spread. ⁸The broomstick should be resting on your shoulders. ⁹Hold onto the ends of the broomstick and swing slowly from side to side.

After reading both paragraphs, it becomes clear that sentence 1 includes the main idea: "you can get a satisfying workout at home using just a chair and a broomstick." Sentences 2–5 deal with using a chair to exercise. Sentences 6–9 are about using the broomstick for exercises.

The author has simply chosen to break the discussion of the main idea down into two smaller paragraphs rather than include all the information in one long paragraph. This relationship between the two paragraphs can be seen clearly in the following outline:

Main idea: You can get a satisfying workout at home using just a chair and a broomstick.

1. The chair, for example, can be used for pushups.

2. The broomstick can be used for waistline and back exercises.

IMPLIED MAIN IDEAS

Sometimes a selection lacks a topic sentence, but that does not mean it lacks a main idea. The author has simply decided to let the details of the selection suggest the main idea. You must figure out what that implied main idea is by deciding upon the point of all the details. For example, read the following paragraph.

In ancient times, irrational behavior was considered the result of demons and evil spirits taking possession of a person. Later, the Greeks looked upon irrational behavior as a physical problem—caused by an imbalance of body fluids called "humors" or by displacement of an organ. In the highly superstitious Middle Ages, the theory of possession by demons was revived. It reached a high point again in the witch hunts of eighteenth-century Europe and America. Only in the last one hundred years did true medical explanations of mental illness gain wide acceptance.

You can see that no sentence in the paragraph is a good "umbrella" statement that covers all the others. We can decide on the main idea by considering all the details and asking, "What is the topic of this paragraph?" (In other words, "Who or what is this paragraph about?") Once we have the topic in mind, we can ask, "What is the primary point the author is trying to make about that topic?" When we think we know the main point, we can test it out by asking, "Does all or most of the material in the paragraph support this idea?"

In the paragraph above, all of the details are about mental illness, so that must be the topic. And what is the general idea all the details are making about mental illness? The details show that people have explained mental illness in many different ways over the years. Although this idea is not stated, you can see that it is a broad enough summary to include all the other material in the paragraph—it is the main idea.

Now read the paragraph below, and see if you can pick out which of the four statements that follow it expresses the main idea. Circle the letter of the statement you choose, and then read the explanation that follows.

> Cutting down on your responsibilities is one way to minimize stress in your life. You can also relax yourself by breathing deeply, rather than taking light, shallow breaths. Peaceful music is also soothing if you focus your attention on it and consciously disregard distracting thoughts. Another good way to release tension is to exercise regularly, which, rather than tiring you out, builds energy and endurance.

a. Cutting down on responsibilities lessens stress.
b. You can relax by breathing deeply.
c. Stress has several harmful effects.
d. There are several ways you can reduce stress in your life.

As we begin to read this paragraph, we might think the topic sentence is the first sentence: "Cutting down on your responsibilities is one way to minimize stress in your life." If that were the main idea, however, then the details in the paragraph would have to be about responsibilities and stress. Such a paragraph might give ways to cut back on responsibilities. But as we continue to read, we find that the paragraph, instead, goes on to give other ways to minimize stress. Thus answer *a* is incorrect—it is too narrow to be the main idea.

Answer *b* is also too narrow to be the main idea—it also mentions only a single way to reduce stress.

Answer *c* is incorrect because the details of the paragraph do not include any information on the harmful effects of stress.

Answer *d* is a correct statement of the main idea. The phrase "several ways you can reduce stress in your life" is a general reference to the four specific ways to minimize stress listed in the paragraph: 1) cutting down on responsibilities, 2) breathing deeply, 3) focusing on peaceful music, and 4) exercising regularly.

➤*Practice 4*

The following paragraphs have unstated main ideas, and each is followed by four sentences. In each case, circle the letter of the sentence that best expresses the unstated main idea.

Remember to consider carefully all of the details and ask yourself, "Who or what is the paragraph about?" Once you discover the topic of the paragraph, ask, "What is the author's main point about the topic?" Then test your answer by asking, "Does all or most of the material in the paragraph support this idea?"

1. Just as I'm about to be kissed by the most gorgeous man I ever laid eyes upon, I am jolted by a "beep . . . beep." That alarm-clock buzzer has ruined more great moments for me than my kid brother and parents combined! I drag myself out of the warm bed and grope around until I find the bathroom, where the tile floor is so cold it numbs my bare feet. Then I'm somehow expected to pick out something neat and clean to wear—a bit of a challenge considering I haven't done any laundry for six weeks now. Once I'm in the kitchen to get my caffeine fix, I must make a special effort not to bite the heads off the people I live with. This is not easy, since they are so darned pleasant and energetic in the morning.

   a. An alarm-clock buzzer is a terrible noise to hear in the morning.
   b. Mornings are not my favorite time of day.
   c. I have trouble finding time to do my laundry.
   d. There ought to be a law against being pleasant and energetic in the morning.

2. Many Americans fear that foreign investors in this country want to take over the American economy from the inside. But in reality, things don't work that way. Of the trillion dollars in foreign investments in this country, three-quarters are in bank deposits or securities—that is, in paper only. Foreign-owned businesses in the U.S., such as hamburger chains and hotels, generate jobs and new growth because they are totally dependent on the local population for staffing and customers. Americans are the ones who must be sought after to become workers, renters, tourists, and patrons. Throughout its history, the U.S. has relied on foreign capital to finance a great deal of its development, but this has never stood in the way of our democracy.

   a. Foreign-owned businesses in America need Americans.
   b. There's no need for Americans to fear foreign influence in this country.
   c. Most of the foreign investment in this country is on paper, not in cash.
   d. Americans need not fear that foreign investors are taking over our economy.

3. Although we can never determine exactly how extensive drug abuse is in the United States, much is known about its effects. Driving under the influence of marijuana is beginning to take its toll in highway deaths and injuries, and perhaps 15 percent of auto accidents are now associated with marijuana. Alcohol, one of our most common drugs, is far more dangerous than its broad social acceptability would imply. Many people recognize alcohol's association with about half of all deaths from automobile accidents. Few know, however, that, compared with non-drinkers, the death rate is twice as high for those who drink five or more drinks at least four times a week or that cirrhosis of the liver (a direct result of alcoholism) is the sixth most common cause of death in the United States. People are also only beginning to realize that alcohol is the third major cause of birth defects in the United States.

a. It is estimated that 15 percent of U.S. auto accidents involve marijuana.
b. Cirrhosis of the liver is a more common cause of death than people realize.
c. The U.S. has a significant drug-abuse problem.
d. Drug abuse is a major problem throughout the world.

Putting Implied Main Ideas into Words

When you read, you often have to *infer*—figure out on your own—an author's unstated main idea, and no one will give you a list of statements to choose from. So you must be able to decide on implied main ideas on your own. The implied main idea that you come up with must not be too narrow to cover all the details in the paragraph, and it also must not be too broad. See if you can put into words the unstated main idea in the following paragraph. Then read the explanation below.

Many people begin their day by waiting for a bus or train. Then they may spend a few minutes waiting for an elevator to get to their offices. Moreover, the elevator may then stop at twenty floors, averaging a wait of twenty seconds each. After work, there's another wait for both an elevator and a bus or train. Most of us also spend a great deal of time waiting in the dentist's office, in line for tickets or fast food, and on the road in barely moving traffic.

What is the implied main idea of this paragraph? _____

_____

To find an implied main idea, consider all of the supporting details. In this case, the supporting details are several examples of daily occurrences when people have to wait. Thus the main idea is a general idea about these examples. At first we may think the main idea is that many people do a lot of waiting during their workday. But that would be too narrow, as the last sentence of the paragraph includes other kinds of waiting. We might also be tempted to say the main idea is that many people spend a lot of time just sitting or standing around. But that would be too broad, as the paragraph discusses only waiting, not other types of sitting and standing around (such as that done while relaxing at a park). In this process of elimination, we have narrowed down the possibilities for the unstated main idea. One way of wording that general idea is: Waiting is a part of many people's lives.

➤ *Practice 5*

Write the implied main ideas of the following paragraphs in your own words.

1. Birds that roost in communities keep warmer and save more energy than those who roost separately. Another advantage to staying in flocks is that many birds are more likely to find food and detect danger than a solitary bird—several pairs of eyes are better than one. In addition, birds that eat on the ground with their flock can more easily escape attack because at least one member of the flock will alert the others. Then, when all the birds fly upward to escape together, they cause confusion, turning a predator's interest away from any one individual. Several small birds may even act together to "mob" a larger intruder and drive it away.

    Implied main idea: _____

    _____

    _____

2. Drivers in Caracas, Venezuela, must follow an odd/even license-number system for driving their cars on any given day. Cars with license plates ending in even numbers can drive downtown only on even-numbered days; those with odd numbers can drive only on odd-numbered days. Similarly, in Los Angeles this past summer every business with one hundred or more employees was forced to set up a ride-sharing program. Such programs involve offering employees incentives for using mass transportation, joining a car pool, or otherwise avoiding driving a car in the city. Even more extreme is Singapore's method of limiting downtown traffic—most private vehicles are entirely banned from large areas of the central city.

    Implied main idea: _____

    _____

    _____

3.   To workers in many developing countries, a job at a modern factory or industrial plant offers more security, more prestige, and better wages than they could hope for from any other work in the local economy. Any risk involved to worker health and safety is considered acceptable and unavoidable. Often, laws regulating health and safety do not even exist because the government does not perceive health and safety as a concern. In addition, there is the fear that such laws might drive away foreign investors. Even if the laws did exist, the funds and staff to carry them out do not.

Implied main idea: _____

_____

_____

➤ Review Test 1

Each of the following groups includes one topic, one main idea (topic sentence), and two supporting details. In the space provided, label each item with one of the following:

    T   (for *Topic*)
    MI   (for *Main Idea*, expressed in a topic sentence)
    SD   (for *Supporting Detail*)

Group 1

_____ a.   How much the human body is worth depends on the basis of calculation.

_____ b.   Based on the values of the chemicals that make up the body, some have calculated its worth to be as low as ninety-eight cents.

_____ c.   How much the human body is worth.

_____ d.   Based on the value of the organs of the body, one doctor has calculated that it is worth at least $169,834.

Group 2

_____ a.   Detoxification is the first step.

_____ b.   Successful treatment of alcoholism.

_____ c.   Finally, attending meetings of Alcoholics Anonymous can be a great help.

_____ d.   Successful treatment of alcoholism involves several stages.

Group 3

_____ a.   The Catholic Church over the last twenty years.

_____ b.   During the last twenty years, the Catholic Church has undergone great changes.

_____ c.   Meatless Fridays and the Latin Mass were eliminated.

_____ d.   Disagreement with papal authority on such topics as birth control and divorce has been widespread among Catholics.

Group 4

_____ a.   Electronic tutors, no larger or more costly than today's calculators, will become as commonplace as the radio.

_____ b.   Technology's effect on education.

_____ c.   Modern technology will change the very nature of our educational system.

_____ d.   Portable electronic libraries, half the size of an average book, will be able to hold all the books ever printed.

➤ *Review Test 2*

A.   The main idea (as expressed in the topic sentence) appears at various places in the following paragraphs. Identify the topic sentence of each paragraph by writing the correct sentence number in the space provided.

1.   ¹Learning another language may seem more challenge than it's worth. ²The advantages to knowing another language, however, make it well worth the hard work. ³A foreign language, for instance, is a window into another culture. ⁴It expresses the way people in that society think and view the world. ⁵To know another language is thus to view life through a new lens. ⁶Knowing another language also provides access to different ways of dealing with problems common to us all. ⁷It is also an advantage in the business world, where multinational partners are becoming more common. ⁸Finally, understanding a different language enables you to look at your own culture from a fresh perspective.

Topic sentence: _____

2.   [1]Individuals sometimes develop amazing strengths by uniting to overcome trouble. [2]At the end of World War II, for example, a group of six children who had lost their parents, their homeland, and their native language were freed from a concentration camp. [3]They were so strongly attached to one another that they refused to be separated even when one became ill with a contagious disease. [4]In the refugee hostel, they resisted being singled out for treats. [5]At mealtimes, each made certain the other five had food before eating. [6]Only after several months had passed and they knew their safety was assured did they show the competiveness and need for attention normal children do.

Topic sentence: _____

3.   [1]When poor countries attempt to set aside land for parks or preserves, they lose the use of valuable natural resources. [2]Such resources may help their people fight poverty and starvation. [3]One environmentalist has suggested a plan to encourage the establishment of parks and preserves in poor nations. [4]According to this plan, rich nations would be taxed to help poor nations that create parks and preserves. [5]The taxes would go into a fund that the poor countries could use as they liked—to protect the parks, to develop agriculture or industry, or for education. [6]In return, the forty-eight tropical-forest nations in Africa, Asia, and the Americas would agree to maintain an extensive park system. [7]If they failed to maintain their preserves, they would lose their fund.

Topic sentence: _____

B. Circle the letter of the sentence that best expresses the implied main idea of paragraph 4. Then write out the implied main idea of paragraph 5.

4.   Lack of gravity changes how astronauts look during their first few days in space. Body fluids at first flow more towards the head, puffing up the face. And no matter how often astronauts brush their hair, it still tends to float loosely around their heads. In addition, because in the absence of gravity open water floats in the air, astronauts are limited in how they clean themselves in space. For example, they have to swallow their toothpaste rather than rinse their mouths out after brushing.

   a. Astronauts' faces puff up in space at first.
   b. The absence of gravity in space influences astronauts' looks and grooming habits.
   c. When astronauts are in space, their hair tends to float loosely about their heads because of the absence of gravity.
   d. Being in space is very challenging in numerous ways.

5.   Once the most popular and affordable form of public transportation in America, streetcars in the early part of this century carried a record 11 billion passengers on 45,000 miles of track. By 1960, however, trolley systems were virtually extinct. Companies backed by General Motors, Firestone Tire and Rubber, Standard Oil, and others with a financial interest in cars and buses had bought and closed up almost every trolley in America. Now, however, public officials are concerned with finding cheaper, more convenient alternatives to subway systems. San Diego was the first to construct a major new trolley line. As ridership soared, second and third lines were added, with more planned for the future. Portland and Sacramento then started theirs, and more than twenty other cities have proposed new trolley lines.

Implied main idea: _____

_____

_____

➤ *Review Test 3*

A. To review what you've learned in this chapter, complete each of the following sentences about main ideas.

1.   The umbrella statement that covers all of the material in a paragraph is its *(topic, topic sentence, supporting detail)* _____

2.   The main idea of a longer selection is often called its *(topic, central point, implied main idea)* _____

3.   To locate the main idea of a selection, you may find it helpful to first decide on its *(topic, central point, implied main idea)* _____

_____

4.   When a paragraph has no topic sentence, we say that its main idea is _____

_____

5.   To help you decide if a certain sentence is the topic sentence, ask yourself, "Is this statement supported by all or most of the _____

_____?"

B. If you think 19th-century women—lacking in careers, exercise classes, and equal opportunities—must have been weaklings with too much time on their hands, you will find the textbook selection below enlightening. After reading the selection, from *America and Its People* (Scott Foresman, 1989), answer the questions that follow on the central point and main ideas. There are also vocabulary questions to help you continue practicing the skill of understanding vocabulary in context.

Words to Watch

Following are some words in the reading that do not have strong context support. Each word is followed by the number of the paragraph in which it appears and its meaning there.

cistern (7): a large container for storing water, especially rain water
Herculean (9): requiring great strength (from Hercules, the strong Greek and Roman mythological hero)
cataclysm (13): disaster
prick (13): bother

HOUSEWORK IN NINETEENTH-CENTURY AMERICA

James Kirby Martin et al.

1 Housework in nineteenth-century America was harsh physical labor. Preparing even a simple meal consumed great time and energy. Prior to the twentieth century, cooking was performed on a coal- or wood-burning stove. Unlike an electric or a gas range, which can be turned on with the flick of a single switch, cast iron and steel stoves were exceptionally difficult to use.

2 Ashes from an old fire had to be removed. Then, paper and kindling had to be set inside the stove, dampers and flues had to be carefully adjusted, and a fire lit. Since there were no thermostats to regulate the stove's temperature, a woman had to keep an eye on the contraption all day long. Any time the fire slackened, she had to adjust a flue or add more fuel.

3 Throughout the day, the stove had to be continually fed with new supplies of coal or wood—an average of fifty pounds a day. At least twice a day, the ash box had to be emptied, a task which required a woman to gather ashes and cinders in a grate and then dump them into a pan below. Altogether, a housewife spent four hours every day sifting ashes, adjusting dampers, lighting fires, carrying coal or wood, and rubbing the stove with thick black wax to keep it from rusting.

4 It was not enough for a housewife to know how to use a cast iron stove. She also had to know how to prepare unprocessed foods for consumption. Prior to the 1890s, there were few factory-prepared foods. Shoppers bought poultry that was still alive and then had to kill and pluck the birds. Fish had to have scales removed. Green coffee had to be roasted and ground. Loaves of sugar had to be pounded, flour sifted, nuts shelled, and raisins seeded.

Cleaning was an even more arduous task than cooking. The soot and smoke from   5
coal- and wood-burning stoves blackened walls and dirtied drapes and carpets. Gas and
kerosene lamps left smelly deposits of black soot on furniture and curtains. Each day,
the lamps' glass chimneys had to be wiped and wicks trimmed or replaced. Floors had
to be scrubbed, rugs beaten, and windows washed. While a small minority of well-to-
do families could afford to hire a cook at $5 a week, a waitress at $3.50 a week, a
laundress at $3.50 a week, and a cleaning woman and a choreman for $1.50 a day, in
the overwhelming majority of homes, all household tasks had to be performed by a
housewife and her daughters.

Housework in nineteenth-century America was a full-time job. Gro Svendsen, a   6
Norwegian immigrant, was astonished by how hard the typical American housewife
had to work. As she wrote her parents in 1862:

> We are told that the women of America have much leisure time but I haven't yet
> met any woman who thought so! Here the mistress of the house must do all the
> work that the cook, the maid and the housekeeper would do in an upper class
> family at home. Moreover, she must do her work as well as these three together
> do it in Norway.

Before the end of the nineteenth century, when indoor plumbing became   7
common, chores that involved the use of water were particularly demanding. Well-to-
do urban families had piped water or a private cistern°, but the overwhelming majority
of American families got their water from a hydrant, a pump, a well, or a stream
located some distance from their house. The mere job of bringing water into the house
was exhausting. According to calculations made in 1886, a typical North Carolina
housewife had to carry water from a pump or a well or a spring eight to ten times each
day. Washing, boiling, and rinsing a single load of laundry used about fifty gallons of
water. Over the course of a year she walked 148 miles toting water and carried over
thirty-six tons of water.

Homes without running water also lacked the simplest way to dispose of garbage: 8
sinks with drains. This meant that women had to remove dirty dishwater, kitchen slops,
and, worst of all, the contents of chamberpots from their house by hand.

Laundry was the household chore that nineteenth-century housewives detested   9
most. Rachel Haskell, a Nevada housewife, called it "the Herculean° task which
women all dread" and "the great domestic dread of the household."

On Sunday evenings, a housewife soaked clothing in tubs of warm water. When   10
she woke the next morning, she had to scrub the laundry on a rough washboard and rub
it with soap made from lye, which severely irritated her hands. Next, she placed the
laundry in big vats of boiling water and stirred the clothes about with a long pole to
prevent the clothes from developing yellow spots. Then she lifted the clothes out of the
vats with a washstick, rinsed the clothes twice, once in plain water and once with
bluing, wrung the clothes out and hung them out to dry. At this point, clothes would be
pressed with heavy flatirons and collars would be stiffened with starch.

The last years of the nineteenth century witnessed a revolution in the nature of   11
housework. Beginning in the 1880s, with the invention of the carpet sweeper, a host of
new "labor-saving" appliances were introduced. These included the electric iron
(1903), the electric vacuum cleaner (1907), and the electric toaster (1912). At the same
time, the first processed and canned foods appeared. In the 1870s, H. J. Heinz

introduced canned pickles and sauerkraut; in the 1880s Franco-American Company introduced the first canned meals; and in the 1890s, Campbell's sold the first condensed soups. By the 1920s, the urban middle class enjoyed a myriad of new household conveniences, including hot and cold running water, gas stoves, automatic washing machines, refrigerators, and vacuum cleaners.

Yet despite the introduction of electricity, running water, and "labor-saving" household appliances, time spent on housework did not decline. Indeed, the typical full-time housewife today spends just as much time on housework as her grandmother or great-grandmother. In 1924, a typical housewife spent about fifty-two hours a week in housework. Half a century later, the average full-time housewife devoted fifty-five hours to housework. A housewife today spends less time cooking and cleaning up after meals, but she spends just as much time as her ancestors on housecleaning and even more time on shopping, household management, laundry, and children.   12

How can this be? The answer lies in a dramatic rise in the standards of cleanliness and childcare expected of a housewife. As early as the 1930s, this change was apparent to a writer in the *Ladies Home Journal*:   13

> Because we housewives today have the tools to reach it, we dig every day after the dust that grandmother left to spring cataclysm°. If few of us have nine children for a weekly bath, we have two or three for a daily immersion. If our consciences don't prick° us over vacant pie shelves or empty cookie jars, they do over meals in which a vitamin may be omitted or a calorie lacking.

Reading Comprehension Questions

Vocabulary in Context

1. The word *slackened* in "any time the fire slackened, she had to adjust a flue or add more fuel" (paragraph 2) means
   a. remained the same.
   b. became less intense.
   c. roared.
   d. grew rapidly.

2. The word *arduous* in "cleaning was an even more arduous task than cooking" (paragraph 5) means
   a. pleasant.
   b. fragrant.
   c. difficult.
   d. proper.

3. The word *toting* in "Over the course of a year she walked 148 miles toting water and carried over thirty-six tons of water" (paragraph 7) means
   a. drinking.
   b. within.
   c. avoiding.
   d. carrying.

4. The word *detested* in "Laundry was the household chore that . . . housewives detested most. Rachel Haskell . . . called it 'the Herculean task which women all dread'" (paragraph 9) means
   a. hated.
   b. adored.
   c. chose.
   d. ignored.

5. The word *myriad* in "By the 1920s, the urban middle class enjoyed a myriad of new household conveniences, including hot and cold running water, gas stoves, automatic washing machines" (paragraph 11) means
   a. ignorance.
   b. decrease.
   c. memory.
   d. large number.

Central Point

6. Which sentence best expresses the author's central point?
   a. Women have always hated housework.
   b. Life in 19th-century America was difficult.
   c. Housework in 19th- and early 20th-century America was a physically demanding, full-time job.
   d. A revolution in the nature of housework occurred in the last years of the 19th century because of numerous new household conveniences.

Main Ideas

7. The second sentence of the selection—"Preparing even a simple meal consumed great time and energy"—is the topic sentence of
   a. paragraph 1.
   b. paragraphs 1 and 2.
   c. paragraphs 1–3.
   d. paragraphs 1–4.

8. Which sentence best expresses the main idea of paragraphs 7–10?
   a. Household tasks related to the use of water were particularly difficult.
   b. Most houses did not have running water.
   c. Numerous gallons of water had to be carried long distances.
   d. Laundry had to be soaked, scrubbed, stirred about in boiling water, rinsed twice, wrung out and dried, and pressed.

9. The topic sentence of paragraph 11 is its
   a. first sentence.
   b. second sentence.
   c. fourth sentence.
   d. last sentence.

10. Which sentence best expresses the implied main idea of paragraph 13?
    a. Giving two or three children daily baths may take as much time as giving a weekly bath to nine children.
    b. There was actually little difference in a housewife's life before and after the so-called "revolution in the nature of housework."
    c. Housework has remained a full-time job despite labor-saving innovations because standards of cleanliness and childcare have risen.
    d. Standards of cleanliness and childcare change over the years.

3

Supporting Details

You know from the previous chapter that the main idea is the umbrella statement covering all of the other material in a paragraph—examples, reasons, facts, and other specific details. All of those specific details are also called *supporting details*—they are the information that backs up and explains the main idea.

MAJOR AND MINOR DETAILS

There are two kinds of supporting details—major and minor. Taken together, the main idea and its major supporting details form the basic framework of paragraphs. The *major details* are the primary points that support the main idea. Paragraphs often contain minor details as well. While the major details explain and develop the main idea, they, in turn, are expanded upon by the *minor supporting details*.

You've already learned that a paragraph's main idea is more general than its supporting details. Similarly, major supporting details are more general than minor supporting details. An important reading skill is the ability to distinguish the major details from the minor ones.

To get a better idea of the role of major and minor supporting details, look again at a main idea considered in the last chapter:

Main Idea

Clearly, TV violence does affect people in negative ways.

This sentence brings to mind the question "Just what is meant by negative ways?" This is where supporting details come in: they clarify and explain. Turn to the next page to see the same main idea with one major supporting detail:

Main Idea and Major Detail

Clearly, TV violence does affect people in negative ways. One study showed that people who watch a great deal of television are especially fearful and suspicious of others.

Now we have a better idea of what the main idea really means. Often, however, the major details themselves are further explained, and that's where the minor support comes in. A major detail introduces a new point, and minor details develop that point. Here is the same paragraph with the main idea in **boldface** and the major details in *italics*; the other sentences are minor details.

Main Idea and Major and Minor Details

Does watching violence on television make people more prone to violence themselves? **Clearly, TV violence does affect people in negative ways.** *One study showed that people who watch a great deal of television are especially fearful and suspicious of others.* They try to protect themselves from the outside world with extra locks on the doors, guard dogs, and guns. *That same study also showed that heavy TV watchers become less upset about real-life violence than non-TV watchers.* It seems that the constant violence they see on TV makes them less sensitive to the real thing. *Another study, of a group of children, found that TV violence increases aggressive behavior.* Children who watched violent shows were more willing to hurt another child in games where they are given a choice between helping or hurting. They were also more likely to select toy weapons over other kinds of playthings.

Now see if you can separate major from minor support in the following paragraph. It begins with the main idea and continues with several major and minor details. Try to locate and put a check in front of the *two* details that give major supporting information about the main idea.

As you read, keep an eye out for certain words that show the writer is adding a new point. Examples of such addition words are *first, next, another, in addition,* and *finally.*

Health Care for the Poor

[1]In view of the overwhelming health problems among the poor, it is important to make massive efforts to prevent such problems, which is usually much less costly than treating them later on. [2]There are a couple of important approaches to take in working to prevent illness among the poor. [3]First of all, there should be a major focus on preventive health services to poor children and their families. [4]Such programs should include immunization schedules, along with parent education on the need for such immunization and help in getting the children to the clinics. [5]The clinics

should emphasize dental care, an often neglected service. [6]More extensive prenatal care is needed. [7]In addition, society must also fight the social conditions of poverty that breed disease. [8]We have to help more low-income people get better housing, free from the rats that bite their babies and the lead paint that poisons their toddlers. [9]We have to help people break out of the cycle of poverty, illiteracy, and unemployment if we are going to make the promise of medical progress become a reality for all our citizens.

Now see if you checked correctly the two major supporting details. You'll find them after the main idea in the following outline of the paragraph:

Main idea: There are a couple of important approaches to take in working to prevent illness among the poor.

Major supporting details:

1. There should be a major focus on preventive health services to poor children and their families.
2. Society must also fight the social conditions of poverty that breed disease.

A more complete outline, showing minor details as well, would be as follows:

Main idea: There are a couple of important approaches to take in working to prevent illness among the poor.

Major and minor supporting details:

1. There should be a major focus on preventive health services to poor children and their families.
   a. Such programs should include immunization schedules, along with parent education on the need for immunization and help in getting children to the clinics.
   b. The clinics should emphasize dental care.
   c. More extensive prenatal care is needed.
2. Society must also fight the social conditions of poverty that breed disease.
   a. We must help low-income people get housing free from rats and lead paint, which poisons toddlers.
   b. We must help people break the cycle of poverty, illiteracy, and unemployment.

Notice how the complete outline about preventing health problems among the poor goes from the general to the specific. The more general statements are clarified and developed by the points beneath them. At a glance, you can see that the major supporting details introduce new points and that the minor details expand on those points. The outline, by its very nature, divides the paragraph into main idea, major supporting details, and minor supporting details.

One excellent way, then, to gain experience in identifying major supporting details is to outline a selection. In doing so, you make clear the relationships between the basic parts of a piece. Recognizing such relationships is an important part of effective study.

HOW TO LOCATE MAJOR DETAILS

By now you may see that to locate major details, you must (1) find the main idea and (2) decide on the points that are *primary support* for that main idea. Practice these steps by reading the paragraph below. Identify and underline the main idea. Then ask yourself, "What are the major points the author uses to back up the main idea?" Finally, fill in the main idea and major details in the outline that follows. The rest of the details in the passage will be minor details.

[1]There is a debate over the value of video games. [2]Critics argue that video games are destructive. [3]The games, they say, distract students from reading and study. [4]Game players spend less time in reading for pleasure, and they have less time to spend on schoolwork. [5]Video games are also viewed as being too violent. [6]For example, Patricia Greenfield, a professor of psychology at the University of California, notes that when she asked one boy why he liked video games better than television, he answered, "On TV, if you want to make someone die, you can't." [7]On the other hand, defenders of video games maintain that the games offer certain benefits. [8]They claim that the games can help improve reasoning ability. [9]To deal with the challenging situations presented by some games, students must develop their ability to think and respond in a quick, logical way. [10]In addition, video games promote a positive view of computers. [11]Students who enjoy the games may respond more readily to learning to use computers in school.

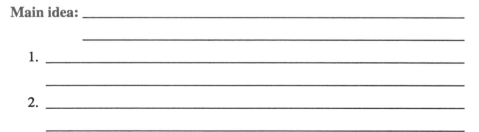

Main idea: _____

_____

1. _____

_____

2. _____

_____

By the time you finished the paragraph, you may have realized that the first sentence presents the main idea: "There is a debate over the value of video games." The rest of the paragraph then develops that idea by introducing and discussing the two sides of that debate. The first major detail is presented in sentence 2: "Critics argue that video games are destructive." The second major detail is given in sentence 7: "On the other hand, defenders of video games maintain that the games offer certain benefits." Sentences 2 and 7, then, contain the major supporting details—the two general ideas that support the main idea.

The other sentences go on to develop those major points—they are the minor supporting details. Minor supporting details may be important to a thorough understanding, but they can be eliminated without removing the author's primary points. Note how the following version of the paragraph—without the minor details—still makes sense.

> There is a debate over the value of video games. Critics argue that video games are destructive. On the other hand, defenders of video games maintain that the games offer certain benefits.

A Note on Maps and Charts

Many students find it helpful to organize material in a very visual way. They may create a *map*, or diagram, to show the relationship between the parts of a selection. A map of the above paragraph on video games might look like this:

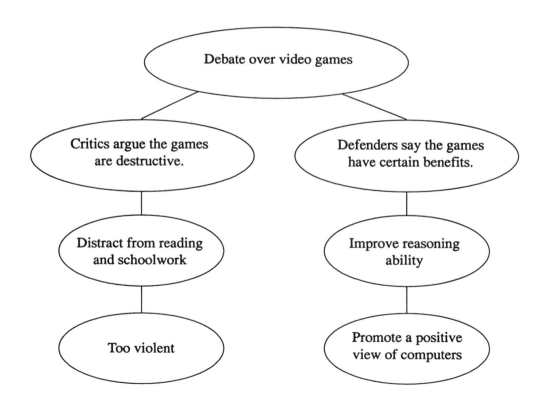

Another visual way of organizing material is to create a chart. A *chart* is an orderly arrangement of information in columns and rows. The chart provides easy, quick reference and is often used for making comparisons or for listing groups of useful facts. Below is an example of a chart.

Debate over Video Games

Destructive:	Beneficial:
Distract students from reading and schoolwork Too violent	Improve reasoning ability Promote a positive view of computers

➤ *Practice 1*

A. The passage below contains three major details. Complete the outline by filling in the main idea and the missing major and minor details.

Biologically, men and women are different in various ways. The differences in anatomy are the most obvious, most notably the differing reproductive systems. Another important anatomical difference is men's greater strength. A second way in which men and women differ is in their genes, which carry the hereditary blueprint for physical development. Genes are carried by chromosomes. The genes of males have two different chromosomes (XY), while females have two similar ones (XX). In addition, more than thirty hereditary disorders, including hemophilia and webbing of the toes, are found only in men. Finally, there are also differences between men's and women's hormones, the chemical substances which our glands secrete. While both sexes have some "male" and "female" hormones, women have more "female" hormones and men have more "male" hormones. Experiments with animals have shown that male hormones can increase aggressiveness and the sex drive.

Main idea: _____

_____

Major detail: 1. *Differences in anatomy* _____

Minor details: a. *Different reproductive systems* _____

b. _____

Major detail: 2. _____

Minor details: a. _____

                  b. *More than thirty hereditary diseases found only in men*

Major detail: 3. *Different balance of hormones*

B. The passage below contains three major details that for study purposes can be organized into a map. Complete the map that follows.

> Consumers concerned about the hazards of noise can reduce noise pollution in many ways. They can buy sound-reduced versions of such ordinarily noisy products as garbage disposals and lawnmowers. They can also use sound-absorbing materials in their home. Carpeting can be installed instead of hard flooring, and cork and fabric can be used in rooms that tend to be noisy. Also, people can become less noisy themselves. They can learn to avoid shouting, to close doors without slamming them, and to play radios, TV sets, and stereos at moderate levels.

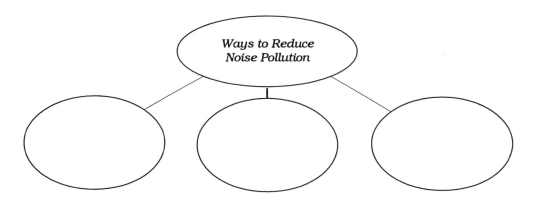

C. The passage below contains supporting details that, for study purposes, can be organized into a chart. Complete the chart that follows the passage.

> Advertisers must consider the various advantages and disadvantages of the mediums available to them. A brief look at television points up some of the issues to be considered. The most important of television's advantages is the ability to reach a mass audience. In addition, this is done with the powerful combination of sight and sound—more effective than if consumers were to only see the ad or only hear it. Also, advertisers can aim their messages at the most likely customers. For example, they can purchase network time to advertise widely available products or local time for local products and services. Or they can buy time on specific types of programs. Thus a kitchen appliance company might advertise on cooking shows. A

disadvantage of TV advertising is that the large number of ads takes away from each ad's impact. Also, television ads are extremely expensive. Creating a TV commercial costs at least $125,000 and showing it on popular prime-time shows costs at least double that amount. Finally, the wide use of VCRs means that many viewers can watch prerecorded shows and bypass the commercials.

Television As an Advertising Medium

Advantages	Disadvantages
1. _____ _____	1. _____ _____
2. _____ _____	2. _____ _____
3. *Aim messages at most likely customers*	3. *VCRs can be used to bypass ads*

READING CAREFULLY

You have seen that major details support the main idea and that minor details expand on the major ones. The minor and major details thus work together to clarify the main idea. For example, let's take another look at the paragraph about watching violence on television. Once again, the main idea is boldfaced, and the major details are italicized. The rest of the sentences are minor details.

Does watching violence on television make people more prone to violence themselves? **Clearly, TV violence does affect people in negative ways.** *One study showed that people who watch a great deal of television are especially fearful and suspicious of others.* They try to protect themselves from the outside world with extra locks on the doors, guard dogs, and guns. *That same study also showed that heavy TV watchers become less upset about real-life violence than non-TV watchers.* It seems that the constant violence they see on TV makes them less sensitive to the real thing. *Another study, of a group of children, found that TV violence increases aggressive behavior.* Children who watched violent shows were more willing to hurt another child in games where they are given a choice between helping or hurting. They were also more likely to select toy weapons over other kinds of playthings.

Clearly, both the major and minor details are helpful for the reader to really understand the main idea. The general ideas that heavy TV watchers are especially fearful and less upset about real-life violence and that children increase aggressive behavior are clarified by the minor details. This illustrates that a careful reading of *both* major and minor details can be important for good comprehension.

Try using your recognition of major and minor details to help you carefully read the textbook passage below. After a close reading, answer the questions that follow.

In the United States, people moved to the suburbs for a variety of reasons. Peter H. Rossi divided these causes for moving to suburbia into two categories. One category is what Rossi called "push" factors. Persons were pushed toward the suburbs by the difficulties associated with life in central cities—crime, pollution, overcrowding, and the like. Rossi's second category of reasons for moving to suburbia was "pull" factors. At the same time that people were trying to escape the difficulties of city life, they were pulled toward suburbia by a desire to live in smaller communities, to own their own homes and gardens, to find better schools for their children, or simply to enjoy the status linked to life in an affluent suburb.

1. In general, the major details of the paragraph are
    a. the things that pushed people to suburbia.
    b. Rossi's two categories of causes for people moving to the suburbs.
    c. the reasons people prefer to live in smaller communities and own their own homes and gardens.

2. Specifically, the major details of the paragraph are
    a. push factors and pull factors.
    b. suburbs and cities.
    c. difficulties associated with life in central cities.

3. *Fill in the blanks*: What are the three specific difficulties mentioned that push people away from the cities? (The answers are minor details.)

    _____

    _____

    _____

4. What are the four things about the suburbs that attract people? (The answers are minor details.)

    _____

    _____

    _____

    _____

The answer to question 1 is *b*. The answer to question 2 is *a*. The answers to question 3 are (1) crime, (2) pollution, and (3) overcrowding. The answers to question 4 are (1) smaller communities, (2) owning one's own home and garden, (3) better schools, and (4) the status linked to wealthy suburbs.

➤ *Practice 2*

Answer the questions that follow the paragraphs.

A.   [1]Sea-land cargo containers were introduced in America in the early 1960s. [2]Uniform in size, these large metal boxes fit neatly into steamships and could be lifted by cranes from ships directly onto flatbed trucks. [3]They enabled importers to keep their merchandise together and protect it from damage and theft. [4]These were positive changes. [5]But the containers outdated New York and other older crowded waterfronts, which lacked the space needed for parking the containers. [6]The containers also destroyed the once-powerful longshoremen's unions, since one giant container crane could easily put a hundred men out of work. [7]In good ways and a few not-so-good ways, sea-land cargo containers changed the course of international trade forever.

1. The main idea of the passage is stated in
   a. sentence 1.
   b. sentence 4.
   c. sentence 7.

2. The major details of this passage are
   a. fitting neatly into steamships and keeping merchandise together.
   b. positive and negative consequences of sea-land cargo containers.
   c. New York's waterfront and other older waterfronts.

3. One advantage of the containers is that they
   a. are uniform in size.
   b. are metal.
   c. require a lot of parking space.

4. According to the author, two disadvantages of sea-land cargo containers are that they outdated older crowded waterfronts and _____

   _____.

5. The answer to question 4 is
   a. the main idea.
   b. a major detail.
   c. a minor detail.

B. In past ages human destruction of the environment may have been so severe that great civilizations were destroyed. The fall of the ancient Mesopotamian civilizations, located in the lush river basin of the Tigris and Euphrates Rivers, has usually been attributed to outside invaders. More recent information, however, indicates that these civilizations in the Fertile Crescent may have fallen victim to increasing environmental stress that eventually reduced their food supplies and weakened their economies. They prospered because they had developed extensive irrigation systems that provided a dependable and plentiful food supply. Their irrigation systems had no drainage, however. Water would evaporate during irrigation, leaving the remaining water with a higher salt content. Over the centuries, then, the land eventually became too salty to grow good crops. With their agricultural base weakened, the Mesopotamian civilizations collapsed.

6. The main idea of the passage is expressed in
   a. the first sentence.
   b. the second sentence.
   c. the last sentence.

7. This passage has just one major detail, an example that illustrates the main idea. One way to state that major detail is:
   a. Some have felt that the ancient Mesopotamian civilizations were destroyed by invaders.
   b. The Mesopotamian civilizations were destroyed because of the stress they put on their environment, which resulted in less food and weakened economies.
   c. When water evaporates, the salt is left behind; as a result, the remaining water is left with a higher salt content.

8. At first, the irrigation systems of the Mesopotamian civilizations
   a. led to a plentiful food supply.
   b. left the land too salty.
   c. were harmed by invaders.

9. *Fill in the blank:* Salt accumulated in the ground water because the irrigation systems had no _____.

10. If there were a second major detail in this passage, it would surely
    a. illustrate how another great civilization was destroyed by weakening of the food supply.
    b. explain why irrigation systems require good drainage systems.
    c. illustrate how human damage to the environment destroyed another great civilization.

➤ *Review Test 1*

A. Complete the outline of the following paragraph by filling in the missing major and minor supporting details.

> No planet outside this solar system has yet been detected. But should such a planet be found, it will have to have a couple of important characteristics to support life as we know it. First of all, the planet's mass must fall into a very narrow range of possible masses. Because life we're familiar with requires oxygen to exist, the planet must have an atmosphere. If the planet's mass is too small, the atmosphere will escape into space. On the other hand, if it's too large, the heat from the interior will evaporate surface water, also essential to life. In addition, the star that the planet revolves around must be exactly the right size. Too big a star will tend to explode before life has a chance to develop around it. Too small a star will hold its planet in such a close orbit that one side will burn up while the other side freezes.

Main idea: To support life as we know it, a planet must have two important characteristics.

Major detail: 1. _____

_____

Minor details: a. *If it were too small, there would be no atmosphere.* ___

b. _____

_____

Major detail: 2. _____

_____

Minor details: a. _____

_____

b. _____

_____

B. Both major and minor details are used to support the main idea (which is boldfaced) in the paragraph below. Separate the major, more general details from the minor ones by completing the map.

> First the good news: Americans are definitely eating more healthful meals. We are consuming greater amounts of such high-fiber foods as whole-grain breads, fruits and vegetables, which are believed to help prevent certain cancers and other diseases. At the same time, we are substituting relatively low-fat foods for higher-fat ones—for example, eating fish instead of red meat, drinking skim milk instead of whole. Fatty foods should be eliminated from our diets since they contribute to a variety of serious ailments. The bad news is that our snack foods are not nearly as healthful. Between meals, we often revert to eating large amounts of fat. For instance,

sales of ice cream and potato chips are going through the roof. Another drawback of the snack foods is that they have almost no fiber. **The conclusion of eating-behavior experts is that we try super-hard to eat healthfully at mealtimes—but then undo some of the good work by "rewarding" ourselves with bad-for-you snacks.**

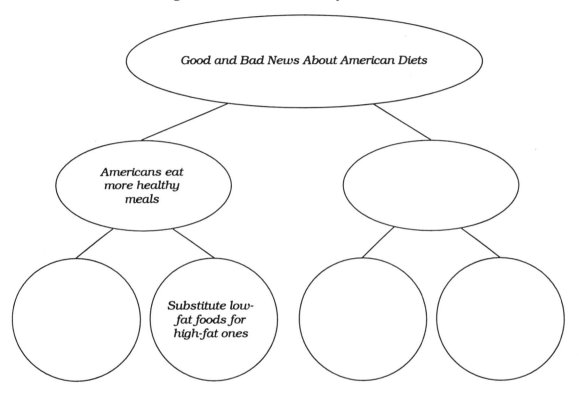

> ➤ *Review Test 2*

A. Answer the questions that follow the passage. Note that the topic sentence is boldfaced.

> **A number of general factors can be identified which reduce the level of dissatisfaction of contemporary industrial workers.** Higher wages give workers a sense of accomplishment apart from the task before them. A shortened workweek has increased the amount of time that people can devote to recreation and leisure, thereby reducing some of the discontent stemming from the workplace. For example, the average industrial worker spent sixty hours a week on the job in 1880, compared with the forty-hour workweek which began in the 1930s. Numerous studies have shown that positive relationships with coworkers can make a boring job tolerable or even enjoyable. Finally, unions have given many workers an opportunity to exercise some influence in decision-making.

1. The major supporting details of the paragraph are several
   a. reasons that higher wages give workers a sense of accomplishment.
   b. causes for the reduction of the level of dissatisfaction of contemporary industrial workers.
   c. comparisons between the average industrial worker's workweek with the average workweek of the 1930s.
   d. factors behind the level of dissatisfaction of contemporary industrial workers.

2. List the major supporting details of the paragraph. (The number of details may differ from the number of lines below.)

   _____

   _____

   _____

   _____

   _____

3. *Fill in the blank:* The average industrial worker of the 1930s worked _____ hours less per week than the average industrial worker of the 1880s.

B. Following the passage below is a question raised by the main idea of the passage. After reading the passage, answer the question by stating the major supporting details.

Suburban settlements have become so varied that even the collective term *suburbs* gives undue support to the stereotype of suburban uniformity. Pollster Louis Harris has divided suburbs into four distinct categories based on income level and rate of growth. Higher-income suburbs are categorized as either affluent bedroom or affluent settled. The affluent bedroom communities rank at the highest levels in terms of income, proportion of persons employed in professional and managerial occupations, and percentages of homeowners. Affluent settled communities tend to be older, and perhaps even declining in population. They are more likely to house business firms and do not serve mainly as a place of residence for commuters.

Harris has recognized that certain suburban areas are composed of individuals and families with low or moderate incomes. Low-income growing communities serve as the home of upwardly mobile blue-collar workers who have moved from central cities. Low-income stagnant communities are among the oldest suburbs and are experiencing the full range of social problems characteristic of the central cities.

What are Harris's four categories of suburbs based on income level and rate of growth?

1. _____

2. _____

3. _____

4. _____

➤ Review Test 3

A. To review what you've learned in this chapter, answer each of these questions about supporting details.

1. *Fill in the blanks:* Major supporting details are more (*general, specific*) _____ than main ideas. Minor supporting details are more (*general, specific*) _____ than major details.

2. *Circle the letter of each of the three answers that apply:* Supporting details can be

    a. reasons   d. main ideas
    b. topics   e. facts
    c. examples   f. central points

3. Label each part of the outline form below with one of the following:

    • Main Idea
    • Major Supporting Detail
    • Minor Supporting Detail

    _____

    1. _____

        a. _____

        b. _____

    2. _____

B. How important to an infant's basic development is the care it receives? This question is addressed in the following selection from the college textbook *Psychology*, by Mary M. Gergen and others (Harcourt Brace Jovanovich, 1989). Read the passage and then answer the questions on supporting details that follow.

To help you continue to strengthen your work on the skills taught in previous chapters, there are also questions on vocabulary in context and central point and main ideas.

Words to Watch

Following are some words in the reading that do not have strong context support. Each word is followed by the number of the paragraph in which it appears and its meaning there.

innate (3): inborn
mutually (3): in a manner in which giving and receiving are equal
reinforcer (4): reward causing a positive response
reciprocated (9): returned

BABY LOVE

Mary M. Gergen et al.

At the base of an infant's social life is its first experience of love. During the first two years, infants normally acquire a basic sense of attachment. By **attachment,** we mean a feeling of dependence, trust, and the desire to be physically close to the major caregiver, usually the mother. Developmentalists such as Erik Erikson believe that the basic trust formed during this period provides the foundation for all other social and emotional development. 1

We do not know how quickly infants develop attachment. Psychologists had once believed that infants in the first few weeks of life were not yet able to distinguish their mother from other people, but recent research indicates that they are able to. By six months or so, they have clearly developed attachment. One indication of this is that many infants will cry if their mothers disappear from sight. Also, children often will show fear and distress in the presence of a stranger. The presence of a caretaker will soothe them. 2

What is the basis of the infant's attachment to its mother? Some learning theorists believe that the attachment between mother and child develops because of the child's ability to cry and smile. Crying and smiling are innate° responses in infants; these responses reflect the child's need states, which the child communicates in a primitive way to parents. The child cries when in distress, and the parent relieves the distress. At this point, the child smiles (which in a sense rewards the parent's actions). The behaviors of parents and infants are *mutually° reinforcing*—the infant provides smiles and the parent provides food and care—so both parties become attached. 3

For some time psychologists thought that the nourishment provided by the parent   4
was the principal reinforcer° for infants, but research suggests that the physical comfort provided by parents may be even more important. Harry and Margaret Harlow conducted several experiments on infant monkeys who were separated from their mothers at birth and reared with *surrogate*, or substitute, mothers. In some cases, the surrogate mother was made of wire with a wooden block for a head. This was not a very cozy mother to cuddle up to. In other cases, the surrogate mother had a soft, cuddly, terrycloth body. In one experiment, the infant monkeys were raised in a cage with both the terrycloth "mother" and the wire "mother." However, only the wire mother was equipped with a milk bottle, so nourishment came from the wire mother alone.

The Harlows and their associates observed the behavior of the infants and   5
discovered an important tendency. The infant monkey had become attached to the terrycloth mother, even though the wire mother provided the food. If an infant monkey was frightened (by sounds, lights, or a new object), it would seek the security of the terrycloth mother. It would feed from the wire mother's bottle, but it spent most of its time with the cloth-covered mother. Also, when an infant monkey proceeded to investigate the case, it would keep one foot on the terrycloth mother and would return and cling to this surrogate mother whenever frightened. These results suggest that *contact comfort* is in many ways more important for attachment than nourishment.

Even though the terrycloth mothers provided the infant monkeys with security,   6
these monkeys did not develop into normal adults. While they were less disturbed than monkeys raised only with wire mothers, as adults they exhibited disturbed behavior. They constantly rocked, sucked on themselves, and behaved in an aggressive manner when released into a group of monkeys. This behavior lasted through their adult lives.

Obviously, the terrycloth and wire mothers were not enough. Attachment to real   7
monkeys seemed important for the young monkeys to develop into proper adults. But need the mother be present for this to occur? Harry Harlow looked at this question as well. He found that infant monkeys that were separated from their mothers and raised with other infants showed more clinging behavior and tended to be more timid as adults than normally reared monkeys. These infants showed some negative effects of being raised without a mother, but they were not so badly affected as infants who were raised completely isolated from other monkeys.

Of course, you may have doubts about generalizing to humans from experiments   8
with monkeys. This is a reasonable doubt. But we should note that apes and monkeys are our closest nonhuman relatives. Thus, we may suspect that some similarities might exist. Also, studies of children brought up in orphanages show that those who are not given the opportunity to form strong attachments to caregivers suffer from social and emotional difficulties.

Harlow also tested whether or not the effects of early isolation could be reversed.   9
In one study, he placed young monkeys who had not been isolated with older monkeys that had been isolated. The younger monkeys showed a lot of clinging behavior, and very little aggressive behavior. The usual response of the younger monkeys was to cling and attach themselves to the older monkeys. Over time, the isolates reciprocated° this behavior, and after six months the isolates behaved much like the younger monkeys. The younger monkeys apparently provided nonthreatening models to the isolates.

Studies of young children in orphanages have shown that giving loving attention 10 and care to formerly neglected babies improves their lives significantly. Listless, dull babies became lively, normal youngsters when they were lovingly cared for. In one study, the children who did not receive loving care became mentally retarded and remained institutionalized all of their lives, while the others who were cared for developed into normal adults living in the community. We should point out that this series of studies merely observed some orphanages; it was not an experiment. It would appear that the effects of the early experience of isolation may be correctable. Recently, a review of twenty studies on early separation of mothers from their children indicated that children do not usually suffer permanent harm from this experience. What seems to matter is that someone give loving care to the infants.

We have emphasized attachment to the principal caretaker, but typically by one 11 year of age children extend their attachments to others, such as the father, grandparents, and other caretakers. Also at this time the fear of strangers, which peaks around eight months, begins to decrease, and will be reduced markedly by the time the child is eighteen months old. The attachment to others provides the foundation for future social relationships.

Reading Comprehension Questions

Vocabulary in Context

1. The word *listless* in "listless, dull babies became lively, normal youngsters when they were lovingly cared for" (paragraph 10) means
   a. well-cared for.
   b. tall.
   c. bright.
   d. inactive.

2. The word *markedly* in "at this time the fear of strangers . . . begins to decrease, and will be reduced markedly by the time the child is eighteen months old" (paragraph 11) means
   a. not at all.
   b. very noticeably.
   c. only rarely.
   d. unfortunately.

Central Point and Main Ideas

3. Which sentence best expresses the central point of the selection?
   a. Infant nourishment is relatively unimportant.
   b. Strong parental "attachment" in infancy appears to form the foundation for normal social development, but the absence of such attachment can be overcome.

      c. In one experiment, infant monkeys preferred surrogate mothers who provided physical comfort to surrogate mothers who fed them; but even physical comfort from a fake parent was insufficient for normal development.

      d. Studies of young children in orphanages suggest that loving care can overcome some of the disadvantages of early neglect.

4. The main idea of paragraphs 4 and 5 is
   a. expressed in the last sentence of paragraph 3.
   b. expressed in the first sentence of paragraph 4 and the last sentence of paragraph 5.
   c. expressed in the second sentence of paragraph 4 and the first sentence of paragraph 5.
   d. implied.

5. Which sentence best expresses the implied main idea of paragraph 9?
   a. Harlow tested whether or not the effects of early isolation could be reversed.
   b. The young monkeys in Harlow's experiment showed a lot of clinging behavior and very little aggressive behavior.
   c. One of Harlow's experiments suggests that it is possible to overcome the effects of early isolation.
   d. One of Harlow's experiments suggests that young monkeys generally make good models for older monkeys.

Supporting Details

6. Some learning theorists believe that infants and mothers form attachment to each other
   a. in all situations.
   b. because their behaviors reinforce one another.
   c. because the mother provides smiles.
   d. when the child is in distress.

7. In forming an attachment,
   a. touch appears to be more important than food.
   b. isolation is best.
   c. monkeys prefer wire mothers over terry cloth mothers.
   d. food appears to be more important than touch.

8-10. Add the details missing in the following partial outline of the reading. Do so by filling in each blank with the letter of one of the sentences in the box below the outline.

Central point: Psychologists' experiments and studies suggest much about the development of infants and young children.

   A. The Harlows' experiments with monkeys suggest important conclusions about how attachments are formed.

       1. _____

       2. Experiments showed that there are fewer but still some negative effects in being raised without a mother but with other infant monkeys.

   B. _____

       1. When Harlow placed previously isolated older monkeys with young normal monkeys, the isolates' behavior became much like that of the normal monkeys.

       2. _____

       3. A review of twenty studies on early separation of mothers and children indicates that the negative effects of such separation can be overcome with loving care.

Details Missing from the Outline:

   a. Monkey and human studies show that it's possible to overcome the negative effects of previous isolation or neglect.

   b. Studies of young children in orphanages have shown that loving attention and care can greatly improve the lives of previously neglected children.

   c. Experiments in which surrogate, non-living mothers were provided for isolated monkeys suggest that contact comfort is more important for attachment than nourishment.

4

Transitions

Consider the following sentences:

Some people hate driving small cars. The gas mileage is good.

Insert the disk into the A drive of the computer. Make sure the power switch is turned on.

You can reduce the number of colds you catch. Wash your hands frequently during the cold season.

Do people hate driving small cars because the gas mileage is good? Is the disk supposed to be inserted before the power switch is turned on? Is washing your hands the only way to avoid catching a cold? We're not sure because the above sentences are unclear. To clarify them, transitions are needed. *Transitions* are words and phrases that signal the relationships between ideas. To show how useful transitions are, here are the same sentences, but this time with transitions to clarify the relationships:

Some people hate driving small cars *even though* the gas mileage is good.

Before inserting the disk into the A-drive of the computer, make sure the power switch is turned on.

You can reduce the number of colds you catch. *For one thing*, wash your hands frequently during the cold season.

Now we know that people hate driving small cars *despite the fact that* the mileage is good, that the disk is inserted *after* the computer is turned on, and that washing hands is *one of several ways* to avoid catching colds. Transitions have bridged the gaps between ideas. In Latin, *trans* means "across," so transitions live up to their name—they carry the reader "across" from one thought to another.

There are a number of ways in which transitions connect ideas and show relationships. Here is a list of the major types of transitions.

1 Words that show addition
2 Words that show time
3 Words that show contrast
4 Words that show comparison
5 Words that show illustration
6 Words that show cause and effect

Each of these kinds of transitions will be explained in the pages that follow.

1 WORDS THAT SHOW ADDITION

Put a check beside the item that is easier to read and understand:

_____ People have dogs for companionship. Dogs are good protection.

_____ One reason people have dogs is for companionship. Dogs are also good protection.

The words *one* and *also* in the second item make the relationship between the sentences more clear. The author is listing reasons for having dogs. One reason is companionship. An additional reason is protection. *One*, *also* and words like them are known as addition words.

Addition words tell you that the writer is presenting one or more ideas that continue along the same line of thought as a previous idea. Such words introduce ideas that *add to* a thought already mentioned. Here are some common addition words:

Addition Words

one	in addition	first of all	furthermore
also	moreover	second	last of all
another	next	third	finally

Examples:

My friend Ellen is so safety-conscious that she had her wooden front door replaced with a steel one. *Also*, she had iron bars inserted on all her apartment windows.

By recycling, the township has saved thousands of dollars in landfill expenses. *Furthermore*, it has made money by selling recycled glass, paper, and metal.

Consumers today want much more information about food products than they did twenty or more years ago. Why? *First of all*, they are much more aware of nutrition than they used to be.

➤ *Practice 1*

Complete each sentence with a suitable transition from the box on the preceding page. Try to use a variety of transitions.

1. One reason Marian left Jack is that he borrowed her credit cards without asking. _____ reason is that he used the cards to buy gifts for other women.

2. Paranoid people often believe that someone is plotting against them. _____, they may believe that everyone is talking about and staring at them.

3. Payroll savings has several advantages. _____, the money is taken out of your paycheck automatically, so you can easily save regularly.

4. One dental warning sign is if a tooth hurts while one eats something sweet. Another sign is sensitivity to hot or cold. A _____ sign is bleeding gums.

5. Living in the mountains can be troublesome. For one thing, heavy rains can create mudslides on local roads. _____, it is sometimes difficult to get a good station on the radio.

2   WORDS THAT SHOW TIME

Put a check beside the sentence that is easier to read and understand:

_____   I fill in the answers to the test questions I'm sure I know. I work on the rest of the exam.

_____   First I fill in the answers to the test questions I'm sure I know. Then I work on the rest of the exam.

The words *first* and *then* in the second item clarify the relationship between the sentences. The author begins work on the rest of the exam after answering the questions that he or she is sure about. *First* and *then* and words like them are time words.

These transitions indicate a **time relationship**. They tell us *when* something happened in relation to something else happening. Here are some common time words:

Time Words

first	next	as	while
then	before	now	during
often	after	until	immediately
when	soon	previously	frequently

Examples:

> *First* I skim the pages of the television guide to see what movies will be on. *Then* I circle the ones I want to record on the VCR.

> For hundreds of years windmills were widely used for such purposes as grinding grain and pumping water. *Now* windmills are coming back into fashion as a source of electricity.

> *During* World War II, meat was rationed.

Helpful Points About Transitions

Here are two points to keep in mind about transitions:

1. Some transition words have the same meaning. For example, *also, moreover,* and *furthermore* all mean "in addition." Authors typically use a variety of transitions to avoid repetition.

2. In some cases the same word can serve as two different types of transition, depending on how it is used. For example, the word *first* may be used as an addition word to show that the author is beginning a series of similar thoughts, as in the following sentence:

> Plant researchers have developed promising new types of apples. *First,* the apples are disease-resistant and don't need pesticides. Moreover, ...

First may also may be used to signal a time sequence, as in this sentence:

> Our English class turned into a shambles this morning. *First,* the radiator began to steam and whistle. Then, ...

➤ *Practice 2*

Complete each sentence with a suitable transition from the box at the top of the page. Try to use a variety of transitions.

1. _____ a great white shark was spotted a half-mile off shore, lifeguards made everyone get out of the water.

2. San Francisco tailor Levi Strauss originally made jeans from canvas. It wasn't _____ the early 1860s that he started using a softer fabric imported from France, which in the United States was called denim.

3. My next-door neighbor _____ lets his grass grow so high that I'm afraid my two-year-old daughter will get lost in his yard.

4. Advances in medical technology have forced doctors to redefine when death actually occurs. _____ the definition of death seemed simple.

5. _____ the summer, our dog Floyd spends most of his day sprawled on the cool tiles of the kitchen floor, panting and drooling.

3 WORDS THAT SHOW CONTRAST

Put a check beside the sentence that is easier to read and understand:

_____ Martha adores her son-in-law despite the fact he hasn't worked in a year.

_____ Martha adores her son-in-law; he hasn't worked in a year.

The second item seems to imply that Martha adores her son-in-law because he hasn't worked in a year. In the first item, the phrase *despite the fact* clarifies the relationship between the two ideas: Even though Martha's son-in-law hasn't worked in a year, she still adores him. *Despite the fact* and words like them are contrast words.

Contrast words inform us that something is going to *differ* from what we might expect. Here are some common contrast words:

Contrast Words

but	in contrast	conversely	on the other hand
however	instead	nevertheless	on the contrary
yet	still	even though	in spite of
although	despite		

Examples:

Some people think they have to exercise every day to stay in shape. *However*, three workouts a week are all they need to do.

Some people look upon eating as something to be done quickly, so they can get on to better things. *In contrast*, other people think eating is one of the better things.

Professional writers don't wait for inspiration. *On the contrary*, they stick to a strict schedule of writing.

➤ *Practice 3*

Complete each sentence with a suitable transition from the box on the preceding page. Try to use a variety of transitions.

1. Many believe that Frankenstein is a monster. _____, "Frankenstein" is the name of the doctor who created the monster, which was never named.

2. _____ the woman's lack of sales experience, the manager of the record store hired her because she knows a lot about popular music.

3. _____ Americans are concerned with fitness, the typical adult can't climb a flight of steps without getting short of breath.

4. Tony wanted to watch the late movie on television; _____, he went to bed early because it was his turn the next morning to get the twins ready for nursery school.

5. Most American-born college students cannot converse in a foreign language. _____, it is a rare student in Europe who cannot speak at least one language besides his own.

4   WORDS THAT SHOW COMPARISON

Put a check beside the sentence that is easier to read and understand:

_____   The computerized scanner has streamlined the supermarket check-out line. Computerized fingerprint identification allows the police to do in seconds what once took two hours.

_____   The computerized scanner has streamlined the supermarket check-out line. Similarly, computerized fingerprint identification allows the police to do in seconds what once took two hours.

The first item makes us wonder, "What has supermarket work got to do with police work?" In the second item, the transition word *similarly* makes it clear that the author is *comparing* the benefits of computerization in both types of work. *Similarly* and words like it are comparison words.

These **comparison words** signal that the author is pointing out a similarity between two subjects. They tell us that the second idea is *like* the first one in some way. Here are some common comparison words:

Comparison Words

like	just as	in the same way	as well
as	likewise	in like manner	equally
just like	similar	in a similar fashion	

Examples:

When buying milk, my mother always takes a bottle from the back of the shelf. *Similarly,* when my father buys a newspaper, he usually grabs one from the middle of the pile.

If movie makers have a big hit, they tend to repeat the winning idea in their next movie, *just like* certain authors who keep writing the same type of story over and over.

When individuals communicate, they are more likely to solve their problems. *In a similar fashion*, countries can best solve their problems through communication.

➣ *Practice 4*

Complete each sentence with a suitable transition from the box on the preceding page. Try to use a variety of transitions.

1. A swarm of locusts looks _____ a massive, dark cloud moving across the sky.

2. My grandmother uses torn bath towels for drying dishes. _____, she turns chipped cups into planters.

3. As a young boy, Edward was often beaten by his parents. Unfortunately, he now treats his own children _____.

4. _____ people put their best feet forward for romance, birds show off their skills or looks during courtship.

5. Dogs can be trained by using a system of rewards. A _____ method can reinforce desirable behavior in children.

5   WORDS THAT SHOW ILLUSTRATION

Put a check beside the sentence that is easier to read and understand:

_____   Even very young children can do household chores. For example, they can run a duster along baseboards or fold napkins for dinner.

_____   Even very young children can do household chores. They can run a duster along baseboards or fold napkins for dinner.

The second item suggests that running a duster along baseboards and folding napkins are the only two chores the author feels young children can do. The words *for example* in the first item make it clear that those chores are examples of ways children can help around the house. *For example* and other words like them are illustration words.

These **illustration words** indicate that an author will provide one or more examples to develop and clarify a given idea. They tell us that a specific idea is *an example* of a general idea. Here are some common illustration words:

Illustration Words

for example	to illustrate	once
for instance	such as	including

Examples:

My grandmother doesn't hear well anymore. *For instance*, whenever I say, "Hi, Granny," she answers, "Fine, just fine."

There are various ways you can save money, *such as* bringing lunch to work and automatically putting aside a small portion of your check each week.

My cousin Dave will do anything on a dare. *Once* he showed up for a family dinner wearing only swimming trunks and a snorkeling mask.

> *Practice 5*

Complete each sentence with a suitable transition from the above box. Try to use a variety of transitions.

1. Throughout history, men have chosen to marry for different reasons. In ancient

    Sparta, _____, men needed wives solely for childbearing.

2. Common courtesies, _____ saying *please* and *thank you*, are becoming less and less common.

3. Your relationship with the customers leaves a great deal to be desired. _____, it is rude to answer the phone by saying, "What do you want? And make it fast."

4. Companies often create their own advertising characters, _____ the Pillsbury Doughboy and Energizer Rabbit.

5. Sometimes drivers don't seem to be paying full attention to their driving. _____, this morning I saw people driving while talking on car phones, combing their hair, and glancing at newspapers.

6   WORDS THAT SHOW CAUSE AND EFFECT

Put a check beside the sentence that is easier to read and understand:

_____   I decided to go away to school. My boyfriend began talking about getting married.

_____   I decided to go away to school because my boyfriend began talking about getting married.

In the first item, we're not sure about the relationship between the two sentences. Did the speaker's boyfriend discuss marriage because she decided to go away to school? Or was it the other way around? The word *because* in the second item makes it clear that the author decided to go away to school as a result of her boyfriend's interest in marriage. *Because* and words like it are cause-and-effect words.

These **cause-and-effect words** signal that the author is explaining *why* something happened or will happen. Here are some common cause-and-effect words:

Cause-and-Effect Words

thus	because	because of	if ... then
as a result	result in	consequently	since
therefore	leads to	accordingly	so

Examples:

My sister became a vegetarian *because* she doesn't want to eat anything that had a mother.

If it gets too humid out, *then* our wooden doors swell up and become hard to open and shut.

Orders built up while company employees took summer vacations. *As a result*, everyone had to work overtime in September.

➤ *Practice 6*

Complete each sentence with a suitable transition from the above box. Try to use a variety of transitions.

1.   _____ the top of the TV gets warm after it has been on for a while, my cat likes to sleep up there.

2.   The fire had quickly destroyed nearby telephone lines. _____, witnesses were unable to call the fire department to report the blaze.

3.   _____ prisons are so overcrowded, district attorneys often use plea bargaining to reduce serious crimes to misdemeanors.

4.   Conflict can be beneficial. For instance, conflict can _____ needed social change.

5.   _____ spectator violence at professional sports events continues to rise, many franchise owners are thinking of prohibiting the sale of beer at games.

➤ Review Test 1

A.   Fill each blank with one of the words in the box. Use each word once.

despite	after	because
another	for instance	

1.   One reason singles join a health club is to get in shape. _____ is that it's a great place to meet people.

2.   _____ Lincoln's assassination, his widow was hysterical for months. In 1875, she was committed for four months to an institution for the insane.

3.   Many products are named after specific individuals. _____, the man who created the Tootsie Roll named it after his daughter, whom he had nicknamed Tootsie.

4.   _____ a learning disability which made it difficult for her to learn to read, Darla worked hard and became a successful businesswoman.

5.   The button factory was built near the river _____ it made buttons out of shells found there.

B.   Fill in each blank with the appropriate transition from the box. Use each transition once.

because	soon	first
however	for example	

I do not like to write. In fact, I dislike writing so much that I have developed a series of steps for postponing the agony of doing writing assignments. _____, I tell myself that to proceed without the proper equipment would be unwise. So I go buy a new pen. This kills at least an hour. Simply holding a shiny new pen, _____, is not enough. The instant I begin to stare at the blank page, I realize that writing may also require thought; so I begin to think deeply about my subject. Soon I feel drowsy. This naturally leads to the conclusion that I need a nap _____ I want to be at my very best when I throw myself into my writing. After a refreshing nap, I again face the blank page. It is usually at this stage that I actually write a sentence or two—disappointing ones. I then wisely decide that I need inspiration, from an interesting magazine or a television movie, _____. _____, I am deeply absorbed in a magazine or movie. If thoughts of my writing assignment should interfere, I comfort myself with the knowledge that, as any artist knows, you can't rush these things.

➤ Review Test 2

A. First, write in the transition that correctly completes each sentence. Secondly, underline the kind of transition you chose.

1. a. _____ the invention of television, people probably spent more of their leisure time reading.

   Nevertheless
   Before
   Because of

   b. The relationship between the two parts of the sentence is one of
      1) addition.
      2) cause and effect.
      3) time.

2. a. We experience a change in the seasons _____ the Earth tilts on its axis as it revolves around the sun.

   because
   just like
   including

   b. The relationship of the first part of the sentence to the second part is one of
      1) illustration.
      2) cause and effect.
      3) comparison.

3. a. If you're having company for dinner, try to get as much done in advance as possible. _____, set the table the day before.

In contrast
Similarly
For instance

    b. The relationship of the second sentence to the first is one of
      1) illustration.
      2) comparison.
      3) contrast.

4. a. My grandfather loves to say, "You're as nervous _____ a long-tailed cat in a roomful of rocking chairs."

after
as
as a result

    b. The relationship expressed by the quotation is one of
      1) cause and effect.
      2) time.
      3) comparison.

5. a. _____ Manny's car stereo was on full blast, I could see his lips moving, but I had no idea what he was saying.

Moreover
Because
Just as

    b. The relationship between the first part of the sentence and the rest of the sentence is one of
      1) comparison.
      2) addition.
      3) cause and effect.

6. a. Originally, type was set by hand, one letter at a time. Today, _____, much of this work is performed by a computer.

for instance
therefore
however

    b. The relationship between the two sentences is one of
      1) contrast.
      2) illustration.
      3) cause and effect.

B. In the spaces provided, write in four major transitions used in the following passage—a cause-and-effect transition, an illustration transition, an addition transition, and a contrast transition.

During the years of the Great Depression, people could afford little entertainment. Going to the movies was a diversion that cost very little. As a result, Hollywood turned out a number of happy, upbeat movies, designed to help people forget their troubles. For example, a top box-office attraction of those dark years was sweet, curly-haired Shirley Temple, the star of twenty-one relentlessly positive movies. Another type of popular Depression movie was the lavish, large-scale musical. Audiences flocked to see these Hollywood spectaculars, despite the fact that their own lives were bleak by comparison.

Cause-and-Effect Transition

7. _____

Illustration Transition

8. _____

Addition Transition

9. _____

Contrast Transition

10. _____

➤ *Review Test 3*

A. To review what you've learned in this chapter, complete each of the following sentences about transitions.

1.   Transitions are words that signal the *(main ideas in, relationships between, importance of)* _____ ideas.

2.   A(n) _____ transition means that the writer is adding to an idea or ideas already mentioned.

3.   A(n) _____ transition signals that two things are alike in some way.

4.   The transition *after* signals a _____ relationship.

5.   The transition *therefore* signals a _____ relationship.

B. Before modern times, family life in quiet rural villages was peaceful and loving, right? Wrong! In the following richly detailed selection from the textbook *Sociology*, Third Edition, by Rodney Stark (Wadsworth, 1989), the common romantic image of preindustrial rural life is shown to be far from true.

This excerpt provides the opportunity to apply your understanding of transitions to a full-length reading. Following the reading are questions on transitions and the relationships they signal. To help you continue reinforcing the skills taught in previous chapters, there are also questions on

   • vocabulary in context
   • central point and main ideas
   • supporting details.

Words to Watch

Following are some words in the reading that do not have strong context support. Each word is followed by the number of the paragraph in which it appears and its meaning there.

dowry (1): the goods, money, or estate that a bride brings to her husband
devastating (3): very effective
abounded with (3): had plenty of
grudgingly (7): with reluctance
perforated (9): penetrated
radically (10): completely

PERSONAL RELATIONSHIPS IN THE NOT-SO-GOOD OLD DAYS

Rodney Stark

Relations between husbands and wives

Only in modern times have most people married for love. In the good old days, most married for money and labor—marriage was an economic arrangement between families. How much land or wealth did the man have? How large a dowry° would the bride bring to her spouse? Emotional attachments were of no importance to parents in arranging marriages, and neither the bride nor the groom expected emotional fulfillment from marriage.

Shorter [a historical researcher] noted an absence of emotional expression between couples and doubted that more than a few actually felt affection. The most common sentiments seem to have been resentment and anger. Not only was wife-beating commonplace, but so was husband-beating. And when wives beat their husbands, it was the husband, not the wife, who was likely to be punished by the community. In France, a husband beaten by his wife was often made to ride backward through the village on a donkey, holding the donkey's tail. He had shamed the village by not controlling his wife properly. The same practice of punishing the husband was frequently employed when wives were sexually unfaithful.

The most devastating° evidence of poor husband-wife relations was the reaction to death and dying. Just as the deaths of children often caused no sorrow, the death of a spouse often prompted no regret. Some public expression of grief was expected, especially by widows, but popular culture abounded with° contrary beliefs. Shorter reported the following proverbs:

> *The two sweetest days of a fellow in life,*
> *Are the marriage and burial of his wife.*
>
> *Rich is the man whose wife is dead and horse alive.*

Indeed, peasants who rushed for medical help whenever a horse or cow   4
took sick often resisted suggestions by neighbors to get a doctor for a sick
wife. The loss of a cow or a horse cost money, but a wife was easily replaced
by remarriage to a younger woman who could bring a new dowry.

Bonds between parents and children

Besides the lack of emotional ties to infants and young children,   5
emotional bonds between parents and older children were also weak. First,
most of the children left the household at an early age. Second, when they did
so, it was largely a case of "out of sight, out of mind." If a child ventured
from the village, he or she was soon forgotten, not just by the neighbors but
by the parents as well. All traces were lost of those who moved away.
According to Shorter, a French village doctor wrote in his diary in 1710 that
he had heard about one of his brothers being hanged but that he had
completely lost track of the others.

Finally, even the children who stayed in the village did not come to   6
love their parents. Instead, they fought constantly with their parents about
inheritance rights and about when their parents would retire, and they openly
awaited their parents' deaths. Shorter concluded that dislike and hatred were
the typical feelings between family members.

Peer group bonds

Surely people in traditional societies must have liked someone.   7
Unfortunately for our image of traditional family life, the primary unit of
society and attachment was not the family but the peer group. The family
provided for reproduction, child rearing (such as it was), and economic
support (often grudgingly°), but emotional attachments were primarily to
persons of the same age and sex *outside* the family.

Wives had close attachments to other wives, and husbands to other   8
husbands. Social life was highly segregated by sex and was based on
childhood friendships and associations. For example, a group of
neighborhood boys would become close friends while still very young, and
these friendships remained the primary ties of these people all their lives. The
same occurred among women. While this no doubt provided people with a
source of intimacy and self-esteem, it hindered the formation of close
emotional bonds within the family.

A woman would enter marriage expecting to share her feelings not with   9
her husband but with her peers. Men reserved intimate feelings for their
peers, too. In this way the weak boundaries defining the household were
perforated° by primary relations beyond the family. Thus, outsiders
determined much that went on within a household. Husbands and wives often
acted to please their peers, not one another.

Of course, sometimes people loved their children, and some couples   10
undoubtedly fell in love. But most evidence indicates life in the preindustrial
household was the opposite of the popular, nostalgic image of quiet, rural
villages where people happily lived and died, secure and loved, amidst their

large families and lifelong friends. It was instead a nasty, spiteful, loveless life that no modern person would willingly endure. Indeed, as industrialization made other options possible, the family changed radically° because no one was willing to endure the old ways any longer.

Reading Comprehension Questions

Vocabulary in Context

1. The word *ventured* in "it was largely a case of 'out of sight, out of mind.' If a child ventured from the village, he or she was soon forgotten" (paragraph 5) means
   a. refused to go.
   b. temporarily went away.
   c. dared going.
   d. stole money or goods.

2. The word *hindered* in "[childhood] friendships remained the primary ties of these people. . . . While this no doubt provided people with a source of intimacy and self-esteem, it hindered the formation of close emotional bonds within the family" (paragraph 8) means
   a. expanded.
   b. got in the way of.
   c. learned from.
   d. helped.

Central Point and Main Idea

3. Which sentence best expresses the central point of the selection?
   a. People should marry for love.
   b. The main ties in preindustrial families were economic, with the primary emotional bonds being between peers.
   c. Life was difficult in preindustrial society.
   d. Social life in preindustrial society, based on childhood associations, was highly segregated by sex.

4. Which sentence best expresses the main idea of paragraphs 5 and 6?
   a. Parents and children had weak attachments to each other.
   b. Children left home at an early age.
   c. Even children who stayed in their parents' village didn't come to love their parents.
   d. Children fought often with their parents about inheritance rights.

5. Which sentence best expresses the main idea of paragraphs 8 and 9?
   a. Wives had close attachments to other wives.
   b. Men reserved intimate feelings for their peers.
   c. Women didn't expect to share their feelings with their husbands.
   d. Social life was segregated by sex and was reserved for peers, who thus got in the way of family life.

Supporting Details

6. Just as the main idea of a paragraph is supported by major details, so is the central point of a longer selection. Following is an outline of the selection. Fill in the missing major detail.

   Relationships in the Not-So-Good Old Days

   A. The ties between husbands and wives were mainly economical; the most common sentiments among them seem to have been negative ones.
   B. The emotional bonds between parents and children were weak.
   C. _____

   _____

Transitions

7. The relationship between the two parts of the sentence below is one of
   a. time.
   b. comparison.
   c. contrast.
   d. cause and effect.

   The loss of a cow or a horse cost money, but a wife was easily replaced by remarriage to a younger woman who could bring a new dowry. (Paragraph 4)

8. The supporting details listed in paragraphs 5 and 6 are introduced with the transitions *first*, *second*, and _____.

9. The relationship of the second sentence below to the first is one of
   a. addition.
   b. time.
   c. illustration.
   d. cause and effect.

   Social life was highly segregated by sex and was based on childhood friendships and associations. For example, a group of neighborhood boys would become close friends while still very young, and these friendships remained the primary ties of these people all their lives. (Paragraph 8)

10. The relationship between the two sentences below is one of
    a. addition.
    b. time.
    c. comparison.
    d. cause and effect.

    . . . the weak boundaries defining the household were perforated by primary relations beyond the family. Thus, outsiders determined much that went on within a household. (Paragraph 9)

5

Patterns of
Organization

To help readers understand their main points, authors try to present supporting details in a clearly organized way. Details might be arranged in any of several common patterns. Sometimes authors may build a paragraph or longer passage exclusively on one pattern; often, the patterns are mixed. By recognizing the patterns, you will be better able to understand and remember what you read.

THE FIVE BASIC PATTERNS OF ORGANIZATION

Here are the most commonly used patterns of organization:

1 Time Order
2 List of Items
3 Comparison and/or Contrast
4 Cause and Effect
5 Definition and Example

All five of the patterns are based on relationships you learned about in the last chapter. All five, then, involve transition words that you should now recognize. The time order pattern, for example, is marked by transitions that show time (*first, then, next, after,* and so on). The list on the next page shows some of the transitions used with each pattern:

Pattern	*Transitions Used*
Time order	Words that show time (*first, then, next, after . . .*)
List of Items	Words that show addition (*also, another, moreover, finally . . .*)
Comparison/Contrast	Words that show comparison or contrast (*like, just as, however, in contrast . . .*)
Cause and Effect	Words that show cause and effect (*because, as a result, since, leads to . . .*)
Definition and Example	Words that show illustration (*for example, to illustrate, such as . . .*)

The following pages provide explanations and examples of each pattern.

1   TIME ORDER

Arrange the following group of sentences into an order that makes sense. Put a *1* in front of the sentence that should come first, a *2* in front of the sentence that comes next, and a *3* in front of the sentence that should be last. The result will be a short paragraph.

_____   The water then begins to expand and rise, to be replaced by cold water from the upper regions of the pot.

_____   In the convection process, water from the bottom of a heating pot begins to move faster.

_____   After this heated water gets to the top, it cools off and sinks, to be replaced by newly heated water from the bottom.

Authors usually present events in the order in which they happen, resulting in a pattern of organization known as *time order*. Clues to the pattern of the above sentences are the transitions then and after. The sentences should read as follows:

In the convection process, water from the bottom of a heating pot begins to move faster. The water then begins to expand and rise, to be replaced by cold water from the upper regions of the pot. After this heated water gets to the top, it cools off and sinks, to be replaced by newly heated water from the bottom.

As a student, you will see time order used frequently. Textbooks in all fields describe events and processes, such as the events leading to the Boston Tea Party, the important incidents in Abraham Lincoln's life, the steps involved for a bill to travel through Congress, or the process of photosynthesis.

The following transition words often signal that a paragraph or selection is organized according to time order:

Time Transitions

first	next	as	while
second	before	now	during
then	after	until	when
since	soon	later	finally

Other signals for this pattern are dates, times, and such words as *stages, series, steps,* and *process.*

The two most common kinds of time order involve a *series of events or stages* and a *series of steps or directions.* Each is discussed below.

Series of Events or Stages

Following is a paragraph that is organized according to time order. Complete the outline of the paragraph by listing the missing stages in the order in which they happen.

The study of volunteers in sleep laboratories has led researchers to believe that humans go through four different stages of sleep in a normal night's rest. Immediately upon falling asleep, people enter stage 1 sleep, also called "light sleep" or "REM" (rapid eye movement) sleep. During this stage the sleeper's brain waves are irregular, his pulse rate is slow, and he is easily awakened. The next period of sleep, stage 2 sleep, is characterized by bursts of fast brain-wave activity called "spindles." During stage 3 sleep, the spindles disappear, and brain waves become long and slow. The sleeper's heart rate, blood pressure, and temperature all drop as well. The deepest level of sleep, during which the sleeper is hardest to awaken, occurs during stage 4 sleep. Extremely slow brain waves known as delta waves are present during this deep-sleep phase.

Main idea: The study of volunteers has led researchers to believe that humans go through four different stages of sleep in a normal night's rest.

1. _____

2. _____

3. *Stage 3: spindles replaced by long, slow brain waves*

4. _____

Here are the three stages of sleep observed in study volunteers that are missing from the outline, along with a few notes on each: Stage 1—light or REM sleep, irregular brain waves, slow pulse, easily awakened; Stage 2—burst of fast brain-wave activity called spindles; Stage 4—deepest level sleep; very slow brain waves called delta waves.

➤ *Practice 1a*

The following passage describes a theoretical sequence of events. Complete the outline of the paragraph by completing the main idea and filling in the missing major details.

Many scientists believe that the birth of our solar system began with death—the death of a star in a brief but enormous explosion. The shock wave from the explosion disturbed a cloud of gas and dust, compressing a portion of it. This compressed gas then became more and more compact, pulling into itself by its own gravity. The process of falling in towards its center heated the gas. Eventually the mass of gas and dust grew hot enough to support thermonuclear fusion reactions. At this point, the sun was born. It was surrounded by cold gas and dust. The radiation of the young sun soon blew away most of this outer material, but a small portion of it condensed to form the Earth and other planets.

Main idea: *One scientific theory says that our solar system* _____

_____

1. *A shock wave from a star's explosion compressed a cloud of gas and* _____

   dust. _____

2. _____

   _____

3. *When the heat was great enough for thermonuclear fusion reactions, the* _____

   sun was born. _____

4. _____

   _____

   _____

Series of Steps or Directions

On the next page is an example of a paragraph in which steps in a process are organized according to time order. Complete the outline of the paragraph that follows by adding the main idea and listing the missing steps in their correct sequence.

A four-step system can make your studying more effective. The first step is to preview an assignment. This includes reading the title, the introduction and conclusion, headings, and other significant parts. Next, read the selection straight through. As you do, mark important ideas, such as definitions and helpful examples. Third, write study notes on the selection in a rough outline form. The marking you did in the second step will help you focus in on the important points for your notes. Finally, recite the ideas in your notes. To help you do this, write key words in the margins of your study notes, and then turn those words into questions. For instance, the key words "three types of rocks" can be converted into the question "What are the three types of rocks?" Recite the answers to the questions until you can answer without referring to your notes.

Main idea: _____

_____

1. _____

_____

2. *Read the selection straight through, marking important parts as you do.*

3. _____

_____

4. _____

_____

You should have added the main idea ("A four-step system can make your studying more effective") and these steps: (1) Preview the selection. (3) Write notes on the selection in a rough outline form. (4) Recite the information in your notes.

➤ Practice 1b

The following passage gives directions that involve several steps that must be done in order. Complete the outline on the next page.

When you feel overwhelmed by a heavy work load, there are several steps you can take to gain control. The first is to list as quickly as possible everything that needs to get done. For a report or assignment, this can mean brainstorming or throwing as many ideas you can think of onto paper in ten minutes, without worrying about order or form. Secondly, divide the tasks into three groups: what has to be done immediately, what can be done within the next week or so, and what can be postponed till a later date. Next, break each task down into the exact steps you must take to get it done. Then, as on a test, do the easiest ones first and go back to the hard ones later. Instead of just worrying about what you ought to be doing, you'll be getting something done. And you'll be surprised at how easily one step leads to another.

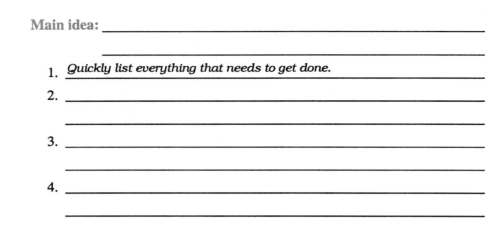

Main idea: _____

_____

1. *Quickly list everything that needs to get done.* _____

2. _____

_____

3. _____

_____

4. _____

_____

2 LIST OF ITEMS

Arrange the following group of sentences into an order that makes sense. Put a *1* in front of the sentence that should come first, a *2* in front of the sentence that comes next, and a *3* in front of the sentence that should be last. The result will be a short paragraph.

_____ In addition, unemployment among Native Americans is far above the national average.

_____ Statistics paint a bleak picture of the quality of life for many Native Americans today.

_____ First of all, the death rate for Navajo babies over eighteen weeks old is two and a half times the national average.

This paragraph begins with the main idea: "Statistics paint a bleak picture of the quality of life for many Native Americans today." The next two sentences go on to list two ways in which statistics show a poor quality of life for many Native Americans, resulting in the pattern of organization known as a *list of items*. The transitions *first of all* and *in addition* introduce the points being listed and indicate their order: "First of all, the death rate for Navajo babies over eighteen weeks old is two and a half times the national average. In addition, unemployment among Native Americans is far above the national average."

A *list of items* refers to a series of details (such as examples, reasons, or facts) that support a point. The items have no time order, so they are listed in the order the author prefers. The transitions used in lists of items tell us that another supporting detail is being added to one or more already mentioned. Following are some transitions that show addition and that often signal a listing pattern of organization:

Addition Transitions

and	in addition	first of all	furthermore
also	moreover	first	last of all
another	next	second	finally

A List of Items Paragraph

The main idea of the paragraph that follows is supported by a list of items. First underline the main idea. Then see if you can count the number of items (major details) in the author's list and also identify the type of item being listed. Note that transitions will help you find the items. After doing this exercise, read the explanation that follows.

A review of the ways America deals with its garbage reveals the problems we face in getting rid of and limiting our waste. First of all, most of the 500,000 tons of waste generated each day in the United States is buried in landfills. Landfills are expensive to construct, fill up rapidly and can contaminate groundwater. Incineration is cheaper and theoretically can pay for itself by producing energy in the form of electricity or steam. The initial construction expense, however, is enormous, and mechanical problems are common. Most disturbing is the potential threat incinerators pose to public health due to the dangerous toxic gases they emit during burning. Finally, an important way to deal with our garbage problem lies in reducing through recycling programs the amount of garbage produced in the first place. It has been estimated that up to 80 percent of our garbage can be eliminated through separation and recycling. To succeed, this method will have to be much more widely used than it is now.

How many items are listed: _____

What type of item is listed? _____

This paragraph consists of a main idea, stated in the topic sentence (the first sentence), followed by a list of three items, all supporting the main idea. The type of item listed in the paragraph is *ways America deals with its garbage* (landfills, incineration, and recycling). Notice that, in contrast to the major details of a time-order passage, the items might have been listed in any order without affecting the main idea of the paragraph.

➤ *Practice 2*

The following passages use a listing pattern. Underline each main idea. Then count the number of major-detail items used to support the main idea. Finally, answer the questions that follow each passage.

1.   The names of many people, real and fictional, have become permanent parts of the English language. General Ambrose Everett Burnside, for one, is remembered because of his long side whiskers—the Civil War-era general lent his name, with its syllables reversed, to the word *sideburns*. Another "person" whose name has been adopted into the language is that of Atlas, a giant from Greek mythology who supported the heavens on his shoulders. An early collection of maps had a picture of Atlas holding up the world, and *atlas* has come to mean any book of maps. Still another name-turned-word is that of Sir Robert Peel, the founder of the London (England) Metropolitan Police. London policemen are still called *bobbies* in honor of Sir Robert.

How many items are listed? _____

What type of item is listed? _____

_____

2.   Preventive medicine sounds ideal as a way of ensuring good health and reducing costs, but how do you actually prevent something from happening? A number of practitioners and health planners have figured out ways of putting preventive medicine into practice. The first way is primary prevention, which consists of actions that keep a disease from occurring at all. An example would be childhood vaccinations against polio, measles, and smallpox. Secondary prevention involves detection before a disease comes to the attention of the physician. An example would be self-examination by women for breast cancer. Tertiary prevention is not very different from medical care and consists of preventing further damage from already existing disease. Controlling pneumonia so it does not lead to death or maintaining a diabetic on insulin are examples of tertiary prevention.

How many items are listed? _____

What type of item is listed? _____

_____

3   COMPARISON AND/OR CONTRAST

Arrange the following group of sentences into an order that makes sense. Put a *1* in front of the sentence that should come first, a *2* in front of the sentence that comes next, and a *3* in front of the sentence that should be last. The result will be a short paragraph.

_____ "Informational" advertising introduces a product that is new to the market, telling consumers what it is, why they need it, and where it's available.

_____ Newly introduced products are generally advertised differently than well-established products.

_____ Established products, on the other hand, can rely on "reminder" advertisements, which provide little hard information about the actual product.

The first sentence of this paragraph is the general one, the one with the main idea: "Newly introduced products are generally advertised differently than well-established products." The word *differently* suggests a contrast pattern of organization. The comparison words *on the other hand* in one of the other two sentences show that types of advertising are indeed being contrasted: "'Informational' advertising introduces a product that is new to the market, telling consumers what it is, why they need it, and where it's available. Established products, on the other hand, can rely on 'reminder' advertisements, which provide little hard information about the actual product."

The *comparison-contrast* pattern shows how two things are alike or how they are different, or both. When things are *compared*, their similarities are pointed out; when they are *contrasted*, their differences are discussed (for example, the difference in advertising used for new and established products).

In our daily lives we compare and contrast things all the time, whether we are aware of it or not. For example, a simple decision such as whether to make a hamburger or a Swiss cheese sandwich for lunch requires us to compare and contrast the two choices. We may consider them both because of their similarities—they both taste good and are filling. We may, however, choose one over the other because of how they differ—a hamburger requires cooking while a cheese sandwich can be slapped together in about thirty seconds. If we are in a rush, we will probably choose the sandwich. If not, we may decide to have a hot meal and cook a hamburger instead.

Here are some common transitions showing comparison and contrast:

Comparison Transitions

like	just like	just as	alike
likewise	equally	resembles	also
similarly	similarities	same	similar

Contrast Transitions

however	on the other hand	different
in contrast	as opposed to	differently
instead	unlike	differs from

A Comparison/Contrast Paragraph

In the following paragraph, the main idea is stated in the first sentence. As is often the case, the main idea suggests a paragraph's pattern of organization. In this case, the transition *same* is a hint that the paragraph may be organized in a comparison-contrast pattern. Read the paragraph, and answer the questions below. Then read the explanation that follows.

In spite of the stereotype of the hardworking Asian immigrant who achieves the American dream against all odds, many refugees from Cambodia, Laos, and Vietnam suffer from the same kind of postwar trauma as Vietnam veterans. Like the returned vets, Asian refugees in this country are haunted by memories of the horrors of war and feel alienated from those who did not share that experience. But unlike the vets, they must deal with being torn apart from their families as well as learning to function in a language and a society foreign to them. Both groups, however, share symptoms common to war survivors, including recurring night terrors, inability to eat or sleep, and chronic depression.

1.   Is this paragraph comparing, contrasting, or both? _____

     _____

2.   What two things are being compared and/or contrasted?_____

     _____

3.   Which three comparison and/or contrast transitions are used in the

     paragraph? _____

This paragraph is both comparing and contrasting—it discusses both similarities and differences. The two things being compared and contrasted are the postwar trauma of refugees from Cambodia, Laos, and Vietnam and the postwar trauma of Vietnam veterans. Two comparison transitions are used—*same* and *like*. One contrast transition is used—*unlike*.

➤ *Practice 3*

The following passages use the pattern of *comparison* or *contrast*. Read each passage and answer the questions which follow.

A. People who move to a foreign country go through an adjustment process that often resembles what newlyweds experience. The first two weeks are the "honeymoon stage," characterized by a rosy fascination with all aspects of the foreign culture. The architecture, food, and people all seem clever and charming. As in marriage, however, reality sets in over the next few months, during the "disillusionment stage." The husband must deal with stockings hanging in the bathroom, and the wife with clothes on the floor. Similarly, the foreign visitor discovers that he must stand in three separate lines at the bank to get a check cashed and that the hot water comes on only once a day. Eventually, of course, the adjustment is made, and foreigners, like newlyweds, can relax and enjoy life within the new situation.

Check the pattern that is used in this paragraph:

_____ Comparison

_____ Contrast

What two things are being compared or contrasted?

1. _____ 2. _____

B. Many investigators report that women are less competitive and more cooperative than men and more concerned with social relationships. Compared to their friendships with men, both men and women report their friendships with women to be higher in intimacy, enjoyment, and nurturance. Judith Hall found that in 94 percent of published studies of adults smiling, females smiled more than males. More recent studies outside the laboratory confirm that women's generally greater warmth is frequently expressed as smiling. When Marianne LaFrance analyzed 9000 college yearbook photos, and when Amy Halberstadt and Martha Saitta studied 1100 magazine and newspaper photos and 1300 people in shopping malls, parks, and streets, they consistently found that females were more likely to smile. In groups, men contribute more task-oriented behaviors, such as giving information, and women contribute more positive social-emotional behaviors, such as giving help or showing support.

Check the pattern that is used in this paragraph:

_____ Comparison

_____ Contrast

What two things are being compared or contrasted?

1. _____ 2. _____

4   CAUSE AND EFFECT

Arrange the following group of sentences into an order that makes sense. Put a *1* in front of the sentence that should come first, a *2* in front of the sentence that comes next, and a *3* in front of the sentence that should be last. The result will be a short paragraph.

_____ Then, if the cold sufferer shakes hands with someone else after touching his nose, he is likely to transfer the germs to the other person.

_____ Since the nose is a major source of cold germs, a cold sufferer can easily become covered with germs by touching his nose.

_____ A handshake can result in the passing of one person's cold germs to another person.

As the words *since, result in,* and *if . . . then* suggest, this paragraph is organized in a *cause-and-effect* pattern. The paragraph begins with the general idea: "A handshake can result in the passing of one person's cold germs to another person." Next comes a more detailed explanation: "Since the nose is a major source of cold germs, a cold sufferer can easily become covered with germs by touching his nose. Then, if the cold sufferer shakes hands with someone else after touching his nose, he is likely to transfer the germs to the other person."

Information that falls into a *cause-effect* pattern addresses itself to the questions "Why does an event happen?" and "What are the results of an event?" In other words, this pattern answers the question "What are the *causes* and/or *effects* of an event?" In some cases, several causes will be a writer's focus; in other cases, several effects will be examined; in yet other instances, there will be a whole series of causes and effects.

Authors usually don't just tell what happened; they try to tell about events in a way that explains both *what* happened and *why*. A textbook section on the sinking of the ship the *Titanic*, for example, would be incomplete if it did not include the cause of the disaster—going at a high speed, the ship collided with an iceberg. Or if the banks of the Mississippi River are flooded, a newspaper will not simply report about the flooding. An article on this event would also tell why the flooding happened—heavy rains caused the river to overflow. An important part of any effort to understand events and processes includes learning about cause-effect relationships.

Explanations of causes and effects very often use transitions such as the following:

Cause-and-Effect Transitions

thus	because	because of	causes
as a result	result in	result	effects
therefore	since	consequently	leads to

A Cause-and-Effect Paragraph

Read the paragraph below and see if you can answer the questions about cause and effect. Then read the explanation to see how you did.

Most of the destruction in the great San Francisco Earthquake of 1906 was the result of fires that the earthquake triggered, and not the actual earthquake tremor. When buildings collapsed or were damaged in the quake, stoves and furnaces were overturned, resulting in the setting of numerous fires around the city. Fallen electrical wires started still other fires. At the same time, the earthquake ruptured the mains that were supposed to supply water for firefighting. Rubble in the streets blocked the paths of fire crews trying to reach burning areas. Thus, San Francisco's firefighters watched helplessly as the fires caused by the earthquake grew and grew until they leveled the city.

1. What was the direct cause of most of the destruction during the great earthquake in San Francisco in 1906?

   _____

2. What events did the earthquake cause which in turn led to fires?

   _____

   _____

   _____

3. What effects of the earthquake interfered with firefighting?

   _____

   _____

4. Which four cause-and-effect transitions are used in the passage?

   _____

The direct cause of most of the earthquake's destruction was fire. The events caused by the earthquake which led to the fires were 1) buildings collapsing and thus knocking down stoves and furnaces and 2) electrical wires being knocked down. The effects of the earthquake that interfered with firefighting efforts were 1) ruptured water mains that could thus no longer provide water for firefighting and 2) rubble in the streets that blocked fire crews. Finally, the cause-and-effect transitions used in the passage are *result, resulting in, thus*, and *caused by*.

➤ *Practice 4*

The three activities that follow (A, B, and C) will give you a sharper sense of cause-and-effect relationships.

A.   The following sentences describe a cause-and-effect relationship. For each sentence, identify both the cause and the effect.

    1. The fruit had fermented, causing the butterflies that sipped its nectar to become drunk.

       Cause:_____

       Effect:_____

    2. The more you smoke, the more you increase your risk of having a heart attack.

       Cause:_____

       Effect:_____

    3. According to a free-lance writer for *People* magazine, a picture of a movie star on the cover sells the most magazines.

       Cause:_____

       Effect:_____

    4. Human behavior is a product of an interaction between our basic biological heritage and the learning experiences of the particular culture in which we happen to live.

       Cause:_____

       _____

       Effect:_____

B.   The following sentences all list either two causes leading to the same effect or two effects resulting from a single cause. Identify causes and effects in each sentence. Here is an example of how to do this activity.

Example

    High winds and hailstones as big as golf balls resulted in $10,000 worth of property damage.

    High winds: *cause*
    Hailstones: *cause*
    Property damage: *effect*

    5. A torn ligament and a fractured ankle bone kept Raheem out of the final football game of the season.

       A torn ligament: _____

A fractured ankle bone: _____

Raheem could not play in the final game of the season: _____

6. Because of the high cost of raising a family and of housing, two-income families have become a way of life in America.

The high cost of raising a family: _____

The high cost of housing: _____

Two-income families being an American way of life: _____

7. Among the reasons that products fail are poor design and poor performance.

Products fail: _____

Poor design: _____

Poor performance: _____

8. We can prevent soil from being blown away by wind or from being washed away by rain simply by planting bushes and trees on the land.

Prevention of soil being blown away: _____

Prevention of soil being washed away: _____

Planting bushes and trees: _____

C. After reading each passage, answer the questions about causes and/or effects.

9. The mid-1970s brought drops in the scores achieved by high school students on the Scholastic Achievement Tests (SAT's). U.S. educators thus became concerned that our schools were not giving students enough grounding in basic academic skills and became convinced that students could best think for themselves if they had better basic skills. As a result, the byword is "back to basics," as schools emphasize these skills as part of standard curricula. One effect of the change is that high school and college students have shown a renewed interest in foreign languages, with the biggest jumps in enrollment in Japanese, Chinese and Russian.

    a. What was the *cause* of educators feeling our schools were not emphasizing basic skills enough? _____

    b. What was the *effect* of educators feeling our schools were not emphasizing basic skills enough? _____

    c. What is one effect of schools emphasizing basic skills as part of the standard courses of study? _____

    _____

10. Throughout millions of years of evolution, groups developed the ability to survive in certain climates. As a result, various peoples may share certain physical characteristics even though they come from very dissimilar racial backgrounds. American Plains Indians, Ethiopians, and Northern Europeans, for example, share the trait of a high-bridged, narrow nose because they all developed in similar cold, dry climates or higher latitudes. A high, narrow nose is an advantage under these conditions because it allows the air in the nasal passage to be moisturized before entering the lungs.

a. What is the *cause* of various groups that come from very different racial backgrounds sharing certain physical traits?_____

_____

b. What is an *effect* of the American Plains Indians, Ethiopians, and Northern Europeans all living in similar cold, dry climates or higher latitudes which are dry? _____

_____

c. What is the effect of a high-bridged, narrow nose on the dry air it breathes in? _____

_____

5   DEFINITION AND EXAMPLE

Arrange the following group of sentences into an order that makes sense. Put a *1* in front of the sentence that should come first, a *2* in front of the sentence that comes next, and a *3* in front of the sentence that should be last. The result will be a short paragraph.

_____ Self-proclaimed psychic Yuri Keller provides another example; he claims to be able to bend metal objects purely by willing them bent.

_____ For instance, participants in a famous series of experiments at Maimonides Hospital in Brooklyn appeared to dream about images being "sent" to them by people in another room.

_____ ESP, or extra-sensory perception, is the name for all supposed mental powers that extend beyond our normal senses.

This paragraph begins with a definition: "ESP, or extra-sensory perception, is the name for all supposed mental powers that extend beyond our normal senses." The second sentence provides an illustration of ESP: "For instance, participants in a famous series of experiments at Maimonides Hospital in

Brooklyn appeared to dream about images being 'sent' to them by people in another room." The third sentence then provides a second example: "Self-proclaimed psychic Yuri Keller provides another example; he claims to be able to bend metal objects purely by willing them bent." The second and third sentences include the illustration transitions *for instance* and *example*. As you can see, the *definition-and-example* pattern of organization includes just what its name suggests: a definition and one or more examples.

To communicate successfully, an author must help readers understand the words and ideas that are being expressed. If a word is likely to be new to readers, the author may take time to include a *definition* before going on. Then, to clarify the definition, which might be too general to be easily understood, the author may present explanatory details, including one or more *examples* to help readers better understand what is meant.

Textbooks often contain definitions and examples. They introduce students to new words and provide examples of how those words are used to make them clearer and more familiar. Typically, the definition appears first, followed by one or more examples. But sometimes the examples are given first and then the definition. And note that definitions may be given without examples, and examples are frequently used to illustrate general statements other than definitions.

Examples are often introduced by transitions like the following:

Example Transitions

for example	to illustrate	one
for instance	such as	specifically
as an illustration	to be specific	including

A Definition-and-Example Paragraph

The following paragraph defines a word, explains it a bit, and then gives an example of it. After reading the paragraph, see if you can answer the questions that follow.

[1]A loss leader is a product or service that sells at a loss but generates customer interest that can lead to a later profit. [2]A classic example of a loss leader is the ice-cream counter at a Thrifty's variety store. [3]Ice-cream cones are sold for less than the cost of the stand, equipment, supplies, and labor. [4]But the ice-cream counter, strategically placed near the store entrance, helps draw customers into the store. [5]Once inside, they often buy other items as well, so the store turns an overall profit. [6]The loss-leader principle is used in many other applications. [7]Television networks take a loss on special events like the Olympic Games because they believe that the viewers they attract will then "stay tuned" for their other, money-making shows.

What term is being defined? _____

What is the definition? _____

In which sentence does the first example begin? _____

How many examples are given in all? _____

      The term *loss leader* is defined in the first sentence—*a product or service that sells at a loss but generates customer interest that can lead to a later profit.* The first example of a loss leader is the ice-cream counter at a Thrifty's variety store; that example is first mentioned in sentence 2. In all, two examples are given, the second one being the fact that television networks take a loss on special events such as the Olympics so that viewers will stay tuned for money-making shows.

➤ Practice 5

The following passages include a definition and one or more specific examples, each marked by a transition. In the spaces provided, write the number of the definition sentence and the number of the sentence where each example begins.

A.   ¹While voluntary associations can be just as efficient (or inefficient) as formal organizations, their focus is generally somewhat different. ²Voluntary associations are organizations established on the basis of mutual interest, whose members volunteer or even pay to participate. ³For instance, the Girl Scouts of America, the American Jewish Congress, the Kiwanis Club, and the League of Women Voters are all considered voluntary associations.

     Definition _____   Example _____

B.   ¹When you write, you speak to your audience as a unique individual. ²Point of view reveals the person you decide to be as you write. ³Like tone, point of view is closely tied to your purpose, audience, and subject. ⁴Imagine you want to convey to students in your composition class the way your grandfather's death—on your eighth birthday—impressed you with life's fragility. ⁵To capture that day's impact on you, you might, for example, tell what happened from the point of view of a child: ⁶"Today is my birthday. ⁷I'm eight. ⁸Grandpa died an hour before I was supposed to have my party." ⁹Or you might choose instead to recount the event speaking as the adult you are today: ¹⁰"My grandfather died an hour before my eighth birthday party." ¹¹Your point of view will obviously affect the essay's content and organization.

     Definition _____   Example _____   Example _____

Topic Sentences and Patterns of Organization

A paragraph's topic sentence often indicates its pattern of organization. For example, the topic sentence of a paragraph you worked on earlier is: *A four-step system can make your studying more effective.* This sentence probably made you suspect that the paragraph goes on to list those four steps. If so, the paragraph would be organized according to time order (a series of steps). When a paragraph turns out to include the information you expect (as it does in that case), then you know you have found the correct pattern.

Another good example is the paragraph you read earlier on a San Francisco earthquake. The topic sentence of that paragraph is: *Most of the destruction in the great San Francisco Earthquake of 1906 was the result of fires that the earthquake triggered, and not the actual earthquake tremor.* The words *result of* suggest that this paragraph may be about causes and effects. And, in fact, most of the paragraph *is* about a chain of causes and effects.

So if you are having trouble recognizing a paragraph's pattern of organization, you may find it helpful to think about its topic sentence. Try, for instance, to guess the pattern of the paragraph with this topic sentence:

> While there are thousands of self-help groups, they all fall into three basic classifications.

The statement that self-help groups "fall into three basic classifications" is a strong indication that the paragraph will list those classifications. The topic sentence helps us guess that the paragraph may be a list of three items—that is, the three classifications.

➤ Practice 6

Circle the letter of the pattern of organization that each topic sentence suggests.

1. Depressed economic times often lead to an increase in spouse abuse and divorce.

   a. Definition and example   b. Cause and effect   c. Comparison/contrast

2. While Randy Jarvis and Octavio Ruiz live only a few miles from one another, their lives are so different they might as well be living in separate countries.

   a. Time order   b. Cause and effect   c. Comparison/contrast

3. There are several steps to remembering your dreams better.

   a. Comparison/contrast   b. Time order   c. Definition and example

4. People considering the purchase of a dog should first ask themselves several questions.

   a. Definition and example   b. Cause and effect   c. List of items

5. An important but little-known field of psychology is that of psycholinguistics, or the study of the psychology of language.

   a. Time order   b. Cause and effect   c. Definition and example

➤ *Review Test 1*

Label each item with the letter of its main pattern of organization. Each pattern is used twice.

a Time order
b List of items
c Comparison and/or contrast
d Cause and effect
e Definition and example

_____ 1. While humans grow until they reach maturity, a lobster will continue to grow for as long as it lives.

_____ 2. Our natural environment includes several visible forms of water: fog, clouds, dew, rain, frost, snow, sleet, and hail.

_____ 3. Because Soviet parents believe that being in cold outside air makes it harder to catch cold, they train their children to tolerate below-freezing temperatures.

_____ 4. *The Tragedy of Hamlet* begins outside the Danish castle, where two officers see the ghost of the murdered King, Hamlet's father. The officers soon decide to tell Hamlet about the ghost. Next we see the new king, Hamlet, and others enter a room of state in the castle.

_____ 5. Jungles are areas of land that are densely overgrown with tropical trees and other vegetation. In South America, the Amazon is the largest jungle.

_____ 6. If farmers alternate crops which take nitrogen from the soil with those that return nitrogen to the soil, then they can plant the same fields year after year.

_____ 7. Newspaper want ads are one of several excellent sources for secondhand goods. Others are garage sales, flea markets, and thrift shops.

_____ 8. Preventive medicine is like changing a car's oil. Just as we must change the oil regularly for a car to operate smoothly, we must have regular checkups with our doctors.

_____ 9. Norms are the standards of behavior accepted as appropriate in a society. In American society, for instance, wearing shoes to places like school and work is a norm.

_____ 10. Abe Lincoln took an unusual path to the Presidency. He lost his first job and then declared bankruptcy. He suffered a nervous breakdown and lost seven political contests before finally being elected to the White House.

> *Review Test 2*

Read each paragraph; then answer the question and complete the outline, map, or chart that follows.

A. The first day care centers in the United States were established by wealthy women in the 1850s. These centers cared for unwed mothers and their offspring. Not until the 1930s, during the Depression, did day care expand much beyond this limited role. The government then created day nurseries to provide free meals for poor children and employment for out-of-work teachers. The establishment of child care facilities increased dramatically during World War II as many women moved into the labor force to replace men away at war. Yet, until the last decade, day care was not nearly so common—or controversial—as it is today.

1. The main pattern of organization of the paragraph is
   a. time order   b. comparison/contrast   c. list of items

2. Complete the map of the paragraph. (You may recall from page 55 that a map, or diagram, is a very visual way of showing the relationship between the main parts of a selection.)

A General History of Day-Care Centers

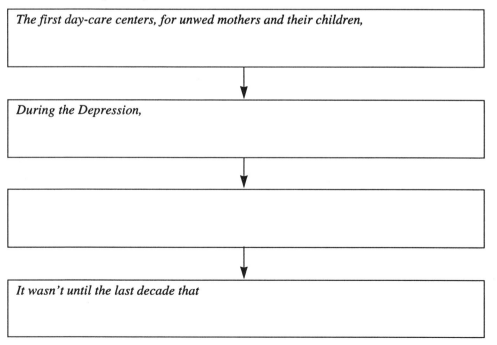

The first day-care centers, for unwed mothers and their children,

↓

During the Depression,

↓

↓

It wasn't until the last decade that

B.   There are several cultural reasons why the aged are stigmatized and oppressed in American society. One is that the members of our society are obsessed with youth. We have traditionally associated a number of highly valued traits with youth: beauty, health, sexual vigor, happiness, usefulness, and intelligence. One consequence is that those considered old are typically believed to be physically unattractive, sickly, asexual, useless, and incompetent.

Second, in our rapidly changing, highly technical society, old people are considered to be unnecessary. Their wisdom represents another age that is irrelevant now. By contrast, in simpler societies where tradition is paramount, the elderly are highly respected, admired, and even revered because they are the repositories for the group's accumulated wisdom. They serve as memories for the group, passing on to the next generation the cherished values, myths, and skills necessary for survival and success.

The elderly constitute a surplus population in yet another way: They are non-producers in a society where production translates into value. As Gornick puts it:

America is one of the worst countries in the world in which to grow old. This is a country in which the only value of a human being is the ability to produce. If you can produce, you are respected and have power; if you can't, you are despised and shunted aside.

Not only are the elderly devalued for their lack of productivity; they are also viewed as social leeches living off the production of the young. They are targets of possible increased resentment as their members grow and, thus, their cost to society increases.

1. The passage
   a. narrates events that illustrate a definition.
   b. compares and contrasts effects.
   c. lists a series of causes.

2. Complete the outline of the paragraph.

   Main idea: There are several cultural reasons why the aged are stigmatized and oppressed in American society.

   1. _____
      _____
   2. _____
      _____
   3. _____
      _____
   4. _____
      _____

C. Animals know their environment by direct experience only; man crystallizes his knowledge and his feelings in phonetic symbolic representations; by written symbols he accumulates knowledge and passes it on to further generations of men. Animals feed themselves where they find food, but man, co-ordinating his efforts with the efforts of others by linguistic means, feeds himself abundantly and with food prepared by a hundred hands and brought from great distances. Animals exercise but limited control over each other, but man, again by employing symbols, establishes laws and ethical systems, which are linguistic means of establishing order and predictability upon human conduct.

1. The main pattern of organization of the paragraph is
   a. time order   b. list of items   c. comparison/contrast

2. The following chart is one way of organizing the information in this paragraph for quick review. Fill in the empty boxes of the chart.

   Main idea: While animals know their environment only through experience, people use spoken and written symbols to accumulate and pass on knowledge.

	Animals	People
Getting food		
Control over others		

D. The crowd is one of the most familiar and at times spectacular forms of collective behavior. It is a temporary, relatively unorganized gathering of people who are in close physical proximity. Since a wide range of behavior is encompassed by the concept, sociologist Herbert Blumer (1946) distinguishes among four basic types of crowd behavior. The first, a casual crowd, is a collection of people who have little in common except that they may be participating in a common event, such as looking through a department-store window. The second, a conventional crowd, entails a number of people who have assembled for some specific purpose and who typically act in accordance with established norms, such as people attending a baseball game or concert. The third, an expressive crowd, is an aggregation of people who have gotten together for self-stimulation and personal gratification, such as at a religious revival or a rock festival. And fourth, an acting crowd is an excited, volatile collection of people who are engaged in rioting, looting or other forms of aggressive behavior in which established norms carry little weight.

1. The paragraph combines two patterns of organization, both
   a. time order and list of items.
   b. comparison and cause-and-effect.
   c. definition-example and list of items.

2. Complete the outline based on the paragraph.

   Main idea: Sociologist Herbert Blumer distinguishes among four types of crowds according to their behavior.

   1. _____
      a. *Definition: a collection of people who have little in common except they may be participating in a common event*
      b. *Example:* _____

   2. _____
      a. *Definition:* _____
      _____
      b. *Examples:* _____

   3. _____
      a. *Definition:* _____
      _____
      b. *Examples:* _____

   4. _____
      a. *Definition:* _____
      _____
      b. *Examples: rioting or looting*

➤ *Review Test 3*

A. To review what you've learned in this chapter, complete each of the following sentences about patterns of organization.

1. A paragraph's pattern of organization is the pattern in which its (*supporting details, main idea, causes and effects*) _____ _____ is or are organized.

2. The pattern in which a series of details are presented in any order the author considers best is called a _____.

3. The pattern in which the details discuss how two or more things are alike or different is a pattern of _____.

4. When a passage provides a series of directions, it uses a _____ order.

5. When textbook authors provide a definition of a term, they are likely to also provide one or more _____ to help make that definition clear.

B. How do you handle the conflicts in your life? Whatever your methods, you will probably recognize them in the following excerpt from the widely-used textbook *Communicate*! Sixth Edition, by Rudolph F. Verderber (Wadsworth, 1990). Following the selection are questions on patterns of organization. To help you continue to strengthen your work on the skills taught in previous chapters, there are also questions on

- vocabulary in context
- central point and main ideas
- supporting details
- transitions.

Words to Watch

Following are some words in the reading that do not have strong context support. Each word is followed by the number of the paragraph in which it appears and its meaning there.

stabilize (1): hold steady
ultimately (1): finally
disengagement (8): becoming free of a situation
martyring (10): sacrificing
coercion (11): force
obscured (12): hidden
degenerate (14): worsen
manipulation (14): unfairly controlling others for one's own purposes

MANAGING CONFLICTS IN RELATIONSHIPS

Rudolph F. Verderber

Will your relationships grow, be strengthened, and stabilize°, or will they wither and ultimately° die? The answer depends a great deal on how you manage conflict within them. Conflict is the clash of opposing attitudes, ideas, behaviors, goals, and needs. Although many people view conflict as bad (and, to be sure, conflict situations are likely to make us anxious and uneasy), conflict is sometimes useful in that it forces people to make choices and to test the relative merits of their attitudes, behaviors, needs, and goals.   1

Conflicts include clashes over ideas ("Charley was the first one to talk." "No, it was Mark" or "Your mother is a battle-ax." "What do you mean, a 'battle-ax'?"); over values ("Bringing home pencils and pens from work is not stealing." "Of course it is" or "The idea that you have to be married to have sex is completely outdated." "No, it isn't"); and, perhaps the most difficult to deal with, over ego involvement ("Listen, I've been a football fan for thirty years, I ought to know what good defense is." "Well, you may be a fan, but that doesn't make you an expert").   2

Patterns of Dealing with Conflict

People engage in many behaviors to cope with or manage their conflicts. Some are positive and some are negative. These many ways may be discussed under five major patterns. Let's consider each in turn.   3

Withdrawal   One of the most common—and certainly one of the easiest—ways to deal with conflict is to withdraw. *Withdrawal* is physical or psychological removal from the situation.   4

Physical withdrawal is, of course, easiest to identify. Dorie and Tom are in conflict over Tom's smoking. When Dorie says, "Tom, I thought you told me that   5 whether you stopped smoking completely or not, you weren't going to smoke around the house. Now here you are lighting up!" Tom may withdraw physically, saying, "I don't want to talk about it" as he goes to his basement workshop.

Psychological withdrawal may be more difficult to detect but every bit as common. Using the same example, when Dorie speaks to Tom about his smoking, Tom sits quietly in his chair looking at Dorie, but while she is speaking, he is thinking about the poker game he will be going to the next evening.   6

Both of these common withdrawal behaviors are negative. Why? Because they neither eliminate nor attempt to manage the nature of the conflict. For instance, when Tom withdraws physically, Dorie may follow him to the basement, where the conflict will be resumed; if not, the conflict will undoubtedly surface later—probably in an intensified manner—when Dorie and Tom try to cope with another issue. When Tom ignores Dorie's comments, Dorie may force Tom to cope with the smoking issue, or she may go along with Tom's ignoring her but harbor a resentment that will surface later.   7

There appear to be two types of situations where withdrawal may work. The first is when the withdrawal is temporary disengagement° used for the purpose of letting the heat of the conflict cool down. When Bill and Margaret begin to argue over having Bill's mother for Thanksgiving dinner, Margaret feels herself get angry about what her mother-in-law had said to her recently about the way she and Bill were raising their daughter. Margaret says, "Hold it a minute, let me make a pot of coffee. We can both relax a bit and then we'll talk about this some more." A few minutes later she returns, temper intact and ready to approach the conflict more objectively. Margaret's action is not true withdrawal; it is not meant as a means of avoiding confrontation. It provides a cooling-off period that will probably benefit both of them. The second case where withdrawal may work is when a conflict occurs between people who communicate infrequently. Jack and Mark work in the same office. At two office gatherings they have gotten into arguments about whether the company really cares about its employees. At the next office gathering Mark avoids sitting near Jack. Withdrawal is a negative pattern only when it is a person's major way of managing conflict.   8

Surrender   *Surrender* means giving in immediately to avoid conflict. Some people are so afraid of being in conflict that they will do anything to avoid it. For instance, Jeff and Marian are discussing their vacation plans. Jeff would like just the two of them to go somewhere together, but Marian has talked with two of their friends who are vacationing the same week about going together. After Jeff mentions that he'd like the two of them to go alone, Marian says, "But I think it would be fun to go with another couple, don't you?" Jeff replies, "OK, whatever you want." In this example Jeff really wants the two of them to go alone, but rather than describe his feelings or give reasons for his position, he gives in to avoid conflict.   9

Surrender is negative for at least two reasons: (1) Decisions should be made on merits and not to avoid conflict. If one person gives in, there is no evaluation of the decision—no one knows what would really be best. (2) Surrender can infuriate the other person. When Marian tells Jeff her thoughts, she would probably like Jeff to see her way as the best. But if Jeff just surrenders, Marian will perceive Jeff not as liking her plan but as martyring° himself. His unwillingness to present his reasons could cause even more conflict.   10

Aggression   The use of physical or psychological coercion° to get one's way is   11
aggression. Through aggression people attempt to force others to accept their ideas.
Through aggression a person may "win," but it seldom does anything positive for a
relationship. Aggression is an emotional reaction to conflict. Thought is short-circuited,
and the person lashes out physically or verbally. Aggression never deals with the merits
of the issue—only who is bigger, can talk louder, or is nastier.

In each of the above patterns, conflict is escalated or obscured°. In none is it   12
managed.

Persuasion   *Persuasion* is the attempt to change either the attitude or the behavior of   13
another person. At times during a conflict one person might try to persuade the other
that a particular action is the right one. Doris and Jack are considering buying a car.
Doris says, "Don't we need room?" Jack, her husband, might reply, "Enough to get us
into the car together, but I don't see why we need more than that." At this point, Doris
and Jack's conflict comes into focus. Now Doris might say, "Jack, remember the other
day when you were cussing out our present car because it doesn't have much back-seat
room? We carry a lot of stuff. I do food shopping, you're always carrying equipment
for men at the lodge, and there are lots of times when we invite another couple to go
somewhere with us." Statements like this one are attempts at resolving the conflict
through persuasion.

When persuasion is open and reasonable, it can be a positive means of resolving   14
conflict. But persuasion can degenerate° into manipulation°. Although persuasive
efforts may fuel a conflict, if that persuasion has a solid logical base, it is at least
possible that the persuasion will resolve the conflict.

Discussion   *Discussion* is verbal problem solving. It involves weighing and   15
considering the pros and cons of the issues in conflict. Discussion is the most desirable
means of dealing with conflict in a relationship; nevertheless, it is often difficult to
accomplish.

Problem-solving might follow the formal method of defining the problem,   16
analyzing the problem, suggesting possible solutions, selecting the solution that best
fits the analysis, and working to implement the decision. For instance, if Jeff and
Marian were discussing, they might focus on the problem of how they should spend
their vacation. They would seek to identify the goals they hoped to meet. They would
suggest places to go and the possibilities of going there with or without others. They
would consider how each possibility would meet their goals. Then they would select
the place and whether to go with their friends.

Reading Comprehension Questions

Vocabulary in Context

1. The word *harbor* in "When Tom ignores Dorie's comments, Dorie . . . may go along with Tom's ignoring her but harbor a resentment that will surface later" (paragraph 7) means
   a. hold onto.
   b. avoid.
   c. give up.
   d. pretend.

Central Point and Main Ideas

2. Which sentence best expresses the central point of the selection?
   a. Many people have a negative view of conflict.
   b. There are five main ways, both positive and negative, with which people deal with conflict.
   c. Conflicts can force people to make choices and to test their attitudes, actions, needs, and aims.
   d. It is better not to intensify or hide conflict.

3. The main idea of paragraph 8 can be found in its
   a. first sentence.
   b. second sentence.
   c. next-to-the-last sentence.
   d. last sentence.

Supporting Details

4. Fill in the missing detail in the outline below of paragraphs 4–8.

   Withdrawal is physical or psychological removal from the situation.

   A. Usually negative results—no attempt to eliminate or manage the conflict

   B. Two types of situations in which withdrawal may work

       1. _____

           _____

       2. When a conflict occurs between people who communicate infrequently

5. _____ TRUE OR FALSE? Discussion is both the easiest and most desirable way of dealing with conflict in a relationship.

Transitions

6. Write down one transition that is used in **paragraph 7**: _____

7. The two addition transitions that introduce major details in paragraph 8 are

   _____ and _____.

Patterns of Organization

8. Just as paragraphs are organized according to patterns, so are longer selections. The overall pattern of organization of this selection is
   a. time order.
   b. cause and effect.
   c. list of items.
   d. comparison and/or contrast.

9. In paragraph 7, examples are used to illustrate
   a. a series of steps in a process.
   b. items in a short list.
   c. a cause-and-effect explanation.
   d. a definition.

10. The pattern of organization of paragraphs 9 and 13 is
    a. time order.
    b. list of items.
    c. contrast.
    d. definition and example.

6

Summarizing and Outlining

Although everyone agrees that summarizing and outlining are valuable skills, they are all too seldom taught. To cite a personal example, while I was asked in high school to prepare summaries and outlines of books, stories, and articles, I was never actually taught how to do so. All of my teachers seemed to assume that someone else was responsible for helping me learn these sophisticated skills.

When I got to college, I had to do even more summarizing and outlining. For instance, many essay exam questions required summaries, that is, brief accounts of large amounts of material. I also had to summarize and outline when writing papers and giving reports, studying class lecture notes, and preparing study sheets on textbook reading assignments. Through necessity, then, I gradually learned how to summarize and outline effectively.

You are well positioned in this book to master summarizing and outlining in a more organized way than I did. What you have learned in the chapters on main ideas, supporting details, transitions and patterns of organization will help you with these two invaluable skills.

UNDERSTANDING SUMMARIES

All of us often summarize in everyday life. For example, in response to someone's question, we might summarize our day by saying:

"I had a good day" or "I had a bad day."

Or we might offer a slightly more specific summary:

"I had an exciting day" or "I had a depressing day" or "I had a busy day."

Or our summary might be even more detailed:

"I had a busy day. I had three classes at school this morning, spent the afternoon in the library doing homework, and then worked at my part-time job for five hours in the evening."

When we make such general statements, we are providing summaries. A *summary* can be defined as the reduction of a large amount of information to its most important points. Just as we can offer a summary of the numerous details of our day, so we can prepare summaries of the numerous details in our college course materials. Read the following two textbook passages, and then look at the summaries of them that follow.

Passage 1

Psychologists have developed a number of suggestions for controlling anger. A sense of humor can often defuse intense anger. By finding something amusing in the situation, you can make tension crumble. Physical exercises have also been effective in controlling anger. Using the added physical strength that intense emotions produce can help to release some pressure. Jogging, racquetball, hitting punching bags, and lifting weights are effective ways to use up physical energy. Relaxation exercises as well have been beneficial in controlling anger. One type of relaxation exercise stresses tensing and relaxing muscles in various parts of your body: your arms, your legs, your feet, and even your nose and tongue. Another relaxation exercise emphasizes deep breathing.

Summary of Passage 1

To control anger, psychologists suggest a sense of humor as well as physical and relaxation exercises.

Passage 2

Compromise is a common and effective way of coping directly with conflict or frustration. We often recognize that we cannot have everything we want and that we cannot expect others to do just what we would like them to do. We then compromise, deciding on a more realistic solution or goal since an ideal solution or goal is not practical. A young person who loves animals and greatly wishes to become a veterinarian may discover he has less aptitude for biology than he had hoped and that dissecting is so distasteful to him that he could never bring himself to operate on animals. By way of compromise, he may decide to become an animal technician, a person who works as an assistant to a veterinarian.

Summary of Passage 2

Compromise is a direct way of coping in which we decide on a more realistic solution or goal since an ideal solution or goal is not practical. For example, a person not good in biology may decide to be an animal technician rather than a veterinarian.

Important Points About Summarizing

1 A summary includes the main idea and often the major supporting details of a selection. In the summary of the first passage above, the main idea and the major details have been combined in one sentence. In the second summary, the main idea is the definition of compromise; it is followed by a brief example that helps make clear the definition. *Note that textbook summaries will often include definitions of key terms followed by condensed examples.*

2 At times a summary may be the main idea and only one or no major details; at other times, the summary may be a main idea followed by several major details. In other words, the length of a summary will depend upon your purpose. Just as a general guideline, though, a paragraph might be reduced to a sentence or two; an article might be reduced to a paragraph; an entire textbook chapter might be reduced to about three or so pages of notes.

3 A summary should *never* include more than one statement of the main idea. Authors—especially textbook authors—often repeat main ideas to make them as clear as possible. When summarizing, you must eliminate such restatements.

To avoid repetition, you must do the clear thinking necessary to truly understand the basic idea or ideas in a selection. You must "get inside" the material and realize fully what it says before you can reduce it to its essentials.

4 Depending on your purpose, a summary can be in the words of the author, or in your own words, or a combination of the two. If you are summarizing textbook material or a class lecture, you may be better off using the words of the author or of your teacher, especially where definitions of important terms are involved. (Notice in the second passage summarized above that the author's definition of *compromise* is used in the summary.) If you are summarizing a story or article as part of a written report, you will be expected to use your own words.

5 Your understanding of patterns of organization can often help you in summarizing material. For example, if a selection is basically a list of items, then you know your summary will also list items. If a selection is mainly a narrative (first this happened, then that happened), then your summary will briefly narrate a series of events. If a selection is mainly a series of definitions and examples, then your summary will provide both, with your focus on selecting and condensing the examples.

A Helpful Step in Summarizing: Recognizing Basic Ideas

Summarizing requires the ability to notice when an author is restating a main idea, rather than presenting another idea on the same topic. As already mentioned, textbook authors and other writers often restate ideas. By doing so, they help ensure clear communication. If the reader does not understand—or only partly understands—one wording of an idea, he or she may understand the idea when it is expressed again, in slightly different words. Effective readers and thinkers develop the ability to recognize such restatements of ideas.

Read the following passage. Then see if you can underline the two topic sentences—the sentences that express the main idea.

> [1]Our attention is selective—we focus on aspects of our environment that are most important to us or that we expect to see. [2]Thus we notice our doctor's receptionist, office hours, and the number of people sitting ahead of us in the waiting room. [3]We may fail to see the piece of modern art that is displayed on a wall. [4]We expect our boss to give us negative feedback, so we miss hearing the nice things he or she has to say. [5]We expect a friend to be a poor cook, so we notice the parts of the meal that are poorly prepared. [6]In the process, we fail to appreciate the parts of the meal that were tasty. [7]The significant issues in our lives and our beliefs act as filters on our environment, greatly determining what will and will not get our attention.

The main idea is first presented in sentence 1; it is then restated in sentence 7. The restatement emphasizes and clarifies the main idea. Keep in mind, then, that different sentences can state pretty much the same idea. For example, the above main idea could be worded in yet another way: "What we notice and what we ignore in our environment is largely determined by what is important to us and by our expectations."

To develop your ability to distinguish a restatement of the main idea from a basically different idea on the same topic, read the following sentence:

> **One reason we don't always listen carefully is that we're often wrapped up in personal concerns that are of more immediate importance to us than the messages others are sending.**

Now decide which three of the six statements below are basically the same in meaning as the above statement and which three are basically different. Put the letter *S* next to the three statements where the meaning is basically the same. After labeling each statement, read the explanations that follow.

_____ 1. Some people listen much more carefully than others.

_____ 2. One way to improve your listening skills is to look the speaker in the eye.

_____ 3. Because of personal distractions, we do not always pay close attention to a speaker.

____ 4. The messages that others convey to us are sometimes very distracting.

____ 5. We sometimes don't listen carefully because our minds are on personal issues.

____ 6. Being preoccupied with our own concerns is one cause of our poor attention to what others are saying.

Explanations:

1. Sentence 1 compares *how* people listen—some listen much more carefully than others. In contrast, the boldfaced statement is about *why* we don't always listen carefully. Although both statements are about listening carefully, they say basically different things about that topic.

2. Sentence 2 is also basically different from the boldfaced statement. Rather than explaining why we do not listen carefully, it is about a way to improve one's listening.

3. Both sentence 3 and the boldfaced sentence express the idea that personal distractions are one reason we don't always listen carefully. Therefore, sentence 3 means basically the same as the boldfaced sentence.

4. This sentence is about how distracting other people's messages can be, but the boldfaced sentence is about personal distractions. The two sentences have two different meanings.

5. Like the boldfaced sentence, this one explains that personal concerns sometimes keep us from listening carefully. Thus this sentence means basically the same thing as the boldfaced sentence does.

6. This sentence also explains that personal ("our own") concerns can keep us from listening carefully. It too is basically the same as the boldfaced sentence.

The following practice will help you develop the ability to recognize multiple statements of the main idea.

➤ *Practice 1*

Carefully read each opening statement (set off in **boldface**). Then decide whether each numbered statement that follows is basically the same in meaning or basically different in meaning from the opening statement. Write an *S* (for *Same*) next to the three statements where the meaning is closest to the original statement.

1. **Not everything that is faced can be changed, but nothing can be changed until it is faced.**

   ____ 1. There's no guarantee that a bad situation will improve, but it certainly will not unless it is confronted.

_____ 2. People are generally not willing to ask for help in solving their problems.

_____ 3. If a problem is to have a chance to be solved, it must be honestly acknowledged.

_____ 4. Since many problems are impossible to solve, it's just as well to ignore them.

_____ 5. All problems can be solved if the people involved will honestly face the situation.

_____ 6. Even a problem that is solvable will not be solved unless it is faced.

2. **We may be motivated to eat by "internal cues," such as hunger pangs or low blood glucose, or "external cues," including attractive food, the time of day, or commercials for food.**

_____ 1. Overweight people are overly influenced by external cues to eat.

_____ 2. There are two types of cues that motivate us to eat: internal and external.

_____ 3. When people are not hungry, external cues to eat have no effect.

_____ 4. The motivators that cause people to eat can be categorized as either "external cues" or "internal cues."

_____ 5. External cues are even more powerful motivators to eat than are internal cues.

_____ 6. We may get the urge to eat because of inner physical conditions or from signals in our environment.

3. **Once we form an opinion of someone, we tend to hang onto it and make any conflicting information fit our image.**

_____ 1. Our first impression of another person is quickly displaced by a second, more accurate impression.

_____ 2. First impressions are very powerful. Even as we learn more about a person, we assume that our first impression was basically correct.

_____ 3. It's important not to allow ourselves to form an immediate impression of someone we've just met.

_____ 4. First impressions are difficult to change even if we learn new information that contradicts them.

_____ 5. First impressions tend to be lasting.

_____ 6. Our first impressions of people will almost invariably be proven correct by what we later learn about them.

Summarizing Short Passages

As stated earlier, many passages of paragraph length can often be reduced to the main idea and one or more major supporting details. This section will give you practice in doing passage-length summaries. It will also introduce outlining, which can be a helpful step in doing summaries.

Read the passage below. Then decide which of the five statements that follow accurately summarizes the essential information of the passage.

> For some people, the need to achieve is low because they actually fear becoming successful. Research by Matina Horner and others shows that this fear of success occurs in both men and women. Why should someone display anxiety over getting ahead in life? Several factors seem to be involved. Horner implies that some individuals may fear that success will bring social rejection. They fear losing their close friends or having people reject them because "now he or she is better than I am." Herb Goldberg suggests that guilt is another factor. People may feel guilty because they somehow "do not deserve to be better than other people." This reaction is sometimes observed in children who succeed better than their parents did. John Sisk indicates that anxiety over losing control may also be important. Successful people typically acquire a lot of money and other material goods. Sisk believes that "affluence like passion means a loss of control." As one gets more success, money, and material things, there is a risk that such things will control what we do. Some people probably worry that they will lose the freedom to act independently.

Circle the letter of the statement that best summarizes the passage.

a. Some men and women have a low need to achieve because they fear that success will bring social rejection, guilt, or loss of control.
b. Some people fear that they will lose the freedom to act independently because of social rejection, guilt, and loss of control.
c. Some people may fear that acquiring a lot of money will mean a loss of freedom to act independently.
d. The low need to achieve is sometimes caused by the fear that success will bring social rejection.

Here is how you could have determined the best answer above—and how you can go about summarizing any passage:

1 First read the entire passage through once. Then reread it, asking yourself, "What is the topic of this passage, and what point is being made about the topic?"

2 As you reread the passage, you'll note that the topic is fear of success: the first several sentences all refer to a fear of success. You'll note also what

is said about the topic: that several factors seem to be involved in this fear of success. You are now ready to put together the implied main idea: "Some people have a low need to achieve because they fear success for various reasons."

3 At almost the same time that you are asking yourself, "What is the topic?" and "What is the point being made about the topic?" you should ask, "What are the major details that support the point?" A further study of the passage reveals that it is basically a list of items—it lists the three reasons, or factors, behind people's fear of success. (Notice that two transition words in the passage—*another* and *also*—help signal that a list is being provided.) The major supporting details of the passage are the three factors: fear of social rejection, feelings of guilt, and anxiety over losing control.

You may find it very helpful while summarizing to do a mini-outline of the passage by numbering the supporting points. On scratch paper or the textbook margin or simply in your head, you might create the following:

> *Point:*   People fear success for various reasons.
> *Support:*   1. fear of social rejection
> 2. feelings of guilt
> 3. anxiety over losing control

Such an outline will help you understand the content and basic relationships in a passage. You can then proceed with summarizing the material.

4 For the above passage, you should have chosen statement *a* as the best summary—it is a one-sentence combination of the main idea and the three major supporting details. Statement *b* is incorrect because the main idea is about the fear of success, not the fear of losing the freedom to act independently. Statement *c* is incorrect because it covers only one minor detail. And finally, statement *d* is incorrect because it is about only one of the three major details.

➤ *Practice 2*

Circle the letter of the statement or statements that best summarize each selection that follows. Your choice should provide the main idea; it may include as well one or more major supporting details.

1. Working conditions in the nineteenth century seem barbaric today: twelve- to fourteen-hour workdays; six- and seven-day weeks; cramped, unsafe factories; marginal wages; and no legal protection. Yet employers seldom had problems motivating their workers: Poverty and unemployment were so widespread that any job was welcome.

a. Working conditions in the nineteenth century were difficult and even dangerous.

b. Workers in the nineteenth century were more highly motivated than their twentieth-century counterparts.

c. Widespread poverty and unemployment made nineteenth-century workers willing to put up with terrible working conditions.

d. Legal protection and wages have improved sharply since the barbaric conditions that prevailed in the nineteenth century.

2. The hallmark of representative democracy is that all citizens have the fundamental right to vote for those who will administer and make the laws. Those in power have often defied this principle of democracy by minimizing, neutralizing, or even negating the voting privileges of blacks. Although the Fourteenth Amendment gave blacks the right to vote after the Civil War, the white majority in the Southern states used a variety of tactics to keep them from voting. Most effective was the strategy of intimidation. Blacks who tried to assert their right to vote were often beaten, sometimes lynched, or their property was destroyed.

a. All citizens of a democracy have a right to vote for those who will administer and make laws, and nobody should try to interfere with that right.

b. Those in power have often interfered with the constitutional voting rights of blacks through various tactics, the most effective being cruel intimidation.

c. After the Civil War, blacks who tried to vote were often beaten.

d. Those in power have often defied the principles of democracy in order to further their own selfish ends.

3. All family systems can be roughly categorized into one of two types. The *extended family* is one in which more than two generations of the same kinship line live together, either in the same house or in adjacent dwellings. The head of the entire family is usually the eldest male, and all adults share responsibility for child-rearing and other tasks. The extended family, which is quite commonly found in traditional, preindustrial societies, can be very large: sometimes it contains several adult offspring of the head of the family, together with all their spouses and children. In contrast, the *nuclear family* is one in which the family group consists only of the parents and their dependent children, living apart from other relatives. The nuclear family occurs in some preindustrial societies, and is the usual type in virtually all modern industrialized societies. In fact, the growing dominance of the nuclear family is transforming family life all over the world.

a. There are two types of families. In the extended family, in which more than two generations of family live together, the head of the family is the eldest male and all adults share in family tasks. This type of family is common in preindustrial societies.

b. There are various types of families. The nuclear family is the most common among modern industrialized societies. The dominance of the nuclear family is transforming family life worldwide.

c. An extended family consisted of two generations of family living together. A nuclear family consists of parents and their dependent children. It occurs in some preindustrial societies and is the usual type of family in just about all modern industrialized societies.

d. There are two basic types of families. The extended family, which is more than two generations living together, is common in preindustrial societies. The nuclear family, made up of parents and their dependent children, is usual in industrialized societies.

UNDERSTANDING OUTLINES

Very often a good way to summarize something is to outline it first. An *outline* is itself a summary in which numbers and letters are often used to set off the main idea and the supporting details of a selection. For example, the passage on page 120 about controlling anger could have been outlined as follows:

Psychologists suggest several ways to control anger.
1. Sense of humor
2. Physical exercises
3. Relaxation exercises

Important Points About Outlining

1 Most outlines start with a main idea (or a title that summarizes the main idea) followed by one or more levels of major and minor details, marked by numbers and letters. The outline above on controlling anger needs only one level of numbers. Most outlines should not need more than two or three levels.

Note that you have already worked with outlines in the chapters on supporting details and patterns of organization. In most cases, you used only one level of symbols. In some instances, as on pages 53, 62, and 112, you used two levels of symbols.

2 When doing an outline, put all points of equal importance at the same distance from the margin. Thus in the outline on controlling anger, all three ways to control anger are placed (and numbered) at the same distance from the margin.

Here is how an outline might look:

MAIN IDEA
    Major Detail
        Minor Detail
        Minor Detail
    Major Detail
        Minor Detail
        Minor Detail

Note that an outline proceeds from the most general to the most specific, from main ideas to major details to minor details.

3   Students sometimes find it helpful to use mapping rather than outlining. In *mapping* you create a visual outline of shapes as well as words. Circles, boxes, and other shapes are used to set off main ideas and supporting details. Elsewhere in this book, mapping or a chart is sometimes used as an alternative to outlining. (See, for example, pages 55, 56, and 57.) While this chapter will focus on outlining, keep in mind that you can at times use maps and charts as well to show the relationships between ideas and details in a selection.

4   Both outlines and summaries are excellent thinking tools that will help you with all your reading and study assignments. Either demands that you work to identify the main idea of a selection and to understand the relationship between it and the major details that develop the idea. *The very act of doing an outline or a summary will help you understand and master the material.*

5   With class lecture notes and textbook reading assignments in particular, outlines and summaries are excellent review materials. Studying an outline or a summary is easier and more productive than repeated rereading of an entire set of notes or entire text chapters. The next part of this chapter offers tips and practice in outlining and summarizing textbook material.

OUTLINING AND SUMMARIZING A TEXTBOOK CHAPTER

I will never forget the first college course for which I had to read and study a great deal of material. For Introduction to Psychology, I had a teacher that students called Shotgun O'Connor. He was so named because during class he shot off dozens (it seemed like hundreds) of ideas. I typically filled up ten or so notebook pages per class, leaving my head spinning and my hand cramped. I remember using up several Bic pens that semester. Besides having to know the lecture material for each test, students also were responsible for three textbook chapters not covered in class.

Three weeks into the semester, I sat down on a Saturday to study for my first exam. With all the class material to cover, I knew I would have to study very efficiently, getting as much out of my time as possible. I spent most of the day reading the three textbook chapters, and that same evening I started to study them. After about two hours of work I had reread and studied the material on the first four pages of the first chapter; I still had almost ninety-two pages to go. I also had a pile of lecture notes to study.

When I realized my problem, I just sat at my desk for a while, wondering what to do. It was then that my roommate, who himself faced a mountain of material to study, suggested we order a pizza. I quickly agreed. I felt like a dying man, so I figured it wouldn't hurt to have a last meal. But the pizza went down in heavy lumps. I knew my days in college were numbered unless I came up with a system for organizing and condensing all the material I had to study.

Here in a nutshell is what I learned to do with the chapters in my psychology book (I used a similar system with my lecture notes):

1 I went through the chapters and marked off all the definitions of key terms, along with an example in each case that made each definition clear for me. Specifically, I would put *DEF* in the margin for a definition and *EX* in the margin for an example.

2 Then I outlined the material, so that basic relationships were clear. I did this mainly by looking for relationships between main headings and subheadings within each chapter. For instance, one of the headings in the first chapter was "The Methods of Psychology." I wrote down that heading and then wrote down and numbered all the subheadings that fit under it:

> *The Methods of Psychology*
>   *1. The Naturalistic-Observation Method*
>   *2. The Experimental Method*
>   *3. The Correlational Method*

3 I also wrote down the definitions of each of these methods, and an example of the method, along with what seemed to be other important details about the method.

4 Then I recorded the next main heading and the subheadings under it. In cases where there were no subheadings, I tried to convert the heading into a basic question and answer the question. For example, one heading in my psychology text chapter was "The Social Relevance of Psychology." I turned that into the question "What *is* the social relevance of psychology?" and then wrote a summary of the textbook author's answer to that question. When I was done, I had reduced thirty-two pages in the textbook chapter down to three pages of notes. I had, in effect, used a combination of outlining and summarizing to condense a large amount of information down to its most important points.

That in a nutshell was my study method: read all the material through once; then go back to pick out definitions and examples, to outline and number the basic relationships in the material, to ask and answer in a condensed way any basic questions of the headings; and finally write it all down in the form of outline and summary notes. I found that the notetaking process was a vital step in both understanding the material and in beginning to remember it.

I next concentrated on studying my notes, which gave me a core of knowledge that I was able to draw upon to deal with Shotgun O'Connor's first test. I scored a low B on that test, and as I became better at outlining and summarizing, my scores on later tests were even better. (A colleague of mine, Gayle Edwards, describes a similar study system in this book on pages 391–397.)

To get a sense of how to outline and summarize textbook material, read the following passage. Then circle the letter—A, B, or C—of the notes that most accurately reflect the content of the passage.

> Anxiety becomes a disorder when fears, ideas and impulses are exaggerated or unrealistic. A person suffering from *anxiety disorder* often has such physical symptoms as sweating, shaking, shortness of breath, and a fast heartbeat. *Phobias*, the most common form of anxiety disorder, are continuing unrealistic fears that interfere with normal living. For instance, instead of fearing only threatening animals, a phobic person may fear all animals, even those that are docile and friendly. People with this phobia may panic at the sight of a harmless snake or mouse.
>
> Eating problems are another form of anxiety disorder. One eating disorder, *anorexia nervosa*, generally begins when young girls grow anxious about becoming overweight. Although they initially want to eat, they eventually completely lose their desire for food. They diet continually, even when they are so underweight that their lives are threatened. The sight of food makes them nauseated. In a related disorder, *bulemia*, the person goes on eating binges and then uses laxatives or vomits to purge herself. Bulimia is believed to be most common among college-age women.
>
> There are also obsessive-compulsive anxiety disorders. *Obsessions* are persistent ideas or impulses that invade people's minds against their will and cannot be gotten rid of by reasoning. One common obsession is an intense fear of germs. Someone with this obsession refuses to shake hands or otherwise come into contact with others. Obsessions often lead to *compulsions*, which are persistent behaviors. Feeling they are never clean, for instance, people obsessed with fears of contamination may become compulsive about hand-washing.

A. Anxiety disorder—an exaggerated or unrealistic fear, idea, or impulse, often with physical symptoms such as shaking or fast heartbeat.

Types:
1. Phobias—unrealistic fear that interferes with daily living, such as of a harmless animal
2. Eating disorders—unrealistic fear of gaining weight

   a. Anorexia nervosa—loss of desire for food
   b. Bulemia—eating binges followed by purging
3. Obsessive-complusive disorders—exaggerated, unrealistic ideas and impulses
   a. Obsession—persistent idea, such as fear of being contaminated by germs
   b. Compulsion—persistent behavior, such as constant hand-washing

B. Anxiety disorder—often includes physical symptoms such as sweating, shaking, shortness of breath, and a fast heartbeat

   Types:
   1. Phobias—fear that interferes with daily living
   2. Anorexia nervosa—loss of desire for food
   3. Bulemia—eating binges followed by purging
   4. Obsession—persistent idea, such as fear of being contaminated by germs
   5. Compulsion—persistent behavior, such as constant hand-washing

C. Anxiety disorder—an exaggerated or unrealistic fear, idea, or impulse, often with physical symptoms such as shaking or fast heartbeat

   Types:
   1. Phobias
      a. Fear that interferes with daily living, such as of a harmless animal
      b. Anorexia nervosa—loss of desire for food
      c. Bulemia—eating binges followed by purging
   2. Obsessive-complusive disorders
      a. Obsession—persistent idea, such as fear of being contaminated by germs
      b. Compulsions—persistent behavior, such as constant hand-washing

To find the best of the three sets of notes, you must do the same thing you would do if you were outlining the passage yourself—identify the main idea and major and minor details. A careful reading of the passage reveals that the main idea of the passage is: "There are various types of anxiety disorders, which are exaggerated or unrealistic fears, ideas, and impulses that often cause such physical symptoms as sweating, shaking, shortness of breath." The major details are the three types of anxiety disorder listed: phobias, eating disorders, and obsessive-compulsive disorders. Thus the outline that best reflects the passage will define and explain *anxiety disorders* and then go on to name and explain the three types listed.

Having analyzed the passage, let's turn to the above sets of notes. Set A defines and explains *anxiety disorder* and goes on to list and explain the three types of anxiety disorder. The important minor details have been listed as well. Set A, then, is a pretty good condensation of the passage.

In contrast, Set B does not account for two of the major-detail categories: eating disorders and obsessive-compulsive disorders. In Set C, the category of eating disorder has been skipped, and anorexia nervosa and bulimia are incorrectly identified as phobias.

➤ *Practice 3*

Read each of the selections that follows. Then circle the letter of the notes that best outline and summarize the material in each selection.

1. Eric Erikson divided adulthood into three stages. In his view the central task of the first stage, young adulthood, is that of achieving *intimacy*. The young person who has a firm sense of identity is eager and able to fuse his or her identity with another person's in a loving relationship, without fear of competition or loss of self. A young person who avoids commitment may experience isolation. In middle age, personal and social concerns merge. Adults who feel they have contributed something of value to society and who are involved in guiding the next generation (as parents or in other roles) experience *generativity*. Those who do not experience stagnation—the sense of going nowhere, doing nothing important. Generativity lays the foundation for *integrity* in old age, a sense of a life well lived. Older people who have achieved integrity are satisfied with the choices they made and feel that had they a second life to live, they would "do it all over again." They see death as the final stop in a meaningful journey.

   A. Erickson's three stages of adulthood
      1. Intimacy—a fusion with another in a loving relationship
      2. Generativity—feeling of contributing something of value
      3. Integrity—a sense of a life well lived

   B. Erickson's stages of adulthood
      1. Intimacy
      2. Isolation
      3. Generativity
      4. Stagnation
      5. Integrity

   C. Erickson's stages of adulthood
      1. Young adulthood
         - intimacy achieved in a loving relationship
         - avoidance of commitment may result in isolation
      2. Middle age
         - generativity achieved by those contributing to society and guiding the young
         - stagnation experienced by those who don't contribute
      3. Old age—integrity achieved through a sense of a life well lived

2.   Across the life span we find ourselves immersed in countless relationships. Few are more important to us than those we have with our **peers**—individuals who are approximately the same age. Peer groups serve a variety of functions. First, they provide an arena in which children can exercise independence from adult controls. Next, peer groups give children experience with relationships in which they are on an equal footing with others. In the adult world, in contrast, children occupy the position of subordinates, with adults directing, guiding, and controlling their activities. Third, peer groups afford a social sphere in which the position of children is not marginal. In them, youngsters can acquire status and achieve an identity in which their own activities and concerns are paramount. And last, peer groups are agencies for the transmission of informal knowledge, sexual information, deviant behaviors, superstitions, folklore, fads, jokes, riddles, and games. Peers are as necessary to children's development as adults are; the complexity of social life requires that children be involved in networks both of adults and peers.

   A. Children need relationships with both adults and peers.
      1. Peer groups provide an arena in which children exercise independence from adult controls.
      2. Peer groups provide adolescents with an impetus to seek greater freedom.
      3. Peer groups give children experience with relationships in which they are on an equal footing with others.
      4. Adult-child relationships allow adults to direct, guide, and control children's activities.
      5. Peer groups provide a social sphere in which children's don't have a marginal position.
      6. Peer groups transmit informal knowledge.

   B. Peer groups, made up of individuals who are about the same age, serve various functions.
      1. Provide an arena in which children can exercise independence from adult controls
      2. Give children experience with being on an equal footing with others, allowing for important different experiences than in adult-child relationships
      3. Provide a social sphere in which children don't have a marginal position
      4. Transmit useful knowledge

   C. Across the life span we find ourselves immersed in countless relationships.
      1. Peer relationships—with individuals who are approximately the same age

    2. Adolescent-adult relationships

    3. Adult-child relationships

    4. Networks of both adults and peers

3.   Our capacity to learn from watching as well as from doing means that the mass media have important socialization consequences for us. The mass media are those organizations—television, radio, motion pictures, newspapers, and magazines—that convey information to a large segment of the public. All the mass media educate. The question is: What are they teaching? The good news from research is that prosocial (positive and helpful) models can have prosocial effects. Children who view a prosocial television diet, including such programs as *Sesame Street* and *Mr. Rogers' Neighborhood*, exhibit greater levels of helping behaviors, cooperation, sharing, and self-control than children who view a neutral or violent diet. Moreover, these programs have a positive effect on language development.

        The bad news from television research is that there is a link between the mayhem and violence on children's programs and aggressive behavior in children. Although televised violence does not harm every child who watches it, many children imitate the violent attitudes and behaviors they see. Prime-time programs depict about five violent acts per hour, and Saturday-morning cartoons average twenty to twenty-five violent acts per hour. By the time most young people leave high school, they have spent more time before a television screen than in the classroom. In the process they will have witnessed some 13,000 murders. Television not only provides opportunities for children and adults to learn new aggressive skills, it also weakens the inhibitions against behaving in the same way. And television violence increases the toleration of aggression in real life—a "psychic numbing" effect—and reinforces the tendency to view the world as a dangerous place.

A.   The mass media have important socialization consequences for us.

    1. The mass media convey information to a large segment of the public.

       a. television

       b. radio

       c. motion pictures

       d. newspapers

       e. magazines

    2. TV research reveals a link between TV violence and aggressive behavior in children.

       a. Violence on TV makes children more aggressive and violent.

       b. TV violence increases toleration of real-life aggression.

       c. TV violence reinforces the tendency to view the world as a dangerous place.

    B. The mass media influence the public.

        1. Researchers have found positive influences.

          a. Prosocial models can have prosocial effects.

          b. Children's programs help language development.

        2. Researchers have found negative influences.

          a. Violence on TV makes children more aggressive and violent.

          b. TV violence increases toleration of real-life aggression.

          c. TV violence reinforces the tendency to view the world as a dangerous place.

    C. The mass media influence the public.

        1. Prosocial models can have prosocial effects.

          - Programs such as *Sesame Street* and *Mr. Rogers' Neighborhood* encourage helping behavior in children who watch.

        2. Children's programs help language development.

        3. Prime-time programs depict about five acts of violence an hour.

        4. TV violence increases toleration of real-life aggression.

          - By the end of high school, more young people have spent more time before a TV than in the classroom.

        5. TV violence reinforces the tendency to view the world as a dangerous place.

          - By high school, children will have witnessed some 13,000 murders on TV.

➤ Review Test 1

A. Carefully read each opening statement (set off in **boldface**). Then decide whether each numbered statement that follows is basically the same in meaning or basically different in meaning from the opening statement. Write an *S* (for *Same*) next to the three statements where the meaning is closest to the original statement.

1. **People are comfortable making statements of fact and opinion, but they rarely disclose their feelings.**

    ____ 1. People are less comfortable in conveying their feelings than they are in expressing facts and opinions.

    ____ 2. Facts and opinions are far more reliable predictors of people's actions than are feelings.

    ____ 3. As people get to know one another better, they talk less in terms of facts and opinions and more in terms of feelings.

    ____ 4. It is easier for people to talk in terms of facts and opinions than about emotions.

    ____ 5. People who keep their emotions closely bottled up tend to be extremely opinionated.

    ____ 6. People rarely express how they feel, being much more comfortable expressing facts and opinions.

2. **If those who have studied the art of writing are in accord on any one point, it is this one: the surest way to arouse and hold the attention of the reader is by being specific and definite.**

_____ 1. Concrete language quickly attracts readers' interest, but does not hold it for very long.

_____ 2. Experts know that if you want your writing to be read and enjoyed, use plenty of specific details and concrete language.

_____ 3. It is not easy to hold the attention of the reader.

_____ 4. Definite and concrete language, say the experts, grabs and holds the reader's attention best.

_____ 5. Readers' attention is difficult to capture, but once you have it, it's easy to keep.

_____ 6. Experience has shown that people prefer reading detailed writing and definite language to more general writing.

B. Circle the letter of the answer that best summarizes each selection that follows.

3. Of all major ethnic groups in the United States, Japanese Americans are most economically successful. There seem to be two major factors involved in the Japanese American "success story." The first factor is that of educational achievement. On the average, both male and female Japanese Americans complete more years of schooling than the general population. For example, while 13 percent of all U.S. males complete college, 19 percent of Japanese American males do. The second factor that helps explain the Japanese American economic success is their assimilation into the larger society. Their high intermarriage rate is evidence of that assimilation. About 40 percent of third-generation Japanese Americans marry non-Japanese Americans. Such merging into mainstream culture helps insure that the doors of economic opportunity swing open for many Japanese Americans.

a. Because of their high assimilation rate, Japanese Americans are the most economically successful of all major ethnic groups in the United States. Their high intermarriage rate is evidence of their assimilation.

b. Of all major ethnic groups in the United States, Japanese Americans are the most economically successful.

c. While 13 percent of all U.S. males complete college, 19 percent of Japanese American males do.

d. Japanese Americans are the most economically successful of all major ethnic groups in the United States because of their high level of educational achievement and their high rate of assimilation into the larger society.

4.   Money does not guarantee victory, but it does guarantee the *opportunity* for victory. Without good financing, potential candidates do not become candidates. With good financing, potential candidates can hire consultants—media experts, pollsters, direct mailing specialists, voice coaches, statisticians, speech writers, and make-up artists—to give their campaigns appeal. Not only do the consultants charge a lot (perhaps $250 per hour) but the technology they employ—computers, interviews, and television—is costly. Because consultants need success in order to build their reputations, they too shun underfunded candidates. One student of consulting concludes that "you need $150,000 just to get in the door to see a consultant."

Indeed, consultants are far more important to candidates than are political parties. Not only have they usurped the role of parties in the campaign (volunteer doorbell ringers are fast becoming a relic of the past) but they also encourage candidates to deemphasize issues and concentrate on image. The "three p's"—polling, packaging, and promotion—are more important than parties, grass-roots support, and the development of strong positions on the issues.

a. Political candidates require good financing for various expenses. Money buys candidates such consultants as media experts, pollsters, direct mailing specialists, voice coaches, statisticians, speech writers and make-up artists.

b. Today's political candidates require money to hire expensive consultants and the technology they use, including computers, interviews and television. Consultants' emphasis on "polling, packaging and promotion" has reduced the importance of parties, grass-roots support, and strong positions on the issues.

c. Today's political campaigns are a fraud. They require the candidates to shun genuine grass-roots support and strong positions in favor of know-nothing, high-tech media consultants and expensive surveys. The consultants themselves care more about building their reputations than they do about electing qualified candidates.

d. Political parties are far less important today than ever. Due to the influence of consultants and the demands of media-centered campaigns, candidates deemphasize issues and concentrate on image. "Polling, packaging, and promotion" have become more important than parties, grass-roots support, and strong positions on the issues.

➤ *Review Test 2*

A. Carefully read each opening statement (set off in **boldface**). Then decide whether each numbered statement that follows is basically the same in meaning or basically different in meaning from the opening statement. Write an *S* (for *Same*) next to the **two** statements where the meaning is closest to the original statement.

1. **A self-fulfilling prophecy is one that comes true because someone's expectations of an event have helped to bring it about.**

    _____ 1. If a person believes strongly that a certain event is going to happen, he may actually influence that event to occur. Such a belief, or prediction, is known as a self-fulfilling prophecy.

    _____ 2. The idea of the self-fulfilling prophecy is based upon a person's certain knowledge ahead of time of how a situation will end.

    _____ 3. A situation is more likely to end well if a person gets help from others in achieving that desired end.

    _____ 4. People only imagine that they have any influence over most situations.

    _____ 5. When people act in ways that cause a situation to end in the manner they expect, their expectation becomes a self-fulfilling prophecy.

    _____ 6. A person's expectations of an event cannot change its outcome, but they may change the person's perception of that outcome.

2. **If only there were evil people somewhere treacherously committing evil deeds, and it were necessary only to separate them from the rest of us and destroy them; but the line dividing good and evil cuts through the heart of every human being.**

    _____ 1. People who appear to be good are in reality only hiding the evil that they have done.

    _____ 2. Since every human being has the potential to do good and evil, we can't get rid of evil simply by getting rid of all the so-called evil people.

    _____ 3. Because the world is not divided between good people and evil people, there's no way to identify and eliminate the evil ones; rather, all people are made up of both good and evil.

    _____ 4. Evil people look so much like the rest of us that it is impossible to identify them.

    _____ 5. Destroying the evil people in the world would make life much safer for the rest of us.

    _____ 6. Getting rid of evil is not so simple: Evil people resemble good people, and in real life, there is no dividing line to separate out the evil ones for us.

B. Circle the letter of the answer that best summarizes the selection that follows.

> Schools play a considerable part in choosing the youth who come to occupy the higher-status positions in society. At the same time, school performance also sorts out those who will occupy the lower rungs in the occupational-prestige ladder. Education is, therefore, a selection process. The sorting is done with respect to two different criteria: a child's ability and his or her social class background. Although the goal of education is to select on ability alone, ascribed social status (the status of one's family, race, and religion) has a pronounced effect on the degree of success in the educational system. The school is similar to a conveyor belt, with people of all social classes getting on at the same time but leaving the belt in accordance with social class—the lower the class, the shorter the ride.

    a. The lower a student's social class, the more likely it is that he or she will leave school early.
    b. The goal of education is to encourage students according to their abilities.
    c. Schools play a large part in selecting the youth who will occupy the higher-status positions in our society, based on the students' ability and social class.
    d. Our educational system sorts out the students who will occupy the higher- and lower-status rungs in our society according to the students' ability and social class.

C. Read the following selection. Then circle the letter of the outline that best condenses the selection.

> The United States is in the midst of a profound change in the age structure of its population, one that will affect virtually every area of national life over the next half century. At present there are over 28 million aged Americans, representing just over one in ten of the population. By the year 2030 there will be over 50 million aged people representing approximately one in every five Americans.
>
> Why has this dramatic change taken place? One reason is that people are living longer: since the beginning of the century, average life expectancy at birth has increased by twenty-eight years. But the main reason is an enormous bulge in the population structure as a result of American's post-World War II "baby boom." In two decades from about 1946 to 1964, some 76 million children were born, representing a third of the total present population. After 1964 the birth rate dropped, creating a "birth dearth," and the rate has remained at a relatively low level since then.
>
> The graying of America will bring about a variety of changes, some of which are already apparent. To begin with, elementary schools and even high

schools all over the nation have closed their doors, and teachers have been thrown out of work. Educational facilities will have to offer more courses in continuing education for older people, or they may have so few students that they will not survive. The medical problems of the aged will become a major growth area in medicine, for American physicians, despite their lack of enthusiasm for this field in the past, are likely to specialize where the greatest market is. Nursing homes, funeral homes, and crematoriums will proliferate. And in all likelihood, the aged will achieve a more respected status in society.

A. The U.S. population is gradually gaining more and more older people, a change which has two main causes and will bring about various changes.
   1. Reasons for the increase in percentage of older Americans
      a. Increase of 28 years in average life expectancy
      b. The aging of the population explosion known as the baby boom
   2. Changes that will result from the graying of America, some already apparent
      a. Changes in education
         1) Fewer elementary and high schools and their teachers needed
         2) More continuing education for older people needed for schools to survive
      b. Growth in certain services
         1) medical services to the elderly
         2) nursing homes
         3) funerals homes and crematoriums
      c. Perhaps a more respected social status for the elderly

B. The graying of America will bring about a variety of changes, some of which are already apparent.
   1. There will be notable changes in the field of education.
      a. Fewer elementary schools and high schools will be needed.
         1) Schools have closed.
         2) Teachers have lost their jobs.
      b. Educational facilities will offer more continuing education courses for the elderly in order to gain sufficient students to survive.
   2. Services for and because of the elderly will grow.
      a. Physicians will specialize more and more where the market is—in medicine for the elderly.
      b. There will be more and more nursing homes.
      c. There will be more and more funeral homes and crematoriums.
   3. Because of their growing power, the elderly are likely to achieve a more respected status in society.

C. The U.S. population is gradually gaining more and more older people, a change which has two main causes and will bring about a variety of changes.
1. Increase of 28 years in average life expectancy
2. The aging of the population explosion known as the baby boom
3. Changes in education
   a. Fewer elementary and high schools and their teachers needed
   b. More continuing education for older people
4. Growth in certain services
   a. Medical services to the elderly
   b. Nursing homes
   c. Funerals homes and crematoriums
5. Perhaps a more respected social status for the elderly

➤ Review Test 3

A. To review what you've learned in this chapter, answer the following questions.

1. Summarizing is a way to (*predict, outline, condense*) _____ material.

2. A summary will always include (*the main idea, all the major details, several minor details*) _____.

3. _____ TRUE OR FALSE? A summary should never include the author's wording.

4. _____ TRUE OR FALSE? A summary should not be shorter than one paragraph.

5. _____ TRUE OR FALSE? Writing an outline can be a helpful step toward writing a summary.

B. Why is it so hard to make, and keep, close friends in our society? How is that parents and children can find they don't know each other well, even though they share the same home? In this selection from their textbook *Psychology of Adjustment and Human Relationships* (McGraw-Hill, 1990), James F. Calhoun and Joan Ross Acocella answer those questions and offer practical suggestions for getting closer to others. The selection will also give you an opportunity to apply your understanding of summarizing and outlining to a full-length selection.

Following the selection are questions on summarizing and outlining. To help you continue reinforcing the skills taught in previous chapters, there are also questions on

- vocabulary in context
- central point and main ideas
- supporting details
- transitions
- patterns of organization.

Words to Watch

Following are some words in the reading that do not have strong context support. Each word is followed by the number of the paragraph in which it appears and its meaning there.

foster (1): encourage
stupefaction (3): numbness
engineer (4): plan
superficial (4): not deep
reciprocate (4): do something in return
institute (5): begin
induced (6): persuaded

MAKING TIME

James F. Calhoun and Joan Ross Acocella

Intimacy feeds on time. Specifically, there are two time-bound factors that foster° intimacy. First is the duration of the relationship; the longer you know a person, the more likely you are to become intimate with him or her. Second is the frequency of informal meetings. For intimacy to grow, you need to see the other person often, and these meetings should occur outside the context of formal roles (employer-employee, teacher-student, clerk-customer). Such roles, because they set rather strict rules for interactions, prevent the sort of relaxed self-revelation, mutual exploration, and general breeze-shooting that promote intimacy.   1

It is precisely the scarcity of these two factors—longstanding relationships and frequent informal meetings—that seems to work against intimacy in our time. As we have seen, modern mobility tends to keep our friendships brief. As for frequent and informal meetings with friends and acquaintances, these have almost gone out of style, at least for the working adult with a family. Neighbors, in general, are discouraged from simply appearing at the back door; good fences make good neighbors, as they say. Friends too are often discouraged from dropping in. We tend to see them, instead, at dinners and parties, where our roles are more strictly defined. Modern styles of architecture and city planning contribute to this lack of opportunity for informal meetings. Gone is the town square, where people used to gather and gossip. Gone is the front porch, where people used to sit and greet their neighbors. The modern American couple is to be found behind closed (and often locked) doors. If you want to see them, call before you come.   2

And what of intimacy within the household? Intimacy certainly stands a better chance among family members. Yet here too modern life presents impediments. A truly astounding proportion of the time that family members spend together is spent not in interaction, but in silence—in front of the television set. (On the average weekday winter evening almost half the population of the United States is sitting, in simultaneous stupefaction°, before the television set.) When family members are not watching television, they are often occupied with instrumental behaviors—practical   3 pursuits aimed at survival or achievement (cooking, homework, household repairs). Not surprisingly, there is little time left over for relaxed interaction: comparing opinions on this or that, checking out how everyone's day was, speculating on what's the matter with Mr. Jones next door, and so forth.

In sum, our society doesn't offer many ready-made opportunities for informal   4
interaction. If you want to increase your intimacy with others, you have to create these opportunities, literally engineer° them. For example, if you would like to move beyond your superficial° acquaintance with the people across the street, ring their doorbell on the spur of the moment and invite them over for something extremely informal—a cup of coffee, a drink on a hot day, a very ordinary dinner (meatloaf, not beef Wellington). If you see them puttering in the garden, go over and chat for a moment. Give and ask. If you buy a crate of tomatoes, send some over. If you need a pie plate, borrow it. The great beauty of intimacy with neighbors is the quality of relaxed, low-demand give and take. If you start this process moving, your neighbors are quite likely to reciprocate°. (And if they don't, you can try the people down the block.)

As for deepening intimacy with friends, try if possible to cut up your interactions   5
into smaller pieces. That is, instead of seeing them for a five-hour dinner party every five weeks, see them for one hour every week—for a glass of wine, a cup of coffee, a walk in the park, or whatever. As more and more American women go to work, the custom of the dinner party is becoming increasingly burdensome. It places too many demands on everyone. The brief, low-demand get-together is generally much more rewarding, both for host and guest. If you institute° it, it's likely to be repeated. If you can't go to the movies with your friends, tell them to come by afterwards. Start throwing informal parties after dinner. If you have to work most of Saturday, invite your friends for breakfast on Sunday. And if you don't have time to make your own coffee cake, just buy one. The important thing is to see your friends, and see them without making a big production of it.

As for intimacy within the family, marriage manuals often advise that spouses go   6
off on cozy vacations together, armed with champagne and frilly underwear, while child-rearing manuals recommend family outings. Again, however, what seems to be needed are not big "togetherness projects" but small and frequent pauses for informal interaction. So plan such pauses. Husband and wife can make a rule that the half hour before dinner is their half hour; the phone is taken off the hook and children are banished from the kitchen while parents have a quiet chat together. Dinnertime itself is an excellent opportunity for relaxed interaction among all family members. Indeed, it is often the one time of the day when the whole family can be induced° to sit down together and talk. If your dinnertime is a social disaster—everyone reading the paper or coming and going at different times or watching television while they eat—make new rules. Dinnertime, you declare, is now sacred. Everybody should show up on time, leave their reading material behind, steer clear of the television knob, and be ready for a chat. This can be immensely fruitful. Through a modest half-hour exchange over dinner every night, you may find out what your son really does after school, what your wife really thinks of your moustache, and much more besides.

To sum up, we can no longer expect intimacy to flower automatically within the   7
family. Our culture has simply created too many substitutes for intimacy-producing interaction. Therefore, if you are seeking a closer relationship with your parents, children, or spouse, you must make the time, frequently and regularly, to sit down quietly and talk with them.

Reading Comprehension Questions

Vocabulary in Context

1. The word *impediments* in "Intimacy certainly stands a better chance among family members. Yet here too modern life presents impediments" (paragraph 3) means
   a. silences.
   b. movements.
   c. obstacles.
   d. occupations.

2. The word *banished* in "Husband and wife can make a rule that the half hour before dinner is their half hour; . . . children are banished from the kitchen while parents have a quiet chat" (paragraph 6) means
   a. invited.
   b. managed.
   c. sent away.
   d. questioned.

Central Point and Main Ideas

3. Which sentence best expresses the central point of the selection?
   a. Families spend too much time in front of the television set.
   b. Intimacy is worth working for.
   c. Since modern life discourages intimacy, achieving close relationships requires special efforts to get together often.
   d. Modern life discourages intimacy because there are fewer unplanned opportunities to spend time with friends and neighbors.

4. Which sentence best expresses the main idea of paragraph 3?
   a. Modern life presents obstacles to family intimacy.
   b. Television interferes with family intimacy.
   c. Today's family members are either watching television or busy with practical activities.
   d. Instrumental behaviors are practical activities aimed at survival or achievement.

Supporting Details

5. According to the authors, you can best encourage intimacy by
   a. watching TV together.
   b. moving to another city for a new job.
   c. inviting friends over occasionally for formal dinners.
   d. seeing friends and family in frequent get-togethers that are easy to plan.

Transitions

6. The first words of each sentence below signal
   a. comparison.
   b. addition.
   c. contrast.
   d. cause and effect.

   First is the duration of the relationship . . . Second is the frequency of informal meetings. (Paragraph 1)

Patterns of Organization

7. The pattern of organization of paragraph 2 is
   a. list of steps in the process of achieving intimacy.
   b. discussion of the causes of the difficulty in achieving intimacy today.
   c. list of ways to achieve intimacy with friends, neighbors, and family.
   d. definition of *intimacy* and several examples of it.

Summarizing and Outlining

8. Complete the following outline of paragraph 1 by filling in the blanks.

   Time is necessary for intimacy in two ways.

   a. _____

   b. _____

9. Which of the following best summarizes paragraphs 2–3?
   a. Modern life makes it difficult to spend the necessary time to develop intimate friendships.
   b. Modern life discourages the long relationships and frequent informal meetings needed for intimacy among friends, neighbors, and family.
   c. The modern American couple is often found behind closed (and often locked) doors, so casual encounters are discouraged.
   d. Instead of interacting with each other frequently, family members spend much of their time watching television in silence or in instrumental behaviors.

10. Complete the following outline of paragraphs 4–6.

    To increase your intimacy with others, you must create opportunities for frequent informal interaction.
    1. To increase intimacy with neighbors, find reasons for brief informal get-togethers.
    2. To increase intimacy with friends, get together more often for shorter periods of time.

    3. _____

    _____

7

Fact and Opinion

On the television police drama *Dragnet*, whenever witnesses began to speak emotionally or to give their own theories, the hero, Sergeant Joe Friday, would ask for "just the facts." He wanted neutral, unbiased information—the kind that can be proven true or false—rather than a witness's interpretation of what happened.

The kind of information Sergeant Friday preferred, however, isn't easy to come by. When most speakers and writers communicate, they include their opinions of a subject. What they say is therefore at least partly biased.

While bias is often unavoidable, many writers do try to remain as objective as possible. News articles and scientific reports are examples of writing in which authors try to be as factual as they can. However, opinions are central to other types of materials, such as editorials, political speeches, and advertisements. Writers of these materials try to convince readers who have different viewpoints to change their minds.

Both facts and opinions can be valuable to readers, but knowing the difference between the two is important in evaluating what is read. Thus, like Sgt. Friday, skilled readers must be able to distinguish *fact* from *opinion.*

Sorting out facts from opinions is something you do already, perhaps without even realizing it. For example, imagine a friend saying, "I saw a science-fiction movie last night about aliens invading Earth. The special effects were great; the aliens looked like reptiles—they had green skin and forked tongues. The acting was terrible, though." Hearing this description, you would probably realize your friend's comments are a mixture of fact and opinion.

FACT

A *fact* is a statement that can be proven true through objective evidence. This evidence may be physical proof or the spoken or written testimony of witnesses. In the friend's comments about the movie, the facts are that it was about aliens invading Earth and that the aliens had green skin and forked tongues. If you wanted to, you could check the truth of these statements by questioning other witnesses or watching the movie yourself.

Following are some more facts—they can be checked for accuracy and thus proven true.

> *Fact:* The Quad Tower is the tallest building in this city.
> (A researcher could go out and, through inspection, confirm that the building is the tallest.)

> *Fact:* Albert Einstein willed his violin to his grandson.
> (This statement can be checked in historical publications or with Einstein's estate.)

> *Fact:* The 1991 Minnesota Twins won the World Series in seven games.
> (Anyone can check sports records to confirm this.)

OPINION

An *opinion* is a statement that cannot be objectively proven true or false. Opinions usually express the beliefs, feelings, or judgments that a person has about a subject. Your friend, for instance, said that the movie's special effects were great and that the acting was terrible. These statements may be reasonable ones with which other people would agree, but they cannot be objectively proven. They are opinions. You might see the movie and reach very different conclusions.

Here are some more opinions:

> *Opinion:* The Quad Tower is the ugliest building in the city.
> (There's no way to prove this statement because two people can look at the same building and come to different conclusions about its beauty. "Ugly" is a *value word*, a word we use to express a value judgment. Value words are signals that an opinion is being expressed. By their very nature, these words represent opinions, not facts.)

> *Opinion:* Einstein should have willed his violin to a museum.
> (Who says? Not his grandson. This is an opinion.)

Opinion: The 1991 Minnesota Twins were the best team in the history of baseball.

(Whether something is "best" is always debatable. "Best" is another value word.)

Writing Facts and Opinions

To get a better sense of fact and opinion, take a few minutes to write three facts about yourself and then to write three of your opinions. Here, for example, are three facts about me and three of my opinions.

Facts about me:

- I am six feet tall.
- I do my writing on a Macintosh computer.
- I have two sisters and one wife.

Three of my opinions:

- Schools, including colleges, should require students to do a great deal of reading.
- Ralph Nader is a true American hero.
- All ads that glamorize smoking and drinking should be banned.

Now write your facts and opinions in the space below:

Facts about you:

- _____
  _____
- _____
  _____
- _____
  _____

Three of your opinions:

- _____
  _____
- _____
  _____
- _____
  _____

More About Fact and Opinion

To sharpen your understanding of fact and opinion, read the following statements and decide whether each is fact or opinion. Put an **F** (for "fact") or an **O** (for "opinion") beside each statement.

_____ 1. No flower is more beautiful than the simple daisy.

_____ 2. Vice President Gerald Ford became president when Richard Nixon resigned in 1974.

_____ 3. Medical statistics show that it is riskier for a woman to have a first child after age 40.

_____ 4. It is stupid for women over 40 to get pregnant.

_____ 5. Redheads should never wear pink or purple—they look awful in those colors.

_____ 6. In Egypt, 96 percent of the land is desert.

_____ 7. There is too much violence in children's television programs.

_____ 8. Joanne's favorite color is purple.

_____ 9. In fact, baseball is the only sport that deserves to be called "America's game."

_____ 10. The prehistoric ruins at Stonehenge in England consist of a circle of upright stone slabs.

Now read carefully the following explanations of the ten items.

1. This is an opinion. Many may easily find flowers they consider more beautiful than the daisy. The word *beautiful* is another value word.

2. This is a fact. Nixon's resignation and Ford's presidency were reported throughout the world.

3. This is a fact that can be verified by checking medical statistics.

4. This is an opinion. Some people might admire the woman who has children in her 40s.

5. This is an opinion. As the value word *awful* suggests, a judgment is being expressed. Many feel that redheads look wonderful in pink and purple.

6. This is a fact, agreed upon and written down by experts who study geography.

7. As the words *too much* suggest, this is an opinion. Some people may conclude there is little harm in children watching violence.

8. This is a fact. The idea that purple is beautiful is an opinion; but that Joanne prefers that color is a fact which can be confirmed by asking her what her favorite color is.

9. This is an opinion, despite the words to the contrary. Fans of sports other than baseball might feel their sport deserves the title "America's game."

10. This is a fact. It has been verified by many archeologists and other witnesses, and many publications include their testimony.

➤ *Practice 1*

Here are short reviews taken from a newspaper movie guide. Some reviews present only factual reports; others contain opinions about the movie as well. Identify the factual reviews with an **F** and the reviews that include both a factual report and an opinion with an **F + O**.

_____ 1. **18 Again! '88.** George Burns, Charlie Schlatter. An 81-year-old wakes up from a car accident with his mind in the body of his 18-year-old grandson.

_____ 2. **Von Ryan's Express, '65.** Frank Sinatra, Trevor Howard. Exciting POW adventure about a daring escape from an Italian prisoner camp.

_____ 3. **Soapdish, '91.** Sally Field, Kevin Kline. The star of a soap opera opposes her ex-lover's return to the daytime drama.

_____ 4. **Lady Sings the Blues, '72.** Diana Ross, Billy Dee Williams. Tough, well-acted but unsatisfying biography of singer Billie Holiday.

_____ 5. **Action Jackson, '88.** Carl Weathers, Craig T. Nelson. An Ivy League Detroit police officer steals an auto tycoon's mistress and stops his gang of assassins.

_____ 6. **The Purple People Eater, '88.** Ned Beatty, Neil Patrick Harris. An alien and a 12-year-old boy form a band and help out oldsters with a benefit concert.

_____ 7. **Butch Cassidy and the Sundance Kid, '69.** Paul Newman, Robert Redford. No other Western is as much sheer fun.

_____ 8. **A Patch of Blue, '65.** Sidney Poitier, Shelley Winters. Moving drama about a man who befriends a mistreated blind girl.

_____ 9. **The Video Dead, '92.** Roxanna Augesen, Rocky Duvall. Ghouls from the movie *Zombie Blood Nightmare* emerge from within a brother and sister's TV.

_____ 10. **Hello, Dolly! '69.** Barbra Streisand, Walter Matthau. Big screen, big star, big bore.

Other Points About Fact and Opinion

There are several added points to keep in mind when separating fact from opinion.

1   Statements of fact may be found to be untrue.

Suppose you went to the science-fiction movie your friend spoke of and discovered the aliens actually had blue rather than green skin. (Perhaps your friend is colorblind.) His statement would then be an error, not a fact. It is not unusual for evidence to show that a "fact" is not really true. It was once considered to be a fact that the world was flat, for example, but that "fact" turned out to be an error.

2   Opinions may be masked as facts.

People sometimes present their opinions as facts, as shown in practice sentence 9 on page 150. Here are two more examples:

In point of fact, neither candidate for the mayor's office is well-qualified.

The truth of the matter is that frozen foods taste as good as fresh foods.

Despite the words to the contrary, the above are not statements of fact but statements of opinion.

3   Remember that value words often represent opinions. Here are examples of value words:

Value Words

best	great	beautiful
worst	terrible	bad
better	lovely	good
worse	disgusting	wonderful

Value words often express judgments—they are generally subjective, not objective. While factual statements report on observed reality, subjective statements evaluate reality. For example, the observation that it is raining outside is an objective one. The statement that the weather is bad, however, is subjective, an evaluation of reality. (Some people consider rain to be good weather.)

4   Finally, remember that much of what we read and hear is a mixture of fact and opinion.

Recognizing facts and opinions is important because much information that sounds factual is really opinion. A political candidate, for example, may say, "My record is outstanding." Voters would be wise to wonder what the value word *outstanding* means to this candidate. Or an advertisement may claim that a particular automobile is "the most economical car on the road today," a statement that at first seems factual. But what is meant by *economical*? If the car offers the most miles per gallon but the worst record for expensive repairs, you might not agree that it's economical.

➤ *Practice 2*

Some of the statements below are facts, and some are opinions. Label facts with an **F** and opinions with an **O**. Remember that facts can be proven, but opinions give personal views.

_____ 1. The island of Puerto Rico has been a U.S. territory since 1898.

_____ 2. Puerto Rico should become our country's fifty-first state.

_____ 3. No hobby is more peaceful than gardening.

_____ 4. According to national surveys, millions of Americans garden.

_____ 5. In 1989, Pete Rose, then Cincinnati Reds' manager, was banned from baseball because of his gambling activities.

_____ 6. Pete Rose did not deserve to be banned from baseball for gambling.

_____ 7. Our company allows each employee ten days of paid sick leave per year.

_____ 8. Too many employees misuse the sick leave policy.

_____ 9. In England, election campaigns last for six weeks.

_____ 10. The United States should also limit campaigns for presidential elections to six weeks.

➤ *Practice 3*

Some of the statements below are facts, and some are opinions; in addition, three include fact and opinion. Label facts with an **F**, opinions with an **O**, and statements of fact *and* opinion with an **F + O**.

_____ 1. My husband is a very attractive man.

_____ 2. My college roommate, a real beauty, dated my husband before we were married.

_____ 3. My husband is six-foot-three and weighs 225 pounds.

_____ 4. Alexander Graham Bell patented the first telephone in 1876.

_____ 5. My niece shouldn't be allowed to talk on the phone as much as she does.

_____ 6. The telephone, found in more than 99 percent of U.S. homes, is the single most significant invention in communication history.

_____ 7. Most people with car phones bought them just to show off while they drive.

_____ 8. Mark Twain, whose real name was Samuel Clemens, died in 1910.

_____ 9. Mark Twain's novel *The Prince and the Pauper* has inspired several movies, including the Eddie Murphy film *Trading Places*.

_____ 10. *The Adventures of Huckleberry Finn*, first published in 1884, is still the best birthday present a 12-year-old boy could receive.

Facts and Opinions in Passages

People tend to accept what they read as fact, but much of what we read is actually opinion. Keeping an eye out for opinion will help you to think for yourself and to question what you read.

Two sentences in the following passage are facts, two are opinions, and one combines fact and opinion. Read the passage, and identify facts with an **F**, opinions with an **O**, and the statement of fact *and* opinion with an **F + O**.

> [1]There were several queens of Egypt by the name of Cleopatra, including the one who ruled in the days of Antony and Caesar. [2]She is one of the most interesting figures in Egyptian history. [3]History records that she was born in 69 B.C. and killed herself almost forty years later. [4]The story of how she killed herself is very easy to believe. [5]Reports say she killed herself with an asp, the Egyptian cobra—a symbol of Egyptian royalty, so there could have been no better way for the queen to end her life.

1. _____   2. _____   3. _____   4. _____   5. _____

Sentence 1 contains facts set down in historical records. Sentence 2 expresses an opinion—some may feel Cleopatra is not one of the most interesting figures in Egyptian history. Sentence 3 contains more facts of history. Sentence 4 contains an opinion—how easy something is to believe will differ from person to person. The last sentence is a mixture of fact and opinion: The beginning parts of the sentence are facts, but what the best way would have been for Cleopatra to end her life is certainly a matter of opinion.

➤ Practice 4

The following passage contains five sentences. Two sentences are facts, two are opinions, and one combines fact and opinion. Identify the facts with an **F**, the opinions with an **O**, and the statement of fact *and* opinion with an **F + O**.

[1]Recently, three thousand California high school students had a physics lesson at an amusement park. [2]A Valencia teacher decided that thrill rides can serve as a living physics lab, a truly wonderful idea. [3]As the students rode the roller coaster, for instance, they took instrument readings to try to learn how much force is needed to keep a person from flying out of the seat. [4]Ordinarily, science courses are terribly dull. [5]This teacher definitely deserves an award for thinking of a such a great way to spice science up for students.

1. _____   2. _____   3. _____   4. _____   5. _____

➤ Review Test 1

A. Three of the statements below are facts, and three are opinions. Identify facts with an **F** and opinions with an **O**.

_____ 1. More copies of the Bible have been sold than of any other book in the world.

_____ 2. People don't spend enough time studying Scriptures.

_____ 3. The world's first "test-tube baby," conceived outside of its mother's body, was born in England in 1978.

_____ 4. People unable to conceive children in the normal way should accept that fact and try to adopt children.

_____ 5. Satin feels wonderful, but it's still not as comfortable as cotton.

_____ 6. Eli Whitney never made any money on his invention, the cotton gin, because he didn't have a valid patent on it.

B. Here are short reviews taken from a newspaper movie guide. Some reviews present only factual reports; others contain opinions about the movie as well. Identify the factual reviews with an **F** and the reviews that include both a factual report *and* an opinion with an **F + O**.

_____ 7. **Fires Within, '91.** Jimmy Smits, Greta Scacchi. After eight years a Cuban exile joins his wife and daughter in Miami where his wife has a lover.

_____ 8. **Sounder, '72.** Cicely Tyson, Paul Winfield. A marvelous film about a family of sharecroppers coming of age during the Depression.

_____ 9. **The Best Years of Our Lives, '46.** Fredric March, Myrna Loy. Story of three WWII veterans adjusting to civilian life won nine Oscars, including best picture, director, and actor.

_____ 10. **Ulzana's Raid, '72.** Burt Lancaster, Bruce Davison. A tough, violent, underrated Western adventure from director Robert Aldrich.

➤ Review Test 2

A. Some of the statements below are facts, and some are opinions; in addition, three include both fact and opinion. Identify facts with an **F**, opinions with an **O**, and statements of fact *and* opinion with an **F + O**.

_____ 1. The magazine *Sports Illustrated* is the best source of behind-the-scenes sports information.

_____ 2. *Sports Illustrated* is owned by the same company that publishes *Time*.

_____ 3. Every winter, *Sports Illustrated* publishes its "Swimsuit Issue," which in a very tasteful way shows semi-nude pictures of women.

_____ 4. A hamburger doesn't taste right without at least a little salt.

_____ 5. Many canned and frozen vegetables contain salt, so people should eat only fresh vegetables.

_____ 6. Salt, which is now common, was once so rare that Roman soldiers were paid with it.

_____ 7. Many countries produce rock and jazz artists, but only Americans can play great country music.

_____ 8. Not even Crystal Gayle can out-sing Dolly Parton.

_____ 9. Some country singers have "crossed over" to record songs in other styles.

_____ 10. It's hard to understand how anyone can appreciate the whiny sound of some country music.

B. Each passage below contains five sentences. Two are facts, two are opinions, and one combines fact and opinion. Identify facts with an **F**, opinions with an **O**, and statements of fact *and* opinion with an **F + O**.

1. [1]In 1988, Northwest Airlines became the first major airline to ban smoking on all domestic flights. [2]Actually, the airlines should have adopted this policy years ago. [3]Due to poor air circulation, no-smoking areas eventually fill up with smoke from the smoking areas. [4]The nonsmokers are thereby forced to inhale some smoke, which is obviously unfair. [5]Of course, the ideal solution to the problem of breathing smoke from other people's cigarettes is simply to make smoking illegal everywhere.

   1. _____   2. _____   3. _____   4. _____   5. _____

2. [1]The Taiwanese are good at coming up with fascinating inventions. [2]Computerized shoes and solar-powered baseball caps were just two of the items at a recent exhibition of inventions in Taiwan. [3]Among the funniest was the "talking" smoke sensor, which says, "Thank you for not smoking" when it senses tobacco smoke. [4]But the weirdest invention of all was the "sanitary table." [5]The surface of this dining table consists of hundreds of sheets of thin plastic that can be peeled off as they become soiled.

   1. _____   2. _____   3. _____   4. _____   5. _____

➤ Review Test 3

A. To review what you've learned in this chapter, complete each of the following sentences about facts and opinions.

1. A (*fact, opinion*) _____ can be proven true through objective evidence.

2. (*Facts, Opinions*) _____ often include words that express judgments.

3. An example of a comparison that expresses a personal judgment is (*taller, more attractive*) _____.

4. Readers would probably expect a(n) (*editorial, political speech, news report, film review*) _____ to be totally factual.

B. Because advertising is such an important part of modern life, we may think of it as a modern business device. But advertising, in fact, has a history that goes back to ancient times. In this reading from the textbook *Introducing Mass Communication* (McGraw-Hill, 1989), Michael W. Gamble and Teri Kwai Gamble describe that history, including some colorful examples of advertising through the years.

Following the reading are questions on facts and opinions. To help you continue reinforcing the skills taught in previous chapters, there are also questions on

- vocabulary in context
- central point and main ideas
- supporting details
- transitions
- patterns of organization
- outlining.

Words to Watch

Following are some words in the reading that do not have strong context support. Each word is followed by the number of the paragraph in which it appears and its meaning there.

assess (1): evaluate
predates (1): came before
transmission (4): passing along
antiquity (4): ancient times
innovation (7): new development
perused (9): read
vehicles (10): media
broadsides (10): large sheets of paper printed with information on public issues
attributed (10): credited
enhance (11): to make more effective
spurred (14): stimulated
proliferation (14): rapid growth
devised (15): invented
facilitates (16): eases

THE DEVELOPMENT OF ADVERTISING

Michael W. Gamble and Teri Kwai Gamble

In order to understand and assess° the role played by advertising in America today, we should briefly examine the role it played in the past. To be sure, advertising predates° America. In fact, the desire to advertise may be part of human nature itself. 1

The earliest advertisements were probably those of the town criers or the signs that marked the location of shops and inns. Whether you lived in ancient Egypt, Rome, or Greece, no doubt you would have heard and responded to the shouts of street 2 vendors who peddled their wares. For example, this verse (or one quite like it) is said to have been used in ancient Athens:

> For eyes that are Shining, for cheeks like the dawn,
> For Beauty that lasts after girlhood is gone,
> For prices in reason, the woman who knows,
> Will buy her cosmetics of Aesclyptos.

Town criers were also used to announce the arrival of ships bearing precious 3
cargoes of wine, spices, and metals. Frequently, a musician accompanied the crier's chants, helping to ensure that he stayed in the right key.

The transmission° of information—a key idea of advertising—extends far back 4
into antiquity°. For instance, this inscription was etched on a Pompeiian wall:

> Traveler
> Going from here to the twelfth tower
> There Sarinus keeps a tavern.
> This is to request you to enter,
> Farewell.

To it may be traced current ads for hotels and motels like Sheraton and Holiday 5
Inn. In like fashion, one actual Roman ad should remind you of ads for today's circuses, boxing matches, or health clubs:

> There will be a dedication or
> Formal opening of Certain Baths.
> Those attending are promised Slaughter
> of Wild Beasts, Athletic Games, Perfume
> Sprinkling, and Awnings to keep off the Sun.

Outdoor signs survived the fall of the Roman Empire and were transformed into 6
the decorative art of inns. Because literacy rates were low, these signs were symbolic of the goods to be found within: a goat indicated a dairy, a mule driving a mill stood for a bakery, and a spinning wheel announced a weaver. This practice enabled those who could not read to identify the nature of the store.

The most significant event in the history of advertising was the invention of 7
movable type by Johannes Gutenberg in 1440. This innovation° led to the use of printed posters, handbills, and newspaper ads. About forty years after the introduction of movable type, the first English advertisement was printed by Caxton of London. It announced a prayerbook for sale and was posted on church doors. *Siquis*, the forerunner of our present want ads, also emerged about this time. Also known as "if anybodys," they usually began with the words, "If anybody desires" or "If anybody knows of." In addition to advertising available positions and services or lost articles, *siquis* were also used to advertise products like tobacco and perfume. However, it was not until the early seventeenth century that the newspaper was born, giving advertising an important push forward.

The first newspaper advertisement appeared in the back of a London newspaper 8
in 1650; it offered a reward for the return of twelve stolen horses. Gradually, ads were used to help sell products like chocolate, real estate, medicine, and coffee. The following is an example of an ad that appeared in 1657:

> In Bartholomew Lane, on the back side of the Old Exchange, the drink called coffee, which is a very wholesome and physical drink, having many excellent virtues . . . is to be sold both in the morning and three o'clock in the afternoon.

Among the virtues noted in the copy were the following:

> It closes the orifices of the stomach, fortifies the heat within, helpeth digestion, quickeneth the spirits, maketh the heart lightsum, is good against eye sores, coughs, or colds, rhumes, consumption, headache, dropsie, gout, scurvey, King's evil, and many others.

Advertising attracted the attention of critics in the eighteenth century. In 1759, Dr. Samuel Johnson, writing in the *Idler*, noted: "Advertisements are now so numerous that they are very negligently perused°, and it is therefore become necessary to gain attention by magnificence of promises and by eloquence sometimes sublime and sometimes ridiculous." 9

In colonial America, advertising appeared in many vehicles°, including newspapers, pamphlets, broadsides°, and almanacs. Benjamin Franklin was the first American newspaper publisher to realize that advertising could provide a major portion of a newspaper's revenue. So significant were Franklin's achievements that he has been dubbed "the father of American advertising." Besides publishing periodicals that contained advertising, Franklin also used advertising to promote his own products, including the Franklin stove. The following copy is attributed° to Ben Franklin: 10

> Fireplaces with small openings cause draughts of cold air to rush in at every crevice and 'tis very uncomfortable as well as dangerous to sit against any such crevice. . . . Women, particularly from this cause (as they sit so much in the house) get cold in the head, rheums, and deflexions which fall into their jaws and gums, and have destroyed early, many a fine set of teeth in these northern colonies.

How do you think the ad created by Franklin compares with today's ads for storm windows and fireplace air circulators? To be sure, both stress the health and comfort benefits to be derived from their use. Besides being an adept copywriter, Franklin is also credited with the following innovations: He surrounded the ads with white space to separate them from each other; he made ads more readable by giving each ad its own large headline; and he used illustrations to enhance° copy. Other patriots followed Franklin's lead and used advertising to promote their own products; for example, Paul Revere used advertising to sell false teeth, and George Washington used advertising to sell real estate. 11

The growth of the penny newspaper soon made advertising big business in America. Volney B. Palmer, the first advertising agent in the United States, started his brokerage service in Philadelphia in 1841. Palmer made his money by contracting to buy large volumes of advertising space at a discount from newspapers and then reselling the space to advertisers at a higher rate. Palmer, however, did not actually prepare the ads. It was not until 1890 that N. W. Ayer and Son, another Philadelphia concern, offered to aid in the preparation of ads as well. N. W. Ayer and Son is credited with being the first advertising agency to function in much the same way as agencies function today; that is, the agency planned, created, and executed advertising campaigns for 12 clients in exchange for a commission paid by the media or fees received from clients.

It remained for magazines to make the sale of products on a national scale a 13 reality. James W. Thompson, the founder of today's J. Walter Thompson agency, is the person responsible for persuading American magazines to accept advertising. Like Volney Palmer, he bought up space magazines had available and resold it to advertisers and other space agents. The readers of many of the national magazines were women, and consequently the most frequently advertised products were soaps, cosmetics, and patent medicines. It was not long before advertisers realized that these ads were capable of creating new markets by influencing the buying habits of readers. Between the end of the Civil War and 1900, advertising expenditures increased from $50 million to $540 million. As the years passed, advertising in magazines and newspapers continued to flourish.

As we know, newspapers and magazines were soon forced to compete with the 14 new electronic media. In the 1920s radio came on the scene, and shortly thereafter television "supplied" and entered the picture. These media would force advertising to evolve from a craft that used words and supporting pictures to promote products into one that relied on spoken words and moving pictures as well as written words to accomplish its objectives. Just as advertising expenditures had built the financial base that spurred° the proliferation° of America's newspapers and magazines, so advertising would help pay for radio and television.

Since World War II, advertising has experienced a steady ascent: $2.8 billion in 15 1945; $9.1 billion in 1955; $15.2 billion in 1965; $23.1 billion in 1972; $54.6 billion in 1980; over $60 billion in 1981; and over $70 billion today. Advertising now accounts for about 2 percent of the gross national product. Through the growth years, the purpose of advertising—to inform as well as persuade—has remained unchanged. And there is little doubt that advertising plays an essential role in our economy. Besides supporting commercial broadcasting, advertising also pays for almost three-quarters of the cost of the newspapers and magazines we read. Without advertising we would have to pay considerably more than we currently pay to read these periodicals, and some plan would have to be devised° to support commercial radio and television as well. In addition, the demand for advertising will undoubtedly contribute to the growth of cable programming in much the same way.

As is apparent, the media are not the only businesses advertising supports. As 16 English historian and essayist Thomas Macaulay wrote: "Advertising is to business what steam is to industry—the sole propelling power. Nothing except the Mint can make money without advertising." Thus, for business, advertising is a tool that facilitates° the presentation and sale of goods to consumers. And for consumers, advertising is a tool that familiarizes them with the marketplace.

History has shown that advertising is the most efficient way to introduce new or 17 improved products and keep an existing product in the public's mind. The only substitute for advertising is personal selling, and a huge amount of money would be needed to fund armies of personal sales representatives. The cost of an average personal business sales call is now estimated to be over $90. If we multiply that number by the estimated audience for a hit television program, or even the circulation figures of a newspaper or magazine, the cost is mind-boggling. The cost of using advertising to reach the public is much less. In fact, you can reach 1,000 prospects through advertising for less than 10 percent of what it costs to talk to one prospect through personal selling.

To various degrees, advertising influences the products you choose to buy by   18
bringing you information about new products, existing products, or product
improvements. To various degrees, advertising induces you to reuse products you have
tried, and it attempts to dispel misconceptions. Advertising acquaints you with the
differences (real or perceived) between product brands as well as the distinguishing
characteristics of companies and institutions. Advertising reveals what a particular
product should do for you when used, and by so doing it gives you criteria for
evaluating the products you currently use. Advertising is simply an important part of
your world.

Reading Comprehension Questions

Vocabulary in Context

1. The word *induces* in "advertising induces you to reuse products you have
   tried" (paragraph 18) means
   a. discourages.
   b. persuades.
   c. confuses.
   d. pays.

Central Point and Main Ideas

2. Which sentence best expresses the central point of the selection?
   a. Today, advertising has a major role in American life.
   b. Advertising helps pay for commercial radio and television.
   c. Gutenberg's invention of the printing press was the most significant event
      in advertising history.
   d. Advertising, which probably began in ancient days and grew rapidly since
      the invention of the printing press, has a major positive role in American
      life.

3. The implied main idea of paragraph 14 is:
   a. Advertising and the electronic media radio and television influenced each
      other's development.
   b. Radios came on the scene in the 1920s.
   c. Television followed radio.
   d. Radio and television allowed advertising to include the spoken word and
      moving pictures.

Supporting Details

4. According to the author, advertising
   a. informs and persuades.
   b. has decreased since World War II.
   c. increases the costs of newspapers and magazines.
   d. was rarely used in colonial America.

Transitions

5. The sentence below begins with a transition that shows
   a. time.
   b. addition.
   c. illustration.
   d. comparison.

   Just as advertising expenditures had built the financial base that spurred the proliferation of America's newspapers and magazines, so advertising would help pay for radio and television. (Paragraph 14)

Patterns of Organization

6. Just as paragraphs have patterns of organization, so do longer selections. The main pattern of organization of the first fourteen paragraphs of this selection is
   a. time order.
   b. list of items.
   c. comparison and contrast.
   d. definition and example.

Summarizing and Outlining

7. Complete the following outline of paragraphs 2–6 by filling in the blank.

   The earliest ads probably used writing and the human voice.

   1. In ancient Egypt, Rome, and Greece, _____

   _____

   _____

   2. After the fall of the Roman Empire, outdoor signs developed into the decorative symbolic signs of inns.

Fact and Opinion

8. Which of the following contains an opinion?
   a. "In fact, the desire to advertise may be part of human nature itself."
   b. "The first newspaper advertisement appeared in the back of a London newspaper in 1650. . . . "
   c. "Advertising attracted the attention of critics in the eighteenth century."
   d. "Volney B. Palmer, the first advertising agent in the United States, started his brokerage service in Philadelphia in 1841."

9. The statement that Franklin is "the father of American advertising" is
   a. a fact.
   b. an opinion.

10. The 1657 ad below contains
   a. only fact.
   b. only opinion.
   c. both fact and opinion.

   In Bartholomew Lane, on the back side of the Old Exchange, the drink called coffee, which is a very wholesome and physical drink, having many excellent virtues . . . is to be sold both in the morning and three o'clock in the afternoon. (Paragraph 8)

8

Inferences

You have probably heard the expression "to read between the lines." When you "read between the lines," you pick up ideas that are not directly stated in what you are reading. These implied ideas are often important for a full understanding of what an author means. Discovering the ideas in writing that are not stated directly is called *making inferences*, or *drawing conclusions*.

INFERENCES IN EVERYDAY LIFE

Consider first how often you make inferences in everyday life. For example, suppose you are driving to get some milk at a store near Main Street on a morning in early July. You've recently moved to this town. You notice a lot of people walking towards Main Street carrying folding chairs. So you infer that something special is happening in town today. As you get closer to Main Street, you hear a band playing. And then you notice a colorful float being towed toward Main Street. Before you even reach Main Street, you have inferred what all the fuss is about—there's going to be a Fourth of July parade.

How did you arrive at these inferences? First of all, you used your experience and general knowledge of people. Secondly, you made informed guesses based on the facts you observed.

Of course, not all your inferences will necessarily prove true. For example, it's possible that the parade will take place much later in the day. Or maybe it has already taken place, and someone is simply moving a float that had been in it. But you can be pretty sure that all those people were carrying chairs so they could sit down for some event, perhaps to hear a band concert. That would explain the band music you heard. In any case, the more evidence you have, the more solid your inferences are. If you saw floats and a band lined up on Main Street, your inference that there's going to be a parade would be stronger yet.

Take a moment now and jot down what you might infer if you experienced each of the following:

1.   An electrical storm continued all morning. When you got home that afternoon, you discovered that the clocks were all twelve minutes slow.

Your inference: _____

2.   Sitting before a mirror, a man draws fine dark wrinkles under his eyes, on his smooth forehead, and around his mouth. Next he streaks his thick black hair with white powder.

Your inference: _____

In the first situation, you probably inferred that the electricity in your home had gone off for twelve minutes. This conclusion is well supported by the fact that an electrical storm had taken place. Of course, it's also possible that your roommate turned all the clocks back twelve minutes, but that is much less likely—unless your roommate is a practical joker.

In the second situation, you probably concluded that the man is applying make-up in order to appear older. There is little evidence, however, for why he is doing that. Maybe he is going to a costume party, or perhaps he's an actor preparing for a performance.

Take a minute now to look at the following *Philadelphia Inquirer* cartoon. What do you think was the artist's intention?

Now put a check by the *two* inferences that are most logically based on the information suggested by the cartoon.

____ 1. The children are enjoying themselves.

____ 2. The house was built on stilts so the children could play underneath it.

____ 3. The children probably seldom watch real television.

____ 4. The cartoonist wishes to emphasize how television keeps children from more active play.

____ 5. The cartoonist means to emphasize the children's creativity in building a realistic sand sculpture.

Here is an explanation of each item:

1. This inference is well supported by the big smiles on the children's faces.

2. This is not a logical inference. Since the house is so close to the water, we can assume that the stilts have a more practical purpose—to keep the house above high tide.

3. This is also an illogical inference. The fact that the children have chosen to watch a fake television set rather than play on the beach suggests that watching TV is a significant part of their lives. Otherwise why would they enjoy just sitting there?

4. This inference is well supported by the cartoon. We can deduce that the cartoonist has purposely contrasted the passive activity of watching TV with an environment in which children are usually quite active.

5. This is not a logical inference. The sand sculpture is not a challenging one— it's basically a square box. In addition, the children's pose—sitting and watching, and not interacting—suggests passivity, not creativity.

Now read the sentence below and put a check by the inference most logically based on the information in the sentence. Then read the explanation that follows.

Victor always sits in the back of his college classrooms.

____ a. Victor dislikes his courses.

____ b. Victor is unprepared for his class.

____ c. Victor feels uncomfortable in the front of the room.

____ d. Victor is farsighted.

The sentence tells us nothing about how Victor feels about his courses, how prepared he is, or how well he sees. Thus answers *a, b,* or *d* are possibilities, but none is directly suggested by the sentence. The correct answer is therefore *c.* Based on the information we are given, we can conclude only that Victor—for some reason—does not like sitting in the front. We are not given enough information to know why he feels this way. (As you will learn in more detail in the "Argument" chapter on pages 220-221, your inferences will be stronger if you don't jump to conclusions that are unsupported or that are only very weakly supported by the available information.)

➤ *Practice 1*

Put a check by the inference *most logically based* on the information provided.

1. The Eskimo language contains at least eighteen words describing different types of ice and snow.

   ____ a. There is really only one type of snow.

   ____ b. The Eskimo language clearly has many times more words than the English language.

   ____ c. The Eskimo language probably also has numerous words for different types of palm trees.

   ____ d. The exact nature of ice and snow is important to the Eskimo way of life.

2. In certain supermarkets, customers hear taped music that includes the quiet message "I am an honest person."

   ____ a. The message is intended to discourage shoplifting.

   ____ b. The supermarket manager is a very honest person.

   ____ c. Shoplifting is a minor problem in those supermarkets.

   ____ d. Most supermarket customers are dishonest.

3. A woman enters her office building, walks past a group of fellow employees without returning their greetings, and goes into her office, slamming the door.

   ____ a. The woman has just been fired from her job.

   ____ b. The woman is very angry at her boss.

   ____ c. The woman is in a bad mood.

   ____ d. The woman has a lot of work to do this morning.

4. Two cash registers are open at a department store. Although one line is shorter than the other, customers keep leaving the short line to stand in the long one.

   ____ a. The cashier at the register with the short line is unpopular.

   ____ b. Some problem is keeping the short line from moving.

   ____ c. People standing in the longer line are receiving discounts on their purchases.

   ____ d. Long lines give people more time to reconsider their purchases.

5. In parts of India, wild animals show almost no fear of the human beings who live near them.

   ____ a. The animals are not very intelligent.

   ____ b. The animals never see humans and so have developed no fear of them.

   ____ c. The animals have been raised as pets by humans.

   ____ d. The humans have never acted aggressively towards the animals.

INFERENCES IN READING

In reading, too, we make logical leaps from the information given in a straightforward way to ideas that are not stated directly. As the scholar S. I. Hayakawa has said, inferences are "statements about the unknown made on the basis of the known." To draw inferences, we use all the clues provided by the writer, our own experience, and logic.

In this book, you have already practiced making inferences in the chapter on vocabulary. There you had to use context clues within sentences to infer the meanings of words. Also, in the chapter on main ideas, you had to "read between the lines" in order to find implied main ideas. The intent of this chapter is to broaden your ability to make inferences about what you read.

Read the following passage and then check the *three* inferences that can logically be drawn from it.

> There is a tribe on the island of New Guinea known as the Cargo Cult. For decades these people have been waiting for a great bird to swoop down from the clouds and drop riches and magical gifts on them. Their whole lives revolve around complicated ceremonies to make this happen. They are waiting for happiness to drop from the sky.
>
> They're not as crazy as they seem. During World War II, huge airplanes did drop boxes of food and magical gifts ranging from mirrors to jeeps. Sometimes they dropped bombs. After the war, a tribal headman made the decision to recreate the wartime conditions and lure back the first big bird. So at every harvest, these people burn almost all their crops. Periodically they destroy their villages, too. Most of the men refuse to work at all, keeping a constant vigil.
>
> Now this decision has been followed by an entire tribe of people for over forty years. And the Cargo Cult isn't just an oddity, either, it's a monumental headache to the government of Papua New Guinea—sometimes the cult members get frustrated and burn other tribes' crops and villages as well as their own. Reasonable explanations make no impression whatsoever. They continue to wait and burn. They are not known to be happy people.

____ 1. During the war, bombs destroyed some of the Cargo Cult's crops.

____ 2. Most of the women also refuse to work.

____ 3. The Cargo Cult members are neighborly.

____ 4. Cult members prefer the gifts they hope will fall from the sky to the sure benefits of work.

____ 5. The cult members feel they need jeeps to survive in the modern world.

____ 6. Waiting for something to bring them happiness has not made the Cargo Cult members happy.

Here is an explanation of each item:

1. This is a logical inference. Because the Cargo Cult members associate receiving "magical gifts" with their crops being destroyed, we can conclude both happened during the war. And because we know that bombs were dropped on New Guinea, we can conclude that the bombs destroyed the crops.

2. This is not a logical inference. In fact, we have reason to believe that most of the women did work. First of all, the author specifically omits them when mentioning that most of the men refuse to work. Secondly, if most of the men refuse to work, probably most women must do work in order for the tribe's work to get done.

3. This is not a logical inference. Most people would agree that burning other people's crops and villages is not a neighborly gesture. And even if we were to assume that the Cargo Cult members only burned crops and villages far away from them (and not those of their neighbors), we would still have no evidence that the Cargo Cult people were neighborly.

4. This is a logical inference. We can observe that the Cargo Cult members, in fact, destroy their crops and villages in hopes of receiving the "magical gifts." Also, it's clear that the men who don't work could be productive if they wished to be.

5. This is not a logical inference. Considering that the cult members think of airplanes as great birds, we cannot infer that these people know the function of jeeps. Nothing in the passage leads us to think otherwise.

6. This is a logical inference. First of all, cult members "are not known to be happy people." This is not hard to believe when we consider the facts that they are constantly waiting for something that is quite unlikely to arrive and that, in the process, they destroy their own food source and village.

Inference Guidelines

The exercises in this chapter provide practice in making careful inferences when you read. Three guidelines to that process are:

1   **Never lose sight of the available information.**   As much as possible, base your inferences on the facts. For instance, because the article states that the cult members think of airplanes as great birds, the reader can infer that the members do not understand what a jeep is or how to operate one.

2   **Use your background information and experience to help you in making inferences.**   For instance, the Cargo Cult passage didn't explicitly state that

the women of the tribe worked, but experience tells us that someone has to do the work of a community. Since most of the men of the tribe did not do that work, it's a pretty good guess that the women did much of it—especially since the author didn't say that the women also refused to work.

The more background information people have, the more accurate their inferences are likely to be. So keep in mind that if your background information in a particular matter is weak, your inferences may be shaky. The Cargo Cult's inference about how to get gifts to drop from the sky is based on a very weak background in the facts of their wartime experience. A doctor's inferences about your rash and fever are likely to be more helpful than those of your car mechanic.

3   **Consider the alternatives.**   Considering alternative interpretations of the facts is one way to zero in on a likely interpretation. Don't simply accept the first inference that comes to mind. Instead, consider all of the facts of a case and all the possible explanations. For example, the doctor analyzing your rash and fever may first think of and then eliminate several possible diagnoses before seriously testing for one or two of the more likely ones.

➣ *Practice 2*

Read the following passages. Then circle the letter of the *most logical answer* to each question, based on the facts given in the passage.

A.   Famous showman and circus owner P. T. Barnum is best known for his famous line "There's a sucker born every minute." He used every opportunity he had to prove the truth of his proverb. For example, when his exhibition of exotic animals and odd human beings became popular, he found that people tended to linger inside. This made it impossible for new paying customers to enter. Barnum solved the problem by hanging a large sign on the wall reading "THIS WAY TO THE EGRESS." Those following the sign found themselves out on the street. *Egress* is another word for *exit*. Barnum was right.

1. From the passage, we can conclude that Barnum
   a. avoided people.
   b. liked to trick people.
   c. had a high opinion of the average person's intelligence.

2. Barnum wanted people to leave the exhibition because
   a. the more quickly they left, the more tickets he could sell.
   b. he didn't like to be crowded.
   c. he wanted to close it.

3. From the wording of the new sign, we can infer that it was purposely designed to look like
   a. an exit sign.
   b. a practical joke.
   c. a sign to another exhibit.

4. It is likely that many people at the exhibition
   a. knew the meaning of *egress*.
   b. sneaked into the exhibition without paying.
   c. left the exhibition without meaning to.

5. From the last sentence, we can conclude that the author feels that people who didn't know or guess the meaning of *egress* were
   a. rare.
   b. suckers.
   c. lucky.

B. No More Tears, a shampoo that does not sting the eyes, was formulated for babies. Realizing that gentleness might appeal to adults as well, Johnson & Johnson marketers launched a promotional campaign featuring mothers and babies washing their hair together. When a healthy share of the adult female shampoo market came its way, the company added former pro football quarterback Fran Tarkenton as a thinning-hair spokesperson. Apparently gentle hair treatment appealed to middle-aged men, too, and the company captured part of still another market segment. Such repositioning—the conscious effort to change consumers' perceptions of a product—may be in order when marketers discover that a product appeals to other market segments.

6. The name and original intended market of the product imply that
   a. consumers will no longer "cry" about high-priced shampoos.
   b. other shampoos sting the eyes, causing tears.
   c. the product has a pleasant smell.

7. We can conclude that Johnson & Johnson was
   a. pleased with the results of its repositioning efforts for No More Tears.
   b. displeased with the results of its repositioning efforts for No More Tears.
   c. reluctant to try repositioning.

8. We can conclude that one reason Johnson & Johnson selected Fran Tarkenton as a spokesperson for No More Tears was that
   a. he is known for clean living.
   b. he would especially appeal to teenage boys.
   c. he would show that using No More Tears was not unmanly.

9. The passage implies that No More Tears is really
   a. a superior hair cleaner.
   b. a gentle shampoo.
   c. overly priced.

10. Repositioning is probably often used to
    a. switch a product's market segment from one group to another.
    b. increase a product's share of an already established market segment.
    c. add a new market segment to a product's already established market segment.

INFERENCES IN LITERATURE

Inference is very important in reading literature. While writers of factual material usually state directly what they mean, creative writers often *show* what they mean. It is up to the reader to infer the point of what the creative writer has to say. For instance, a non-fiction writer might write the following:

> Marian was angry at her father.

But the novelist might write:

> Marian's eyes narrowed when her father spoke to her. She cut him off in mid-sentence with the words, "I don't have time to argue with you."

The author has *shown* us the anger with specific detail rather than simply stating the fact of the anger. To understand imaginative writing, then, you must often use your inference skills—just as you do in everyday life.

Applying inference skills can increase your appreciation of such literary forms as novels, short stories, plays, essays, autobiographies, and poetry. Poetry, especially, by its nature implies much of its meaning. Implications are often made through comparisons. For example, Emily Dickinson begins one of her poems:

> Hope is the thing with feathers
> That perches in the soul
> And sings the tune without the words,
> And never stops at all.

Dickinson here compares hope with a singing bird. This implies, among other things, that hope is a sweet and welcome thing.

Looking at Poetry

Read the poem on the next page, and then circle the letter of the most logical answer to each question, based on the words and images in the poem. After you do so, read the explanations.

milestone: a stone post set up to show the distance in miles on a road

Sixty-Eighth Birthday

As life runs on, the road grows strange
With faces new, and near the end
The milestones into headstones change,
'Neath every one a friend.

James Russell Lowell

1. The speaker is
   a. very young.
   b. sixty-eight.
   c. an unknown age.

2. The poet compares life to a
   a. road with milestones.
   b. new face.
   c. friend.

3. The poem suggests that birthdays are
   a. strange roads.
   b. milestones on the road of life.
   c. friends.

4. The third line of the poem means that
   a. turning points go to our heads.
   b. change is good.
   c. eventually the road of life ends in death.

5. The poem implies that as we get older,
   a. we gain more friends.
   b. more and more of our friends die.
   c. our friends become strangers to us.

Here is an explanation for each of the five inferences:

1. The answer to the first question is *b*. The poem, of course, doesn't come out and say that the speaker is sixty-eight, but the title strongly implies it—what other purpose would there be for that title?

2. The answer to question 2 is *a*. The comparison of life to a road is implied in the first and third lines, which suggest that life runs on a road marked by milestones along it.

3. By describing life as a road with milestones, the poet implies that birthdays can be considered the milestones—the distance markers. The answer to question 3 is thus *b*.

4.   The third line of the poem says that life's milestones turn into headstones, which are stone markers set onto graves. This clearly implies that the road of life ends in death, so the answer to question 4 is *c*.

5.   The answer to the final question is *b*. The point that more and more of our friends die is fully made in the fourth line, where the speaker says that under all of the headstones are friends.

➤ Practice 3

Following are the first three stanzas of William Blake's poem "The Fly." Read the poem, and then circle the letters of the *five* inferences most solidly based on it.

The Fly

Little Fly,
Thy summer's play
My thoughtless hand
Has brushed away.

Am not I
a fly like thee?
Or art thou not
A man like me?

For I dance,
and drink, and sing,
Till some blind hand
Shall brush my wing.

William Blake

1.   The speaker has
      a. played with the fly.
      b. lightly brushed the fly away.
      c. killed the fly.

      (*Hint*: The speaker's hand has "brushed away" the fly's "summer's play," according to the first stanza.)

2.   The speaker compares himself to
      a. summer's play.
      b. a fly.
      c. a dance.

      (*Hint*: The speaker asks, "Am not I / A fly like thee? / Or art thou not / a man like me?")

3. The speaker feels his life is
   a. not worth living.
   b. enjoyable.
   c. not enjoyable.

   (*Hint*: The speaker symbolically describes his life in the first two lines of the third stanza.)

4. We can conclude that the image of a wing being brushed symbolizes
   a. dancing.
   b. drinking.
   c. dying.

   (*Hint*: In the last stanza, the speaker implies that his dancing, drinking and singing will end when "some blind hand / Shall brush [his] wing.")

5. The speaker feels death comes
   a. according to a plan.
   b. at random.

   (*Hint*: The poet uses the images of a "thoughtless [meaning *careless*] hand" and a "blind hand.")

Looking at Prose

Read the following short essay by noted science-fiction writer Isaac Asimov. Then put a check by the *five* inferences most solidly based on the words and images in the essay. After you do so, read the explanations.

KP: work with the "kitchen police," soldiers who assist the army cooks
bents: talents
oracles: messages from the gods
foist: force
arbiter: judge
indulgently: done to go along with someone's wishes
raucously: loudly
smugly: in a self-satisfied way

What Is Intelligence, Anyway?

What is intelligence, anyway? When I was in the Army, I received a kind of aptitude test that all soldiers took and, against a normal of 100, scored 160. No one at the base had ever seen a figure like that, and for two hours they made a big fuss over me. (It didn't mean anything. The next day I was still a buck private with KP as my highest duty.)

All my life I've been registering scores like that, so that I have the complacent feeling that I'm highly intelligent, and I expect other people to think so, too. Actually, though, don't such scores simply mean that I am very good at answering the type of academic questions that are considered worthy of answers by the people who make up the intelligence tests—people with intellectual bents similar to mine?

For instance, I had an auto repairman once, who, on these intelligence tests, could not possibly have scored more than 80, by my estimate. I always took it for granted that I was far more intelligent than he was. Yet, when anything went wrong with my car, I hastened to him with it, watched him anxiously as he explored its vitals, and listened to his pronouncements as though they were divine oracles—-and he always fixed my car.

Well then, suppose my auto repairman devised questions for an intelligence test. Or suppose a carpenter did, or a farmer, or, indeed, almost anyone but an academician. By every one of those tests, I'd prove myself a moron. And I'd be a moron, too. In a world where I could not use my academic training and my verbal talents but had to do something intricate or hard, working with my hands, I would do poorly. My intelligence, then, is not absolute but is a function of the society I live in and of the fact that a small subsection of that society has managed to foist itself on the rest as an arbiter of such matters.

Consider my auto repairman, again. He had a habit of telling me jokes whenever he saw me. One time he raised his head from under the automobile hood to say, "Doc, a deaf-and-dumb guy went into a hardware store to ask for some nails. He put two fingers together on the counter and made hammering motions with the other hand. The clerk brought him a hammer. He shook his head and pointed to the two fingers he was hammering. The clerk brought him nails. He picked out the sizes he wanted, and left. Well, Doc, the next guy who came in was a blind man. He wanted scissors. How do you suppose he asked for them?"

Indulgently, I lifted my right hand and made scissoring motions with my first two fingers. Whereupon my auto repairman laughed raucously and said, "Why, you dumb jerk, he used his voice and asked for them." Then he said, smugly, "I've been trying that on all my customers today." "Did you catch many?" I asked. "Quite a few," he said, "but I knew for sure I'd catch you." "Why is that?" I asked. "Because you're so goddamned educated, Doc, I knew you couldn't be very smart."

And I have an uneasy feeling he had something there.

___ 1. Asimov believed that academic abilities are not necessarily better than other skills.

___ 2. Asimov believed that he was not really intelligent.

___ 3. Asimov knew he was intelligent in the way which is measured by IQ tests.

___ 4. Asimov probably actually knew a great deal about cars.

___ 5. Asimov's cars needed numerous repairs.

___ 6. Asimov respected his automotive repairman's abilities.

___ 7. The riddle fooled Asimov because he wasn't particularly familiar with hardware stores.

___ 8. The riddle fooled Asimov because he didn't think about the difference between being unable to speak and unable to see.

___ 9. The auto repairman's definition of *smart* is having common sense.

___ 10. The auto repairman's definition of *smart* is having lots of schooling.

Here are explanations of each item:

1.   This is a logical inference. Asimov indicates that, despite his superior performance on academic tests, he is dependent on people who might perhaps not score high on these tests, such as an auto repairman, a carpenter, or a farmer. The reader can assume that, because of this dependence, Asimov believes that his academic abilities are not necessarily better than other skills.

2-3.   Asimov wrote that he consistently scored high on IQ tests. And he did not imply that his own type of intelligence—that measured by the tests—is not valid, only that other types of skills are also valid. You should, then, have checked inference 3 but not 2.

4.   Given Asimov's dependence on his auto repairman whenever anything went wrong with his car, we can safely conclude he knew little about cars. This is not a logical inference.

5.   This is not a well-supported inference. Nothing in the reading suggests that Asimov's cars needed repairing especially often.

6.   This is a well-supported inference. First of all, Asimov depended greatly on the repairman to take good care of his car. In addition, he always listened to his repairman's comments on his car "as though they were divine oracles"— messages from the gods.

7-8.   The answer to the riddle stems from the difference between the communication abilities of a dumb person and those of a blind person. Familiarity with hardware has nothing to do with it—the riddle's story could take place in another type of store and still have the same point. Therefore, you should have checked inference 8, but not 7.

9-10.   The auto repairman knew that Asimov was very educated, yet he said that Asimov "couldn't be very smart." Thus being well-educated must not have been the repairman's definition of *smart*. And since the repairman implied that only a smart person would be able to answer his riddle, we can assume his idea of *smart* was having the common sense to analyze the difference between the dumb man and the blind man. You should, then, have checked inference 9 but not 10.

➤ *Practice 4*

Following is a short story written by Langston Hughes, a poet and fiction writer who emerged as a major literary figure during the Harlem Renaissance of the 1920s. Read the story, and then circle the letters of the *five* inferences most solidly based on it.

Early Autumn

When Bill was very young, they had been in love. Many nights they had spent walking, talking together. Then something not very important had come between them, and they didn't speak. Impulsively, she had married a man she thought she loved. Bill went away, bitter about women.

Yesterday, walking across Washington Square, she saw him for the first time in years.

"Bill Walker," she said.

He stopped. At first he did not recognize her, to him she looked so old.

"Mary! Where did you come from?"

Unconsciously, she lifted her face as though wanting a kiss, but he held out his hand. She took it.

"I live in New York now," she said.

"Oh"—smiling politely. Then a little frown came quickly between his eyes.

"Always wondered what happened to you, Bill."

"I'm a lawyer. Nice firm, way downtown."

"Married yet?"

"Sure. Two kids."

"Oh," she said.

A great many people went past them through the park. People they didn't know. It was late afternoon. Nearly sunset. Cold.

"And your husband?" he asked her.

"We have three children. I work in the bursar's office at Columbia."

"You're looking very . . . " (he wanted to say old) ". . . well," he said.

She understood. Under the trees in Washington Square, she found herself desperately reaching back into the past. She had been older than he then in Ohio. Now she was not young at all. Bill was still young.

"We live on Central Park West," she said. "Come and see us sometime."

"Sure," he replied. "You and your husband must have dinner with my family some night. Any night. Lucille and I'd love to have you."

The leaves fell slowly from the trees in the Square. Fell without wind. Autumn dusk. She felt a little sick.

"We'd love it," she answered.

"You ought to see my kids." He grinned.

Suddenly the lights came on up the whole length of Fifth Avenue, chains of misty brilliance in the blue air.

"There's my bus," she said.

He held out his hand, "Good-by."

"When . . . " she wanted to say, but the bus was ready to pull off. The lights on the avenue blurred, twinkled, blurred. And she was afraid to open her mouth as she entered the bus. Afraid it would be impossible to utter a word.

Suddenly she shrieked very loudly, "Good-by!" But the bus door had closed.

The bus started. People came between them outside, people crossing the street, people they didn't know. Space and people. She lost sight of Bill. Then she remembered she had forgotten to give him her address—or ask him for his—or tell him that her youngest boy was named Bill, too.

1.   Authors of fiction often choose settings that symbolically reflect their story. In this case, the characters' stage of life is echoed in the author's choices of
     a. city and park.
     b. season and time of day.
     c. transportation and temperature.

2.   Hughes portrayed the awkwardness of the meeting by indicating a contrast between
     a. the woman's and Bill's jobs.
     b. New York City and Ohio.
     c. what the characters say and what they mean.

3.   The suggestion that Bill was still young but the woman was not implies that
     a. she was actually many, many years older than he.
     b. her life has aged her more rapidly than his life has aged him.
     c. he was an exercise buff who had taken especially good care of himself.

4.   The story suggests that Bill
     a. did not regret having not married the woman.
     b. plans on inviting the woman and her husband over for dinner.
     c. still wished nothing had come between him and the woman when they were young.

5.   The last few words of the story suggest that
     a. the boy was really Bill's son.
     b. the woman regretted naming her youngest son Bill.
     c. the woman had thought of Bill with so much longing that she named a son after him.

➤ Review Test 1

A.   After reading each passage, put a check by the *two* inferences that are most firmly based on the given facts.

1.   There is a joke that says there is only one holiday fruitcake in the world. Supposedly, it gets passed from one person to the next to the next. Raisin haters especially detest fruitcake, since raisins are the most common fruit in the cakes. Fruitcakes last so long partly because they are soaked in brandy, but the result of this soaking is a damp heavy cake resembling a dark, moist brick.

     ____ a. Brandy has the ability to preserve some food.
     ____ b. Fruitcakes can be kept unrefrigerated up to a year.
     ____ c. The fruitcake in the joke gets passed from person to person because no one wants it.

2. Researchers say that bones found in the mountains of Colorado are believed to have belonged to a "supersaurus" that may have been more than one hundred feet long. Bones recovered so far at the site include a pelvis that is six feet tall. The supersaurus is thought to have weighed about thirty tons. Researchers hope the complete skeleton, when found, will help them understand how such a huge animal could survive by eating only plants.

   ___ a. The supersaurus weighed more than any other known dinosaur.

   ___ b. The supersaurus was a vegetarian.

   ___ c. The supersaurus lived only in North America.

   ___ d. Researchers continue looking for bones at the Colorado location.

   ___ e. The researchers are all from the University of Colorado.

3. President Lyndon Johnson had a love of giving gifts. He especially enjoyed giving electric toothbrushes to friends, admirers and even enemies. To his biographer Doris Kearns, he explained why. "I give 'em toothbrushes," said LBJ, "because then I know that from now until the end of their days they will think of me the first thing in the morning and the last at night."

   ___ a. Johnson wanted people to think of him.

   ___ b. He cared deeply about healthy teeth.

   ___ c. He had no enemies.

   ___ d. Johnson gave electric toothbrushes to all of his staff.

   ___ e. Johnson expected an electric toothbrush to last a long time.

B. Eight statements follow the passage below. Read the passage, and then check the *four* statements which are most logically supported by the information given.

   The elimination of jobs because of superautomation is not limited to industrial factories. Offices are increasingly electronic. Engineers and architects now draw three-dimensional designs, update them, test them, and store them almost instantaneously in a computer. Agriculture employs robot fruit pickers and sheepshearers, computerized irrigation systems that use sensors to calculate water and fertilizer needs in different parts of a field, and automated chicken houses. Retail stores, banks, and brokerage houses use on-line transaction processing to obtain instant information and to conduct transactions. Laser scanning and bar codes are transforming the physical handling of goods by retailers and wholesale distributors. A final example of technological change affecting jobs is the widespread use of televisions, telephones, and personal computers for the purposes of home banking and shopping.

   ___ 1. Computers will soon replace engineers and architects.

   ___ 2. There will be more jobs for people who run and repair electronic devices.

___ 3. One function of superautomation is the handling and storage of information.

___ 4. Restaurants can't benefit from superautomation.

___ 5. Machines can help company employees accomplish more.

___ 6. Superautomation requires few adjustments from society.

___ 7. Superautomation has advantages and disadvantages.

___ 8. Laser technology is limited to the business world.

➤ Review Test 2

A. Following is an excerpt from "To Build a Fire," a short story by Jack London. Read the excerpt. Then, for each item, circle the letter of the answer most logically based on the information in the passage.

> As he turned to go on, he spat speculatively. There was a sharp, explosive crackle that startled him. He spat again. And again, in the air, before it could fall to the snow, the spittle crackled. He knew that at fifty below spittle crackled on the snow, but this spittle had crackled in the air. Undoubtedly it was colder than fifty below—how much colder he did not know. But the temperature did not matter. He was bound for the old claim on the left fork of Henderson creek, where the boys were already. They had come over across the divide from the Indian Creek country, while he had come the roundabout way to take a look at the possibilities of getting out logs in the spring from the islands in the Yukon. He would be in to camp by six o'clock; a bit after dark, it was true, but the boys would be there, a fire would be going, and a hot supper would be ready. As for lunch, he pressed his hand against the protruding bundle under his jacket. It was also under his shirt, wrapped up in a handkerchief and lying against the naked skin. It was the only way to keep the biscuits from freezing. He smiled agreeably to himself as he thought of these biscuits, each cut open and sopped in bacon grease, and each enclosing a generous slice of fried bacon.

1. The man was
   a. not surprised at how cold it had become.
   b. alarmed at the lateness of the hour.
   c. not afraid about being alone in the cold weather.

2. The man would reach camp
   a. about six o'clock in the morning.
   b. in several hours.
   c. the next day.

3. The man
   a. looked forward to camp.
   b. wished he didn't have to go to that camp.
   c. had never planned on meeting the boys at the camp.

4. The man carried food for
   a. his dinner at camp.
   b. his lunch that day.
   c. the boys.

5. The biscuits
   a. were kept from freezing by the man's body heat.
   b. seemed distasteful to the man.
   c. were wrapped in a bag.

B. Following is James Stephens's poem "Hate." Read the poem, using the definitions as necessary, and then check the *five* inferences most solidly based on it.

nigh: near
writhing: twisting
grimace: a twisting of the face that expresses contempt
stern: unfriendly
cast: thrown
relate: tell

Hate

My enemy came nigh,
And I
Stared fiercely in his face.
My lips went writhing back in a grimace.
And stern I watched him with a narrow eye.
Then, as I turned away, my enemy,
That bitter heart and savage, said to me:
"Some day, when this is past,
When all the arrows that we have are cast,
And fail to find a story to relate,
It may seem to us then a mystery
That we could hate each other."
                    Thus said he,
And did not turn away,
Waiting to hear what I might have to say.
But I fled quickly, fearing if I stayed
I might have kissed him as I would a maid.

____ 1. At first, the speaker is not afraid to face his enemy.

____ 2. The speaker showed no emotion as he faced his enemy.

____ 3. When his enemy came near, the speaker intended to attack him.

____ 4. His enemy threatens to throw an arrow at him.

____ 5. His enemy suggests that there is very little reason for them to hate each other.

____ 6. The enemy's heart was not as bitter as the speaker had thought.

____ 7. At the end, the speaker is afraid of his enemy's attacks.

____ 8. At the end, the speaker is afraid he might not act like an enemy.

____ 9. The enemy was afraid of the speaker.

____10. The poet is suggesting that people do not have to hate each other.

➤ *Review Test 3*

A. To review what you've learned in this chapter, complete each of the following sentences about inferences.

1. An inference is a conclusion that is (*directly stated, suggested*) _____ by the author.

2. When making inferences, it is (*a mistake, useful*) _____ to use our own experience as well as the author's clues.

3. When making inferences, it is (*a mistake, useful*) _____ to use our sense of logic as well as the author's clues.

4. Drawing inferences is a key skill in reading literature because writers of fiction do not so much (*tell, show*) _____ us what they mean as (*tell, show*) _____ us with specific details.

B. Why are so many young people involved in drunk driving accidents? The following article, originally published in the *Washington Post*, provides one answer—and gives you an opportunity to apply your understanding of inferences to a full-length piece.

Following the reading are questions on inferences. To help you continue reinforcing the skills taught in previous chapters, there are also questions on

- vocabulary in context
- central point and main ideas
- supporting details
- transitions
- patterns of organization
- summarizing
- fact and opinion.

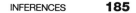

Words to Watch

Following are some words in the reading that do not have strong context support. Each word is followed by the number of the paragraph in which it appears and its meaning there.

sustained (1): suffered
disproportionately (4): out of proportion
goaded (5): prodded
lethal (5): deadly
monitor (6): oversee
formidable (8): inspiring dread and wonder
tomes (8): scholarly books
drones (9): bores
annuity (10): annual income
access (12): right to use

SELLING THE YOUNG ON DRINKING

Colman McCarthy

1 An eighteen-year-old Long Island woman came home from the hospital a few days ago. She had been recuperating from a fractured skull and other injuries sustained° in a car crash that for a moment in mid-March jolted the nation out of its casual indifference to highway slaughter.

2 The crash commanded attention for the body count alone: nine of ten teen-agers were killed in Mineola, N.Y., at 2 A.M. by a freight train when their van didn't make it through a flashing railroad crossing. The group—good students from good families—had been to a party. While there, it later came out, the driver and others in the van had had a few drinks.

3 I remember this tragedy for other reasons besides the size of the death toll. The crash occurred a few miles from where I grew up. I know the crossing. The accident also reminded me that my closest boyhood pal died at 16 in a similar car crash in a race against a train.

4 But I think of this latest tragedy mostly because this is the peak of the high school and college drinking season. Graduation parties and proms mean that cars and the drug alcohol will combine in a suicide stakes that will see a statistical rise in the number of teen-age fatalities and drunk-driving arrests, a number that is already disproportionately° high.

5 Of late, the police and the courts, goaded° to action by citizen groups angered and sickened by drinking drivers who turn highways into death traps, have been taking action. But no hopes should be raised. Through the legal system, we are sending the young one message—that it's wrong, stupid and lethal° to drive and drink—but through advertising, we send another: drink up, it's Miller time, it's a Stroh's night, head for Busch country, let it be Lowenbrau.

Unlike teen-age sex, or teen-age crime, which seem to have created mini-   6
industries to monitor° them, few studies on the effects of alcohol advertising on youth
have been made. But the ones we do have are telling.

In one study, researchers from the Scientific Analysis Corp. in San Francisco   7
reported that beer and hard liquor dominated the national advertising in college
newspapers. In the sample of thirty-two papers, half of the ads were for alcohol. The
ads were not merely pitches for brands. They were life-style ads with cynical anti-
education themes.

One representative ad, the researchers reported, "shows three students coming out   8
of a bookstore. Walking one behind the other, the first and last students are burdened
down with a stack of formidable° looking tomes° while the student in the middle
joyously carries three six-packs of beer. His smile is in contrast to their concern. The
caption reads: 'Now Comes Miller Time.'

"Our hero isn't worrying about term papers, reading assignments and finals. He   9
has a better way to cope. The hard work involved in getting an education is compared
with another life style which gives beer drinking a high priority. The beer drinker
emerges as a charming rascal, the serious students as worried drones°."

The alcohol ads in dailies published in large universities, some of which take in   10
$1 million annually in advertising, are payoffs that marketing executives are willing to
gamble for. The researchers quoted one executive: "Let's not forget that getting a
freshman to choose a certain brand of beer may mean that he will maintain his brand
loyalty for the next twenty or twenty-five years. If he turns out to be a big drinker, the
beer company has bought itself an annuity°."

The buying is good. The Campus Alcohol Information Center at the University of   11
Florida studies beer-drinking habits of students visiting Daytona Beach during spring
break in 1981. Fifty-four percent of the men and thirty-two percent of the women said
they consume five or more cans of beer per sitting.

When the besotted young take to the highways to kill themselves—and us if we   12
venture into the war zones—they are right to judge adult society as hypocritical.
Legislatures do not restrain the advertising practices of the alcohol industry: no
warning notices about the nation's most dangerous drug, no banning from radio or
television, no limitations on access° to college newspapers.

We ensure that every hour is the industry's happy hour.   13

Reading Comprehension Questions

Vocabulary in Context

1. The word *besotted* in "the besotted young take to the highways to kill
   themselves—and us" (paragraph 12) means
   a. overgrown.
   b. drunk.
   c. organized.
   d. sober.

Central Point and Main Ideas

2. Which sentence best expresses the central point of the selection?
   a. According to one study, some students drink a great deal of beer.
   b. Because alcohol ads are uncontrolled, adult society's message against drunk driving is hypocritical.
   c. All advertising should be limited.
   d. The legal system is sending out a strong message against drunk driving.

3. Which sentence best expresses the main idea of paragraph 10?
   a. Some university dailies make a lot of money on advertising.
   b. Alcohol companies have a lot to gain by advertising in college dailies.
   c. A freshman may find a brand of beer he or she is willing to stick with.
   d. Not all freshmen end up drinking throughout their lives.

Supporting Details

4. _____ TRUE OR FALSE? No studies have yet been made on the effect of alcohol advertising on young people.

Transitions

5. The relationship of the second sentence below to the first is one of
   a. addition.
   b. time.
   c. contrast.
   d. comparison.

   Of late, the police and the courts, goaded to action by citizen groups angered and sickened by drinking drivers who turn highways into death traps, have been taking action. But no hopes should be raised. (Paragraph 5)

Patterns of Organization

6. Paragraph 5 contrasts
   a. police with the courts.
   b. driving with drinking.
   c. the old and the young.
   d. the legal system's message on drunk driving with advertising's message.

Summarizing

7. Which of the following best summarizes paragraphs 7–10?
   a. Using life-style ads with anti-education themes, alcohol advertisers— aiming for long-term customers—advertise heavily in college newspapers.
   b. The national advertising in college newspapers is dominated by alcohol advertisements.
   c. The alcohol ads in college newspapers stress anti-education lifestyle themes in which drinking is depicted as more admirable than studying.
   d. Marketing executives pay large sums for ads in campus newspapers in order to win the long-term brand loyalty of students.

Fact and Opinion

8. The sentence below contains
   a. a fact.
   b. an opinion.
   c. both a fact and an opinion.

   In the sample of thirty-two papers, half of the ads were for alcohol. (Paragraph 7)

Inferences

9. We can conclude the author feels that
   a. all advertising should be limited.
   b. if there were fewer alcohol ads, young people would drink less.
   c. our nation is doing an acceptable job in fighting drunk driving.
   d. because of all the alcohol ads, students bear no responsibility for drinking and driving.

10. In paragraph 12, the author implies
    a. legislatures should restrain the alcohol industry's advertising practices.
    b. warning notices on the dangers of alcohol should be required.
    c. college newspapers should not have unlimited alcohol ads.
    d. all of the above.

9

Purpose
and Tone

An important part of reading critically is realizing that behind everything you read is an author. This author is a person who has a reason for writing a given piece and who works from a personal point of view. To fully understand and evaluate what you read, you must recognize *purpose*—the reason why the author writes. You must also be aware of *tone*—the expression of the author's attitude and feeling. Both purpose and tone are discussed in this chapter.

PURPOSE

Authors write with a reason in mind, and you can better evaluate what is being said by determining what that reason is. The author's reason for writing is also called the *purpose* of a selection. Three common purposes are:

- **To inform**—to give information about a subject. Authors with this purpose wish to give their readers facts.

- **To persuade**—to convince the reader to agree with the author's point of view on a subject. Authors with this purpose may give facts, but their main goal is to promote an opinion.

- **To entertain**—to amuse and delight; to appeal to the reader's senses and imagination. Authors with this purpose entertain in various ways, through fiction and nonfiction.

Read each of the three paragraphs that follow and decide whether the author's main purpose is to inform, to persuade, or to entertain. Write in your answers, and then read the explanations that follow.

1. All states should pass laws protecting our children from being paddled or hit in the classroom. In forty-one states, it is still legal to discipline children in school with physical force. This type of discipline is a disgrace. There are many more humane and effective ways of handling unruly students.

   Purpose: _____

2. The worst recorded epidemic of all time was the bubonic plague, also called the Black Death. It swept Europe, Asia and Africa from 1346 to 1353. So deadly was this disease that it killed one third of all the population of these continents. The plague was spread by fleas infected with bacteria from diseased rats.

   Purpose: _____

3. If business were as good as my aim, I'd be on Easy Street. Instead I've got an office on East Trout Street and a nasty relationship with my creditors. That's me, Gill Catfish, the meanest law enforcer outside of Sand Valley Fishpolice. I'm not the type to flounder around. Yeah, I'm a private eye used to muddy waters.

   Purpose: _____

In the first paragraph, the writer's purpose is *to persuade* readers that states should pass laws against physical punishment in the classroom. This is clear because the author begins by clearly saying what states *should* do. In addition, the author claims that disciplining with physical force "is a disgrace" and that there are better ways of handling unruly students. These are statements used to convince us, rather than to inform us. The purpose of the second paragraph is *to inform*. The author is mainly providing readers with factual details about the Black Death. Finally, the playful and silly details about the fishy detective tell us that the purpose of paragraph three is *to entertain* with humor.

At times, writing may blend two purposes. An informative article on losing weight, for example, may include comic touches, or a persuasive letter to the editor may contain factual information. Remember in such cases to focus on the author's primary purpose. Ask yourself, "What is the author's main idea?" That will help you determine his or her principal intention.

Keep in mind as well that persuasive writing may include numerous facts—it can actually be mainly factual. But in such a case, the author may have included only those facts that support his or her point of view.

> *Practice 1*

Label each item according to its main purpose: to inform (**I**), to persuade (**P**), or to entertain (**E**).

_____ 1. The vanilla bean is the fruit of a particular orchid.

_____ 2. I read the obituaries every morning; if I don't find my name, I get dressed and go to work.

_____ 3. Television networks should reduce the number of commercials shown during children's programs.

_____ 4. During the American Revolution, some colonists remained loyal to the British.

_____ 5. If you want him to abandon all women except you, wear Abandon perfume.

_____ 6. Many people in my family are seafood eaters. When they see food, they eat it.

_____ 7. In microwave ovens, electromagnetic energy creates heat from inside food by heating up the food's water molecules.

_____ 8. Auto manufacturers should be required to place air bags on all new cars. This simple safety feature would save thousands of lives each year.

_____ 9. The reason that koala bears appear so calm and sleepy-eyed is that they are slightly drugged from the eucalyptus leaves they feed on.

_____ 10. I had an uncle who knew when he was going to die; the warden told him.

> *Practice 2*

Label each of the following passages according to its main purpose: to inform (**I**), to persuade (**P**), or to entertain (**E**).

_____ 1. If we accept the notion that one goal of the judicial system is to rehabilitate people, our recidivism rate—the percentage of those released from prison who are later arrested for other crimes—shows how inadequate our criminal justice system really is. Depending on the particular study, this rate runs somewhere between 30 and 80 percent. The crime rate among former prisoners is actually much higher, for the recidivism rate represents only those who are rearrested. Part of the reason for recidivism is a penal system that produces contempt and hatred—attitudes hardly conducive to law-abiding behavior. To lower our recidivism rate, we must reform our penal system.

_____ 2. I don't see how knitting got the reputation of being relaxing. How can anyone relax knowing it will take two and a half years to complete a project? Some claim that listening to TV while knitting a sweater is pleasant, but how good can it be to know that by the time you finish the sweater, the person for whom you were making it is another size? And how relaxed can you be after losing a stitch and then poking an awkward needle through dozens of fallen loops only to discover that you missed a stitch twenty-five loops ago? I'll try knitting only when I'm already relaxed enough to tolerate the aggravation. Now I find it more restful to mow the lawn.

_____ 3. At the beginning of the twentieth century, school administrators in Paris wanted to relieve overcrowding by removing youngsters who did not have the capacity to benefit from an academic education. They called in the psychologist Alfred Binet and asked him to devise a test to identify those children. The test that Binet developed was the precursor of a wide variety of tests that try to assign intelligence a numerical score. Binet's approach focused on finding children who were least likely to benefit from an education. Today, intelligence testing is also used to identify children with special strengths who can benefit from a richer teaching program.

TONE

A writer's tone reveals the attitude he or she has toward a subject. Tone is expressed through the words and details the writer selects. Just as a speaker's voice can project a range of feelings, a writer's voice can project one or more tones, or feelings: anger, sympathy, hopefulness, sadness, respect, dislike, and so on. Understanding tone is, then, an important part of understanding what an author has written.

To appreciate the differences in tone that writers can employ, read the following statements of employees of fast-food restaurants:

"I hate this job. The customers are rude, the managers are idiots, and the food smells like dog chow." (*Tone:* bitter, angry.)

"I have no doubt that flipping burgers and toasting buns will prepare me for a top position on Wall Street." (*Tone:* mocking, sarcastic.)

"I love working at Burger Barn. I meet interesting people, earn extra money, and get to eat all the chicken nuggets I want when I go on break." (*Tone:* enthusiastic, positive.)

"I'm not excited about wearing fluorescent green polyester uniforms, but the managers are willing to schedule me around my classes, and the company offers scholarships to hardworking employees." (*Tone:* fair-minded, objective.)

Below is a list of words commonly used to describe tone. Note that two different words may refer to the same tone or similar tones—for example, matter-of-fact and objective, or comic and humorous. Brief meanings are given in parentheses for some of the words.

A List of Words That Describe Tone

straightforward	cheerful
matter-of-fact	joyous
objective	light-hearted
serious	amused
formal	humorous
informal	comic
solemn	playful
bitter	outspoken (*spoken boldly and freely*)
sorrowful	impassioned (*filled with passion and strong feeling*)
depressed	tolerant (*respecting of other views and behavior*)
distressed	remorseful (*filled with guilt over a wrong one has done*)
angry	outraged (*very angered*)
critical	sarcastic (*making sharp or wounding remarks; ironic*)
cruel	mocking (*ridiculing; sneering; holding up for scorn*)
hesitant	scornful (*looking down on someone or something*)
fearful	ironic (*meaning the opposite of what is expressed*)
anxious	arrogant (*conceited*)
alarmed	irreverent (*lacking respect*)
tragic	cynical (*believing the worst of others*)
self-pitying	indignant (*angry about something unfair or mean*)
disbelieving	revengeful (*wanting to hurt someone in return for an injury*)
surprised	vindictive (*very revengeful*)
regretful	malicious (*spiteful; intentionally harmful*)
sympathetic	contemptuous (*expressing great scorn and disgust*)
compassionate	ambivalent (*uncertain about a choice*)
loving	optimistic (*looking on the bright side of things*)
sentimental	pessimistic (*looking on the gloomy side of things*)
forgiving	desperate (*having a great desire or need for something*)
excited	grim (*harsh; dealing with unpleasant subjects*)

Note: Most of the words in this box reflect a feeling or judgment. In contrast, *matter-of-fact* (sticking only to the facts) and *objective* (without prejudice; not affected by personal feelings) describe communication that does not express personal bias and feeling.

More About Tone

Below are five statements expressing different attitudes about an old car. Five different tones are used:

optimistic	disappointed	tolerant
humorous	angry	

Label each statement according to which of these five tones you think is present. Then read the explanation that follows.

_____ 1. Unfortunately, this car is a lot less reliable than I'd like.

_____ 2. It's not the greatest car in the world, but it usually takes me where I have to go.

_____ 3. If car dealers weren't so dishonest, I wouldn't have bought this piece of junk for so much money.

_____ 4. Even though the car has a problem now and then, I bet it'll keep running forever.

_____ 5. This car is so old it's eligible for an antique-vehicle license plate.

The first item has a disappointed tone because of the words *unfortunately* and *less reliable than I'd like*. In the second item, the phrase *usually takes me where I have to go* shows the writer's accepting attitude, giving the item a tolerant tone. The tone of the third item is angry because of the writer's clearly stated resentment of car dealers, of the car itself, and of its price tag. The bet in the fourth item that the car will "keep running forever" gives that item an optimistic tone. And finally, the obvious exaggeration in the last item imparts a humorous tone.

A Note on Irony

One commonly used tone is that of *irony*. When writing has an ironic tone, it says one thing but means the opposite. Irony is found in everyday conversation as well as in writing. Following are a few examples; notice that the quotation in each says the opposite of what is meant.

If your dog is slow to learn, you might say, "Yeah, Russ is a regular Albert Einstein."

After your first class with a sourpuss teacher, you might comment to a classmate, "What a ray of sunshine that guy is."

If someone is unusually attractive and talented, we might remark, "Poor Laura. She's got absolutely nothing going for her."

After seeing your favorite basketball team play its worst game ever, you might comment, "I knew they wouldn't disappoint me."

If the price tag on a shirt you like is double what you'd expect, you might mutter, "What a bargain."

Irony also refers to situations in which what happens is the opposite of what we might expect. We could call it ironic, for example, if a man bites a dog. So another way for a writer to be ironic is to describe such situations. Here are a few more examples of this type of irony:

Marge couldn't seem to get pregnant, so she and Fred adopted a baby. Three months later, Marge was pregnant.

Gina loved dancing, but her boyfriend Eddie didn't dance well. So she insisted he take dancing lessons. As a result, he signed up for lessons and fell in love with his dancing teacher.

The doctor told Mr. Lawrence he'd better exercise if he wanted to stay healthy. So Mr. Lawrence began jogging. One day while jogging across a street, he was hit by a truck and died instantly.

➤ *Practice 3*

A. Below are five statements expressing different attitudes about a blind date. Five different tones are used:

pessimistic	self-pitying	ironic
enthusiastic	angry	

For each statement, write the tone that you think is present.

_____ 1. Me go on a blind date? Oh sure, I've always wanted to meet Dracula's daughter.

_____ 2. I just know I'm going to hate this guy my mother's making me go out with. These things never work out.

_____ 3. No way I'm going on a blind date! You've got a lot of nerve trying to set me up. What do you think I am—desperate?

_____ 4. I'd love it if you'd fix me up with your cousin from out of state. It sounds like a lot of fun.

_____ 5. Oh, I suppose I'll go on a blind date. That's probably the only kind of date I can get.

B. The following conversation between a mother and son involves five of the tones shown in the box below. For each statement, write the tone that you think is present.

self-mocking	threatening	solemn	contented
sympathetic	matter-of-fact	amused	forgiving
arrogant	mildly regretful		

_____ 6. The country life is quiet and peaceful. I didn't know what happiness was until we moved here.

_____ 7. I know I'm going to love it here once I figure out which end of a cow to milk and stop trying to gather eggs from the rooster.

_____ 8. If rents weren't so ridiculously high in the city, we wouldn't be forced to live like country hicks.

_____ 9. I sometimes wish we had not moved to the country. We've lost touch with some old friends, and shopping malls are not around the corner.

_____10. The cost of living in the country is lower.

➤ *Practice 4*

Each passage illustrates one of the tones in the box below. In each space, put the letter of the tone that best applies. Don't use any letter more than once.

Remember that the tone of a selection reflects the author's attitude. To find the tone of a paragraph, ask yourself what attitude is revealed by its words and phrases.

a. threatening	c. matter-of-fact	e. embarrassed	g. critical
b. depressed	d. optimistic	f. hypocritical	h. admiring

_____ 1. Your room is a pigsty! How can you live like this? Can't you even carry your dirty clothes to the hamper? You brag about your weight-lifting abilities, but it seems that socks and underwear are too heavy for you. But don't worry. Pretty soon your socks will walk across the room themselves—they're that dirty and smelly.

_____ 2. If Superman had a sidekick, it would probably be a flea. This remarkable insect can jump 150 times its own length—easily the equivalent of Superman's jumping a tall building in a single bound. It can also accelerate fifty times faster than the space shuttle, survive for months without eating, and be quick-frozen for a year and then brought back to life. All in all, the flea would make a terrific "Super Bug."

_____ 3. I wish I were dead. I just can't take it anymore. Nobody cares about me. My parents are too busy to even ask how I'm doing. I don't have any real friends. Sure, they'll say they're my friends, but they're never around when I need them. I just feel lousy all the time. I cry myself to sleep every night, and I hate getting up in the morning. I don't even care if I pass or fail in school. I don't care about anything.

_____ 4. Since the earliest of times, people have considered the pearl to be one of nature's most beautiful creations. To the oyster, however, it is not valuable, as the pearl is actually a disease of that mollusk. It begins when a tiny piece of sand finds its way into the oyster's shell, where it soon starts to irritate the flesh. In self-protection, the oyster covers the irritant with a calcium-based substance called nacre. But the presence of a foreign body inside the shell continues to annoy the oyster. The mollusk responds by adding thicker coats of nacre, resulting in a pearl.

_____ 5. Much has been written about the so-called death of the family. However, I do not believe that there has been such a death at all. Who said a family must be defined as a mother, a father, and children living in one home? What about the warmth in so many single-parent families? And what of the special intimacy of couples who have no children, through choice or necessity? And surely a divorced father enjoying a summer visit with his children may still be considered "family." In all these situations we still find love and sharing of values. I strongly believe that in the future, families will be less limited by tradition and freer to rejoice in their relationships, whatever they may be.

➤ *Review Test 1*

A. In the space provided, indicate whether the primary purpose of each passage is to inform (**I**), to persuade (**P**), or to entertain (**E**).

_____ 1. It is a tragic fact that the annual number of deaths due to automobile accidents has increased steadily over the years. This is largely because drivers and passengers are careless about using seat belts. So be sure to buckle up, and buckle up your children too. It just might save a life.

_____ 2. Identical twins occur in about one in 250 births; fraternal twins happen about twice as often. But scientists now believe that twins are conceived far more often than they are born. Recent studies show that up to 70 percent of human pregnancies that start out with two embryos end with only one child born. The "vanishing twin syndrome" usually occurs when, for reasons unknown, one of the twins stops developing and is re-absorbed by the mother's body.

_____ 3. Edward took a sip of the purple potion, and his feet began to glow. One more sip and they disappeared. By the time the glass was empty, it looked like it was floating in air—he was entirely invisible. Figuring he had about two hours, he immediately ran to the car. He went out of his way to drive the back roads so no one would notice a "driverless" car. When he reached the apartment building, he parked in back. He glanced up and saw a light in Rita's apartment.

_____ 4. When plans are announced to build a residential facility for recovering mental patients, community feeling often runs high. Neighbors worry that the former mental patients will be dangerous or that property values in the area will fall. In fact, recovering mental patients make fine, responsible neighbors. They are very rarely violent; instead, they are people who have sought help for their emotional problems and are dealing successfully with them. As to their effect on property values, that depends almost entirely on the attitude of the new facility's neighbors. People should welcome such a residence as a constructive addition to their community.

B. Each of the following passages illustrates one of the tones in the box below. In the space provided, put the letter of the tone that best applies to each passage. Use four different tones.

   Remember that the tone of a selection reflects the author's attitude. To find the tone of a paragraph, ask yourself what attitude is revealed by its words and phrases.

a. joyous	c. frightened	e. forgiving	g. amused
b. objective	d. sentimental	f. impassioned	h. comic

_____ 1. Men and women of this university, why permit yourselves to be limited by old-fashioned gender roles? You don't have to be accountants just because you're male! And you don't have to be teachers and nurses just because you're female! Rise up! Demand your right to equal job opportunities! Join SASS, Students Against Sexual Stereotyping. Only if we unite can we overcome thousands of years of prejudice.

_____ 2. I wished the guy in the seat behind the bus driver would stop looking at me like he did. He gave me the creeps. I was really glad when my stop came and I could get off the bus. It didn't take me long to realize, however, that he was getting off too. "Please God, let him go the other way," I thought. I turned toward home. The streets were darker and emptier than I remembered they could be. His footsteps followed mine. When I walked faster, he did too. When I crossed to the other side, he crossed too. Finally, I began to run. My vision was blurred by the tears in my eyes.

_____ 3. The shrew, a small animal similar to a mouse or a mole, measures two inches long from the tip of its nose to the tip of its tail. It weighs only a few ounces. Despite its small size, the shrew has a bite as deadly as that of a poisonous snake and eats as much as two times its own weight each day. It successfully attacks and kills animals much larger than itself. Its main weapons are tiny needle-like teeth and a deadly saliva, which contains an unusually strong poison. A special gland in the shrew's mouth produces this venom.

_____ 4. Toronto had better dirty up if it wants to make it as a film capital. American movie directors like working in the Canadian city, where their dollars go further and restrictions are few. But they complain that Toronto is too clean to double for many U.S. locations. One American film crew working in Toronto needed to find a dark, dirty alley to shoot a particular scene. They couldn't. So they created one, dumping bags of garbage in one well-kept street. The alley looked just right— until the film crew left for dinner and a helpful Toronto public works crew came by and cleaned up the mess.

➤ *Review Test 2*

This activity will give you practice in recognizing purpose and tone in the same passage. Read each paragraph, and then circle your answers to the questions that follow.

A. Umbrellas have feet, invisible little feet. How else can we explain the fact that the rascals are forever sneaking off, stealing away from the spots where we perfect humans are sure we put them? Time and again, it's the same story: A crack of thunder, and the sky unleashes a flood. We reach for our trusty umbrella only to find an empty space. But it was there, we insist. Where did it disappear to? Perhaps it's next to the sunglasses, which, in case you didn't know, have wings.

1. The primary purpose of this paragraph is to
   a. teach readers about umbrellas and sunglasses.
   b. persuade readers to be more careful about where they keep umbrellas.
   c. amuse readers by poking fun at a minor human problem.

2. The tone of this paragraph can be described as
   a. playful and humorous.
   b. surprised and regretful.
   c. objective.

B. How tired I am of the constant griping I hear about the United States Postal Service. Why can't people recognize a bargain when they see one? Do you realize what services your first class stamp guarantees you? For only pennies, your urgent letter may cross the country—even to Hawaii or Alaska—in only a few days. For that same small amount, you may have your mail forwarded when you move. In some cases, the same piece of mail can be forwarded more than once—all on one stamp. It's high time to stop complaining about the Postal Service and to support it instead.

3. The primary purpose of this paragraph is to
   a. inform readers of postal services that are available.
   b. persuade readers to appreciate the Postal Service.
   c. entertain readers with postal anecdotes.

4. The overall tone of this paragraph can be described as
   a. matter-of-fact.
   b. tolerant.
   c. indignant.

C. Every weekend athlete is acquainted with the sudden crippling pain known as a "stitch in the side." The stitch is actually a cramp in the diaphragm, the muscle that separates the abdomen from the chest cavity. When you breathe too heavily in a short period of time—as during a burst of athletic activity— the diaphragm suffers an oxygen shortage and reacts with the painful cramp. To relieve a stitch in your left side, say experts, lift your hands over your head and stretch far to the right while breathing slowly and regularly. Reverse your stretch for a stitch on the right.

5. The primary purpose of this paragraph is to
   a. inform readers what a "stitch in the side" is and how to relieve it.
   b. persuade readers to recognize and relieve a "stitch in the side."
   c. entertain readers with the silly details of a "stitch in the side."

6. The overall tone of this paragraph can be described as
   a. sarcastic.
   b. sad.
   c. matter-of-fact.

D. Nothing disturbs me more than those citizens who treat our country like an open garbage pit. I am referring to people who toss from their cars soda cans, crumpled tissues and what have you. I also have in mind the individual who casually drops candy wrappers, empty cigarette packs, and other junk when walking along public streets. This type of uncaring behavior is also behind our country's most "popular" form of art—graffiti. Americans ought to have more pride in their environment.

7. The primary purpose of this paragraph is to
   a. present facts on the environment.
   b. persuade people not to mess up the environment.
   c. amuse people with stories about silly behavior.

8. The general tone of this paragraph can be described as
   a. forgiving.
   b. critical.
   c. cheerful.

➤ Review Test 3

A. To review what you've learned in this chapter, answer the following questions.

1. What is the purpose of each of the types of writing below? Label each according to their usual main purpose: to inform, to persuade, or to entertain.

   A news report: _____

   A mystery novel: _____

   An editorial: _____

2. *Complete the sentence:* The tone of a selection reveals the author's _____ toward his or her subject.

3. An ironic comment is one that means the _____ of what is said. For example, if everything goes wrong after a person gets up in the morning (there is no hot water for the shower, milk for the cereal is sour, a pool of oil is under the car, and so on) a person might ironically make which of the following statements? *(Circle one letter.)*
   a. "What a lousy start to the day."
   b. "What a great day this is going to be."
   c. "Good grief. What did I do to deserve this?"

B. Not so many years ago, major-league baseball was "for whites only." It took the courage of two unusual men, Jackie Robinson and Branch Rickey, to break baseball's color line. This selection on how they helped change history is a chance to apply your understanding of purpose and tone to a full-length selection.

Following the reading are questions on purpose and tone. To help you continue to strengthen your work on the skills taught in previous chapters, there are also questions on

- vocabulary in context
- central point and main ideas
- supporting details
- transitions

- patterns of organization
- summarizing and outlining
- fact and opinion
- inferences.

Words to Watch

Following are some words in the reading that do not have strong context support. Each word is followed by the number of the paragraph in which it appears and its meaning there.

rampant (6): widespread
staunch (7): strong
raucous (14): harsh-sounding
cantankerous (21): ill-tempered
tumultuous (31): noisy
adulation (31): great admiration

HE WAS FIRST

John Kellmayer

1   Today few people under 50 can remember what it was like *not* to see blacks in professional baseball.

2   But until April 15, 1947, when Jackie Robinson played his first game with the Brooklyn Dodgers, the world of major-league baseball was a whites-only world.

3   The transition was not an easy one. It took place largely because Branch Rickey, owner of the Dodgers, held on to a dream of integrating baseball and because Jackie Robinson had the character, talent, and support to carry him through an ugly obstacle course of racism.

4   Even before he arrived in professional baseball, Robinson had to combat discrimination. Robinson entered the army with a national college reputation as an outstanding athlete. Still, he was denied permission to play on the football and baseball teams at Fort Riley, Kansas, where he was stationed. He had been allowed to practice with the football team, but when the first game against an opposing team came up, Robinson was sent home on a pass. His exclusion from the baseball team there was more direct. A member of that team recalls what happened: "One day we were out at

the field practicing when a Negro lieutenant came out for the team. An officer told him, 'You have to play with the colored team.' That was a joke. There was no colored team." Robinson walked silently off the field.

Eventually, Robinson was granted an honorable discharge, and soon after he 5 signed a contract to play baseball in the Negro American League.

At this time Branch Rickey was waiting for his opportunity to sign a black 6 ballplayer and to integrate major-league baseball. He understood not only that the black ballplayer could be good box office but that bigotry had to be fought. While involved with his college baseball team, he was deeply moved by a nasty scene in which his star catcher, an outstanding young black man, was prohibited from registering at a hotel with the rest of the team. Rickey then became determined to do something about the rampant° racism in baseball.

By 1944, the social climate had become more accepting of integration, in large 7 part because of the contribution of black soldiers in World War II. Also, when the commissioner of baseball, a staunch° opponent of integration, died in 1944, he was replaced by a man named Happy Chandler. Chandler was on record as supporting integration of the game—"If a black man can make it at Okinawa and go to Guadalcanal, he can make it in baseball."

Rickey knew the time had come. He began searching for the special black 8 ballplayer with the mix of talent and character necessary to withstand the struggles to follow. When he learned about a star player in the Negro American League named Jackie Robinson, he arranged to meet with him.

At their meeting, Rickey said, "Jack, I've been looking for a great colored 9 ballplayer, but I need more than a great player. I need a man who will accept insults, take abuse, in a word, carry the flag for his race. I want a man who has the courage not to fight, not to fight back. If a guy slides into you at second base and calls you a black son of a bitch, I wouldn't blame you if you came up swinging. You'd be right. You'd be justified. But you'd set the cause back twenty years. I want a man with courage enough not to fight back. Can you do that?"

Robinson thought for a few minutes before answering, "If you want to take this 10 gamble, I promise you there'll be no incidents." The promise was not easily made. Robinson had encountered plenty of racism in his life, and he was accustomed to fighting for black rights. He was known by his teammates in the Negro American League to have a fast temper. Consequently, keeping his promise to Rickey was going to require great personal will.

After signing with the Dodgers in October, 1945, Robinson did not have to wait 11 long to put his patience to the test. Even before he began to play with the Dodger organization, he and his wife, Rachel, encountered the humiliation of Southern racism.

It began when the Robinsons flew from Los Angeles to spring training in Florida, 12 two weeks after they got married. On a stop in New Orleans, they were paged and asked to get off the plane. They later learned that, in the South, whites who wanted seats on a flight took preference over blacks already seated. Their places had been given to a white couple. They had to wait a day to get another flight and then were told to get off for yet another white couple at a stop in Pensacola, Florida. The Robinsons then had to take a segregated bus the rest of the way to Jacksonville, where Branch Rickey had a car waiting for them. Of that trip, Rachel Robinson later said, "It sharpened for us the drama of what we were about to go into. We got a lot tougher thereafter."

Soon after, during an exhibition game in Florida, Jackie suffered another   13
humiliation, the first of many more to come on the diamond. During the first inning of
that game, a police officer came onto the field and told Jackie, "No niggers don't play
with no white boys. Get off the field right now, or you're going to jail." Jackie had no
choice but to walk quietly off the field. Not one of his teammates spoke up for him
then.

Robinson's assignment to the Dodger minor-league team in Montreal was   14
evidence of Rickey's careful planning for the breaking of the color barrier, as there was
little racism in the Canadian city. That fact became important in supporting the spirits
of Jackie and Rachel against the horrible outpouring of hate that greeted him at each
stop on the road. Baseball historian Robert Smith wrote that when Robinson first
appeared in Syracuse, "the fans reacted in a manner so raucous°, obscene, and
disgusting that it might have shamed a conclave of the Ku Klux Klan." It was during
that game that a Syracuse player threw a black cat at Jackie and yelled, "Hey, Jackie,
there's your cousin." In Baltimore, the players shouted racist insults, threw balls at his
head, and tried to spike him. In addition, as would be the case at many stops through
the years, Jackie wasn't allowed to stay at the same hotel as the rest of the team.

Robinson's manager at Montreal was Clay Hopper, a Mississippi native   15
adamantly opposed at first to the presence of a "nigger" on his ballclub. When Hopper
first saw Robinson, he commented, "Well, when Mr. Rickey picked one, he sure picked
a black one." Later, Rickey once stood near Hopper during a game when Robinson
made a superb dive to make an out, and Rickey commented that Robinson seemed
"superhuman." Hopper's reply was, "Do you really think a nigger's a human being?"

No civil rights legislation could have turned Clay Hopper around the way Jackie   16
Robinson did. By the end of a season in which Robinson led his team to the minor
league World Series, Hopper told Robinson, "You're a great ballplayer and a fine
gentleman. It's been wonderful having you on the team." Hopper would later remark to
Rickey, "You don't have to worry none about that boy. He's the greatest competitor I
ever saw, and what's more, he's a gentleman."

It was clear that Jackie Robinson's next stop was the big league, the Brooklyn   17
Dodgers. Not surprisingly, though, the prospect of a black major-league player was not
met by all with open arms. Just how much resistance there was, however, could be seen
in the meeting of the baseball club owners in January of 1947 in which every owner but
Rickey voted against allowing Jackie to play.

Fortunately, commissioner Happy Chandler had another point of view. He later   18
told Rickey, "Mr. Rickey, I'm going to have to meet my maker some day. If He asked
me why I didn't let this man play, and I answered, 'Because he's a Negro,' that might
not be a sufficient answer. I will approve of the transfer of Robinson's contract from
Montreal to Brooklyn." So the color barrier was broken, and Robinson became a
member of the Brooklyn Dodgers.

Robinson's talent meant less to some of the Brooklyn players than race. The   19
prospect of a black teammate prompted a Dodger outfielder, a Southerner by the name
of Dixie Walker, to pass among the other Southern players a petition urging Rickey to
ban Robinson from their team. Walker gathered signatures and momentum until he
approached shortstop Pee Wee Reese, a Kentucky native. Robinson had originally been
signed on as a shortstop and could have posed a real threat to Reese's job. Nonetheless,
Reese refused to sign the petition. As one of the leaders of the Brooklyn "Bums,"

Reese's acceptance of Robinson was of great importance in determining how the rest of the Dodgers would react to him.

As expected, his presence triggered an ugly racial response. It began with hate 20 mail and death threats against him and his wife and baby boy. In addition, some of his teammates continued to oppose him. Some even refused to sit near him.

The opposing teams, however, were much worse, and the hatred was so intense 21 that some of the Dodger players began to stand up for Jackie. In Philadelphia, players cried out such insults as, "They're waiting for you in the jungles, black boy," and "Hey, snowflake, which one of you white boys' wives are you dating tonight?" The first Dodger to stand up for Robinson on the field was a Southerner, the cantankerous° Eddie "The Brat" Stankey. When the Phillies pointed their bats at Robinson and made machine-gun-like noises in a cruel reference to the threats on his and his family's lives, Stankey shouted, "Why don't you yell at someone who can answer back?" The Phils' response was a chorus of "nigger lover."

Other opposing teams were no better. In an early-season game in Cincinnati, for 22 example, players yelled such indignities as, "You nigger sonofabitch, you shoeshine boy," to Jackie, and, "How can you play with this nigger bastard?" to Pee Wee Reese. Rex Barney, who was a Dodger pitcher then, described Reese's response: "While Jackie was standing by first base, Pee Wee went over to him and put his arm around him, as if to say, 'This is my man. This is the guy. We're gonna win with him.' Well, it drove the Cincinnati players right through the ceiling, and you could have heard the gasp from the crowd as he did it."

In the face of continuing harassment, Jackie Robinson, a hot-tempered young 23 man who had struggled against racism all his life, chose to fight his toughest battle, not with his fists or foul language, but with the courage to not fight back. Instead, he answered his attackers with superior play and electrifying speed.

Within the first month of the '47 season, it became apparent that Robinson could 24 be the deciding factor in the pennant race. His speed on the basepaths brought an entirely new dimension to baseball. Robinson used bunts and fake bunts and steals and fake steals to distract opposing pitchers and force basic changes in strategy in the game.

Undoubtedly, one reason many Dodger players rallied around Robinson was that 25 they saw him as a critical, perhaps *the* critical factor in their pursuit of the pennant. Like Rickey, their motives reflected a mixture of personal ambition and a genuine concern for doing what was right.

And many did do what was right, even off the field. For example, Robinson at 26 first waited until all his teammates had finished their showers before he would take his. One day, outfielder Al Gionfriddo patted Robinson on the butt and told him to get into the showers with everybody else, that he was as much a part of the team as anyone. Robinson smiled and went to the showers with Gionfriddo.

The ballplayers' wives also extended the hand of friendship to Robinson and his 27 wife. Pitcher Clyde King related an incident that was typical of the efforts put forth to make the Robinsons feel part of the Dodger family. At Ebbets Field, an iron fence ran from the dugout to the clubhouse, keeping the fans from the players. After the games, the Dodger wives would be allowed inside the fence to wait for their husbands. Rachel Robinson, reluctant to join the other wives, would wait for Jackie outside the fence among the fans. King remembers that his own wife, Norma, a North Carolina girl, insisted that Rachel join her and the other Dodger wives inside.

For Jackie, a series of such small but significant events may have meant the 28
difference between making it and exploding under the enormous pressure that followed
him throughout that first baseball season.

As the season passed, he not only gained the support of many of his teammates 29
but of much of the baseball world in general. On September 12, *Sporting News*, the
bible of baseball, selected Robinson as its Rookie of the Year—the first of many
prestigious awards he would receive during his term with the Dodgers.

In the article announcing the award, there was a quote from none other than Dixie 30
Walker, the same Dodger who had started the petition in the spring to ban Robinson
from playing for Brooklyn. Walker praised Robinson for his contributions to the club's
success, stating that Robinson was all that Branch Rickey had said and more.

On September 22, the Dodgers defeated the St. Louis Cardinals to clinch the 31
National League pennant—against a team in whose town Jackie had to stay in a
"colored" hotel. Fittingly enough, the following day was proclaimed Jackie Robinson
Day at the Dodger ballpark. Robinson was honored with a tumultuous° outpouring of
affection from the Brooklyn fans, an unbroken peal of adulation° that shook the very
foundations of Ebbets Field.

Americans learned something that year about competition and excellence, about 32
character and race. The fire that Jackie Robinson fanned swept across the years to
follow, resulting in a permanent change in the makeup of the game. He had
demonstrated that blacks could not only play on the same field with white players; they
could excel. People brought their families hundreds of miles to see him play. The
floodgates opened for the signing of the black ballplayer. The same major-league team
owners who voted against hiring blacks soon followed Rickey's lead. In the next few
years came Willie Mays, Ernie Banks, Henry Aaron, and more—an endless list of
black stars.

For some, Jackie Robinson is simply one of the greatest second basemen of all 33
time. For others, he is much more. He is an individual who stood up and opposed the
ugliness of racism with a relentless intensity. He was the first to brave the insults and
the ignorance, the first to show that major league baseball could be raised from the
depths of segregation. His victory is a model of what one determined person can
accomplish.

Basic Skill Questions

Vocabulary in Context

1. The word *adamantly* in "Robinson's manager at Montreal was Clay Hopper,
   a Mississippi native adamantly opposed at first to the presence of a 'nigger'
   on his ball club" (paragraph 15) means
   a. weakly.
   b. stubbornly.
   c. secretly.
   d. pleasantly.

2. The word *momentum* in "Walker gathered signatures and momentum until he approached shortstop Pee Wee Reese" (paragraph 19) means
   a. money.
   b. opposition.
   c. force.
   d. defeat.

Central Point and Main Ideas

3. Which sentence best expresses the central point of this selection?
   a. Until 1947, there were no blacks in professional baseball.
   b. Jackie Robinson, a man of principle and courage, became the best second baseman in baseball.
   c. Baseball became integrated because of the courage of Branch Rickey and Jackie Robinson, who proved blacks could excel in major-league baseball.
   d. The integration of American society was not easily accomplished.

4. Which sentence best expresses the main idea of paragraph 7?
   a. Happy Chandler became baseball commissioner in 1944.
   b. Black soldiers fought for the United States during World War II.
   c. A commissioner of baseball who was opposed to integration died in 1944.
   d. By 1944, society had become more open to integrating baseball.

Supporting Details

5. Robinson encountered racism
   a. on and off the field in both the North and the South.
   b. only during baseball games.
   c. mainly in Canada.
   d. until he joined the major leagues.

6. _____ TRUE OR FALSE? During Robinson's first year with the Dodgers, none of his teammates accepted him.

Transitions

7. The sentence below expresses a relationship of
   a. addition.
   b. comparison.
   c. cause and effect.
   d. illustration.

   By 1944, the social climate had become more accepting of integration, in large part because of the contribution of black soldiers in World War II. (Paragraph 7)

8. The relationship of the second sentence below to the first is one of
   a. contrast.
   b. illustration.
   c. cause and effect.
   d. time order.

> Other opposing teams were no better. In an early-season game in Cincinnati, for example, players yelled such indignities as, "You nigger sonofabitch, you shoeshine boy," to Jackie and, "How can you play with this nigger bastard?" to Pee Wee Reese. (Paragraph 22).

Patterns of Organization

9. The pattern of organization of paragraph 3 is
   a. time order.
   b. definition and example.
   c. cause and effect.
   d. comparison and/or contrast.

10. The pattern of organization of paragraph 12 is
    a. time order.
    b. list of items.
    c. definition and example.
    d. comparison and/or contrast.

Advanced Skill Questions

Summarizing and Outlining

11. Complete the following outline of paragraph 7 by filling in the blank.

    By 1944, integration was more socially acceptable.
    1. Black soldiers had made a significant contribution during World War II.

    2. _____

    _____

12. Which statement best completes the following summary of paragraphs 19–22?

    Upon joining the Brooklyn Dodgers, Robinson faced extreme racism from many of his teammates and opponents.

    a. Dixie Walker, for instance, passed a petition among the Dodgers to ban Robinson from the team.
    b. Robinson received hate mail and death threats against himself and his family.
    c. Some of Robinson's teammates even refused to sit next to him.
    d. Some of Robinson's teammates, however, stood up for him.

Fact and Opinion

13. Which of the following is a statement of opinion?
    a. "The transition was not an easy one."
    b. "Robinson walked silently off the field."
    c. "In addition, as would be the case at many stops through the years, Jackie wasn't allowed to stay at the same hotel as the rest of the team."
    d. "On September 12, *Sporting News*, the bible of baseball, selected Robinson as its Rookie of the Year."

14. Which of the following is a statement of fact?
    a. "No civil rights legislation could have turned Clay Hopper around the way Jackie Robinson did."
    b. "Other opposing teams were no better."
    c. "For Jackie, a series of such small but significant events may have made the difference between making it and exploding under the enormous pressure. . . ."
    d. "King remembers that his own wife, Norma, a North Carolina girl, insisted that Rachel join her and the other Dodger wives inside."

Inferences

15. The author implies that some of Robinson's Dodger teammates
    a. resented the intense racism of the opposing teams and fans.
    b. taught him a lot about baseball strategy.
    c. opposed him more as they won more games.
    d. had little influence on how he stood the pressure of his first major-league season.

16. _____ TRUE OR FALSE? The author implies that the Dodgers won the 1947 National League pennant largely because of Jackie Robinson.

17. Which of the following inferences is best supported by paragraph 19?
    a. All Southern players were racist.
    b. Pee Wee Reese felt no threat from Jackie Robinson.
    c. Reese put principle ahead of personal concern.
    d. Without Pee Wee Reese, baseball would never have become integrated.

Purpose and Tone

18. The main purpose of this selection is
    a. to inform readers about how major-league baseball became integrated.
    b. to persuade readers that Jackie Robinson was the greatest second baseman of all time.
    c. to simply entertain readers with an account of Jackie Robinson's first major-league season.

19. The author's tone when discussing Robinson is
    a. totally objective.
    b. admiring.
    c. lighthearted.
    d. sentimental.

20. In which paragraph of the reading did the author first show, through his choice of words, his attitude toward Jackie Robinson?

    Paragraph _____

10

Argument

An argument is often thought of as an emotional experience where people's feelings get out of control, leaving them ready to start throwing things. However, the term *argument* also has a more formal meaning. It refers to a method of reasoning—*using reasons to support or to come to a conclusion.* For instance, several reasons may lead you to conclude that certain performers or sports stars don't deserve to get paid as much as they do. You might also use reasons to convince your brother to eat a healthier diet, to decide whether to buy a new or a used car, or to determine that you should quit your old job and take on a new one.

Argumentation, then, is a part of our everyday thinking. It is the reasoning process by which we make decisions, judgments, and predictions. It is thus central to many of the papers that we write, and it is a basic structure in much of the material that we read. Very often the two most important things we must do as *writers* are to:

1 Make a point.
2 Support the point.

Very often the two most important things we must do as *readers* are to:

1 Recognize the point.
2 Recognize and evaluate the support for the point.

The concern of this chapter is to help you apply the skills of good argument in what you read. The skilled and critical reader is one who is able to identify the point of an argument, the support for the argument, and the validity of that support.

This chapter will help you learn to analyze and evaluate arguments. First you will learn to distinguish between the point of an argument and the reasons that support it. In the rest of the chapter you will learn to recognize common errors in reasoning that make for poorly supported arguments.

THE BASICS OF ARGUMENT: POINT AND SUPPORT

A good argument is one in which a point is stated and then persuasively and logically supported. Here is a point:

Point: The Beef and Burger Shop is a poor fast-food restaurant.

This statement hardly discourages us from visiting the Beef and Burger Shop. "Why do you say that?" we might legitimately ask. "Give your reasons." Support is needed so we can decide for ourselves whether a valid point has been made. Suppose the point is followed by these three reasons:

1. The burgers are full of gristle.
2. The roast beef sandwiches have a chemical taste.
3. The fries are lukewarm and soggy.

Clearly, the details provide solid support for the point. They give us a basis for understanding and agreeing with the point. In light of these details, our mouths are not watering for lunch at the Beef and Burger Shop.

We see here, then, a small example of what clear thinking in an argument is about: making a point and providing support that truly backs up that point. (Another way to describe a valid argument is: a conclusion supported by logical reasons.)

Let's look at another example:

Point: My neighbors are inconsiderate.

We don't really yet know if the neighbors are inconsiderate. We might trust the opinion of the person who made the statement, but we don't know for sure until supporting details enable us to judge for ourselves. Here are details:

1. They play their stereo very loud late at night.
2. They let their children play on my front lawn.
3. They don't stop their dog from running into my back yard.

Again, the solid support convinces us that a logical point has been made.

In everyday life, of course, people don't simply say, "Here is my point" and "Here is my support." Nor do writers state their basic ideas so directly. Even so, the basic structure of point and support is still at work beneath the surface, and you will benefit enormously from developing the ability to discover and evaluate it.

To help you distinguish, first of all, between point and support for that point—or a conclusion and reasons for that conclusion—do the following activity.

➤ *Practice*

In each group of statements, one statement is the point, and the other statement or statements are support for the point. Identify each point with a **P**, and identify each statement of support with an **S**.

Hint: If you can insert the word *because* in front of a sentence, you probably have a statement of support. For example, we could say, "*Because* the burgers are full of gristle, *because* the roast beef sandwiches have a chemical taste, and *because* the fries are lukewarm and soggy, I've come to this conclusion: the Beef and Burger Shop is a poor fast-food restaurant."

1. _____ Jackie plays fairly, practices hard, and is full of team spirit.
   _____ Jackie will be a good captain for her basketball team.
   _____ Team members like and respect Jackie.

2. _____ Our town ought to require all residents to recycle bottles and cans.
   _____ If we collect glass and cans, the town can earn money by selling them to recyclers.
   _____ The more the town recycles, the less money it must pay for garbage removal.

3. _____ Mass transportation helps people who can't afford a car.
   _____ Increased use of mass transportation would reduce air pollution from cars.
   _____ The government should fund more mass transportation.
   _____ Mass transportation is more energy-efficient than automobile use.

4. _____ I had better buy two new suits and ties.
   _____ My wardrobe is made up of the jeans and sweaters I needed for my old job.
   _____ My new job requires a more formal look.

5. _____ A large new park will benefit our community.
   _____ Joggers who risk accidents by running along the roadside will be able to jog in the park.
   _____ Kids who play ball in the streets can play in a safer place.
   _____ A park provides wholesome opportunities for people to meet their neighbors.

USING POINT-SUPPORT TO EVALUATE RELEVANCE

Once you identify the point and reasons of an argument, you need to decide if each reason given is logical support for the point. The first question you might ask about a reason is if it is even relevant. In their enthusiasm for an argument, people often bring up irrelevant support. For example, in trying to convince you to lend him some money this week, a friend might say, "You didn't lend me money last week when I needed it." But that is really beside the point; the question is whether or not you should lend him money this week, or perhaps at all.

An excellent way to develop your skill at recognizing relevant support is to work on simple point-support outlines of arguments. By isolating the reasons of an argument, such outlines help you think about whether each reason is truly relevant. (They also demonstrate how outlining or summarizing a reading can help you evaluate it better.)

Consider the following outline. The point of the argument is followed by six "reasons," only three of which are relevant support for the point. See if you can circle the numbers of the three relevant statements of support.

Point: Pigs make good pets.

1. When a pig weighs over 180 pounds, it is called a hog.
2. Pigs are friendly and intelligent.
3. In 1965, a pig named "Old Faithful" gave birth to thirty-six piglets in one litter.
4. Pigs are easily housebroken.
5. Pigs, like people, can get sunburn.
6. Pigs can be taught to walk on a leash.

Now read the following comments on the six items to see which ones you should have circled and why.

1. This statement provides a good reason why hogs are *not* good pets, but it says nothing to support the idea that pigs make good pets.

2. People tend to like pets who like them back and with whom they can interact. You should have circled the number to this item.

3. Admittedly, Old Faithful's accomplishment is nothing to oink at, but how many pet owners want thirty-six more pets than they started out with?

4. Given modern standards of cleanliness, being easily housebroken is even more attractive to many pet owners than friendliness or a genius IQ. You should also have circled the number to this item.

5. Most people would prefer a pet for whom they wouldn't have to buy a lifetime supply of sunscreen.

6. Since a common activity for humans and pets is taking a walk outdoors, the ability to keep the animal under control outdoors is often important. *Six* is thus the third number you should have circled.

➤ *Practice*

Each point below is followed by six items, three of which logically support the point, and three of which do not. In the spaces provided, write the letters of the three items that logically support each point.

1. **Point:** High-heeled shoes are a health risk.
    a. Women do not wear high-heeled shoes when participating in sports events.
    b. Although males have worn high-heeled shoes in some cultures and historical periods, they do not wear high-heeled shoes in our society.
    c. Long-term wearing of high-heeled shoes increases the likelihood of developing back and foot disorders.
    d. Many women wear high-heeled shoes to work.
    e. High-heeled shoes increase the risk of falling on a slippery surface.
    f. High, pointed heels easily catch in sidewalk cracks and gratings, resulting in falls.

    Items that logically support the point: _____   _____   _____

2. **Point:** People of all ages can benefit from a hobby.
    a. Some people become so obsessed with crossword puzzles that they spend all their waking hours doing them.
    b. Stressed-out adults can find healthful relaxation in a hobby they enjoy.
    c. A hobby can help a retired person adjust to and enjoy a more leisurely schedule.
    d. Gardening may be the most popular hobby in the country.
    e. Hobbies help people develop talents and skills that may otherwise be ignored.
    f. It can be difficult for commuters to find time in their busy lifestyle for a hobby.

    Items that logically support the point: _____   _____   _____

3. **Point:** Compact discs are a great improvement over records.
    a. Lightweight and small, compact discs are much easier than records to transport and store.
    b. Compact disks aren't marred by scratches, pops, and clicks, as records often are.
    c. Before compact discs came on the scene, eight-track tapes were quite popular.
    d. A compact disc player uses a laser beam to "read" the digital programming on the disc.
    e. Compact discs reproduce sound more purely than records do.
    f. A record cannot substitute for a live performance.

    Items that logically support the point: _____   _____   _____

4.   **Point:** Cities should build more bicycle lanes.
   a. Some roads are too narrow to make room for bicycle lanes.
   b. Cycling is an event in the summer Olympics.
   c. More bicycle lanes would reduce pollution by encouraging people to bike more and drive less.
   d. Cyclists would be safer if they could ride in lanes separate from automobile traffic.
   e. Bicycles can have different gears.
   f. With cycling lanes, more people would be encouraged to get beneficial exercise from cycling.

   Items that logically support the point: _____   _____   _____

MORE ABOUT ARGUMENTS: ERRORS IN REASONING

Learning about some common errors in reasoning will help you to spot weak points in arguments. The rest of this chapter will familiarize you with some of those errors, also known as *fallacies*. Specifically, you'll look at these unsound reasoning patterns:

Four Fallacies That Ignore the Issue:

   • Changing the Subject
   • Circular Reasoning
   • Personal Attack
   • Straw Man

Four Fallacies That Overgeneralize or Oversimplify Issues:

   • Hasty Conclusion
   • False Cause
   • False Comparison
   • Either-Or Fallacy

Following are explanations of these eight common types of fallacies. Exercises throughout give you practice in spotting them.

Fallacies That Ignore the Issue

Fallacy 1. Changing the Subject

This method of arguing tries to divert the audience's attention from the true issue by presenting evidence that actually has nothing to do with the argument. You have already had experience with this method in the activity on pages 215–216, where you had to separate relevant support from support that was beside the point. Here are two more examples:

I think you should buy a bird, not a dog. Many dogs shed all over the house.
(Saying that many dogs shed is beside the point; it is possible to buy a dog that does not shed.)

The congressman is clearly an able leader. He has a warm family life and attends church every Sunday.
(Mention of the congressman's family and church life sidesteps the issue of just how able a leader he is.)

This fallacy is also called a *red herring*. In a fox hunt, drawing a red herring across the dogs' path causes them to lose the scent, allowing the fox to escape. Someone who changes the subject when arguing may hope the audience will lose track of the real point of the argument.

Now read the following paragraph and try to find the sentence that does *not* support the point, which is in the first sentence.

> [1]When you go to college, you should live off campus. [2]In a rented apartment you can enjoy the privacy and convenience of your own kitchen and bathroom. [3]College meal plans are available if you'd rather not do your own cooking. [4]Even though they give you more living space than a dormitory room, off-campus apartments can be found for the same price or less. [5]An off-campus apartment is usually quieter than a dorm. [6]It also gives you a better chance to develop a sense of the larger community the town or city in which your college is located.

Sentences that support the point of this argument must help prove that you should live off campus when you go to college. Whether or not to sign up for a college meal plan has nothing to do with the issue of living off campus. Therefore, sentence 3 is irrelevant to the argument in this paragraph.

➤ *Practice 1*

One sentence in each paragraph below does *not* support the point of the argument. Read the paragraph, and then decide which sentence is not relevant to the argument. To help you decide if a sentence is irrelevant or not, ask yourself, "Does this have anything to do with the point that is being proved?"

1. [1]The level of airline safety has dropped sharply since deregulation. [2]Airline fleets are old and wearing out, and the companies skimp on maintenance. [3]Passengers are herded like cattle and made to sit through what seem like endless delays. [4]The air-traffic control system is short on skilled controllers and depends on out-of-date equipment. [5]Thus near-misses in midair have doubled.

    Which of the following statements does *not* contribute to the author's conclusion that airline safety has dropped sharply since deregulation?

    a. Sentence 2   c. Sentence 4

    b. Sentence 3   d. Sentence 5

2.   [1]*Night Vision* is a superbly written mystery-thriller. [2]The movie's plot is completely believable yet complex enough to keep audiences guessing. [3]Because they have such fully developed personalities, the characters offer fascinating glimpses into human psychology. [4]The heroine is played by the brilliant French film star Madeline Bertot. [5]Fast-paced and witty, the dialogue contains many insightful comments on modern life. [6]The script definitely deserves an Oscar nomination for best screenplay.

Which of the following does *not* support the author's conclusion that *Night Vision* is a superbly written mystery-thriller?

    a. Sentence 2   c. Sentence 4

    b. Sentence 3   d. Sentence 6

Fallacy 2. Circular Reasoning

Part of a point cannot reasonably be used as evidence to support it. That type of argument is called *circular reasoning*, also known as *begging the question*. A simple and obvious example of such reasoning is: "Mr. Green is a great teacher because he is so wonderful at teaching." The supporting reason given in this point itself ("he is so wonderful at teaching") is really the same as the conclusion ("Mr. Green is a great teacher"). We still do not know why he is a great teacher. No real reasons have been given—the statement merely has repeated itself.

Can you spot the circular reasoning in the following arguments?

1. Vitamins are healthy, for they improve your well-being.
2. Since people under 21 are too young to vote, the voting age shouldn't be lowered below age 21.
3. Abortion is an evil practice because it is so wrong.

Let's look more closely now at these arguments:

1.   The word *healthy*, which is used in the conclusion, conveys the same idea as *well-being*.

2.   The author uses the idea that people under 21 are too young to vote as both the conclusion *and* the reason of the argument. No real reason is given for *why* people under 21 are too young to vote.

3.   The claim that abortion is wrong is simply a restatement of the idea that it is an evil practice.

In all these cases, the reasons merely repeat an important part of the conclusion. The careful reader wants to say, "Tell me something new. You are reasoning in circles. Give me supporting evidence, not a repetition."

➤ *Practice 2*

Circle the number of the one item that contains an example of circular reasoning.

1. My wife wants to participate in the local amateur theater group, but I don't want all those actors flirting with her.
2. Sports cars continue to be popular because so many people like them.
3. Phil would make a good salesman. He was an excellent halfback in college and has extensive factory experience.
4. Fran thinks I should break up with Randy because he gambles and drinks. But what does she know? She hasn't been able to find a boyfriend herself in three years.

Fallacy 3. Personal Attack

This fallacy often occurs in political debate. Here's an example:

> Senator Snerd's opinions on public housing are worthless. He can't even manage to hold his own household together, having been married and divorced three times already.

Senator Snerd's family life may or may not reflect a weakness in his character, but it has nothing to do with the value of his opinions on public housing. This kind of fallacy ignores the issue under discussion and concentrates instead on the character of the opponent.

Sometimes personal attacks take the form of accusing people of taking a stand only because it will benefit them personally. For instance, here's a personal attack on a congressman who supports the Equal Rights Amendment (ERA): "He doesn't care about the ERA. He only supports it in order to get more women to vote for him." This argument ignores the congressman's detailed defense of the ERA as a way to ensure equal rights for both men and women. The key to recognizing personal attack is that it always involves an opponent's personal life or character, rather than simply his or her public ideas.

➤ *Practice 3*

Circle the number of the one item that contains an example of personal attack.

1. My wife wants to participate in the local amateur theater group, but I don't want all those actors flirting with her.
2. Sports cars continue to be popular because so many people like them.
3. Phil would make a good salesman. He was an excellent halfback in college and has extensive factory experience.
4. Fran thinks I should break up with Randy because he gambles and drinks. But what does she know? She hasn't been able to find a boyfriend herself in three years.

Fallacy 4. Straw Man

An opponent made of straw can be defeated very easily. Sometimes, if one's real opponent is putting up too good a fight, it can be tempting to build a scarecrow and battle it instead. For example, take the following passage from a debate on the death penalty.

> Ms. Collins opposes capital punishment. But letting murderers out on the street to kill again is a crazy idea. If we did that, no one would be safe.

Ms. Collins, however, never advocated "letting murderers out on the street to kill again." In fact, she wants to keep them in jail for life rather than execute them. This fallacy suggests that the opponent favors an obviously unpopular cause— when the opponent really doesn't support anything of the kind.

➤ Practice 4

Circle the number of the one item that contains an example of straw man.

1. My wife wants to participate in the local amateur theater group, but I don't want all those actors flirting with her.
2. Sports cars continue to be popular because so many people like them.
3. Phil would make a good salesman. He was an excellent halfback in college and has extensive factory experience.
4. Fran thinks I should break up with Randy because he gambles and drinks. But what does she know? She hasn't been able to find a boyfriend herself in three years.

Fallacies That Overgeneralize or Oversimplify

Fallacy 5. Hasty Conclusion

To be valid, a point must be based on an adequate amount of evidence. Someone who makes an inference on the basis of insufficient evidence is coming to a *hasty conclusion*. For instance, the fact that you didn't receive a gift from your mother on your birthday this year can mean several things—she forgot, she is angry, she is broke, the mail is late, and so on. In such a case, one must have more information before reaching a specific conclusion. If, having no more information, you nevertheless conclude that your mother is angry at you, you are jumping to a hasty conclusion—a conclusion based on too little evidence.

Here is another example of a hasty conclusion:

> Two Chinese girls took an art course with me last semester, and they were the best students in the class. Obviously, the Chinese people have a natural talent for art.

Forming a generalization about the quarter of a billion Chinese people in the world based on two examples is an illogical and hasty conclusion.

In the argument below, three supporting reasons are given, followed by four possible conclusions. Three of the conclusions cannot logically be drawn from the small amount of evidence given. Choose the one conclusion that you think is valid and put a check mark beside it. Then read the explanation that follows.

1. Lately Valerie has looked thinner and paler than usual.
2. She used to go to all the parties, but now she stays home in the evenings.
3. At work, she has been seen crying in the ladies' room.

Which of the following is a valid conclusion that can be drawn from the evidence above?

____ a. Valerie is seriously ill.

____ b. Something is troubling Valerie.

____ c. Valerie has broken up with her boyfriend.

____ d. Valerie owes a great deal of money.

The correct answer is *b*. From her behavior, we can safely conclude that something is troubling Valerie, but we have very little evidence about what is troubling her. The fact that she hasn't been going to parties makes us wonder whether or not she's broken up with her boyfriend, but we have absolutely no other evidence to support that conclusion. Thus answer *c* is is a hasty conclusion. The fact that Valerie hasn't been looking well makes us wonder if she's seriously ill. But we have no other evidence for that conclusion either, so answer *a* is also a hasty conclusion. Finally, except for the evidence showing Valerie is troubled in some way, answer *d* has no evidence at all to support it, so it too is a hasty conclusion.

➤ *Practice 5*

Check the sentence that states a valid conclusion based on the supporting evidence in each group below. Remember that the point, or conclusion, should follow logically from the evidence. Do not jump to a conclusion that is not well supported.

Group 1

- Our neighbors have been bringing lots of cartons into their house recently.
- There's a "For Sale" sign in our neighbors' front yard.
- This Saturday, our neighbors held a big yard sale.

Which of the following conclusions is best supported by the evidence above?

____ a. Our neighbors are moving.

____ b. Our neighbors are in debt and need to raise money.

____ c. Our neighbors need to get out of town in a hurry.

____ d. Our neighbors are retiring.

Group 2

- The first stray cat, Gino, followed Janet home from the mailbox, crying, and Janet couldn't come in the house without him.
- Janet found Marbles huddled on the porch in the snow and brought him in out of the cold.
- One spring, Bella jumped in the basement window, so scared that Janet didn't dare put her back outside again.

Which of the following conclusions is best supported by the evidence above?

___ a. Janet has dozens of pets at home.

___ b. Janet is softhearted.

___ c. People must drop off unwanted cats near Janet's house.

___ d. Janet should be a veterinarian.

Fallacy 6. False Cause

You have probably heard someone say as a joke, "I know it's going to rain today because I just washed the car." The idea that someone can make it rain by washing a car is funny because the two events obviously have nothing to do with each other. However, with more complicated issues, it is easy to make the mistake known as the fallacy of *false cause*. The mistake is to assume that because Event B follows Event A, Event A has *caused* Event B.

Cause-and-effect situations can be difficult to analyze, and people are often tempted to oversimplify them by ignoring other possible causes. To identify an argument using a false cause, look for alternative causes. Consider this argument:

The Macklin Company was more prosperous before Ms. Williams became president. Clearly, she is the cause of the decline.

(*Event A:* Ms. Williams became president.
Event B: The Macklin Company's earnings declined.)

What other possible causes could have been responsible for the decline? Perhaps the policies of the previous president are just now affecting the company. Perhaps the market for the company's product has changed. In any case, it's easy but dangerous to assume that just because A *came before* B, A *caused* B.

➤ *Practice 6*

Circle the number of the one item that contains an example of false cause.

1. In Vermont we leave our doors unlocked all year round, so I don't think it's necessary for you New Yorkers to have three locks on your front doors.
2. The waiter went off duty early, and then the vase was discovered missing, so he must have stolen it.

3. Picasso was clearly the greatest artist of modern times since his paintings are better than anyone else's.
4. Eat your string beans, or you won't grow up strong and healthy.

Fallacy 7. False Comparison

When the poet Robert Burns wrote, "My love is like a red, red rose," he meant that both the woman he loved and a rose are beautiful. In other ways—such as having green leaves and thorns, for example—his love did not resemble a rose at all. Comparisons are often a good way to clarify a point. But because two things are not alike in all respects, comparisons (sometimes called *analogies*) often make poor evidence for arguments. In the error in reasoning known as *false comparison*, the assumption is that two things are more alike than they really are. For example, read the following argument.

It didn't hurt your grandfather in the old country to get to work without a car, and it won't hurt you either.

To judge whether or not this is a false comparison, consider how the two situations are alike and how they differ. They are similar in that both involve a young person's need to get to work. But the situations are different in that the grandfather didn't have to be at work an hour after his last class. In fact, he didn't go to school at all. In addition, his family didn't own a car he could use. The differences in this case are more important than the similarities, making it a false comparison.

➤ Practice 7

Circle the number of the one item that contains an example of false comparison.

1. In Vermont we leave our doors unlocked all year round, so I don't think it's necessary for you New Yorkers to have three locks on your front doors.
2. The waiter went off duty early, and then the vase was discovered missing, so he must have stolen it.
3. Picasso was clearly the greatest artist of modern times since his paintings are better than anyone else's.
4. Eat your string beans, or you won't grow up strong and healthy.

Fallacy 8. Either-Or

It is often wrong to assume that there are only two sides to a question. Offering only two choices when more actually exist is an *either-or fallacy*. For example, the statement "You are either with us or against us" assumes that there is no middle ground. Or consider the following:

People opposed to unrestricted free speech are really in favor of censorship.

This argument ignores the fact that a person could believe in free speech as well as in laws that prohibit slander or that punish someone for yelling "Fire!" in a crowded theater. Some issues have only two sides (Will you pass the course, or won't you?), but most have several.

➤ Practice 8

Circle the number of the item that contains an example of the either-or fallacy.

1. In Vermont we leave our doors unlocked all year round, so I don't think it's necessary for you New Yorkers to have three locks on your front doors.
2. The waiter went off duty early, and then the vase was discovered missing, so he must have stolen it.
3. Picasso was clearly the greatest artist of modern times since his paintings are better than anyone else's.
4. Eat your string beans, or you won't grow up strong and healthy.

➤ Review Test 1

A. In each group of statements, one statement is the point, and the other statement or statements are support for the point. Identify each point with a **P,** and identify each statement of support with an **S.**

   Hint: If you can insert the word *because* in front of a sentence, you probably have a statement of support.

1. _____ The next time my house has a water problem, I'm going to call a plumber.

   _____ When I tried to replace one pipe under the sink, I broke two others.

   _____ The toilet I fixed now makes a clunking noise every time it's flushed.

2. _____ Georgia Blake barely has enough to live on after paying for tuition and books, but she is young and full of energy.

   _____ Since Mrs. Grady's husband died, her house seems too big, the chores too hard, and the evenings too lonely.

   _____ Georgia Blake should live with Mrs. Grady for awhile.

3. _____ I might throw up the hot dogs I ate for lunch.

   _____ For me, riding the fair's Terrible Twister roller coaster is a terrible idea.

   _____ I might fall out or pass out.

   _____ I'm fearful that the cars will derail, sending me to my death in the livestock pens.

4. _____ We rely on the police to keep our neighborhoods and cities safe.

_____ Police officers should be rewarded for putting their lives in danger.

_____ Police salaries must be raised.

_____ Higher salaries would encourage qualified young people to join the police force.

B. Each point below is followed by six items, three of which logically support the point, and three of which do not. In the spaces provided, write the letters of the three items that logically support each point.

5. **Point:** Barbara Freedman is the best candidate for governor.

a. She is a good leader.
b. She's an outstanding athlete.
c. Unlike the other candidates, she has successfully served as the mayor of a large city.
d. She has never run for governor before.
e. Her knowledge of the issues is far more extensive than that of the other candidates.
f. Her mother is a college administrator, and her father is a professor.

Items that logically support the point: _____ _____ _____

6. **Point:** We should use more solar energy.

a. Unlike oil and coal, energy from the sun is unlimited.
b. We're not sure how safe nuclear energy is.
c. Solar energy is non-polluting.
d. Wind and water power have been used for centuries.
e. Solar energy is less effective in gray climates.
f. Solar energy is extremely cost-effective.

Items that logically support the point: _____ _____ _____

➤ *Review Test 2*

A. Circle the letter of the *irrelevant* sentence in each paragraph—the sentence that changes the subject.

1. ¹The death penalty is a vital tool in the fight against crime. ²Knowing that they will die if they are caught, potential killers will think twice about committing murder. ³And when a murderer is caught, the death penalty is the only sure guarantee that these criminals will not escape or be released to repeat their crimes. ⁴Some murderers who have not been executed and instead were released on parole went on to kill other victims. ⁵Finally, let us remember that the victims of murder were shown no mercy and given no second chance.

    Which of the following is *not* relevant to the author's conclusion that the death penalty is a vital tool in the fight against crime?

    a. Sentence 2   c. Sentence 4
    b. Sentence 3   d. Sentence 5

2. ¹The current generation will have a better financial future if workers save for retirement instead of counting on the Social Security program. ²Saving will also provide today's workers with some of the discipline their "I want it all now" generation so sorely needs. ³Social Security benefits already have been reduced to accommodate a shrinking labor pool and a growing number of retirees. ⁴In addition, the government has had to start taxing a percentage of the benefits, lessening them even more. ⁵At this rate, if the program isn't completely bankrupt by the early twenty-first century, monthly Social Security checks will be very small.

    Which of the following is *not* relevant to the author's conclusion that workers must save for retirement instead of counting on Social Security?

    a. Sentence 2   c. Sentence 4
    b. Sentence 3   d. Sentence 5

B. Circle the letter of the fallacy contained in each argument below.

3. Trashy novels are a waste of time to read because there is nothing worthwhile in them.
    a. Circular reasoning *(a statement repeats itself rather than providing a real supporting reason to back up an argument)*
    b. Personal attack *(the argument shifts to irrelevant personal criticism)*
    c. Straw man *(an argument is made by claiming an opponent holds an extreme position and then opposing that extreme position)*

4. All those people who do not support anti-handgun legislation must want to see another one of our presidents get shot.

a. Circular reasoning *(a statement repeats itself rather than providing a real supporting reason to back up an argument)*
b. Personal attack *(the argument shifts to irrelevant personal criticism)*
c. Straw man *(an argument is made by claiming an opponent holds an extreme position and then opposing that extreme position)*

C. Check the sentence that states a valid point based on the supporting evidence in each group below. Remember that the point, or conclusion, should follow logically from the evidence. Do not jump to a conclusion that is not well-supported.

Group 1

- The weatherman said this would be a mild winter, but the temperature has been in the teens for the past three weeks.
- There was no storm warning in the forecast today, but the winds were so severe our fishing boat almost capsized.
- The forecast on the radio said it would be sunny all day, but the ballgame was rained out.

5. Check the conclusion that is most strongly based on the evidence above.

____ a. People's poor treatment of the environment affects the ozone layer and causes changes in the weather.

____ b. Always expect the opposite weather from what the weather reports predict.

____ c. It is impossible to ever correctly predict the weather.

____ d. Weather prediction is not always accurate.

Group 2

- A final review of your notes the night before the exam will help you remember them better.
- If you read the test directions carefully before you begin the exam, you'll be unlikely to waste time doing the wrong thing.
- If you answer the questions you are sure of first, the test won't end before you answer all the questions you know.

6. Check the conclusion that is most strongly based on the evidence above.

____ a. Getting good grades is very easy if you follow a few simple guidelines.

____ b. All good students answer the test questions they are sure of first.

____ c. Certain helpful hints can improve students' examination skills.

____ d. Test directions are often very tricky.

D. Circle the letter of the fallacy contained in each argument below.

7.   Since Senator Nelson was elected, the world has moved steadily toward peace and democracy. What better reason can there be to re-elect him?
   a. False cause *(the argument assumes that the order of events alone shows cause and effect)*
   b. False comparison *(the argument assumes that two things being compared are more alike than they really are)*
   c. Either-or *(the argument assumes that there are only two sides to a question)*

8.   If we do not have universal and total nuclear disarmament now, we face the certainty of a worldwide nuclear disaster.
   a. False cause *(the argument assumes that the order of events alone shows cause and effect)*
   b. False comparison *(the argument assumes that two things being compared are more alike than they really are)*
   c. Either-or *(the argument assumes that there are only two sides to a question)*

➤ Review Test 3

A. To review what you've learned in this chapter, complete each of the following sentences about evaluating arguments.

1.   Often the two most important things we must do when we read are to identify the _____ of a selection and also the _____ that backs it up.

2.   A valuable step in reading, writing, or speaking clearly is to first prepare a(n) _____.

3.   A fallacy is an error in (*reading, reasoning, changing the subject*) _____ that makes an argument illogical.

4.   The fallacies of personal attack and straw man are specific versions of (*circular reasoning, changing the subject, hasty conclusion*) _____ because they present evidence that is beside the point.

5.   Assuming that there are only two sides to a question is called the (*false cause, false comparison, either-or*) _____ fallacy.

B. When does obedience go too far? Here is a chance to apply your understanding of arguments to a textbook selection that addresses that question.

Following the selection from *Psychology* (Harcourt Brace Jovanovich, 1989) are questions on argument. To help you continue to strengthen your work on the skills taught in previous chapters, there are also questions on

- vocabulary in context
- central point and main ideas
- supporting details
- transitions
- patterns of organization

- summarizing and outlining
- fact and opinion
- inferences
- purpose and tone.

Words to Watch

Following are some words in the reading that do not have strong context support. Each word is followed by the number of the paragraph in which it appears and its meaning there.

critical (1): crucial
confederate (3): associate
sadistic (7): cruel

OBEDIENCE: MILGRAM'S CONTROVERSIAL STUDIES

Mary M. Gergen et al.

One of the most direct forms of social influence is the demand for *obedience:* people follow orders because an authority figure tells them to. In most societies, obedience plays a critical° role in social control. We obey parents, teachers, police, and other officials. Since many rules, laws, and commands from authority have a positive value, obedience is a major foundation of social life and behavior. However, obedience can go too far! Soldiers in Nazi Germany obeyed the orders of their superiors and, as a result, millions of people were slaughtered. More recently, 900 men, women, and children died in a mass suicide in Guyana. The leader of the community, James Jones, gave the order for everyone to drink a poisoned juice, and they did.

In these two instances, we seem to be observing extreme cases of blind obedience. Some might say that instances of blind obedience, where the commands of authority contradict moral and human principles, are extremely rare. But are they? Social psychologist Stanley Milgram set out to find out.

In a series of experiments, Milgram solicited subjects drawn from all walks of life through newspaper advertisements. In the ads, subjects were told they would be paid for participating in a psychology study at Yale University. Volunteers were paired and were told that one would be the "teacher" and the other the "learner" in a study to test the effect of shock on learning. The person designated as learner and the person designated as teacher were seemingly determined by a random draw. Then the learner was seated in an adjoining room, and his arms were strapped to his chair. Electrodes were attached to his arms. At this point, the learner (actually a confederate° of Milgram's) mentioned that he had a slight heart condition.

The teacher was then escorted to a separate room and seated in front of an 4 impressive, complicated-looking machine, which the experimenter referred to as a shock generator. The machine had a series of switches with labels from 15 volts ("slight shock") to 450 volts ("danger—severe shock").

The teacher was given a somewhat painful sample shock (45 volts) so he or she 5 could have an idea of what the learner would be experiencing. After the sample shock, the experimenter told the teacher to read over the intercom a list of pairs of words so the learner could memorize them. The experimenter then instructed the teacher to read one word of each pair along with four alternatives. It was now the learner's job to pick out the right response. If the response was correct, the teacher was to proceed to the next word. If the response was incorrect, the teacher's task was to give the learner a shock. The teacher was told to start at 15 volts and to proceed up the scale toward 450 volts.

During the experiment, the learner got some items right and others wrong. However, as the experiment progressed, the learner made errors more and more 6 frequently. Each error increased the amount of shock given. In one condition of this experiment, the learner made no response to the shocks until they reached the 300-volt level; then he yelled and complained about the shock and pounded on the wall, shouting "Let me out of here." The learner did this on several occasions. Finally, he stopped responding to the test. Regardless of what the learner said or did, the experimenter told the teacher to continue to read the words and to test for the right answer; if the learner gave an incorrect answer or no answer, the teacher was instructed to administer the next higher level of shock.

As the learner began to scream with pain, the teachers usually became upset and 7 jittery. Many broke out in nervous laughter. Some threatened to quit the experiment. What would you have done? What do you think the average subject did? Would they go on or would they stop? Milgram was curious about this question and asked a group of psychiatrists to predict what percentage they thought would obey the experimenter's demands. They estimated that only half of 1 percent (that is, 1 person in 200) of the population would be sadistic° enough to obey. But they were clearly wrong.

Readers are usually surprised to learn that 65 percent of the subjects who served 8 as teachers obeyed the experimenter's commands and delivered shocks up to the maximum (450 volts), even though the learner objected, screamed, and begged to be released. Of course, in actuality, the learner was a confederate of Milgram's, never actually received any shocks, and answered the word-pair questions according to a prearranged schedule. However, the confederate was well-trained, and his faked pain and protests were well-staged and seemed quite real to the subject.

The finding that two-thirds of the subjects went along with the experimenter's 9 commands suggests that obedience is not just to be found in Nazi Germany or in Jonestown. Rather, obedience seems to be a common response to the commands of authorities. In fact, after examining hundreds of sessions, Milgram failed to find any background, socioeconomic, or personality factors that predicted who would obey the experimenter's commands and who would not.

The important question, of course, is why did so many people obey? Milgram 10 thought that people obeyed because they perceived the experimenter to be a legitimate authority; he had the right to dictate behaviors and demands because he was in the role of a scientist. Presumably, obedience to legitimate authorities is something we learn early in life and retain throughout adulthood. As long as we recognize the authority as legitimate, we are subject to its influence.

Milgram's research has been strongly criticized for being unethical and misleading. Certain critics have objected to his misuse of people as subjects. They argue that the subjects should not have been led to believe that they may have killed someone. Other critics have suggested that the laboratory experiments were not adequate demonstrations of obedience in real life because the subjects would have felt it was a "science game" and would simply have been playing a cooperative role. However, despite these objections, Milgram's work seems to have had a substantial social impact. It would appear that people rather readily acquiesce to authority figures, whether they are army officers, religious leaders, or scientists. Given the consequences of obedience, Milgram's works stand out as an important contribution to psychology and as a warning for our society. 11

Basic Skill Questions

Vocabulary in Context

1. The word *solicited* in "Milgram solicited subjects . . . through newspaper advertisements" (paragraph 3) means
   a. sought.
   b. forgot.
   c. denied.
   d. imitated.

2. The words *acquiesce to* in "It would appear that people rather readily acquiesce to authority figures, whether they are army officers, religious leaders, or scientists" (paragraph 11) mean
   a. oppose.
   b. obey.
   c. question.
   d. converse with.

Central Point and Main Ideas

3. Which sentence best expresses the central point of the selection?
   a. Psychological experiments can reveal much about human behavior in various situations.
   b. Stanley Milgram has conducted psychological research that has been strongly criticized for being unethical and misleading.
   c. An experiment conducted by Stanley Milgram showed that people will often blindly obey authority.
   d. Electrical shocks should not be administered as part of a psychological experiment.

4. Which sentence best expresses the main idea of paragraph 10?
   a. Scientists are authority figures.
   b. Milgram concluded that people tend to obey anyone they recognize as a legitimate authority.

    c. Milgram wondered why so many people obeyed the experimenter in his experiment.

    d. Milgram was surprised to be considered a legitimate authority figure.

Supporting Details

5. In Milgram's experiment, the "teachers" were
    a. associates of Milgram.
    b. students at Yale.
    c. recipients of shocks.
    d. from all walks of life.

6. _____ TRUE OR FALSE? Psychiatrists were able to accurately predict the results of Milgram's experiment.

7. According to the author, obedience to legitimate authority is probably
    a. always dangerous.
    b. often painful.
    c. learned early in life.
    d. senseless.

Transitions

8. The relationship expressed by the sentence below is one of
    a. time.
    b. addition.
    c. contrast.
    d. cause and effect.

    Soldiers in Nazi Germany obeyed the orders of their superiors and, as a result, millions of people were slaughtered. (Paragraph 1)

9. The relationship of the second sentence below to the first is one of
    a. addition.
    b. comparison.
    c. contrast.
    d. illustration.

    [Psychiatrists] estimated that only half of 1 percent (that is, one person in 200) of the population would be sadistic enough to obey. But they were clearly wrong. (Paragraph 7)

Patterns of Organization

10. The overall pattern of organization of paragraphs 3–6 is one of
    a. steps in a process.
    b. list of items.
    c. cause and effect.
    d. definition and example.

Advanced Skill Questions

Summarizing and Outlining

11. Write in the missing paragraph numbers in the following limited outline of the reading.
    1. Introduction (paragraphs 1–2)
    2. The experiments' procedure (paragraphs 3–6)
    3. The experiments' expected results and actual results (paragraphs ___–___)
    4. The experiments' significance (paragraphs ___–___)
    5. Conclusion (paragraph 11)

12. Which of the following statements best summarizes paragraphs 3–6?
    a. Psychologist Stanley Milgram solicited subjects from all walks of life for a series of experiments involving shocks.
    b. During Milgram's experiments, the "learner" would mention that he or she had a slight heart condition. Also, he or she would complain about the shocks and sometimes yell, "Let me out of here." The "teachers," however, didn't seem to become sufficiently sympathetic to the "learners."
    c. To convince volunteers that actual shocks were being used on the "learner," they were given somewhat painful sample shocks (45 volts).
    d. Milgram's experiments involved telling volunteers from all walks of life that they were testing the effect of shock on learning by administering increasingly painful shocks; the "learners," accomplices of Milgram, made errors and complained about the shocks.

Fact and Opinion

13. The statement that "Milgram's works stand out as an important contribution to psychology" (paragraph 11) is
    a. a fact.
    b. an opinion.
    c. a fact and opinion.

Inferences

14. Based on Milgram's results, it is reasonable to conclude that
    a. people should not participate in any psychology experiments.
    b. events like the mass suicide in Jonestown could happen again.
    c. teaching vocabulary can be especially difficult.
    d. most people don't really mind hurting another person.

15. The author suggests that
    a. Milgram's research sheds little light on obedience.
    b. paid volunteers are more likely to obey than non-paid volunteers.
    c. people should be more questioning of authority figures.
    d. there is little reason for obedience in contemporary societies.

Purpose and Tone

16. Based on the reading—including its last sentence—we might conclude that the author's intention was
    a. only to inform.
    b. both to inform and to persuade.
    c. to entertain and to persuade.

17. The author's attitude toward Milgram's experiment is
    a. totally objective.
    b. mainly critical.
    c. generally approving.
    d. largely lighthearted.

Argument

18. Label the point of the following argument based on the reading with a **P**; label the two statements of support for the point with an **S**. Note that one statement should not be labeled—it is neither the point nor the support of the argument.

    _____ Sixty-five percent of the "teachers" in Milgram's experiment obeyed the command to deliver shocks up to the maximum (450 volts).

    _____ Milgram's experiment has been criticized as not representing obedience in real life.

    _____ People tend to obey those they consider legitimate authorities.

    _____ James Jones's followers obeyed him to the point of committing suicide.

19. Label the point of the following argument based on the reading with a **P**; label the two statements of support for the point with an **S**. Note that one statement should not be labeled—it is neither the point nor the support of the argument.

    _____ Participants may have felt that academic researchers would not allow anyone to be genuinely hurt.

    _____ Obedient soldiers in Nazi Germany killed millions of people.

    _____ Milgram's experiment does not represent obedience in real life.

    _____ Participants in the experiment may have felt they were simply cooperating in a "science game."

20. The statement "Milgram's experiment shows that nobody should obey authority figures" can be considered an example of which fallacy?
    a. False cause *(the argument assumes that the order of events alone shows cause and effect)*
    b. Hasty conclusion *(the argument comes to a conclusion based on insufficient evidence)*
    c. Circular reasoning *(a statement repeats itself rather than providing a real supporting reason to back up an argument)*
    d. Straw man *(an argument is made by claiming an opponent holds an extreme position and then opposing that extreme position)*

Part II

MASTERY TESTS

VOCABULARY IN CONTEXT: Test 1

Figure out the meanings of the following five words by studying them in context. Then complete the matching and fill-in test that follows.

1 **adept**
(ə-dept′)

Unfortunately, Lloyd is more **adept** at spending money than at making it.

The pizza maker was so **adept** at tossing dough in the air that a small crowd gathered outside the window to watch her.

2 **assessment**
(ə-ses′-mənt)

Workers don't complain about the manager's **assessments** of their work. He always evaluates them fairly, even when he's critical.

Friends loved my report on the themes in rap lyrics, but my teacher's **assessment** was different—he gave me a C.

3 **collaborate**
(kə-lab′-ə-rāt′)

When Ron and I **collaborated** on a science fair project, we found it difficult to work together.

The first major work on which composer George Gershwin and his lyricist brother Ira **collaborated** was *Lady Be Good*, a 1924 Broadway musical that included the song "Fascinating Rhythm."

4 **emanating**
(em′-ə-nāt′-ing)

The delicious smell of baking bread **emanating** from the kitchen reminded me how hungry I was.

Raw sewage **emanating** from a pipe near the beach was the source of the ocean's unhealthy pollution.

5 **lethal**
(lē′-thəl)

A boxer's hands are considered **lethal** weapons because he is capable of killing with them.

Jan was afraid her son had eaten a **lethal** number of earthworms, so she was relieved to learn not only that earthworms aren't fatal, but they are high in protein.

A. Match each word with its definition.

1. adept _____ coming out of

2. assessment _____ deadly

3. collaborate _____ evaluation

4. emanating _____ work together

5. lethal _____ expert; very skilled

(Continues on next page)

B. Fill in each blank with one of the words in the box. Use each word once.

adept	assessment	collaborate
emanating	lethal	

6. When my time comes, I want to die of a(n) _____ dose of chocolate pudding.

7. That little boy is _____ at looking totally innocent even when he's not.

8. _____ from the kennel was an almost constant chorus of barks and cries.

9. Although Andy wants me to _____ with him on writing a social studies report, he wants to get all the credit.

10. The voters' _____ of the governor was that he had not done enough to keep down taxes.

VOCABULARY IN CONTEXT: Test 2

Figure out the meanings of the following five words by studying them in context. Then complete the matching and fill-in test that follows.

1 **chronic**
(kron'-ik)

Chronic smokers are at a higher risk of developing lung cancer than occasional smokers.

Even though Barry did his job well, he was fired because of his **chronic** lateness.

2 **circumvent**
(sûr'-kəm-vent')

Our only chance to make it to the meeting on time by car is to **circumvent** the crowded traffic downtown.

Hoping to **circumvent** a flood of complaints about his proposal to cut city wages, the mayor called a press conference to defend his decision.

3 **decipher**
(di-sī'-fər)

Our aunt's handwriting is so hard to **decipher** that we're tempted to buy her a typewriter.

Because Albert Einstein's handwriting was so difficult to read, experts were required to **decipher** his notes.

4 **loath**
(lōth)

According to a Gallup Poll, out of all the household tasks, people are by far the most **loath** to wash dishes.

Ed, a strict vegetarian, is **loath** to eat animal products of any kind.

5 **seclusion**
(si-kloo'-zhən)

After a noisy day among people at work, I enjoy the **seclusion** I feel in driving home alone.

Prisoners who cause trouble are sometimes put into **seclusion**, in a room where they cannot see or talk to anyone.

A. Match each word with its definition.

1. chronic   _____ to avoid; to bypass

2. circumvent   _____ very unwilling; reluctant

3. decipher   _____ continuing; constant

4. loath   _____ to read something hard to make out; to make out

5. seclusion   _____ the state of being removed or far from others

(Continues on next page)

B. Fill in each blank with one of the words in the box. Use each word once.

chronic	circumvent	decipher
loath	seclusion	

6. Around April 1, Ralph goes into _____ in the den and doesn't come out until his taxes are done.

7. Our boss is a _____ complainer; he always finds fault with somebody or something.

8. Why are all prescription forms so hard to _____?

9. The children were having such a good time at the amusement park that they were _____ to go home.

10. The thief was able to _____ the burglar alarm by entering the house through a skylight.

VOCABULARY IN CONTEXT: Test 3

Figure out the meanings of the following five words by studying them in context. Then complete the matching and fill-in test that follows.

1 **imminent**
(im′-ə-nənt)

Animals seem to sense when an earthquake is **imminent**— their behavior changes just as the disaster is about to occur.

As he left the hospital room, the visitor said, "Goodnight." However, his sick friend, knowing death was **imminent**, said, "Goodbye."

2 **lucrative**
(loo′-krə-tiv)

Working for the environmental organization was not a **lucrative** job, but it had rewards other than money.

The PTA's flea market was very profitable last year; this year it wasn't so **lucrative** because it rained off and on the entire weekend the flea market took place.

3 **plight**
(plīt)

Touched by the **plight** of the unemployed during the recession, the President signed a bill extending unemployment benefits.

Many people's financial **plight** is the result of their own unwise use of credit cards.

4 **selective**
(si-lek′-tiv)

If Harry had been as **selective** about his wives as he is about his fabulous cars, he never would have gotten divorced even once.

When it comes to chocolate, I'm not **selective**—any old chocolate will do.

5 **ubiquitous**
(yoo-bik′-wi-təs)

An early morning walk through the city showed me that the homeless are **ubiquitous**—there was a blanket-wrapped figure on every steam vent I passed.

Advertising is **ubiquitous** in our society; one firm even sells ad space on the inside of stalls in public restrooms.

A. Match each word with its definition.

1. imminent _____ profitable

2. lucrative _____ careful in choosing

3. plight _____ being, or seeming to be, everyplace at once

4. selective _____ about to occur

5. ubiquitous _____ troubled situation

(Continues on next page)

B. Fill in each blank with one of the words in the box. Use each word once.

imminent	lucrative	plight
selective	ubiquitous	

6. The _____ graffiti in our society show a common disrespect for the public environment.

7. Many people think show business is very _____, forgetting that more than half the shows mounted close early and lose money.

8. What is being done about the _____ of the homeless?

9. Crowds gathered in the park when it was announced that the Pope's arrival was _____.

10. My mother thinks I'm too fussy about who I go out with, but I like to think of myself as _____.

VOCABULARY IN CONTEXT: Test 4

Figure out the meanings of the following five words by studying them in context. Then complete the matching and fill-in test that follows.

1 **devoid**
(di-void′)

Superman has magical talents, including X-ray vision and the ability to fly, but Batman is totally **devoid** of such superpowers.

When you read about the horrors of Nazi Germany and of slavery, you wonder how people can be so **devoid** of feeling for other humans.

2 **diligent**
(dil′-i-jənt)

I wish I'd been more **diligent** about practicing piano when I was younger. It would be nice to be able to play well now.

A good doctor will be **diligent** about keeping up with the medical journals and learning new techniques.

3 **ostentatious**
(os′-ten-tā′-shəs)

The exotic dancer's **ostentatious** costumes were all covered in brightly colored sequins and feathers.

After winning the lottery, the Moores redecorated their house in an **ostentatious** manner, to show off their new wealth.

4 **pretext**
(prē′-tekst)

The thief got into Mrs. Barkley's house with the **pretext** that his car broke down and he needed to use her phone.

Faith told Roberto that she called him to get today's math assignment, but that was a **pretext**; she just felt like talking to him.

5 **rampant**
(ram′-pənt)

When I was a girl, poison ivy was **rampant** in fields near our home, but today such troublesome weeds are held in check with various weed killers.

With the discovery of penicillin, infections that were once **rampant** could finally be controlled.

A. Match each word with its definition.

1. devoid (of)   _____   showy; intended to impress others

2. diligent   _____   an excuse; a reason or purpose given to hide the truth

3. ostentatious _____   widespread; growing without being slowed down or stopped

4. pretext   _____   hard-working; persistent and careful in work

5. rampant   _____   without; lacking   *(Continues on next page)*

243

B. Fill in each blank with one of the words in the box. Use each word once.

devoid	diligent	ostentatious
pretext	rampant	

6. Margaret disliked _____ displays of wealth, such as thick gold bracelets and expensive fur coats.

7. We must stop the violent crime so _____ in parts of our big cities.

8. A(n) _____ worker, Martin patiently made his way up through the ranks of the company, from stock boy to vice president.

9. Grandma's needing a ride to the store was just a _____ to get Dolores out of the house while her friends gathered in the basement for her surprise party.

10. The French fries were so thin, dry, and _____ of taste that they seemed like splinters of wood.

VOCABULARY IN CONTEXT: Test 5

Figure out the meanings of the following five words by studying them in context. Then complete the matching and fill-in test that follows.

1 **covert**
(kuv′-ərt)

The bearded biker lounging against his Harley was actually a police officer on a **covert** assignment.

Jake's public image was that of a businessman, but he had a **covert** position with the CIA.

2 **saunter**
(sôn′-tər)

Having no destination in mind, I **sauntered** around the city, casually investigating neighborhoods and parks.

Each morning the fifth-graders **saunter** into class as if they've got all week, but when the last bell of the day rings, they run out as if the school's on fire.

3 **skeptical**
(skep′-ti-kəl)

Although she was **skeptical**, Emma agreed to try the new ointment to see if it would really remove the wart on her chin.

When Vidal said he was born in France, I was **skeptical** because he doesn't have even a trace of a French accent.

4 **utilitarian**
(yo͞o-til′-i-târ′-ē-ən)

The gold watch with diamond numbers was beautiful, but it had no **utilitarian** value since it no longer kept time.

Native Americans hunted for **utilitarian** reasons only, to feed and clothe their families.

5 **verify**
(ver′-ə-fī′)

The sales clerk asked the customer to **verify** his identity by showing her a driver's license with a photo.

The police had the suspect **verify** her story by naming witnesses who had seen her in another town on the day of the crime.

A. Match each word with its definition.

1. covert   _____ to prove the truth of something with evidence

2. saunter   _____ secret; hidden

3. skeptical   _____ practical

4. utilitarian   _____ to walk leisurely

5. verify   _____ doubting; questioning

(Continues on next page)

B. Fill in each blank with one of the words in the box. Use each word once.

covert	saunter	skeptical
utilitarian	verify	

6. You can _____ that a company doesn't have a bad reputation by checking with the Better Business Bureau.

7. Museums are buying _____ objects that are especially beautiful as well as useful.

8. I am always _____ of advertising claims. After all, an advertiser will never tell about a product's weak points.

9. Detective Blake welcomed _____ assignments investigating drug sales; she found undercover work exciting.

10. I love to _____ up and down the aisles of bookstores, leisurely looking at covers and titles, stopping now and then to look more closely at something especially interesting.

VOCABULARY IN CONTEXT: Test 6

Figure out the meanings of the following five words by studying them in context. Then complete the matching and fill-in test that follows.

1 **negligible**
(neg′-li-jə-bəl)

The small car was a twisted wreck, but the tractor-trailer it had struck suffered **negligible** damage—a broken headlight.

The difference in price between the two VCRs was **negligible,** so the customer chose the one with more features.

2 **ostracized**
(os′-trə-sīzd′)

The religious sect **ostracized** people it considered sinners, barring them from services or even conversations with sect members.

Ostracized by his former friends, the AIDS victim died a lonely death among strangers.

3 **proficient**
(prə-fish′-ənt)

Some historians consider George Washington to have been a **proficient** military leader, ranking him with such geniuses as Napoleon and Alexander the Great.

Scott practiced his gymnastic routine until he was **proficient** enough to do it almost perfectly every time.

4 **spontaneous**
(spon-tā′-nē-əs)

A really good actor will appear to be **spontaneous** when performing no matter how often he or she has rehearsed.

Before young children become self-conscious, they are wonderfully **spontaneous,** doing whatever they feel like doing.

5 **superimposed**
(so͞o′-pər-im-pōzd′)

A sign with a large *X* **superimposed** on a burning cigarette informed us that smoking wasn't allowed.

The design on Pete's T-shirt featured a giant surfer **superimposed** over a small map of California.

A. Match each word with its definition.

1. negligible   _____ barred or banished; shunned

2. ostracized   _____ behaving freely; acting from a natural feeling

3. proficient   _____ insignificant; slight

4. spontaneous   _____ put on or over something

5. superimposed   _____ expert; skillful   *(Continues on next page)*

247

B. Fill in each blank with one of the words in the box. Use each word once.

negligible	ostracized	proficient
spontaneous	superimposed	

6. I tried to look _____ when inviting Rick to the movies, so he would think it was a spur-of-the moment idea, not something I'd been nervously planning for days.

7. For the colored illustrations in the picture book, one transparency was _____ over another.

8. By learning study and test-taking techniques, you can make yourself a(n) _____ student.

9. Just because Elliot wasn't athletic, the other sixth-graders _____ him during recess.

10. Lynn was such an impractical perfectionist that she would retype a paper if it had only a tiny error, something as _____ as a space missing between two words.

MAIN IDEAS: Test 1

Circle the letter of the correct topic of each paragraph. (To find the topic, remember to ask yourself, "Who or what is the paragraph about?") Then circle the letter of the main idea—the author's main point about the topic.

1. A good place to flirt is while waiting in line, says Sara McCormack Hoffman. Hoffman, who teaches a class on the joy of flirting at the Open University in Minneapolis, says there are better and worse places to flirt. Another good place is in a store or shop, where you can talk about merchandise. Hoffman says the worst places include bars, where there are high-pressure situations with loud music and alcohol, and the things you say may go unheard or unremembered.

    Topic: a. Waiting in Line   c. Flirting
                    b Therapy   d. Minneapolis

    Main idea: a. Waiting in line is a good environment for flirting.
                     b. In Minneapolis, there is an Open University.
                     c. There are good and bad places for flirting, according to one therapist.
                     d. Sara McCormack Hoffman is a marriage and family therapist in Minnesota.

2. Power, the ability to control the behavior of others, takes different forms. Force, which the Italian statesman Machiavelli called "the method of beasts," is the use of physical coercion. Another type of power is authority, which is the power behind the laws and rules of society. Influence is also a form of power. When a person is able to control the behavior of others beyond any authority he has to do so, that is influence at work.

    Topic: a. Force   c. Machiavelli
                    b. Power   d. Authority

    Main idea: a. Social laws and rules illustrate the power of authority.
                     b. Power has several forms.
                     c. Force is the use of coercion to control the behavior of others.
                     d. Machiavelli, an Italian statesman, called force "the method of beasts."

(Continues on next page)

3. Cocaine is regarded today as a major social evil and as a medical problem of vast proportions. Only a century ago, however, cocaine was believed to be a harmless stimulant and cure-all. Highly respectable scientists such as psychoanalyst Sigmund Freud experimented with cocaine. The original 1886 formula for Coca-Cola included three parts coca leaves (the source of cocaine) to one part cola nut. The original Coca-Cola was advertised not only as a refreshing beverage, but as a medicine to "cure all nervous afflictions—Sick Headache, Neuralgia, Hysteria, Melancholy, Etc."

Topic: a. Cocaine   c. Coca-Cola
              b. Sigmund Freud   d. Cure-Alls

Main idea: a. Cure-alls were popular a century ago.
              b. Sigmund Freud experimented with cocaine.
              c. Cocaine is regarded today as a major social evil and as a huge medical problem.
              d. A century ago, cocaine was believed to be a harmless stimulant and cure-all.

4. A child will probably make a face when offered a slice of lemon and reject it. Adults, however, often enjoy sprinkling lemon juice on certain foods. The difference in this sensitivity to flavors lies in the taste buds, the thousands of tiny taste receptors that line the tongue. The sensitivity to flavors is determined by the number of taste buds in the mouth. Young children's tongues are loaded with taste buds and are especially sensitive; therefore, sour or spicy flavors seem more intense to them. Adults seek out spicy or bitter foods to stimulate their smaller supply of taste buds.

Topic: a. Lemon   c. Spicy Flavors
              b. Children and Adults   d. Sensitivity to Flavors

Main idea: a. Children and adults differ in various ways.
              b. The sensitivity to flavors is determined by the number of taste buds in the mouth.
              c. Young children's tongues are loaded with tastebuds.
              d. Adults often enjoy sprinkling sour lemon juice on foods and in beverages, and they seek out spicy or bitter foods.

MAIN IDEAS: Test 2

Each of the following groups of statements includes one topic, one main idea (topic sentence), and two supporting ideas. Identify each item in the space provided as either the topic (**T**), main idea (**MI**), or a supporting detail (**SD**).

Group 1

_____ a. One bite from a piranha's triangular-shaped teeth can sever a person's finger or toe.

_____ b. The piranha.

_____ c. For its size, the 8- to 12-inch piranha is the most dangerous of all fish.

_____ d. A school of piranha can strip a 400-pound hog down to a skeleton in just a few minutes.

Group 2

_____ a. Joint custody of the children has become more common.

_____ b. The number of men with sole custody of children has also grown.

_____ c. Alternatives to the mother getting sole child custody have increased in recent years.

_____ d. Alternative child-custody arrangements.

Group 3

_____ a. Benjamin Franklin discovered that lightning was an electrical charge.

_____ b. In addition to being a statesman, Franklin was a scientist.

_____ c. Benjamin Franklin's work.

_____ d. Franklin invented bifocals, the Franklin stove, and an electric storage battery.

(Continues on next page)

Group 4

_____ a.   Bureaucracies are divided into departments and subdivisions.

_____ b.   Bureaucracies.

_____ c.   Through a division of labor, individuals specialize in performing one task.

_____ d.   Bureaucracies have certain characteristics in common.

Group 5

_____ a.   As early as 1905, Yale's star player, James Hogan, received part of the profits from the sale of game programs.

_____ b.   College football and corruption have been linked as long as colleges have had football teams.

_____ c.   During the school term each season, the university gave Hogan a ten-day vacation in Cuba.

_____ d.   Corruption in college football.

MAIN IDEAS: Test 3

The following selections have main ideas (topic sentences) that may appear at any place within the paragraph. Identify the topic sentence of each paragraph by filling in the correct sentence number in the space provided. For the one paragraph in which there are two topic sentences, write in both numbers.

1. ^{1}Although they don't have as many opportunities to enjoy them, animals have just as many whims about their food as people. ^{2}One horse owner discovered the peculiarities of his animal's food preferences quite by accident one day when the horse stole a piece of watermelon from a nearby picnic table. ^{3}The horse ate it, rind and all, and methodically spit out every seed. ^{4}Another person reported that her collie always begged for succotash but ate only the sauce and corn, leaving every lima bean behind.

    Topic sentence(s): _____

2. ^{1}Most people think of the surface of the far reaches of the oceans as lifeless and forbidding. ^{2}In some oceans, however, small surface-dwelling insects known as marine waterstriders combine many talents that allow them to live on the ocean's surface. ^{3}They use the middle pair of their three pairs of legs like oars to glide and sometimes scoot around on the water's surface. ^{4}They find mats and deposit eggs on debris that floats on the water. ^{5}And their robust and hairy bodies repel water so that they will not take it on and get heavy enough to sink.

    Topic sentence(s): _____

3. ^{1}Recent research has provided techniques for significantly improving short-term and long-term memory. ^{2}Short-term memory can be improved by rote rehearsal and chunking. ^{3}Rote rehearsal involves repeatedly going over something in your head, and chunking is a method of organizing long lists into chunks of seven or fewer. ^{4}Long-term memory can be improved by organizing material for meaningful association. ^{5}For example, the more associations that can be made between new information and information already known, the more likely it is you'll remember. ^{6}Another organizing technique is mnemonics, or the use of memory-aiding formulas. ^{7}An example of a mnemonic device is using the acronym HOMES as a clue to recall the names of the five Great Lakes: Huron, Ontario, Michigan, Erie, and Superior. ^{8}Memory, then, can be improved by using these simple methods.

    Topic sentence(s): _____

(Continues on next page)

4.   [1]Police officers complain that they arrest perpetrators who are soon let out on the street. [2]Judges argue that they are bound by laws that force them to free defendants, some of whom may be guilty as charged, on technicalities. [3]Government officials lament that they don't have the funds or space to build new prisons. [4]And many citizens charge that either the police, the judges or the government—or all of the above—are not doing their job. [5]Clearly, the way the huge problem of crime is being handled angers and frustrates many segments of our society.

Topic sentence(s): _____

5.   [1]Have you ever wondered why products come in the colors they do? [2]For instance, why is toothpaste often green or blue and shampoo often golden-yellow? [3]Manufacturers pick the colors that are associated with qualities consumers value in certain products. [4]For example, it's known that blue symbolizes purity to most people and that green is refreshing. [5]These are both desirable qualities in toothpastes. [6]Manufacturers also know that golden-yellow symbolizes richness (as in real gold or egg yolks), so they frequently choose this color for shampoos and cream rinses—products in which consumers value richness. [7]Baby products, such as body lotion, are often tinted pink because that is a color commonly associated with softness and gentleness—the very qualities consumers want for their baby's care.

Topic sentence(s): _____

MAIN IDEAS: Test 4

A. The following selections have main ideas (topic sentences) that may appear at any place within the paragraph. Identify the topic sentence of each paragraph by filling in the correct sentence number in the space provided.

1. ¹One writer spent 900 hours over the course of eight years watching the action in singles bars and learning about male/female relationships. ²Although men may think of themselves as the aggressors, says this writer, it is really women who call the shots when a courtship is beginning. ³He has observed that women are the ones who pick a potential mate out of the crowd. ⁴They position themselves near the man they've selected, and with a glance or a smile invite him to make contact. ⁵Similarly, as conversation begins, the woman initiates each increasingly intimate stage. ⁶Her continuing eye contact, moving closer, and touching the man all signal her permission for him to make further advances. ⁷In most cases, the woman's signals are so subtle that the man is only subconsciously aware of them.

    Topic sentence: _____

2. ¹Changing a career in midlife can be pretty scary, yet many people are doing just that, and for most it's a good idea. ²At age 20, who can know what's the best thing to do for the next fifty years? ³Since people change as they age, a profession that seemed promising at first can become drudgery ten years later. ⁴One option for some who want to change careers is to make a business out of a hobby. ⁵One man who likes to work with his hands, for example, started a now-successful handyman service. ⁶Others make a midlife change by going to college or a trade school to begin a new career. ⁷They often benefit greatly, as older students bring to their studies experience, judgment and motivation that younger students just don't have.

    Topic sentence: _____

3. ¹In everyday advertising, one observes many obvious attempts to package and sell products and ideas (toothpaste, aspirin, presidential candidates) through clever influence tactics. ²On a personal level, many people claim that such blatant attempts at persuasion are so pitifully obvious that they are not much affected by them. ³But success stories abound. ⁴The sales of Benson & Hedges 100s cigarettes increased sevenfold during a four-year period of heavy advertising. ⁵The Mattel Toy Company increased company

(Continues on next page)

size twenty-four-fold after they began to extensively advertise on television. [6]Grape-Nuts, a venerable but nearly forgotten cereal, experienced a sudden 30 percent increase in sales when a well-known natural foods enthusiast began plugging this rather bland cereal. [7]It appears that tremendous numbers of consumers set aside their skepticism even though they know the message is an obvious attempt to sell a product.

Topic sentence: _____

B. The following paragraphs have unstated main ideas. Each paragraph is followed by four sentences. After reading each paragraph, circle the letter of the sentence that best expresses the implied main idea.

4.   One factor that kept FM radio from developing as much as AM was that more people had AM receivers than FM receivers, and it was not possible to pick up FM on a standard AM radio. Moreover, many of the same people who owned AM stations owned FM stations; to simplify the programming effort, they would broadcast the same show over both frequencies. Third, after World War II, the Federal Communications Commission (FCC) moved FM from the place it had originally occupied on the broadcast spectrum; this made all existing FM radios useless.

   a. Standard AM radios could not pick up FM.
   b. Several factors held back FM radio's development.
   c. Many owners of AM stations also owned FM stations.
   d. By moving FM to a different broadcast spectrum, the FCC made all existing FM radios useless.

5.   Orangutans are intelligent apes that live in the forests of the Asian islands of Sumatra and Borneo. Because of a growing human population, those forests are being cut down for lumber and to create farmland. The less forest there is, the fewer the orangutans that can be supported. To add to the problem, orangutans reproduce very slowly. On average, females have just two or three babies over their lifetimes. Today, there are only two thousand orangutans in Borneo and even fewer in Sumatra.

   a. Orangutans live in the forests of Sumatra and Borneo.
   b. Forests are being cut down worldwide for lumber and to create farmland.
   c. The future of orangutans in Sumatra and Borneo is threatened.
   d. Orangutans are intelligent apes that reproduce very slowly.

MAIN IDEAS: Test 5

The following selections, all taken from college textbooks, have main ideas that may appear at any place within the paragraph. Identify the topic sentence of each paragraph by filling in the correct sentence number in the space provided.

1. [1]At the turn of the century, fewer than 20 percent of women worked outside the home. [2]Over the past several decades, the employment picture has changed appreciably. [3]In 1960, some 35 percent of American women were working outside the home. [4]Today the figure is 55 percent (the percentage of men is 76 percent). [5]Women hold 44 percent of all available jobs, and since 1980, they have taken 80 percent of the new jobs created in the economy. [6]Less than 11 percent of women today are the stereotyped "housewife"—a married woman, not in the labor force, with children at home. [7]Indeed, most women prefer to work.

    Topic sentence: _____

2. [1]Greek and Roman orators used a topical system of mnemonics to memorize long speeches. [2]They would visit a large house or temple and walk through the rooms in a definite order, noting where specific objects were placed within each room. [3]When the plan of the building and its contents were memorized, the orator would go through the rooms in his mind, placing images of material to be remembered at different places in the rooms. [4]In order to retrieve the material during the speech, he would imagine himself going through the building and, by association, would recall each point of his speech as he came to each object and each room.

    Topic sentence: _____

3. [1]Five years ago, how did you feel about nuclear power? about South African apartheid? about your parents? [2]If your attitudes have changed, are you aware of the extent of the change? [3]To answer such questions, experimenters have asked people whose attitudes have been altered to recall their pre-experiment attitudes. [4]The result of the study is unnerving: People often insist that they have always felt much as they now feel. [5]For example, Daryl Bem and Keith McConnell (1970) took a survey among Carnegie-Mellon University students. [6]Buried in it was a question concerning student control over the university curriculum. [7]A week later the students agreed to write an essay opposing student control. [8]After doing so, their attitudes shifted toward

(Continues on next page)

greater opposition to student control. [9]When asked to recall how they had answered the question a week previously, they "remembered" holding the opinion that they now held and denied that the experiment affected them.

Topic sentence: _____

4.   [1]Sociologists use three different models to explain how societies operate. [2]The "functional" model regards a society as a system that brings people together to accomplish needed tasks. [3]A functional sociologist, for example, sees our educational system as a means of providing people with the variety of skills needed to keep our society working. [4]In contrast, the "conflict" model sees a society as a system in which some people take advantage of others. [5]A conflict sociologist sees our educational system as designed to make sure that the children of the privileged get the best schooling and the most opportunities. [6]Finally, the "interactionist" model in sociology looks not at society as a whole, but at how individuals and small groups deal with one another. [7]An interactionist sociologist looks not at the whole educational system, but at how different students cope with school.

Topic sentence: _____

5.   [1]In one tribe in New Guinea, aggression is encouraged in boys from early infancy. [2]The child cannot obtain nourishment from his mother without carrying on a continuous battle with her. [3]Unless he grasps the nipple firmly and sucks vigorously, his mother will withdraw it and stop the feeding. [4]In his frantic effort to get food, the child frequently chokes—an annoyance to both himself and his mother. [5]Thus the feeding situation itself is "characterized by anger and struggle rather than by affection and reassurance" (Mead, 1939). [6]The people of another New Guinea tribe are extremely peaceful and do everything possible to discourage aggression. [7]They regard all instances of aggression as abnormal. [8]A similar tribe—the Tasaday of the Philippines—has been discovered. [9]These people are extremely friendly and gentle. [10]They possess no weapons for fighting or food-gathering; in fact, they are strict vegetarians who live off the land. [11]Evidence of this sort suggests that, rather than being basically aggressive animals, human beings are peaceful or aggressive depending upon their early childhood training.

Topic sentence: _____

MAIN IDEAS: Test 6

A. The following selections taken from college textbooks have main ideas (topic sentences) that may appear at any place within the paragraph. Identify the topic sentence of each paragraph by filling in the correct sentence number in the space provided.

1. ^{1}Unlike many lower animals that use their noses to detect mates, predators, and prey, humans do not depend on their sense of smell for survival. ^{2}Nevertheless, the sense of smell in humans is incredibly sensitive: Only a few molecules of a substance reaching the smell receptors are necessary to cause humans to perceive an odor. ^{3}Certain substances that give off a large number of molecules that dissolve easily in the moist, fatty tissues of the nose can be detected in especially small amounts. ^{4}Decayed cabbage, lemons, and rotten eggs are examples.

    Topic sentence: _____

2. ^{1}An old saying has it that "Many hands make light the work." ^{2}Thus we might expect that three individuals can pull three times as much as one person and that eight can pull eight times as much. ^{3}But research reveals that whereas persons individually average 130 pounds of pressure when tugging on a rope, in groups of three, they average 351 pounds (only 2.5 times the solo rate) and in groups of eight only 546 pounds (less than 4 times the solo rate). ^{4}One explanation is that faulty coordination produces group inefficiency. ^{5}However, when subjects are blindfolded and believe they are pulling with others, they also slacken their effort. ^{6}Apparently when we work in groups, we cut down on our efforts, a process termed social loafing.

    Topic sentence: _____

3. ^{1}A century ago, medical practice left much to be desired. ^{2}In the late 1800s, surgeons still operated with bare hands, wearing the same clothes they had worn on the street. ^{3}Their shoes carried in the debris of the streets and hospital corridors. ^{4}Spectators were often permitted to observe operations, gathering around the patient within touching distance of his incision. ^{5}Surgeons used surgical dressings made from pressed sawdust, a waste product from the floors of sawmills. ^{6}Surgical instruments were washed in soapy water, but not heat-sterilized or chemically disinfected. ^{7}The mortality rate following operations in many hospitals was as high as 90 percent.

    Topic sentence: _____

(Continues on next page)

259

B. The following paragraphs, taken from college textbooks, have unstated main ideas. Each paragraph is followed by four sentences. After reading each paragraph, circle the letter of the sentence that best expresses the implied main idea.

4.   Some parents cannot meet the physical, psychological and financial stresses of parenthood; they may abuse, neglect, or abandon their children or become physically or emotionally ill themselves. Most, however, cope to a greater or lesser degree. Parents often turn to support systems such as family, friends, and neighbors, or get help from professionals and from books and articles on child rearing. Adoptive parents develop, basically, much as biological parents, even though they face special experiences and have to deal with special challenges. Successful parents tend to define their situation positively, putting parental responsibilities first; they concentrate on one set of responsibilities at a time; and they are willing to compromise their standards (such as those for neatness or promptness) when necessary.

   a. Some parents abuse, neglect or abandon their children.
   b. Adoptive parents face special experiences and have special challenges to deal with.
   c. Different people respond differently to the stresses and demands of parenthood.
   d. Parents can get help in parenting from support systems, professionals, and books and articles on child rearing.

5.   Blue-collar workers have little or no control over their work. The routes to mobility seem closed to them. Advanced technology (computerized automation, robotics) undermines the value of their skills. Experiences on the job rub in the low status of labor. On-the-job regimentation resembles that in the military. White-collar workers may have more control over their work, but they have no more job security than blue-collar workers and, in many cases, earn less. The fact that many office workers have attended college and have higher expectations and more skills than their jobs warrant makes their on-the-job experience all the more frustrating. As a young female college graduate put it, "I didn't go to school for four years to type. I'm bored; continuously humiliated."

   a. White-collar workers have no more job security than blue-collar workers.
   b. Blue-collar and white-collar workers experience different kinds of job discontent.
   c. White-collar work, in general, is more satisfying than blue-collar work.
   d. Many office workers who have attended college have higher expectations and more skills than their jobs warrant.

SUPPORTING DETAILS: Test 1

A. Complete the map of the following paragraph by filling in the two major details.

> Alcoholism can be attributed to two types of causes. First of all, heredity plays a definite part in alcoholism. Thirty-five genetic factors account for a tendency to alcoholism. If more than half of these factors are passed on from parent to child, the risk of acquiring the disease is great. Environment can also play a part in alcoholism. Children who grow up in the home of an alcoholic, for example, may experience many disappointments in family members. Having learned to trust no one but themselves, they often turn to alcohol for comfort.

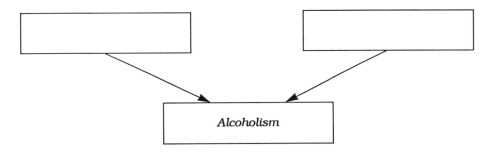

B. Complete the outline of the following paragraph by filling in the main idea and the missing major details.

> There are a few differing theoretical points of view on television violence. Supporters of the catharsis theory contend that the viewing of scenes of aggression helps to purge the viewers' own aggressive feelings. In other words, experiencing violence indirectly may make the individual less likely to commit a violent act. In contrast, the supporters of the stimulation theory maintain that seeing scenes of violence helps to stimulate an individual to behave more violently. The last group, the supporters of the null theory, maintain that fictionalized violence has no influence on real violence.

Main idea: _____

1. *The catharsis theory* _____

2. _____

3. _____

(Continues on next page)

C. Fill in the outline of the following paragraph.

      Symbols can be classified in two basic ways. Referential symbols are those which denote real objects in the external world. The word *door* is a referential symbol: it refers to an object or a class of objects whose existence in the external world can be objectively proven. If someone asks you what a door is, you can simply point to a door. Expressive symbols, on the other hand, refer to objects or events that cannot be established in the external world. The meanings they communicate are often emotional and highly personal. The word *God* is an expressive symbol. To some it may evoke feelings of love and brotherhood; to others it may evoke fear; to still others it may carry no particular emotional meaning.

Main idea: _____

_____

1. _____

    Example: _____

2. _____

    Example: _____

SUPPORTING DETAILS: Test 2

A. Complete the outline of the following paragraph. Note that the main idea is boldfaced.

There are two main forms of survey, and each has its own advantages. One type of survey is the interview. An interview can obtain a high response rate because people find it more difficult to turn down a personal request for an interview than to throw away a written questionnaire. In addition, a skillful interviewer can go beyond written questions and probe for a subject's underlying feelings and reasons. Questionnaires, the second main form of survey, also have two advantages. They are cheaper than interviews, especially when large samples are used. Moreover, since the questions are written, the researcher knows that there is a guarantee of consistency, whereas five interviewers can ask the same question in five different ways.

Major detail: 1. _____

Minor details: a. *Can obtain a high response rate* _____

                 b. _____

                           _____

Major detail: 2. _____

Minor details: a. _____

                 b. _____

(Continues on next page)

B. Prepare a map of the paragraph by completing the main heading and filling in the four major details.

The family is sometimes described as the backbone of society. It performs several essential social functions that are not equally provided by any other structure. For example, the socialization process of new members of each generation occurs first and foremost within the family. Peer groups, schools, churches, and the mass media also play their roles in instructing children to be integrated and functioning members of their society, but such socialization remains primarily a family function. The family also helps regulate sexual activity within a society. The taboo against having sexual relations with or marrying close relatives encourages the continual forming of new ties outside the family, thereby strengthening the larger society. Families also function as providers of social placement. That is, children automatically inherit many important social determinants, such as race, religion, and social class, according to the family to which they are born. The family is expected as well, although not always realistically, to provide material and emotional security to its members. The family is usually a person's most important primary group, and family members generally have intense and enduring relationships with one another that are expressed in both material and emotional terms.

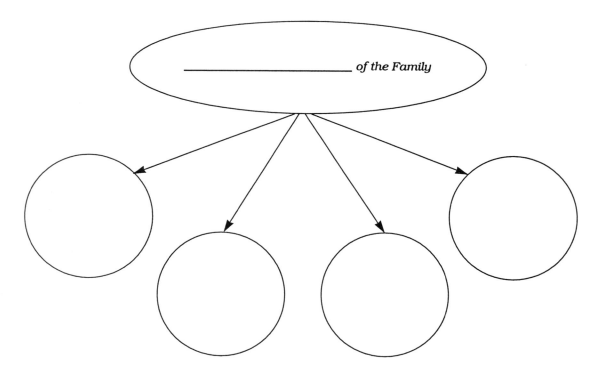

_____ of the Family

SUPPORTING DETAILS: Test 3

A. Below each of the following passages is a question raised by the main idea of the passage. After reading each passage, answer the question by stating the major supporting details.

> Functional illiteracy—the inability to read and write well enough to carry out everyday activities—is a complex social problem that stems from several sources. One source of the problem is our educational system. Our schools tend to pass children from one grade to the next even when their level of learning is woefully deficient. The community also contributes to functional illiteracy. Local businesses and agencies, indifferent to education, do not work with schools toward improving children's motivation and learning. Still another source is the home. Millions of children grow up with illiterate parents who do not give them the opportunity or encouragement to learn language skills.

What are the sources of functional illiteracy?

1. _____

2. _____

3. _____

> The graying of our population has several causes. A combination of high birthrates in the late-nineteenth and early- to mid-twentieth centuries and high immigration rates in this country swelled our population with people now in the over-65 brackets. As the large "baby boom" generation (born in the late 1940s and the 1950s) ages, the proportion of old people in our population will reach its peak about a third of the way through the twenty-first century, after which it will drop again. Furthermore, medical advances have lengthened our average life expectancy. Fewer people now die in childhood and early adulthood, and new medicines and procedures are keeping many old people alive who once would have succumbed to a variety of illnesses.

What are the causes of the graying of our population?

4. _____

5. _____

6. _____

(Continues on next page)

B. Carefully read the following textbook paragraph, and then answer the questions that follow.

> The arrival of police can turn a mild situation into a dangerous one. For example, a Poor People's March in Detroit turned into a riot when police inside a meeting hall tried to force people out and police outside the hall tried to push them in. Many of the ghetto riots of the 1960s were sparked by police action. Police attempts to make an arrest for a traffic violation may lead to a high-speed chase, causing injury and death that might not have occurred otherwise. Stepped-up enforcement of the narcotics laws is in part responsible for shifting the drug traffic from local, amateur groups to highly sophisticated and skilled criminal organizations.

7. The major details of this paragraph are
   a. a list of all types of events in which the police intervene.
   b. reasons for various types of dangerous social situations.
   c. illustrations of police making situations more dangerous.
   d. police attempts to make an arrest for traffic and drug violations.

8. The first sentence provides
   a. the main idea.
   b. a major detail.
   c. a minor detail.

9. *Fill in the blank:* The paragraph includes (*two, three, four or five?*) _____ major supporting details.

10. According to the passage, greater enforcement of the narcotics laws can make drug crimes more dangerous because
    a. police action can spark riots.
    b. the criminals become more sophisticated.
    c. the drug dealers become more numerous.
    d. the police succumb to the temptations of drugs.

SUPPORTING DETAILS: Test 4

A. The following two paragraphs from a textbook share one topic sentence. Carefully read the passage, and then answer the questions that follow.

[1]Without doubt, our moods color our thinking. [2]To West Germans enjoying their team's World Cup soccer victory and to Australians emerging from a heartwarming movie, people seem goodhearted, life in general seems wonderful. [3]Put in a happy mood, the world seems friendlier, decisions come more easily, good news more readily comes to mind. [4]When we feel happy, we think happy and optimistic thoughts.

[5]Let our mood turn gloomy, and our thoughts switch onto a different track. [6]Off come the rose-colored glasses; on come the dark glasses. [7]Now the bad mood primes our recollections of negative events. [8]Whereas formerly depressed people recall their parents the same as do never-depressed people, currently depressed people recall their parents as having been rejecting and punitive. [9]When a black mood strikes, our relationships seem to sour, our self-image takes a dive, our hopes for the future dim, people's behavior seems more sinister.

1. The first *major* supporting detail of this passage is
   a. happy moods give us happy and optimistic thoughts.
   b. people seem goodhearted and life seems wonderful to World Cup soccer victors.
   c. people seem goodhearted and life seems wonderful to Australians emerging from a heartwarming movie.
   d. our moods color our thinking.

2. Sentence 1 provides
   a. the main idea.
   b. a major detail.
   c. a minor detail.

3. Sentence 5 provides
   a. the main idea.
   b. a major detail.
   c. a minor detail.

4. Sentence 8 provides
   a. the main idea.
   b. a major detail.
   c. a minor detail.

5. According to the passage, moods can influence
   a. our decisions.   c. our self-image.
   b. our memories.   d. all of the above.   *(Continues on next page)*

B. Carefully read the paragraph, and then answer the questions that follow.

[1]"Paralanguage" relates to the sounds we hear. [2]It concerns how something is said, not what is said. [3]A major category of paralanguage is vocal characteristics, of which there are several. [4]Pitch refers to the highness or lowness of your voice. [5]Fortunately, most people speak at a pitch that is about right for them, although a few persons talk using notes that are too high or too low for their voice. [6]The loudness of the tone you make is its volume. [7]Each person, regardless of size, can make his or her voice louder. [8]If you have trouble talking loudly enough to be heard in a large classroom, work on increasing pressure from the abdominal area on exhalation. [9]Our rate of speech is the speed at which we talk. [10]Although most of us utter between 140 and 180 words per minute, the optimal rate is a highly individual matter. [11]The test of rate is whether listeners can understand what you are saying. [12]The tone, the timbre, or the sound of your voice is referred to as its quality. [13]The best vocal quality is a clear, pleasant-to-listen-to voice. [14]Problems of quality include nasality (too much resonance in the nose on vowel sounds), breathiness (too much escaping of air during phonation), harshness (too much tension in the throat and chest), and hoarseness (a raspy sound to the voice).

6. In general, the major details of this paragraph are
   a. sounds.
   b. types of voices.
   c. pitches of voices.
   d. vocal characteristics.

7. Specifically, the major details of the paragraph are
   a. paralanguage, sound, and voices.
   b. pitches that are about right, too high, and too low.
   c. pitch, volume, rate of speech, quality.
   d. tone, timbre, sound, and quality of the voice.

8. Sentence 3 provides
   a. the main idea.
   b. a major detail.
   c. a minor detail.

9. Sentence 8 provides
   a. the main idea.
   b. a major detail.
   c. a minor detail.

10. *Fill in the blank*: One problem of voice _____ is harshness.

SUPPORTING DETAILS: Test 5

A. Carefully read the passage below, and then answer the questions that follow.

[1]The people of the Republic of Abkhasia in the southwest corner of the former Soviet Union have the distinction of living, on the average, longer than any other people on earth. [2]In one village of twelve hundred people studied by anthropologists, for example, almost two hundred people were over the age of 81.

[3]Although there is no proven explanation for the longevity of the Abkhasians, a few theoretical explanations have been advanced. [4]Perhaps the centuries of grueling warfare in Abkhasia have allowed only the most physically sturdy to survive and pass on their genes. [5]The Abkhasian diet, low in saturated fat, lacking caffeine, but high in fruits and vegetables, may be a component. [6]The regular exercise that is a part of the Abkhasian agricultural lifestyle may also help explain the villagers' long lives. [7]Researchers also suggest that the Abkhasian culture, which expects all members to perform meaningful work and provides all members with a clear sense of identity, may produce in the most elderly citizens a healthful sense of being needed and valued members of their communities.

1. In general, the major details of the second paragraph are
   a. problems of the Abkhasians.
   b. possible reasons for the Abkhasian longevity.
   c. examples of Abkhasian lifestyle.
   d. components of the Abkahsian diet.

2. The first major detail of the second paragraph is
   a. a proven explanation.
   b. a sturdy genetic heritage.
   c. regular exercise.
   d. the Abkhasian diet.

3. The third major detail of the second paragraph is
   a. the survival of the physically sturdy.
   b. no caffeine.
   c. regular exercise.
   d. a sense of being needed and valued members of the community.

4. *Fill in the blank*: The main idea of the second paragraph can be found in sentence _____.

(Continues on next page)

B.   Complete the map of the following passage by completing the heading and filling in the missing major and minor details.

Poverty is distributed within the American population according to a number of factors. First, those at both ends of the spectrum of age are most likely to be poor. More children under the age of 18—22.4 percent—were poor in 1984. Americans over the age of 65 are also at greater risk of poverty—in 1984, 14.1 percent of them were officially designated as being poor. Race and ethnicity are also related to one's chances of living in poverty. Blacks are three times as likely as whites to be poor, and poverty is also relatively high among Hispanics. Gender also plays a role in economic status. Women are increasingly more likely to be poor than men are—a pattern often described as the feminization of poverty. Of all poor adult Americans, 62 percent are women and 38 percent are men. About half of all poor families are households headed by a woman in which no husband is present.

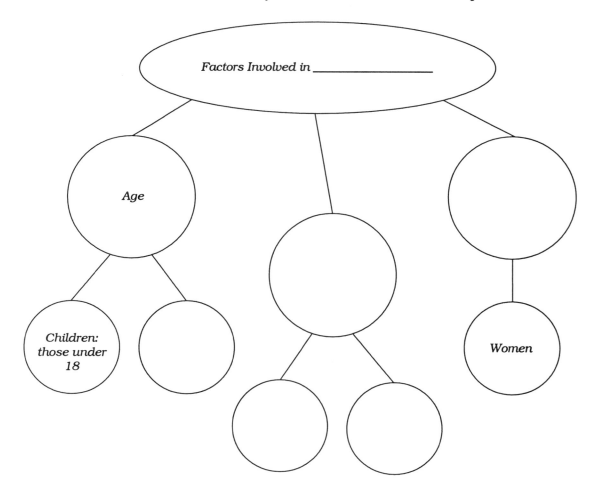

SUPPORTING DETAILS: Test 6

A. Carefully read the textbook passage below, and then answer the questions that follow.

> [1]Like most mass movements, evangelical Protestantism was more divided than it appeared to outsiders. [2]Fundamentalists, believing that the Holy Spirit had not spoken to individuals directly since the time of Christ, focused their attention on the literal words and messages of the Bible as the key to divine guidance. [3]Pentacostalists, on the other hand, insisted that the Holy Spirit still moved the faithful directly; some believers spoke "in tongues," their bodies and voices contorted by the spirit in them. [4]Thus a fundamentalist like the Reverend Jerry Falwell had strong theological disagreements with a Pentacostalist like the Reverend Pat Robertson. [5]Still, evangelicals found a good deal of common ground in what they saw as the corruptions of American society. [6]They rejected feminism in favor of the patriarchal family, in which men were the breadwinners and spiritual heads and women raised children in the home. [7]They attacked the Supreme Court for decisions which they believed helped open the floodgates of pornography. [8]The demand of homosexuals for "gay rights" particularly offended their belief that the Bible condemned homosexuality as an unqualified sin.

1. One way to state the implied main idea of this paragraph is:
   a. Evangelical Protestantism was divided.
   b. Evangelical Protestants shared some views.
   c. The two main types of evangelical Protestants are Fundamentalists, which include Reverend Jerry Falwell, and Pentacostalists.
   d. Fundamentalist and Pentacostalist evangelical Protestants had differences and similarities.

2. Sentences 1 and 5 express
   a. major details.
   b. minor details.

3. The minor supporting details of this paragraph are
   a. points of disagreement and agreement between fundamentalists and Pentacostalists.
   b. people who represent the evangelical Protestant movement.
   c. ways in which evangelicals believe American society has been corrupted.
   d. categories of conservative Christians.

(Continues on next page)

4. According to the paragraph, evangelical Protestants were mainly divided on
   a. the corruptions of American society.
   b. gay rights.
   c. prayer.
   d. theology.

5. Pentacostalists believed that speaking "in tongues"
   a. occurred only during the time of Christ.
   b. is evidence of the Holy Spirit's presence.
   c. was offensive.
   d. usually occurs among women.

6. The idea that evangelicals saw corruptions in American society is supported

   by *(one, two, three, or four?)* __three__ examples that are minor details.

B. Complete the outline of the following paragraph by filling in the main idea and the major details.

Note: The number of answer lines given does not necessarily indicate the number of major details in the passage.

There are stages to children's play. Initially, they engage in solitary play. They may show a preference for being near other children and show some interest in what those others are doing, but their own individual play runs an independent course. Solitary play is eventually replaced by parallel play, in which children use similar materials (such as a pail and toy shovel) and engage in similar activity (such as digging sand), typically near one another; but they hardly interact at all. By age 3, most children show at least some cooperative play, a form that involves direct child-to-child interaction and requires some cooperative role-taking. Examples of such role-taking can be found in the "pretend" games that children use to explore such mysteries as adult relationships (for example, games of "Mommy and Daddy") and other children's anatomy (for example, games of "doctor").

Main idea: __stages of play_____

_____Solitary_____

_____Cooperative_____

_____

_____

_____

_____

_____

TRANSITIONS: Test 1

A. Fill in each blank with the appropriate transition from the box. Use each transition once.

furthermore	in contrast	for instance
because of	similarly	

1. Many animals, such as the tiger, live relatively solitary lives. Others, _____, live in social groups. The gorilla lives in a group consisting of a male, his harem, and their children.

2. Watching television helps me pass the time when I'm on an exercise bike. _____, listening to music on my Walkman makes jogging seem to go by faster.

3. Drinking is dangerous in combination with pregnancy, driving, and drugs. _____, excessive drinking can lead to liver disease.

4. In Antarctica, there are pools of water amidst the frozen environment. Scientists believe that the water doesn't freeze _____ hot spots in the land beneath the pools. The only life form that lives in the water is one type of bacteria.

5. It is possible to be addicted to something other than drugs or alcohol. _____, many people are addicted to gambling, caffeine, and even television.

(Continues on next page)

B. Fill in each blank with the appropriate transition from the box. Use each transition once.

because	including	but
like	as a result	

My last car was the most aggravating object I have ever owned. On rainy days, it would start quickly, fooling me into thinking it was okay, (6)_____ as soon as I got out on the highway, it would begin to buck, cough, and backfire. Pushing down too hard on the accelerator was (7)_____ sticking my foot into a heap of mashed potatoes. In addition to being a rainy-day problem, the car was also a gasoline hog. I got only about ten to twelve miles per gallon—probably (8)_____ I spent so much time warming the car up to keep it from stalling. In addition, there was much rattling from various parts of the car, (9)_____ the dashboard, the radio, and a dozen other things I could never identify. Before long, pieces actually started falling off. Once the window handle came off in my hand when I pulled up to a toll booth. The door lock on the driver's side also broke off. (10)_____, I couldn't lock the car, and sure enough, someone stole it. It gives me endless pleasure to know that there's at least one car thief out there who got exactly what he deserved.

TRANSITIONS: Test 2

A. Fill in each blank with the appropriate transition from the box. Use each transition once.

but	finally	such as
while	for example	

The idea that sport is good for both the athlete and society is a popular one in American life. Former President Gerald Ford, himself a football player (1)_____ he was at the University of Michigan, summarized this belief when he stated: "Few things are more important to a country's growth and well-being than competitive athletics. If it is a cliché to say that athletics builds character as well as muscle, then I subscribe to the cliché." (2)_____ whether or not sport builds character is a debatable matter. There are those who argue that sport selects from a pool of youth those individuals who are already inclined to be competitive, industrious, and disciplined. Youths who lack these traits are likely to avoid sport, drop out, or be cut from a team. Moreover, critics of sport ask, "How do you define 'character'?" Does it include characteristics (3)_____ empathy, honesty, and integrity? If so, what becomes of Vince Lombardi's claim that "Winning isn't everything; it's the only thing"? Are unrestrained aggression, violence, and cheating—even the use of health-endangering steroids—acceptable in the pursuit of victory? The fact is that sport is not necessarily such an uplifting experience. (4)_____, heavyweight champion Larry Holmes reveals that a key to his success was to say to himself before entering the ring: "I have to change. I have to leave the goodness out and bring all the bad in, like Dr. Jekyll and Mr. Hyde." (5)_____, sporting events are often occasions for drinking and rowdy behavior.

(Continues on next page)

B. Fill in each blank with the appropriate transition from the box. Use each transition once.

another	examples	reasons
since	even though	

If you want to satisfy your sweet tooth yet avoid calories, try reaching for something red. A study shows that people consistently find red beverages to be sweeter and more satisfying than drinks of other colors— (6)_____ they have the same sugar content. Scientists offer a couple of (7)_____ for this reaction to red. The researcher who conducted the study gives this explanation: "Nature uses bright colors to teach us what tastes good. We learn in early childhood that the sweetest fruits are the ripest, and the ripest ones are red." Apples, cherries and peaches are just some (8)_____ of fruits that redden as they ripen. The researcher, who heads a university food-science department, offers (9)_____ reason for the study's results: Red is widely considered an upbeat, attractive color, and (10)_____ visual appeal is part of taste appeal, we are predisposed to like any edible that is red.

TRANSITIONS: Test 3

First, write in the transition that correctly completes each sentence. Secondly, underline the kind of transition you chose.

1. a. Craig repeatedly dropped courses when it was too late to get a refund; _____, his parents refused to continue paying for his education.

    in the same way
    as a result
    for example

    b. The relationship indicated by the transition is one of
    1) cause and effect.
    2) illustration.
    3) comparison.

2. a. _____ going to the doctor's office, write down all your questions.

    Despite
    Just like
    Before

    b. The relationship indicated by the transition is one of
    1) comparison.
    2) time.
    3) contrast.

3. a. Kay loves Phillip, _____ she doesn't want to marry him.

    thus
    but
    moreover

    b. The relationship between the two clauses is one of
    1) cause and effect.
    2) contrast.
    3) addition.

4. a. Buckminster Fuller designed geodesic domes— lightweight yet very strong structures—for various purposes. _____ he designed a two-mile dome to cover Manhattan.

    Similarly
    However
    Once

    b. The relationship of the second sentence to the first is one of
    1) comparison.
    2) illustration.
    3) contrast.

5. a. My sister's bleached-blond punk hairdo makes her look _____ to a dandelion in bloom.

    next
    similar
    accordingly

    b. The relationship expressed by the sentence is one of
    1) cause and effect.
    2) comparison.
    3) time.

(Continues on next page)

6. a. Judging by the teenager's party, it seems her parents are irresponsible. First of all, there was no adult supervision. _____, wine and beer were served.

  Moreover
  In contrast
  For example

 b. The relationship of the last sentence to the sentence before it is one of
  1) contrast.
  2) addition.
  3) illustration.

7. a. Social Security benefits may be cut to reduce the budget. _____, retirement planning may be more important than ever.

  In addition
  However
  Therefore

 b. The relationship between the two sentences is one of
  1) contrast.
  2) comparison.
  3) cause and effect.

8. a. At the amusement park, Robin begged until her father took her on the ferris wheel. _____, once the wheel began to move, she started to cry.

  So
  However
  Moreover

 b. The relationship of the second sentence to the first is one of
  1) addition.
  2) cause and effect.
  3) contrast.

9. a. Audience members complained because the ushers had continued to seat people _____ the play had started.

  to illustrate
  because
  after

 b. The relationship indicated by the transition is one of
  1) time.
  2) cause and effect.
  3) illustration.

10. a. To attract subscribers, one news magazine offers a solar-powered calculator as a bonus. _____, one sports magazine will send subscribers a free video of sports "bloopers."

  Yet
  Similarly
  For instance

 b. The relationship of the second sentence to the first is one of
  1) comparison.
  2) contrast.
  3) cause and effect.

TRANSITIONS: Test 4

This test will check your ability to recognize the relationships (signaled by transitions) within and between sentences. Read each passage and answer the questions that follow.

A. ¹The aging of our population will have far-reaching implications for what life will be like in the years to come. ²For one thing, society will need to provide many support services to the frail elderly, many of whom will have outlived their savings and will not be able to pay for their own care. ³Moreover, as the over-65 population becomes more influential at the polls and in the marketplace, we're likely to see changes in governmental programs, in television programming, in new products, in housing patterns, in population shifts from state to state, and so forth. ⁴The possibilities for change are virtually infinite.

1. In sentence 2, the phrase "for one thing"
   a. signals that what follows will be the only information of its type provided.
   b. indicates a comparison between today's society and the future's older society.
   c. introduces the first of two or more ways in which society will change.
   d. tells us that one change is being added to changes named earlier.

2. The relationship of sentence 3 to sentence 2 is one of
   a. addition.   c. time.
   b. contrast.   d. cause and effect.

B. ¹A Utah prison inmate has come up with a dramatic way of applying for more paper for his legal motions. ²His application is written on toilet paper. ³In this document, the prisoner explains that although he is allowed only twenty-five pieces of writing paper a week, he needs fifty. ⁴Furthermore, he writes that insufficient writing paper is a denial of his legal rights. ⁵He concludes by apologizing for using toilet paper, which is the only other paper available to him. ⁶The court clerk who accepted the unusual petition said, "I stamped it as carefully as I could."

3. Sentence 3 expresses a relationship of
   a. addition.   c. comparison.
   b. contrast.   d. cause and effect.

4. The relationship of sentence 4 to sentence 3 is one of
   a. addition.   c. cause and effect.
   b. contrast.   d. illustration.

(Continues on next page)

C.   [1]It's the largest school of its kind in the United States. [2]It's also a school unlike most others. [3]Students learn in classrooms lined not with books, but with slot machines. [4]Instead of sitting at desks, they work at craps and blackjack tables. [5]Classes have names like Psychology of Gaming and Casino Law. [6]Believe it or not, this is a community college—it's Atlantic Community College's Casino Career Institute. [7]Like other community colleges, it provides relatively low-cost training for jobs in local industries. [8]But this is Atlantic County, New Jersey. [9]Here the main industry is Atlantic City's hotels and casinos.

5. The relationship between the two parts of sentence 4 is one of
    a. comparison.   c. contrast.
    b. illustration.   d. addition.

6. The relationship between the two parts of sentence 7 is one of
    a. contrast.   c. time.
    b. illustration.   d. comparison.

D.   [1]Not only do we perceive attractive people as likable, but we also perceive likable people as physically attractive. [2]Perhaps you can recall individuals who, as you grew to like them, became more attractive, their physical imperfections no longer so noticeable. [3]For example, Alan Gross and Christine Crofton had University of Missouri-St. Louis students view someone's photograph after reading a favorable or unfavorable description of the person's personality. [4]Those portrayed as warm, helpful, and considerate were perceived as more attractive. [5]Other researchers have found that as we discover someone's similarities to us, the person begins to seem more attractive. [6]Moreover, the more in love a woman is with a man, the more physically attractive she finds him. [7]To paraphrase Benjamin Franklin, if Jill's in love, she's no judge of Jack's handsomeness.

7. The relationship of sentences 3 and 4 to sentence 1 is one of
    a. time.   c. contrast.
    b. illustration.   d. cause and effect.

8. The relationship of sentence 6 to the two sentences before it is one of
    a. time.   c. addition.
    b. contrast.   d. comparison.

TRANSITIONS: Test 5

A. This part of the test will check your ability to recognize the relationships (signaled by transitions) within and between sentences. Read each passage and answer the questions that follow.

Passage 1

[1]In a chilly region of northeast England, a huge collection of artifacts has been uncovered, giving us a window on life in the year 100 A.D. when Roman soldiers and their families colonized a local hill fort. [2]Among the oldest historical documents found in Great Britain are letters written in Latin by six hundred people to their relatives in Rome. [3]On four thin wooden tablets, for instance, a man named Octavius complains because the roads are so bad. [4]In another letter, a Roman mother consoles her son in this desolate outpost and says she has sent him socks and underwear.

1. The relationship of sentences 3 and 4 to sentence 2 is one of
   a. contrast.   c. illustration.
   b. cause and effect.   d. comparison.

2. The relationship of sentence 4 to sentence 3 is one of
   a. addition.   c. contrast.
   b. comparison.   d. illustration.

Passage 2

[1]Although cultural norms and our environment produce many of the apparent differences between the sexes, scientific studies have shown some differences between men and women that seem to be inborn. [2]Studies have confirmed that the average female is more empathic, more able to share the feelings of those around her. [3]For instance, one study found that when male and female newborns hear another baby cry, the female babies are more likely to join in. [4]Other studies have shown males to do better in matters of hand-eye coordination. [5]This could explain why boys consistently do better in geometry and some of the sciences.

3. The relationship between the two parts of sentence 1 is one of
   a. addition.   c. illustration.
   b. contrast.   d. cause and effect.

4. The relationship of sentence 3 to sentence 2 is one of
   a. cause and effect.   c. time.
   b. illustration.   d. comparison.

(Continues on next page)

5. The relationship between sentences 4 and 5 is one of
   a. addition.
   b. contrast.
   c. cause and effect.
   d. illustration.

B. The five transitions in the box have been removed from the textbook passage below. Read the passage carefully to see which transition logically fits in each answer space. Then write in each transition.

Note: You may find it helpful to check (✓) each transition after you insert it into the passage.

such as	on the other hand	therefore
also	because	

In American culture, except in a few well-defined situations, touching is linked with intimate interpersonal relationships and is (6)_____ taboo for most other types of relationships. Many Americans refrain from touching others in more casual encounters for fear their behavior might be misconstrued or simply (7)_____ they are afraid of or do not like physical contact. When they must stand in line, Americans will usually form an orderly, single line in which everyone waits patiently for a turn. In Arab countries, (8)_____, lines are almost unheard of; in most gatherings, behavior (9)_____ pushing and touching is involved and is not considered distasteful. American children learn relatively young to kiss their relatives hello and goodbye. Spanish children frequently kiss not only their relatives but (10)_____ adult friends and acquaintances when they encounter them or depart from them.

TRANSITIONS: Test 6

A. This part of the test will check your ability to recognize the relationships (signaled by transitions) within and between sentences. Read each passage and answer the questions that follow.

Passage 1

[1]Susan Brodt and Philip Zimbardo brought shy and not-shy college women to the laboratory and had them converse with a handsome male who posed as a fellow subject. [2]Prior to the conversation, the women were cooped up in a small chamber and blasted with loud noise. [3]Some of the shy women (but not others) were told that the noise would leave them with a pounding heart, a common symptom of social anxiety. [4]Thus when these shy women later talked with the man, they were able to attribute their pounding hearts and any difficulties in the conversation to the noise rather than to their shyness or social inadequacy. [5]Compared to the shy women who were not given this handy explanation for their pounding hearts, these shy women were no longer so shy. [6]Like the non-shy women, they talked fluently once the conversation got going and asked questions of the man. [7]In fact, unlike the other shy women (whom the man could easily spot as shy), these shy women were to him indistinguishable from the not-shy women.

1. The relationship between the information in sentences 1 and 2 is one of
   a. cause and effect.   c. time.
   b. contrast.   d. comparison.

2. The relationship between sentences 3 and 4 is one of
   a. addition.   c. cause and effect.
   b. comparison.   d. contast.

3. Sentence 6 expresses a relationship of
   a. contrast.   c. addition.
   b. comparison.   d. time.

Passage 2

[1]The Anasazi Cliff Dwellers of Colorado, ancestors of today's Pueblo Indians, have always been venerated for their skill in constructing the elaborate maze of communal living quarters known as Mesa Verde. [2]They were also admired for their success in farming and irrigating the dry canyons of the Southwest. [3]However, new evidence of some less civilized customs has surprised many anthropologists and put the Anasazi culture in a whole

(Continues on next page)

new light. [4]Among the charred bones found in a ceremonial chamber were stacks of human remains. [5]Those people had been decapitated, dismembered, and roasted over an open fire, indicating that the skilled architects were also confirmed cannibals.

4. The relationship of sentence 2 to sentence 1 is one of
   a. addition.
   b. contrast.
   c. cause and effect.
   d. time.

5. The relationship of sentence 3 to sentences 1 and 2 is one of
   a. illustration.
   b. cause and effect.
   c. contrast.
   d. comparison.

B. The following five transitions have been removed from the textbook passage below. Read the passage carefully to see which transition logically fits in each answer space. Then write in each transition.

Note: You may find it helpful to check (✓) each transition after you insert it into the passage.

such as	finally	because
however	first	

     Sociologists and anthropologists typically divide subcultures into three types: racial groups, ethnic groups, and regional groups. Membership in the (6)_____ group, the racial group, is determined by genetically transmitted, physically observable traits to which people attach social meaning, both within the group and outside it. Membership in the ethnic group is determined by culturally transmitted, learned traits. Thus racial groups are not considered ethnic groups. For one thing, they are too large and too widespread to have recognizable, homogeneous cultures that can be transmitted. (7)_____, some racial subgroups do share certain cultural characteristics, (8)_____ language patterns; to the extent that their members share culturally transmitted traits, racial subgroups may be viewed as ethnic groups. (9)_____, a regional group is so classified (10)_____ its members exhibit certain values and tastes that are prevalent within their geographic area.

PATTERNS OF ORGANIZATION: Test 1

A. 1-5. Arrange the scrambled sentences below into a logical paragraph by numbering them *1, 2, 3, 4,* and *5* in an order that makes sense. Then circle the letter of the primary pattern of organization used.

Note that transitions will help you by clarifying the relationships between sentences.

_____ First of all, don't pick the most popular spot in town; it may be full of couples, and service to a single diner may be rushed.

_____ And finally, bring a book to read or a small amount of paperwork if you still feel self-conscious about dining alone.

_____ There are several tricks to feeling more comfortable when you are dining alone at a restaurant.

_____ Instead, try small ethnic restaurants, where eating alone is a more common sight.

_____ If in doubt, call ahead to ask if a restaurant encourages solo dining.

6. The passage's main pattern of organization is
a. cause and effect.   c. comparison.
b. list of items.   d. definition and example.

B. For each passage, write the number of the topic sentence in the space provided. Then circle the letter of the answer that identifies the primary pattern of organization of the passage.

7-8. ¹In the Bavarian, French, and Italian Alps, once-magnificent forests are slowly being destroyed by the effects of air pollution. ²Trees dying from pollution lose their leaves or needles, allowing sunlight to reach the forest floor. ³During this process, grass prospers in the increased light and pushes out the native plants and moss which help to hold rainwater. ⁴The soil thus loses absorbency and becomes hard, causing rain and snow to slide over the ground instead of sinking into it. ⁵This in turn results in erosion of the soil. ⁶After a heavy rain, the eroded land finally falls away in giant rockslides and avalanches, destroying entire villages and causing life-threatening floods.

Topic sentence: _____

Passage's main pattern of organization:
a. Definition and example
b. Cause and effect
c. Comparison

(Continues on next page)

285

9-10.   [1]A Pyrrhic (pir´-ik) victory is a victory won at such great cost that it amounts virtually to a defeat. [2]A good example of such a victory is provided by the person whose name the term comes from: Pyrrhus, a Greek mercenary general who invaded Italy and attacked the Romans in 281 B.C. [3]Pyrrhus defeated the Roman army sent against him, but his own army suffered terrible losses. [4]"One more such victory and I am ruined," he exclaimed. [5]The Battle of Borodino in 1812 was another classic instance of a Pyrrhic victory. [6]Napoleon's invading French army defeated a defending Russian army near Moscow and occupied the city. [7]But the French suffered so greatly from the battle and the winter that followed that the invasion turned into a disaster that cost Napoleon his throne.

Topic sentence: _____

Passage's main pattern of organization:
a. Time order
b. Definition and example
c. Cause and effect

PATTERNS OF ORGANIZATION: Test 2

A. 1-5. Arrange the scrambled sentences below into a logical paragraph by numbering them *1, 2, 3, 4,* and *5* in an order that makes sense. Then circle the letter of the primary pattern of organization used.

Note that transitions will help you by clarifying the relationships between sentences.

_____ During prolonged or severe labor, some newborns suffer from a specific type of asphyxia, known as birth asphyxia.

_____ The word comes from a Greek word meaning *stopping of the pulse.*

_____ Another tragic instance of asphyxia is the lack of oxygen suffered when a curious child becomes trapped accidentally inside a discarded trunk or refrigerator.

_____ Asphyxia is the medical term for the lack of oxygen in the body, leading to brain damage, or in prolonged cases, death.

_____ Yet another example is the mild asphyxia sometimes suffered by smokers as fumes containing tar and other gases replace the oxygen in their lungs.

6. The passage's main pattern of organization is
    a. time order.   c. contrast.
    b. cause and effect.   d. definition and example.

B. For each passage, put the number of the topic sentence in the space provided. Then circle the letter of the answer that identifies the primary pattern of organization of the passage.

7-8. ¹The M&M/Mars Company has had several changes of heart about red M&M's. ²In 1976, the Food and Drug Administration banned the use of Red Dye No. 2 as a food coloring after tests showed massive doses caused tumors in rats. ³Soon after, the company became concerned about consumer reaction and stopped producing red M&M's, even though they were made with FDA-approved red dyes. ⁴However, after nine years, red M&M's made a brief reappearance, in 1985 Christmas red-and-green holiday packs. ⁵According to company sources, this was followed by a huge popular demand for the red candies from such people as the University of Tennesee student who founded the Society for the Restoration and Preservation of Red M&M's. ⁶Two years after the red-and-green holiday packs were sold, red M&M's made their official permanent comeback in the regular variety package.

Topic sentence: _____

(Continues on next page)

Passage's main pattern of organization:
a. List of items
b. Comparison
c. Time order

9-10. [1]When the British colonized the New World in the seventeenth century, they brought their wives and families with them to establish communities. [2]Unlike them, Portuguese explorers who colonized Brazil in the 1500s arrived alone and lived in groups that were exclusively male. [3]Without any kind of family or community structure, these men lived in a frontier atmosphere that encouraged sexual exploitation of native Indian women and, later, African women who were brought in as slaves. [4]In contrast to those in the British colonies, white men and women of other races cohabited freely in Brazil, as did the generations that followed. [5]Because of this difference in the ways Brazil and the United States were colonized, racism became a dividing factor in this country, whereas most of Brazilian society today is mixed and racial conflict is almost unknown there.

Topic sentence: _____

The passage
a. defines colonization and illustrates that term in a time order.
b. presents a series of events in the order in which they happened.
c. contrasts the ways two countries were colonized and the two results.

PATTERNS OF ORGANIZATION: Test 3

A. 1-5. Arrange the scrambled sentences below into a logical paragraph by numbering them *1, 2, 3, 4,* and *5* in an order that makes sense. Then circle the letter of the primary pattern of organization used.

Note that transitions will help you by clarifying the relationships between sentences.

_____ The other group of pupils responded best to seeing the lessons, either written on the blackboard or printed on hand-out sheets.

_____ By the middle of the school year, one fourth-grade teacher was able to identify two different types of learners in her class.

_____ The teacher noted that the visual learners, unlike the listeners, often had difficulty following her spoken directions, even if she repeated them.

_____ These listeners had no trouble memorizing facts spoken by the teacher and were often heard repeating the lessons out loud to themselves so that they might learn them better.

_____ One group seemed to learn best by listening.

6. The passage's main pattern of organization is
   a. time order.   c. comparison.
   b. contrast.   d. cause and effect.

B. For each passage, put the number of the topic sentence in the space provided. Then circle the letter of the answer that identifies the primary pattern of organization of the passage.

7-8. [1]Crows, magpies, blue jays, and ravens—classified as corvids, or members of the crow family—display the highest level of intelligence in the bird world. [2]Captive crows and magpies, for example, have been taught to count, read clocks, open and close match boxes, and tie knots. [3]Jackdaws have been known to retrieve small bright household trinkets they have stolen, and blue jays can relocate thousands of acorns they have hidden away in remote spots. [4]Possibly the most amazing example of these birds' intelligence is the well-documented ability of hooded crows to pull up fishing lines from untended iceholes and steal a fisherman's entire catch.

Topic sentence: _____

The passage
a. contrasts types of birds.
b. explains why corvids are intelligent.
c. lists examples of the main idea.

(Continues on next page)

289

9-10.   ¹Shame exists in all cultures. ²But in Western culture in general and the United States in particular, shame is self-oriented, while in a country like Japan it is linked not to the self but to others. ³In America, if a child fails an exam, the child might feel terrible and be ashamed. ⁴A Japanese child, on the other hand, would be ashamed not because he or she failed but because the failure resulted in shame for the child's parents. ⁵Shame shows up in a similar way in the workplace. ⁶In Japan, if a company doesn't make a profit as a result of worker laziness, the worker will be ashamed. ⁷It's very hard to think of any American worker feeling ashamed that General Motors didn't make a profit. ⁸The Japanese corporation works because it is part of a social system in which the failure of the individual reflects upon the group. ⁹One feels shame for letting down the group, not the self.

Topic sentence: _____

Passage's main pattern of organization:
a. Time order
b. Contrast
c. Comparison

PATTERNS OF ORGANIZATION: Test 4

A. 1-5. Arrange the scrambled sentences below into a logical paragraph by numbering them *1, 2, 3, 4,* and *5* in an order that makes sense. Then circle the letter of the primary pattern of organization used.

Note that transitions will help you by clarifying the relationships between sentences.

_____ A part-time job provides a way to interact with others and escape the feeling of being trapped at home.

_____ But researchers at the University of Wisconsin are discovering that a part-time job away from home is good for new mothers for various reasons.

_____ Last, a regular paycheck, in addition to being an economic necessity for many, can reaffirm one's worth.

_____ New mothers today often agonize about whether or not to work outside the home after the baby is born.

_____ Working also occupies a lot of time that might be spent worrying about the baby or about one's parental abilities.

6. The passage
   a. provides a series of events in a new mother's life.
   b. lists reasons for new mothers to take part-time jobs.
   c. compares benefits and drawbacks of part-time jobs for new mothers.
   d. defines and illustrates part-time jobs for mothers.

B. For each passage, put the number of the topic sentence in the space provided. Then circle the letter of the answer that identifies the primary pattern of organization of the passage.

7-8. [1]The tendency for members of a group to conform to the prevailing opinions in the group is called *groupthink*. [2]Once a tentative decision has been made, members withhold information or opinions that might cast doubt on that course of action. [3]They do not want to be seen as criticizing their colleagues or as "rocking the boat." [4]If outside experts raise questions about the wisdom of their decision, members unite in opposing and discrediting the new information. [5]The classic example of "groupthink" occurred during President Kennedy's administration. [6]Kennedy sought the advice of a small group of trusted advisers in deciding whether to support the Bay of Pigs invasion of Cuba in 1961. [7]Although several advisers had strong objections to the plan, not one expressed doubts. [8]As far as Kennedy knew, his advisers were unanimously in favor. [9]The invasion was a military and public relations disaster.

(Continues on next page)

Topic sentence: _____

Passage's main pattern of organization:
a. List of items
b. Comparison
c. Definition and example

9-10.   [1]Lyle Rosenbaum and Steven Leventhal had no reason to suspect that their lives were unusual until they were 27 years old. [2]Then Lyle Rosenbaum walked into the same room with Steve Leventhal, and suddenly he was standing face to face with himself. [3]Steven and Lyle were identical twins who had been separated at birth. [4]During all those years, neither one had known that the other existed. [5]Having finally met, Lyle and Steven learned over the next several months that despite being separated from birth, their lives had been remarkably similar. [6]In meeting after meeting, they discovered identical interests, habits, and even quirks. [7]Some were expectable. [8]Both had done well in school, and both had prematurely gray hair. [9]But some of the similarities were almost spooky. [10]When they held a glass, both "held their pinkies in the air." [11]Both loved Donna Summer records, both owned the same make of car, both had been married since their late teens, both were nonsmokers despite having been raised in smoking households.

Topic sentence: _____

The passage combines the patterns of
a. time order and comparison.
b. contrast and definition-example.
c. list of items and cause-effect.

PATTERNS OF ORGANIZATION: Test 5

Read each textbook passage; then answer the question and complete the outline or map that follows.

A. Counselors use four main approaches of therapy on couples who seek their help. Psychodynamic therapy follows the idea that a couple's problems reflect unconscious conflicts within each individual and attempts to resolve them by bringing these hidden tensions to light. Family systems therapy concerns itself with identifying and breaking the destructive patterns that create a troubled relationship. Here the focus is not on the individual but on the organization of the relationship. Behavioral therapy looks at the observable actions and tries to change destructive behaviors by using results-oriented strategies like negotiation and compromise. Cognitive therapy analyzes the way each partner thinks about the other and attempts to point out the errors in those perceptions.

1. The passage
    a. narrates and explains causes.
    b. lists and defines.
    c. compares and illustrates.

2-5. Complete the outline of the paragraph.

Four main approaches of therapy for couples seeking help

1. _____ *—attempts to bring unconscious conflicts*

    to light _____

2. _____

    _____

3. _____

    _____

4. _____

    _____

(Continues on next page)

B.   Monogamy, or the practice of marrying one man and one woman only to one another, is just one of several marriage types that occur throughout the world. A separate but related form of marriage is serial monogamy, which allows a person to have several spouses in a lifetime, but only one at a time. There are two forms of polygamy, which allows persons to have multiple spouses at the same time. One variety is polygyny, in which one man has several wives at once. The other is polyandry, in which women are allowed multiple husbands.

6.   The main pattern of organization of the paragraph is
a. time order   b. list of items   c. cause and effect

7-10. Complete the map of the paragraph by filling in the missing heading and major and minor details.

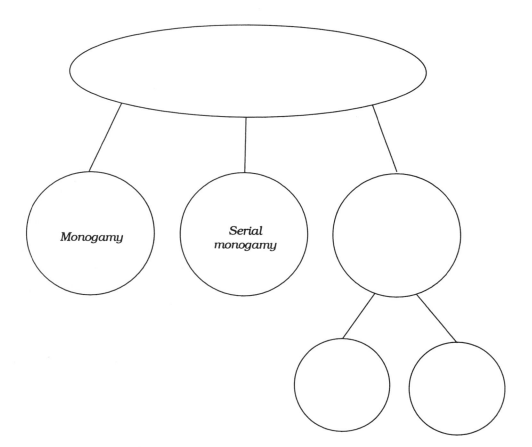

PATTERNS OF ORGANIZATION: Test 6

Read each textbook passage; then answer the question and complete the outline or map that follows.

A.   Forgetting can be embarrassing, inconvenient, and unpleasant. Why do you forget? There are several possibilities. For one thing, it is possible that you are not aware that the event occurred. Your sensory register may not have received the input. This type of problem is not usually referred to as forgetting, since you never really experienced or learned the information. Another possibility is that although you experienced something, you never processed it into short-term and long-term memory. Many memories of events are temporary and are not stored in either short-term or long-term memory. The third possibility is the area of greatest interest to psychologists. Items or events have been stored in long-term memory but are now difficult to bring back. Such recovery problems may be the result of repression, interference, disuse, or other factors.

   1. The paragraph is mainly a list of
      a. examples.
      b. causes.
      c. comparisons.
      d. definitions.

2-5. Complete the outline of the paragraph by filling in the heading and the three missing major details.

   _____

      1. _____

      2. _____

      3. _____

(Continues on next page)

B. Social class affects our *style of life*, the magnitude and manner of our consumption of goods and services. Convenience foods—TV dinners, potato chips, frozen pizza, and Hamburger Helper—are more frequently on the menus of lower-income than higher-income households. Lower-class families drink less vodka, scotch, and imported wine, but consume more blended whiskey and beer. Families in the middle and upper classes tend to buy furniture one piece at a time from specialty stores; lower-class families are more likely to buy matched sets from discount department stores or regular furniture stores. And lower-income families spend more of their leisure time watching television than do higher-income families.

6. The one pattern of organization *not* used in the paragraph is
   a. definition and example.
   b. time order.
   c. comparison and/or contrast.
   d. list of items.

7-10. Complete the chart of the passage by filling in the main idea and the blank boxes.

Main idea: _____

_____

Social class:

Style-of-life examples:		Lower Income	Higher Income
	Convenience foods	More	Less
	Alcoholic beverages	More blended whiskey and beer	More vodka, scotch, and imported wine
	Furniture		One piece at a time
	TV-watching		

SUMMARIZING AND OUTLINING: Test 1

A. Carefully read each opening statement (set off in **boldface**). Then decide whether each lettered statement that follows is basically the same in meaning or basically different in meaning from the opening statement. Write an *S* (for *Same*) next to the *two* statements where the meaning is closest to the original statement.

1-2. **Adults who were mistreated as children have a greater tendency to be violent than those who were not mistreated.**

_____ a. Children should never be yelled at.

_____ b. Children who are mistreated have little choice but to become violent adults.

_____ c. Violent adults tend to be people who were mistreated as children.

_____ d. The tendency toward violence, while powerful, can be controlled.

_____ e. A mistreated child is more likely to become a violent adult than is a child who is not mistreated.

_____ f. We could overcome the problem of violence in our society if only we tried harder.

3-4. **Tension headache, a condition common among people who suppress their emotions (and thus build up tension in their bodies), is usually caused by a tightening of the muscles of the head and neck.**

_____ a. Headaches of all kinds are caused by the tightening of muscles in the head and neck, a common symptom among people who suppress their emotions.

_____ b. Learning to relax will not affect the pain of a tension headache.

_____ c. People who suffer from tension headaches tend to have very aggressive personalities.

_____ d. Tension headaches are usually caused by tight head and neck muscles, common among those who hold back their emotions and thus tighten their muscles.

_____ e. When people bottle up their emotions, the stress they feel tends to tighten the muscles in their heads and necks.

_____ f. Tension headaches usually have a physical cause—tight head and neck muscles; that muscle tightness, in turn, has a psychological cause—the restraining of emotions.

(Continues on next page)

B. Again, carefully read each opening statement (set off in **boldface**). Then decide whether each lettered statement is basically the same in meaning or basically different in meaning from the opening statement. Write an *S* (for *Same*) next to the *three* statements (not two, as in the first part of the test) where the meaning is basically the same.

5-7. **Advertising research reveals that the most effective ads invoke both reasons ("You'll get whiter whites with Detergent X") and emotions ("the brand to use if you care about your family").**

_____ a. People whose emotions are easily touched are the most influenced by advertising.

_____ b. Research shows that the most effective ads are those which appeal to consumers' feelings about their families.

_____ c. Research shows that the most effective ads appeal to consumers' sense of logic and their feelings.

_____ d. Ads work best, research says, when they appeal both to consumers' rational and emotional sides.

_____ e. Consumers often buy products entirely on the basis of the emotional appeal of the advertising for those products.

_____ f. A combination of logical and emotional appeals works best in advertising, according to research.

8-10. **Compensation is stressing a strength in one area to hide a shortcoming in another.**

_____ a. We need to defend ourselves against people who try to make their weaknesses less noticeable than their strengths.

_____ b. Compensation involves having strengths and shortcomings in about equal amounts.

_____ c. When people wish to conceal a weakness of theirs, they may use compensation and emphasize a strength in another area instead.

_____ d. In order to hide a personal flaw, we may emphasize one of our strengths; this is called compensation.

_____ e. There are various ways in which we can conceal our weak points and emphasize our strong points.

_____ f. We are said to be using compensation when we emphasize a strength of ours in order to hide a defect.

SUMMARIZING AND OUTLINING: Test 2

A. Carefully read each opening statement (set off in **boldface**). Then decide whether each lettered statement that follows is basically the same in meaning or basically different in meaning from the opening statement. Write an *S* (for *Same*) next to the *two* statements where the meaning is closest to the original statement.

1-2. **Not all cultures have viewed death with fear; some have seen it in a neutral or even positive light, as a state of peace or a sleeplike trance.**

_____ a. Although many cultures have feared death, others have been more accepting of it as a neutral or positive state.

_____ b. Most cultures fear death as a sleeplike trance.

_____ c. Although a few cultures have feared death, most regard it in a neutral sense, as neither good nor bad.

_____ d. More and more cultures view death in a positive light.

_____ e. The world's cultures have looked upon death in various ways: fearfully, neutrally, or positively—as a peaceful sleeplike state.

_____ f. Death should be viewed in a positive light.

3-4. **No one denies that new evidence can change people's beliefs; our contention is simply that such changes generally occur slowly, and that more compelling evidence is often required to alter a belief than to create it.**

_____ a. People's beliefs can be changed by new evidence.

_____ b. It is usually takes more time and persuasive evidence for people to modify a belief than to create a new belief.

_____ c. People are slower to adopt a new belief than they are to modify an existing belief.

_____ d. Beliefs that change quickly generally do not last long.

_____ e. Changing an established belief happens slowly and takes more convincing evidence than is required to establish a new belief.

_____ f. Children's beliefs are more easily changed than those of adults.

(Continues on next page)

B. Again, carefully read each opening statement (set off in **boldface**). Then decide whether each lettered statement is basically the same in meaning or basically different in meaning from the opening statement. Write an *S* (for *Same*) next to the *three* statements (not two, as in the first part of the test) where the meaning is basically the same.

5-7. **When the straight commission plan is used, salespeople are paid an agreed-upon percentage of the price of everything they sell; under this plan, the salesperson receives no pay until a sale is made.**

_____ a. The straight commission plan is less fair to salespeople than a combined salary and commission plan.

_____ b. A salesperson working strictly on commission earns only a specified percentage of the sales he or she makes.

_____ c. Salespeople working on commission often earn more money than salespeople working for a salary.

_____ d. Under the straight commission plan, salespeople are paid only an agreed-upon percentage of the price of each sale.

_____ e. The percentage that a salesperson on commission earns on a sale depends upon how long he or she has been working for a company.

_____ f. The earnings of salespeople on the straight commission plan are made up of a percentage of the price of whatever they sell.

8-10. **Regression is a defense mechanism in which a person avoids assuming responsibility by pretending that he or she is unable to do something instead of admitting to being simply unwilling.**

_____ a. When people avoid responsibility by saying they are unable to do what is required when they are really unwilling, they are using the defense mechanism of regression.

_____ b. People are more understanding when you tell them you can't do something than they are when you tell them you don't want to, which may account for the defense mechanism of regression.

_____ c. If you say you don't want to do something, you cannot later be held responsible for the outcome of others' actions.

_____ d. When you pretend you can't do something instead of admitting you don't want to, you are using a defense mechanism called regression.

_____ e. People who consistently avoid taking responsibility by pretending to be incapable soon lose the respect of those around them.

_____ f. Regression is the defense mechanism of making the pretense of inability instead of admitting unwillingness.

SUMMARIZING AND OUTLINING: Test 3

A. Carefully read each opening statement (set off in **boldface**). Then decide whether each lettered statement that follows is basically the same in meaning or basically different in meaning from the opening statement. Write an *S* (for *Same*) next to the *three* statements where the meaning is closest to the original statement.

1-3. **When we are looking for a mate, we tend to zero in on potential partners whose ethnic, religious, economic, and educational background closely approximates our own.**

_____ a. People tend to seek a life partner with socioeconomic, educational, and religious experience much like their own.

_____ b. Marriages between people from extremely different backgrounds are usually not happy.

_____ c. The reason that people marry others from similar backgrounds is they have little opportunity to get to know other kinds of people.

_____ d. Most people look for mates with backgrounds that resemble their own.

_____ e. Most people do not deliberately search for potential marriage partners.

_____ f. Most people want their mate to be someone with a similar cultural, economic, and educational background.

4-6. **Many people object to the idea of asking for details when they are criticized; their resistance grows from confusing the act of listening open-mindedly to a speaker's comments with accepting them.**

_____ a. Paying close attention to someone's criticism of you means that you agree with whatever they are saying.

_____ b. Many resist asking for the details of others' criticism of them because of the belief that merely listening to the criticism means admitting it is true.

_____ c. Confusing listening objectively to criticism with accepting it leads many people to resist asking for details when criticized.

_____ d. Listening open-mindedly to criticism of oneself will soon lead one to accepting those comments.

_____ e. Many don't wish to hear detailed criticism of themselves because they think paying attention to the criticism would mean agreeing with it.

_____ f. The best way to deal with criticism you believe is unfair is to refuse to ask the critic to supply any details.

(Continues on next page)

B. Circle the letter of the answer that best summarizes each selection that follows.

7. Emotions seem to be part of what makes us human. But what are they for? Do emotions merely make life more interesting, or are they actually necessary? Psychologists asking these questions have identified three functions of emotions. First, emotions help prepare us for action. As an example, if we saw an angry dog charging towards us, our emotional reaction (fear) would trigger changes in our nervous system, thus preparing us to run away. Emotions also help shape our future behavior. Again, when we feel fear of the dog, we learn to avoid similar situations. Finally, emotions help regulate social interaction. Our observation of other people's emotional states determines how we respond to them. For example, if we notice that another person is experiencing fear, we may be moved to comfort and reassure him.

   a. One important way in which emotions are helpful is in shaping our future behavior. Our fear of dangerous situations, for instance, helps us to avoid them in the future.

   b. Psychologists have distinguished three functions of emotions in our lives. Emotions can prepare us to take action, shape our future behavior, or regulate our social interaction.

   c. Psychologists have studied the necessity of emotion in human life. Emotions appear to be part of what makes us uniquely human.

   d. Psychologists have observed that emotions help prepare us for action. For example, the fear generated by seeing an angry dog charging toward us can prepare us to run away.

8. Why is prostitution considered a social problem? Different groups and different historical periods provide different answers. Those who object to prostitution can be divided into four categories. The first group objects for moral reasons. Some say that prostitution is immoral because it involves sexual behavior between people who are not married to one another, others that the selling of sex is what makes prostitution deviant, and still others that prostitutes and their customers are sexually deviant because they engage in unusual sexual activities. A second group considers prostitution to be part of a larger social problem—the injustice of society. Prostitution exploits the body, degrades the spirit, and continually subjugates women to men. A third group contends that prostitution is a social problem because it ruins "good" neighborhoods. The fourth sees prostitution as a social problem because it violates the law.

   a. Prostitution has always been a problem, with different historical periods having different reasons for considering prostitution to be immoral.

   b. The fact that it involves sexual behavior between unmarried people is the most widespread reason for considering prostitution a social problem.

   c. The immorality of prostitution, its role in larger social problems, its damaging effects upon neighborhoods, and its illegal nature are all equally valid reasons to consider it a serious social problem.

   d. People who consider prostitution a social problem object to it either on the grounds that it is immoral, that it plays a role in larger societal injustices, that it damages neighborhoods, or that it's against the law.

SUMMARIZING AND OUTLINING: Test 4

A. Carefully read each opening statement (set off in **boldface**). Then decide whether each lettered statement that follows is basically the same in meaning or basically different in meaning from the opening statement. Write an *S* (for *Same*) next to the *three* statements where the meaning is closest to the original statement.

1-3. **Courage is not the absence of fear; it is seeing your fear in a realistic perspective and choosing to function in spite of the risk.**

_____ a. Courageous people are not those who don't feel fear—they are people who confront their fear and act bravely anyway.

_____ b. Only a very foolish person would never have fear.

_____ c. Courage does not mean having no fear, but realistically facing fear and acting despite it.

_____ d. Truly courageous people are those who have trained themselves to never experience fear, despite the situation.

_____ e. People who are unaware of fear are just as courageous as people who choose to function in spite of their fear.

_____ f. Courage means seeing a frightening situation realistically—as opposed to having no fear—and still functioning.

4-6. **High population growth rates assault the environment in two ways— through increased resource depletion and pollution.**

_____ a. Family planning is essential if we are to preserve the environment.

_____ b. Pollution and overuse of resources are the negative environmental effects of a high rate of population growth.

_____ c. Using up our natural resources and pollution are two important ways in which our environment is being harmed.

_____ d. A high rate of population growth harms the environment by exhausting natural assets and contaminating the natural surroundings.

_____ e. Pollution and overuse of resources are the ways in which great increases in population injure the environment.

_____ f. The environment is damaged by increased resource depletion, pollution, and high population growth rates.

B. Circle the letter of the answer that best summarizes each selection that follows.

7. If the 1950s had a symbol, it was the automobile: big, boxy, glittering with chrome, sprouting ever more outrageous fins, and careening down the road with the roar of an overpowered V-8 engine. A four-door Plymouth, Ford, or Chevy sedan served

(Continues on next page)

both for commuting and for driving the family to church. Rich kids and young-at-heart adults drove sporty convertibles. Harried suburban housewives preferred a station wagon to tote children and groceries. For the upwardly mobile executive or celebrity, a Cadillac, Lincoln, or Imperial was a must. Their huge wheelbases, Torque Flight transmissions, and feather-touch power steering gave them about as much feel for the road as a slab of ice slaloming down the road.

a. Executives and celebrities in the '50s drove huge Cadillacs, Lincolns, or Imperials. Those cars had huge wheelbases, expensive transmissions, and sensitive power steering that blotted out any sense of the road one was on.

b. People in different segments of society have different automotive needs. Families tend toward four-door sedans, the rich and young-at-heart prefer sporty convertibles, overly busy housewives like station wagons, and executives and celebrities go for the expensive, fancy cars.

c. The 1950s were symbolized by large, powerful, showy cars that came in various models to suit the needs and desires of various segments of the population.

8. The American criminal justice system is not equipped to deal with white-collar crime. Unlike a robbery, a stock or insurance fraud is complex and difficult to unravel. Local law enforcement officials commonly lack the skills and resources necessary to tackle crimes outside the sphere of street crime. Federal agencies will handle only the more serious white-collar crimes. And the handful of white-collar criminals who are prosecuted and convicted are given a slap on the wrist. Street criminals who steal $100 may find their way to prison, while the dishonest executive who embezzles $1 million may receive a suspended sentence and a relatively small fine. Federal statistics indicate that embezzlers at banks steal nine times more than bank robbers. Yet whereas only 17 percent of the embezzlers go to jail, 91 percent of bank robbers end up in jail.

a. The American criminal justice system is not equipped to deal with white-collar crime. Local law enforcement officials don't have the skills or resources to tackle crimes outside the sphere of street crime. And federal law enforcement officials are interested only in the most serious white-collar crimes.

b. The American criminal justice system does a poor job dealing with white-collar crime. White collar crime includes stock and insurance fraud, which is difficult to understand. The most serious white collar crime is handled by the federal government.

c. Our criminal justice system handles white-collar crime poorly. Local officials aren't equipped to handle it, and federal agencies handle only the more serious white-collar crimes. Also, the punishments in this arena are unjust, as even the worst white-collar criminals usually receive much milder sentences than street criminals.

SUMMARIZING AND OUTLINING: Test 5

1. Circle the letter of the answer that best summarizes the selection that follows.

    Sometimes people tell us nice things about ourselves in order to influence us: "You really look nice today." "That was a very intelligent decision." Or they tell us they share our views on things: "I also agree with your position on the Middle East." "You took the words right out of my mouth." Such attempts at influence are called flattery.

    A common saying is that "flattery will get you everywhere." While it sometimes works, it can also fail to get results. Andrew Colman reports that it works best with people who have a good self-image. They are more likely to believe the nice things said because they fit their image. On the other hand, people with a poor self-image are likely to reject such attempts. Telling them they are nice, have good ideas, and other complimentary things does not fit their image. Coleman also notes that flattery is typically more successful when it comes from someone who has higher status than us. We find such people more credible than those of lower status. Thus a teacher could more easily influence a student; a parent, a child; an army general, a private; and a company president, a clerk through flattery. It would be more difficult for flattery to work in the opposite direction.

    a. According to Andrew Colman, flattery is the effort to influence people through complimenting them or agreeing with them. Examples of remarks intended to flatter include "You look nice today" and "I also agree with your position on the Middle East."
    b. A common saying is that "flattery will get you everywhere," but this is unlikely to be true with people with a poor self-image.
    c. Flattery is the effort to influence through positive attention. According to Andrew Colman, flattery works best with people who have a good self-image and when it comes from someone with higher status.
    d. According to Andrew Colman, flattery is typically more successful when it comes from someone of higher status since we find such people more credible than those of lower status. Thus a teacher could probably successfully influence a student through flattery.

2. Circle the letter of the outline notes that best summarize the selection that follows.

    According to Margaret Mead, children typically pass through three stages in developing a self: an imitation stage, a play stage, and a game stage. In the first stage, children imitate other people without understanding what they are doing. They may "read" a book, but the behavior lacks meaning for them. Even so, such imitation is important because children are preparing themselves to take the stance of others and act as they do. In the play stage, children act such roles as mother,

(Continues on next page)

police officer, teacher, Mrs. Elliot, and so on. They take the role of only one other person at a time and "try on" the person's behavior. The model, typically a person central to the child's life, is termed by sociologists a significant other. For instance, a two-year-old child may examine a doll's pants, pretend to find them wet, and reprimand the doll. Presumably the child views the situation from the perspective of the parent and acts as the parent would act.

Whereas in the play stage children take the role of only one other person at a time, in the game stage they assume many roles. Much as in a baseball game, a person must take into account the intentions and expectations of several people. For instance, if the batter bunts the ball down the third-base line, the pitcher must know what the catcher, the shortstop, and the first, second, and, third basemen will do. In the game, children must assume the roles of numerous individuals in contrast to simply the role of one other person. To do so, they must abstract a "composite" role out of the concrete roles of particular people. These notions are extended to embrace all people in similar situations—the "team." In other words, children fashion a generalized other—they come to view their behavior from the standpoint of the larger group or community.

A. Margaret Mead's stages of child self-development
  1. Imitation stage—imitating others' behavior that has no meaning for child
  2. Preparation for the mature attitude and behavior of others
  3. Play stage—acting the role of a one other person at a time
  4. "Trying on" the behavior of a significant other
  5. Game stage—assuming and taking into account many roles
  6. Viewing one's behavior from the standpoint of a larger group or community

B. How children develop
  1. They prepare themselves to take the stance of others and act as they do.
  2. They take the role of only one other person at a time and "try on" the person's behavior.
  3. They assume many roles.

C. Margaret Mead's view of child self-development: three stages
  1. Imitation stage—imitating others' behavior that has no meaning for child
    - Function: preparation for the mature attitude and behavior of others
    - Example: a child "reads" a book
  2. Play stage—acting the role of one other person at a time
    - Function: "Trying on" the behavior of a significant other
    - Examples: Acting like mother, police officer, teacher
  3. Game stage—assuming and taking into account many roles
    - Function: viewing one's behavior from the standpoint of a larger group or community
    - Example: baseball pitcher interacting with other team members

SUMMARIZING AND OUTLINING: Test 6

1. Circle the letter of the answer that best summarizes the selection that follows.

> In its moderate form, the black power movement encouraged blacks to recover their cultural roots and achieve a new sense of identity. African clothes and natural hairstyles became popular. On college campuses black students pressed universities to hire black faculty, institute black studies programs, and provide segregated social and residential space. Black militants, on the other hand, saw black power as an element of a broader Marxist ideology that held violence to be a useful revolutionary tool. The most militant among militants was the Black Panther Party of Oakland, California. The Panthers, led by Huey P. Newton and Eldridge Cleaver, shocked white sensibilities by calling for the black community to arm themselves.

  a. The Black Panther Party, led by Huey Newton and Eldridge Cleaver, represented a more accurate expression of the black power movement than did the university-centered trend to reclaim blacks' heritage and sense of identity.

  b. The moderate form of the black power movement emphasized the recovery of blacks' cultural heritage, while the militant form, as seen in the Black Panthers, emphasized the need for a violent, Marxist-based revolution.

  c. The black power movement led to greater popularity of African fashions, changes in university programs, and the formation of the Black Panther Party.

  d. Because of the black power movement, African styles became popular. In addition, black students on college campuses pressed for the hiring of more black faculty members, the addition of black studies programs, and segregated social and residential space.

2. Read the following selection. Then circle the letter of the outline notes that best summarize the selection.

> The autonomic nervous system is composed of all the neurons that carry messages between the central nervous system and all the internal organs of the body. The autonomic nervous system consists of two branches: the sympathetic and parasympathetic divisions. These two divisions act in almost total opposition to each other, but both are directly involved in controlling and integrating the actions of the glands and the smooth muscles within the body.
>
> The nerve fibers of the sympathetic division are busiest when you are frightened or angry. They carry messages that tell the body to prepare for an emergency and to get ready to act quickly or strenuously. In response to messages from the sympathetic division, your heart pounds, you breathe faster, your pupils enlarge, and digestion stops.
>
> Parasympathetic nerve fibers connect to the same organs as the sympathetic

(Continues on next page)

307

nerve fibers, but they cause just the opposite effects. The parasympathetic division says, in effect, "Okay, the heat's off, back to normal." The heart then goes back to beating at its normal rate, the stomach muscles relax, digestion starts again, breathing slows down, and the pupils of the eyes get smaller. Thus, the parasympathetic division compensates for the sympathetic division and lets the body rest after stress.

A. The body's response to emergencies: the sympathetic division and the parasympathetic division
  1. Function: prepares body for emergency when someone is frightened or angry
  2. Physical responses: pounding heart, faster breathing, enlarged pupils, halted digestion
  3. After the emergency: the parasympathetic division
     a. Function: normalizes the body after an emergency
     b. Physical responses: return to normal heart rate, relaxed stomach muscles, resumed digestion, normalized breathing, reduced pupil size

B. The autonomic nervous system: two-branched system that controls and integrates the work of the glands and smooth muscles through neurons carrying messages between the central nervous system and all the internal organs
  1. Sympathetic division
     a. Function: prepares body for emergency when someone is frightened or angry
     b. Physical responses: pounding heart, faster breathing, enlarged pupils, halted digestion
  2. Parasympathetic division
     a. Function: normalizes the body after an emergency
     b. Physical responses: return to normal heart rate, relaxed stomach muscles, resumed digestion, normalized breathing, reduced pupil size

C. The sympathetic division of the autonomic nervous system prepares the body for emergencies when the person is frightened or angry.
  1. When someone is frightened or angry, the nerve fibers are busiest; they then carry messages.
     a. This prepares the body for an emergency.
     b. This prepares the body to act quickly or strenuously.
     c. In response, your body changes in various ways.
        1) Your heart pounds.
        2) You breathe faster.
        3) Your pupils enlarge.
        4) Your digestion stops.
  2. After the emergency, the parasympathetic division causes the body to relax.
     a. Your heartbeart normalizes.
     b. Your breathing slows down.
     c. Your pupils get smaller.
     d. The stomach muscles relax.

FACT AND OPINION: Test 1

A. Five of the statements below are facts, and five are opinions. Identify statements of fact with an **F** and statements of opinion with an **O**.

_____ 1. The United States government was given the right to tax its citizens in 1913 in the 16th Amendment to the Constitution.

_____ 2. It is unfair for elderly people living on fixed incomes to have to pay income taxes.

_____ 3. Ranchers should not be allowed to hunt and trap wolves.

_____ 4. Timber wolves mate for life.

_____ 5. Japanese geishas are women trained to entertain men through singing, dancing and amusing talk.

_____ 6. Few Western women can match the grace and charm of the professional geisha.

_____ 7. The best time of the year to visit New England is in the fall when the trees change color.

_____ 8. Douglas Corrigan got the nickname "Wrong Way" Corrigan in 1938 when he landed his airplane in Ireland instead of his destination— Long Beach, California.

_____ 9. Corrigan accomplished his solo flight in twenty-eight hours in a $900 airplane.

_____ 10. Not even Disney World surpasses Disney's greatest contribution to American culture—Mickey Mouse.

(Continues on next page)

B. Here are short reviews taken from a newspaper movie guide. Some reviews provide only factual reports; others contain opinions about the movie as well. Identify the factual reviews with an **F**; identify reviews that also contain an opinion with an **F + O**.

_____ 11. **The Survivors, '83.** Walter Matthau, Robin Williams. Michael Ritchie's disappointing social satire about two unemployed men thrown together when they're stalked by a professional hit man.

_____ 12. **Five Graves to Cairo, '43.** Franchot Tone, Anne Baxter. Exciting mystery has a wartime setting, behind German lines in Egypt while Rommel is pummeling North Africa.

_____ 13. **Live Wire, '92.** Pierce Brosnan, Ron Silver. A bomb expert must save Washington from a terrorist who makes ordinary things explode.

_____ 14. **Silver Streak, '76.** Gene Wilder, Jill Clayburgh. Entertaining comedy-thriller about an innocent man enmeshed in an international murder plot.

_____ 15. **Hooper, '78.** Burt Reynolds, Jan Michael Vincent. Above-average Reynolds smash-'em-up about Hollywood stunt men.

_____ 16. **Body Parts, '91.** Jeff Fahey, Lindsay Duncan. A psychologist loses his arm in an accident and gets another grafted on, from a serial killer.

_____ 17. **Hot Stuff, '79.** Dom DeLuise, Suzanne Pleshette. A weak comedy about four cops trying to trap crooks.

_____ 18. **Mermaids, '90.** Cher, Winona Ryder. A teenager, her kid sister, and their mother move to a new town in the early 1960s.

_____ 19. **Network, '76.** Faye Dunaway, Peter Finch. Muddled but effective satire of television-news ethics.

_____ 20. **In the Heat of the Night, '67.** Sidney Poitier. Oscar-winning mystery about a Philadelphia cop caught up in a murder investigation in an unfriendly Mississippi town.

FACT AND OPINION: Test 2

A. Four of the statements below are facts, and three are opinions; in addition, three include both fact and opinion. Identify facts with an **F**, opinions with an **O**, and statements of fact *and* opinion with an **F + O**.

_____ 1. Train travel is far more romantic and educational than traveling by air.

_____ 2. Traveling by train is slower than flying, but the added interest of the trip makes the extra time worthwhile.

_____ 3. The number of people who travel by train has gone down steadily since commercial air travel was introduced.

_____ 4. Beaches along the East Coast are occasionally closed because of rubbish in the water, including sewage and vials of blood from medical laboratories.

_____ 5. The poisoning of our oceans is the most shameful legacy we can leave to future generations.

_____ 6. Severe punishments should be given to those guilty of illegal dumping in the ocean, many of whom have not yet been identified.

_____ 7. Retrievers and other hunting dogs are bred to have mouths that won't damage the game they bring back.

_____ 8. Vacant buildings ought to be turned into apartment buildings for the homeless.

_____ 9. The Roman city of Pompeii, destroyed by a volcanic eruption in 79 A.D. that preserved parts of it, remains the most interesting record we have of life at that time.

_____ 10. Bakeries, toolmakers' shops and restaurants, as well as graffiti on the walls, tell us something of what life was like in Pompeii at the time of the eruption.

(Continues on next page)

B. Each paragraph below includes five sentences. Three sentences express facts, and two express opinions. In the spaces provided, identify facts with an **F** and opinions with an **O**.

[11]Hunter "Patch" Anderson, M.D. is the founder of the Gesundheit Institute of Arlington, Virginia. [12]The institute is probably the world's most unusual. [13]It is dedicated to promoting health through laughter. [14]Anderson himself has a weird sense of humor. [15]He sometimes wears bright mismatched socks, a fish-shaped necktie and a rubber clown nose.

11. _____   12. _____   13. _____   14. _____   15. _____

[16]The greatest fraud ever committed was the presentation of the radio drama *The War of the Worlds*. [17]On October 30, 1938, the Mercury Theater of the Air presented the play about Martians invading Earth. [18]The broadcast proved beyond doubt that people will believe anything they hear. [19]Panic set in among listeners who believed the play was reality; the panic centered around Grovers Mill, New Jersey, where—in the play—the aliens had landed. [20]Hundreds of listeners were treated for shock and hysteria in hospital emergency rooms.

16. _____   17. _____   18. _____   19. _____   20. _____

FACT AND OPINION: Test 3

A. Some of the statements below are facts, some are opinions, and two include both fact and opinion. Identify facts with an **F**, opinions with an **O**, and statements of fact *and* opinion with an **F + O**.

_____ 1. The first zoo in the United States was the Philadelphia Zoological Gardens, which opened in 1874.

_____ 2. It's unfair for zoos to display animals in small cages and confining exhibit areas.

_____ 3. It's unfortunate that the koala, hunted for both fur and food, is now an endangered species.

_____ 4. The koala, a native of Australia, gets all its nourishment from one tree, the eucalyptus; it doesn't even need to add water to its diet.

_____ 5. Every nature-loving person should be a member of the World Wildlife Federation, an organization working on behalf of endangered species.

_____ 6. About 12,000 years ago, the wildlife in Alaska included elephants, lions, and camels.

_____ 7. The Internal Revenue Service has the power to seize the property of people who cheat on taxes.

_____ 8. Cheating on taxes isn't as bad as some other crimes, such as robbery.

_____ 9. A university study shows that heavy drug use seriously affects a teenager's transition to adulthood.

_____ 10. The most appropriate sentence for convicted drug pushers is life imprisonment.

(*Continues on next page*)

B. Each paragraph below contains five sentences. Some sentences express facts, and some express opinions. In addition, each paragraph includes one statement of fact and opinion. Identify facts with an **F**, opinions with an **O**, and statements of fact *and* opinion with an **F + O**.

[11]Americans celebrate some of the strangest holidays in the world. [12]Regional celebrations around the country include Graveyard Cleaning and Decoration Day and the Rattlesnake Roundup. [13]In Churubusco, Indiana, Turtle Day celebrates Oscar, a six-foot-long turtle. [14]Oscar was spotted by a local minister and farmer in 1948. [15]The least appealing of all American holidays must be Buzzard Day, which is the day the buzzards return to Hinckley, Ohio.

11. _____   12. _____   13. _____   14. _____   15. _____

[16]Since 1969, Miles Laboratories has manufactured Flintstone vitamins for children. [17]The vitamins come in the shape of cave-dwelling cartoon characters Fred Flintstone, Wilma Flintstone, Barney Rubble, Dino the dinosaur, children Pebbles and Bamm Bamm, and even Fred's car. [18]Curiously absent from the cast of vitamin characters is one of the most interesting of the Flintstone characters, Betty Rubble. [19]Spokespeople at Miles Laboratories say that when Betty is shrunk to vitamin size, she is too easily confused with Wilma. [20]Some way really ought to be found to include Wilma in the Flintstone vitamin group.

16. _____   17. _____   18. _____   19. _____   20. _____

FACT AND OPINION: Test 4

A. Some of the statements below are facts, some are opinions, and some include both fact and opinion. Identify facts with an **F**, opinions with an **O**, and statements of fact *and* opinion with an **F + O**.

_____ 1. P. T. Barnum's first "Greatest Show on Earth" circus opened in 1871, and it thoroughly lived up to its name.

_____ 2. Strong men, wild animal acts, and clowns were some of the attractions featured in Barnum's early circuses.

_____ 3. Today, the best circuses are to be found in Russia.

_____ 4. The first *Encyclopaedia Britannica* was published in 1771 in three volumes.

_____ 5. In a stroke of genius, the designers of the encyclopedia's fifteenth edition organized it according to an "outline of knowledge."

_____ 6. The fifteenth edition, which appeared in 1974, is made up of about 43 million words—words on every topic worth knowing about.

_____ 7. Nevertheless, the *Encyclopaedia Britannica* is entirely too expensive.

_____ 8. Visitors to the town of Winslow, Arizona, can see a meteor crater that is three-quarters of a mile across and six hundred feet deep.

_____ 9. The Winslow crater is one of the greatest natural wonders of America.

_____ 10. Every day, millions of meteors fall into our atmosphere, where the friction burns them down to nothing.

(Continues on next page)

315

B. Each paragraph below contains five sentences. Some sentences express facts, and some express opinions. In addition, each paragraph includes one statement of fact and opinion. Identify facts with an **F**, opinions with an **O**, and statements of fact *and* opinion with an **F + O**.

[11]A researcher who studied "fetal soap addiction" claims that babies can get interested in soap operas before they are born. [12]According to the study, unborn babies whose mothers regularly watch a soap opera become very familiar with the program's musical theme and voices. [13]Although it's hard to believe, the study says that after these babies are born, they will stop crying and calmly watch the soap opera whenever it comes on. [14]While this information is fascinating, such studies are a waste of taxpayers' money. [15]Instead, scientists should stick to issues that will improve our health and our environment.

11. _____   12. _____   13. _____   14. _____   15. _____

[16]Margaret Sanger is the most important figure in the history of family planning. [17]As one of eleven children, Sanger, born in 1883, witnessed difficulties in her mother's life that had been caused by her frequent pregnancies. [18]As an adult, Sanger worked as a maternity nurse and became further interested in helping women limit the size of their families. [19]She sought repeatedly to learn more about contraception, but ridiculously outdated sexist attitudes made such information almost impossible to get. [20]Sanger persisted and succeeded in opening the world's first birth control clinic in Brooklyn in 1916.

16. _____   17. _____   18. _____   19. _____   20. _____

FACT AND OPINION: Test 5

A. Five of the following textbook excerpts are facts, four are opinions, and three include both fact and opinion. Identify facts with an **F**, opinions with an **O**, and statements of fact *and* opinion with an **F + O**.

_____ 1. The age of the average soldier serving in Vietnam was 19, compared with 26 for World War II.

_____ 2. Not only was Henry Clay an outstanding leader; he was also the most charming and colorful of American statesmen.

_____ 3. Trained as a psychoanalyst in Germany, Karen Horney came to the United States in 1934.

_____ 4. American painting in the early 19th century was of a quality comparable to that of contemporary European work.

_____ 5. It would be impossible to find a more representative figure of the Italian Renaissance than Leonardo da Vinci, creator of *The Last Supper* and *Mona Lisa.*

_____ 6. On April 4, 1968, Martin Luther King, Jr., traveled to Memphis to lead a demonstration in support of striking sanitation workers; he was assassinated that same day.

_____ 7. From a prison cell, King produced one of the most eloquent documents of the civil rights movement, his "Letter from Birmingham Jail."

_____ 8. It is advertising that provides the financing for for-profit television.

_____ 9. Ross Perot clearly was the best candidate in the 1992 presidential race.

_____ 10. Perhaps the most disturbing problem that vexed the nation in the Carter years was a soaring, double-digit inflation rate, which went all the way up to 13 percent.

_____ 11. Nothing illustrated better the raucous and intolerant quality of nationalism than the organization and growth of the Ku Klux Klan.

_____ 12. We can dream in black and white and in color.

(Continues on next page)

B. Identify factual sentences with an **F**, sentences that express opinion with an **O**, and the one sentence containing both fact *and* opinion with an **F + O**.

> [13]The 1955 movie *The Conqueror*, which starred John Wayne in the role of Mongol ruler Genghis Khan, was for several reasons one of the worst movies of all time. [14]To begin with, Wayne was ridiculously miscast in this movie. [15]Also, the movie was shot in the canyonlands of Utah, where the ground and air were contaminated by radioactive fallout from atomic bomb tests in nearby Nevada. [16]By 1988, ninety-one of the 220 people who worked on the set of *The Conqueror* had developed cancer, and forty-six, including Wayne, had died of it. [17]The fallout from the bomb tests is certainly to blame for all those cases of cancer.

13. _____   14. _____   15. _____   16. _____   17. _____

C. Read the following passage from the book *Biologic: Environmental Protection by Design* by David Wann. Then identify each listed excerpt from the passage as either fact (**F**) or opinion (**O**).

> It is well documented that existing automobile prototypes are far more efficient than today's cars and that some get more than 80 miles per gallon. Our first strategy should be to insist that they be put on the market. Burning far less fuel will automatically reduce pollution. . . .
>
> We don't want only one type of car. We need electric cars for some uses and organically fueled cars for other uses. And we need to think about leasing, sharing, and co-owning vehicles, too. Several apartment complexes across the country have successful car-sharing programs. Participants sign up for "cartime" and make their travel arrangements accordingly, thus avoiding the need for families to own second cars. This works especially well when a long-distance car is only used occasionally. In such a case, a "city car" (maybe electric) could meet most of a family's requirements with high efficiency.

18. _____ Our first strategy should be to insist that they be put on the market.

19. _____ Burning far less fuel will automatically reduce pollution.

20. _____ We need electric cars for some uses and organically fueled cars for other uses.

FACT AND OPINION: Test 6

A. Read the following textbook excerpts and identify facts with an **F**, opinions with an **O**, and the *two* statements that mix fact *and* opinion with an **F + O**.

_____ 1. In the fourteenth century a fascinating chapter of history began when the warlike Aztecs came down from the north and founded a city on an island in Lake Tezcoco.

_____ 2. Blacks constitute the largest racial minority group in the United States, numbering roughly 28.5 million persons and representing about 13 percent of the population.

_____ 3. As a general, Washington was not a brilliant strategist like Napoleon.

_____ 4. As secretary of state under Lincoln and Andrew Johnson, William Henry Seward averted direct European interference in the Civil War through skillful diplomacy, and the breadth of his intellect and vision led him to dream dreams beyond those of most politicians.

_____ 5. While fifteenth-century Venice was a city of narrow, crooked alleys and canals, nineteenth-century Boston was increasingly developed in a gridlike pattern, with rows of parallel streets crisscrossing others at right angles.

_____ 6. The major aim of consumer education should be to teach consumers how to spend their money, time, and energy to bring expressed wants into harmony with considered needs.

B. Read the following textbook passage. Identify each listed excerpt from the passage as either a fact (**F**) or an opinion (**O**).

Uncle Tom's Cabin was one of the most important and controversial of American novels. Written by Harriet Beecher Stowe, the novel was a young woman's response to the Fugitive Slave Act. Although the act was probably responsible for sending only about three hundred slaves back to the South, Stowe was outraged by it, calling it a "nightmare abomination."

Uncle Tom's Cabin, or Life Among the Lowly first appeared in serial form in the *National Era*, an abolitionist journal. Although simplistic and often overly melodramatic, the novel was also deeply affecting. Indeed, sales reached 300,000 copies within a year. However, not everyone welcomed Stowe's work. In the South, Stowe was criticized as naive or a liar. In one

(Continues on next page)

infamous incident, she received an anonymous parcel containing the ear of a disobedient slave. When Stowe was faced with the charge that the book was deceitful, she answered with *A Key to Uncle Tom's Cabin*, which provided documentation that every incident in the novel had actually happened.

In 1862, Lincoln met Harriet Beecher Stowe and reportedly said, "So you're the little woman that wrote the book that made this great war." Indeed, although the copies sold can be counted, the emotional impact of Stowe's novel will never be fully known.

7. _____ *Uncle Tom's Cabin* was one of the most important and controversial of American novels.

8. _____ Written by Harriet Beecher Stowe, the novel was a young woman's response to the Fugitive Slave Act.

9. _____ Although simplistic and often overly melodramatic, the novel was also deeply affecting.

10. _____ When Stowe was faced with the charge that the book was deceitful, she answered with *A Key to Uncle Tom's Cabin*, which provided documentation that every incident in the novel had actually happened.

INFERENCES: Test 1

A. Read each passage below. Then check the *two* statements after each passage which are most logically supported by the information given.

1. "Does the chili have any meat in it?" the woman asked. "No," answered the waiter. "I'll have chili, then." The waiter was disappointed, since chili was one of the restaurant's least expensive items. "The lobster special is delicious," he suggested, "and healthy." The woman shook her head and responded, "Not for the lobster."

____ a. The woman is a vegetarian.

____ b. The woman was brought up as a vegetarian.

____ c. The waiter was hoping to get a larger tip for a more expensive meal.

____ d. The woman is on a tight budget.

____ e. The woman was alone.

2. In 1935, Harry S. Truman (who would become President eleven years later) had just been elected to the U.S. Senate. As a brand-new senator from the Midwest, he was concerned that some of his more experienced colleagues might consider him "a sort of hick politician" who did not deserve to be part of such an important group of lawmakers. But another senator, Ham Lewis, put him at his ease. "Don't start out with an inferiority complex," Lewis told Truman. "For the first six months, you'll wonder how you got here. After that, you'll wonder how the rest of us got here."

____ a. This was Truman's first elected office.

____ b. Truman was concerned about what the other senators thought of him.

____ c. Truman felt he was not qualified to be a senator.

____ d. Ham Lewis was a close friend of Senator Truman.

____ e. Ham Lewis felt Truman's confidence as a senator would grow.

(Continues on next page)

B. Ten statements follow the passage below. Read the passage, and then check the *six* statements which are most logically supported by the information given.

Where does that road go? How does a television set work? What is that tool used for? Answering these questions may have no obvious benefit for you. You may not expect the road to take you anywhere you need to go, or the tool to be of any use to you. Exploration and curiosity appear to be motives activated by the new and unknown and directed toward no more specific a goal than "finding out." Even animals will learn a behavior just to be allowed to explore the environment. The family dog will run around a new house, sniffing and checking things out, before it settles down to eat its dinner.

Animals also seem to prefer complexity, presumably because more complex forms take longer to know and are therefore more interesting. Placed in a maze that is painted black, a rat will explore it and learn its way around. The next time, given a choice between a black maze and a blue one, it will choose the blue one. Apparently the unfamiliarity of the unknown maze has more appeal.

____ 1. It is boring to ask questions if the answers have no obvious practical benefit.

____ 2. We are curious about the unknown.

____ 3. Curiosity is always stronger than great hunger.

____ 4. Curiosity is what separates people from animals.

____ 5. Curiosity leads to exploration.

____ 6. A simple problem is often less interesting than a complex one.

____ 7. Mazes are challenging to rats.

____ 8. Rats are more curious than dogs.

____ 9. Given a choice between a familiar blue maze and an unfamiliar white one, a rat will probably choose the white one.

____ 10. Variety is interesting for its own sake.

INFERENCES: Test 2

A. Read the two passages below. Then check the *two* statements after each passage which are most logically supported by the information given.

1. Early Americans were not as conservative as we might imagine. Marriage and birth records show that in rural New England in the late 1700s, nearly a third of the brides were pregnant. But few pregnant women were abandoned by their lovers in that era. Sexual relations were considered part of a serious courtship. If pregnancy occurred, it just hurried up a marriage that would have taken place anyway.

    ____ a. Most rural New Englanders in the late 1700s felt that birth out of wedlock was acceptable.

    ____ b. Adultery was widespread among eighteenth-century rural New Englanders.

    ____ c. In the late 1700s, premarital sex was not uncommon among rural New Englanders.

    ____ d. In rural New England in the late 1700s, relatively few children were born to unwed mothers.

    ____ e. In the late 1700s, most brides in rural New England were teenagers.

2. Today's media have created some frustrating—and expensive—problems for parents of young girls. Every day, in magazines and on TV, their daughters see great-looking models in the latest clothes, dancing and singing about some new product. These ads create requests—for press-on nails, acid-washed jeans, hip new haircuts, and so on. The list is endless. It strains the mind and the pocketbook, and it leaves me wondering: "What ever happened to just playing store?"

    ____ a. The author dislikes the looks of acid-washed jeans.

    ____ b. The author is male.

    ____ c. The author feels parents have fewer problems with young boys than with young girls.

    ____ d. The author feels it would be better for young girls to be less concerned with fashion.

    ____ e. The author probably feels it is more wholesome for young girls to play store than to wear press-on nails.

(Continues on next page)

B. Ten statements follow the passage below. After reading the passage, check the *six* statements which are most logically supported by the information given.

In Miami, Florida, Judge Stanley Goldstein presides over a "drug court" in which defendants are offered a simple choice: going to trial, with the risk of conviction and a jail term, or entering a one-year treatment program under the supervision of the court. The designers of the program expected it to save the city the expense of trials and incarcerations, but it has yielded benefits that have surprised even them. Of the 1,700 accused persons who have completed the Miami treatment program, only 3 percent have been re-arrested for drug use. Before the treatment option was introduced, the recidivism rate was 33 percent. In Portland, Oregon, a "drug court" similar to the one in Miami has been introduced, and it's resulting in similarly low recidivism rates.

_____ 1. All drug defendants in Miami and Portland choose the treatment option.

_____ 2. Treatment can be a more effective remedy than punishment for dealing with illegal drug abuse.

_____ 3. Miami and Portland will probably continue to offer drug-abuse defendants the option of a treatment program.

_____ 4. Drug trials and incarceration are expensive in Miami.

_____ 5. Drug trials and incarceration are not as expensive in other parts of the country.

_____ 6. The courts that use a treatment program probably have some system for checking whether participants are using drugs.

_____ 7. Society is always better off when criminals are punished.

_____ 8. The drug treatment program in Miami is cheaper than the trials and incarcerations there.

_____ 9. The drug-treatment programs in Miami and Portland will be of little interest to other cities.

_____ 10. New programs may have unexpected results.

INFERENCES: Test 3

A. Read the passage below, taken from *The Plug-In Drug: Television, Children and Family* by Marie Winn, using the definitions as necessary. Then circle the letter of the answer to each item that is most logically supported by the information given.

deferred: put off   *inchoately:* imperfectly   *enervated:* weakened
induced: caused   *resume:* begin again

Not unlike drugs or alcohol, the television experience allows the participant to blot out the real world and enter into a pleasurable and passive mental state. The worries and anxieties of reality are as effectively deferred by becoming absorbed in a television program as by going on a "trip" induced by drugs or alcohol. And just as alcoholics are only inchoately aware of their addiction, feeling that they control their drinking more than they really do ("I can cut it out any time I want—I just like to have three or four drinks before dinner"), people similarly overestimate their control over television watching. Even as they put off other activities to spend hour after hour watching television, they feel they could easily resume living in a different, less passive style. But somehow or other while the television set is present in their homes, the click doesn't sound. With television pleasures available, those other experiences seem less attractive, more difficult somehow.

A heavy viewer (a college English instructor) observes: "I find television almost irresistible. When the set is on, I cannot ignore it. I can't turn it off. I feel sapped, will-less, enervated. As I reach out to turn off the set, the strength goes out of my arms. So I sit there for hours and hours."

1. The author compares being wrapped up in TV to
   a. the real world.
   b. a drug or alcohol "trip."
   c. more lively activities.

2. The author thus implies that watching television is
   a. addictive.
   b. easy to control.
   c. not pleasurable.

3. From the passage we can conclude that the author feels television
   a. is never really interesting.
   b. usually helps us face our problems.
   c. generally takes the place of more worthwhile activities.

(Continues on next page)

4. From the passage we can conclude that educators
   a. are less likely to be TV addicts.
   b. can be TV addicts.
   c. are more likely to be TV addicts.

B. Read the excerpt below from the article "Language of Advertising" by Charles O'Neill. Then check the *six* statements which are most logically supported by the information given.

premise: underlying condition

> No advertisement, no matter how carefully engineered and packed with information, has even a remote chance of succeeding unless it attracts our attention in the first place. Of the 560 advertising messages waiting for us each day, very few (author Alvin Toffler estimates 76) will actually obtain our conscious attention. The remaining 484 are screened out. The people who design and write ads recognize that this screening process takes place; they anticipate and accept it as a basic premise of their business. Nonetheless, they expend a great deal of energy to guarantee that their ads are among the few that penetrate the defenses and distraction which surround us. The classic, all-time-favorite device used to penetrate the barrier is sex. The perfect sex ad is simply headlined "SEX," with the text running something like this: "Now that we've got your attention. . . ." Whether it takes the sex approach or another, every successful advertisement contains a "hitch": a word or image intended to bring us into the ad. The hitch is usually one or a set of strong visuals (photos or illustrations with emotional value) or a disarming, unexpected set of words.

_____ 1. Advertisers compete for the consumer's attention.

_____ 2. Most ads are probably about equally successful in getting the consumer's attention.

_____ 3. Both pictures and words can attract the consumer's attention.

_____ 4. Sex is a common "hitch."

_____ 5. Sex is used only in ads for products related to sex and romance.

_____ 6. We are drawn to ads with important technical information.

_____ 7. We are drawn to ads with great emotional appeal.

_____ 8. Consumers don't really care about the nature of the product being advertised.

_____ 9. A shocking ad warning about drugs will gain more attention than a quiet, factual ad.

_____ 10. Ad designers and writers try to manipulate consumers into paying attention to their ads.

INFERENCES: Test 4

A. Following is Carl Sandburg's well-known poem "Fog." Read the poem, and then for each question, circle the letter of the answer that is most solidly based on the poem.

haunches: the part of a four-legged animal from the uppermost part of the legs and backward

Fog

The fog comes
On little cat feet.

It sits looking
Over harbor and city
On silent haunches
And then moves on.

1. Sandburg compares the way the fog moves to
   a. the way a cat moves.
   b. movement near a harbor.
   c. a city's rhythm.

2. Through this comparison, Sandburg implies that the fog
   a. sings.
   b. moves quickly and quietly.
   c. floats along like the water at a harbor.

3. Sandburg continues the comparison in the second stanza with the word
   a. *harbor.*
   b. *city.*
   c. *haunches.*

4. In the second stanza, Sandburg implies that the fog
   a. never stays.
   b. stays too long.
   c. stays for a while and then leaves.

5. Sandburg's poem portrays fog as
   a. dangerous.
   b. bothersome.
   c. quiet.

(Continues on next page)

B. Ten statements follow the passage below, from *A Son of the Middle Border*, an autobiographical account by Hamlin Garland. First read the passage carefully, using the definitions as necessary. Then circle the numbers of the *five* statements which are most logically supported by the information given.

imperative: commanding   *dismal:* gloomy
confronted: faced   *resolution:* firm determination
impassive: expressionless   *mused:* thought it over
countenance: face

Slipping from my weary horse, I tied her to the rail and hurried up the walk toward the doctor's bell. I remembered just where the knob rested. Twice I pulled sharply, strongly, putting into it some part of the anxiety and impatience I felt. I could hear its imperative jingle as it died away in the silent house.

At last the door opened and the doctor, a big blond handsome man in a long nightgown, confronted me with an impassive face. "What is it, my boy?" he asked kindly.

As I told him he looked down at my water-soaked form and wild-eyed countenance with gentle patience. Then he peered out over my head into the dismal night. He was a man of resolution, but he hesitated for a moment. "Your father is suffering sharply, is he?"

"Yes, sir. I could hear him groan.—Please hurry."

He mused a moment. "He is a soldier. He would not complain of a little thing—I will come."

_____ 1. At the time of this narrative, the speaker is a boy.

_____ 2. The speaker's ride had been a very short one.

_____ 3. The speaker had been to the doctor's house before.

_____ 4. The doctor was alone in the house.

_____ 5. The doctor was not expecting a visitor.

_____ 6. It had been raining.

_____ 7. The speaker did not admire the doctor.

_____ 8. The speaker was very afraid of the doctor.

_____ 9. The doctor concluded that the soldier's problem deserved immediate attention.

_____ 10. The doctor had been a soldier himself once.

INFERENCES: Test 5

A. Following is a well-known poem by A. E. Housman (1859-1936). Read it; then answer each question by circling the inference most solidly based on "When I Was One-and-Twenty."

crowns, pounds, guineas: forms of English money
fancy: desire
in vain: with little consequence
rue: sorrow or regret

When I Was One-and-Twenty

When I was one-and-twenty
I heard a wise man say,
"Give crowns and pounds and guineas
But not your heart away;
Give pearls away and rubies
But keep your fancy free."
But I was one-and-twenty,
No use to talk to me.
When I was one-and-twenty
I heard him say again,
"The heart out of the bosom
Was never given in vain;
'Tis paid with sighs a-plenty
And sold for endless rue."
And I am two-and-twenty,
And Oh, 'tis true, 'tis true.

1. To "give . . . your heart away" is a figure of speech meaning
   a. to fall in love.
   b. to be generous.
   c. to feel sick.

2. To "keep your fancy free" is a figure of speech meaning
   a. be kind.
   b. don't spend a lot of money.
   c. don't desire only one person.

3. The wise man's advice was:
   a. It's best not to be rich.
   b. It's better to give riches away than to fall in love.
   c. An inexpensive romance is never harmful.

(Continues on next page)

4. When the speaker says, "But I was one-and-twenty, / No use to talk to me," the meaning is that he or she
   a. sought out the wise man's advice.
   b. misunderstood the wise man's advice.
   c. ignored the wise man's advice.

5. The speaker accepted the wise man's advice when
   a. the speaker was twenty-one.
   b. the speaker first fell in love.
   c. the speaker, at the age of twenty-two, had a disappointing romance.

B. Ten statements follow the excerpt below from *Hunger of Memory*, an autobiographical account by Richard Rodriguez. Check the *five* statements which are most logically supported by the information given.

> I remember, to start with, that day in Sacramento, in a California now nearly thirty years past, when I first entered a classroom—able to understand about fifty stray English words. The third of four children, I had been preceded by my older brother and sister to a neighborhood Roman Catholic school. But neither of them had revealed very much about their classroom experiences. They left each morning and returned each afternoon, always together, speaking Spanish as they climbed the five steps to the porch. And their mysterious books, wrapped in brown shopping-bag paper, remained on the table next to the door, closed firmly behind them.
>
> An accident of geography sent me to a school where all my classmates were white and many were the children of doctors and lawyers and business executives. On that first day of school, my classmates must certainly have been uneasy to find themselves apart from their families, in the first institution of their lives. But I was astonished. I was fated to be the "problem student" in class.
>
> The nun said, in a friendly but oddly impersonal voice: "Boys and girls, this is Richard Rodriguez." (I heard her sound it out: *Rich-heard Road-ree-guess*.) It was the first time I had heard anyone say my name in English. "Richard," the nun repeated more slowly, writing my name down in her book. Quickly I turned to see my mother's face dissolve in a watery blur behind the pebbled-glass door.

_____ 1. Rodriguez's classmates must have been older than he was.

_____ 2. Before he entered the classroom, Rodriguez knew little about school.

_____ 3. The Rodriguez family spoke Spanish at home.

_____ 4. Rodriguez knew that, despite the language barrier, he would have no problems relating to his classmates.

_____ 5. Rodriguez did not get along with his older brother and sister.

_____ 6. Rodriguez's parents were probably not doctors, lawyers, or executives.

_____ 7. The other students in the class probably did not speak Spanish.

_____ 8. The nun disliked Spanish children.

_____ 9. The Rodriguez family was not Roman Catholic.

_____ 10. One of Rodriguez's problems in class must have been not understanding much of what was said.

INFERENCES: Test 6

After reading each textbook selection, circle the letter of the best answer to each question.

A. Even the pupils of our eyes communicate. E. H. Hess and J. M. Polt of the University of Chicago measured the amount of pupil dilation while showing men and women various types of pictures. The results of the experiment were very interesting: a person's eyes grow larger in proportion to the degree of interest one has in an object. For example, men's pupils grew about 18 percent larger when looking at pictures of a naked woman, and the degree of dilation for women looking at a naked man's picture was 20 percent. Interestingly enough, the greatest increase in pupil size occurred when women looked at a picture of a mother and an infant. A good salesperson can increase profits by being aware of pupil dilation, as Edward Hall describes. He was once in a Middle Eastern bazaar, where an Arab merchant insisted that a customer looking at his jewelry buy a certain piece that the shopper had been ignoring. But the vendor had been watching the pupils of the buyer's eyes and had known what the buyer really wanted.

1. We communicate through our pupils
   a. consciously.
   b. rarely.
   c. unconsciously.
   d. in undetectable ways.

2. Hess and Polt's research shows that
   a. men's and women's interests are consistently the same.
   b. women are not particularly interested in sex.
   c. our minds affect our bodies.
   d. women's pupils are larger than men's.

B. There is an old joke about a man who was asked if he could play a violin and answered, "I don't know. I've never tried." This is psychologically a very wise reply. Those who have never tried to play a violin really do not know whether they can or not. Those who say too early in life and too firmly, "No, I'm not at all musical," shut themselves off prematurely from whole areas of life that might have proved rewarding. In each of us there are unknown possibilities, undiscovered potentials—and one big advantage of having an open self-concept rather than a rigid one is that we shall continue to expose ourselves to new experiences and therefore we shall continue to discover more and more about ourselves as we grow older.

(Continues on next page)

3. The author implies that
   a. self-discovery ought to be a life-long process.
   b. most people are very talented musically.
   c. most people have an open self-concept.
   d. all of the above.

C.   The English regarded the northern part of North America as a place that only the mad French could endow with possibility. English fishermen who strayed from Newfoundland to the coast of Acadia and New England carried home descriptions of the long, lonely stretch of coast, washed by the waves of the slate gray Atlantic. Long winters of numbing cold and heavy snowfalls alternated with short summers of steamy heat. There were no minerals worthy of mining, no crops worthy of export, no large population of natives suitable for enslaving. To prospective investors and settlers, the Chesapeake, with its temperate climate and long growing season, appeared a more likely spot. In truth, of course, Indian tribes had successfully inhabited the territory that came to be called New England for at least ten thousand years. Each spring they set fires while the forests were still wet, to burn away the underbrush and make traveling and hunting easier. Such burnings encouraged the growth of deer and other game populations and gave New England forests an almost parklike appearance.

4. We can conclude that the English of this era believed
   a. the French to be less sensible than themselves.
   b. slavery was acceptable.
   c. farming and mining were desirable pursuits.
   d. all of the above.

5. The passage suggests that New England
   a. had a climate similar to that in the Chesapeake area.
   b. was more inhabitable than the English believed.
   c. was clearly more beautiful than the Chesapeake area.
   d. had more minerals to mine than the English realized.

PURPOSE AND TONE: Test 1

A. In the space provided, indicate whether the primary purpose of each sentence is to inform (**I**), to persuade (**P**), or to entertain (**E**).

_____ 1. Sixty million years ago, the horse's ancestors were only about a foot tall.

_____ 2. For the sake of our already overcrowded schools, Paulsen City must turn down this proposed housing development.

_____ 3. My brother says that I was so ugly as a kid that my mother had to tie a pork chop around my neck to get our dog to play with me.

_____ 4. Cosmetic companies that test their products on animals don't deserve your business; please buy from cruelty-free companies instead.

_____ 5. U.S. coins are withdrawn from circulation when they become so worn or bent that they will no longer pass through a bank's automatic sorting machine.

B. Each of the following passages illustrates better than the others one of the five different tones identified in the box below. In the space provided, put the letter of the tone that applies to each passage. Use each tone once.

a. encouraging	c. amused	e. angry and bitter
b. critical	d. matter-of-fact	

_____ 6. Somewhere around midterm, almost every student feels like saying, "I just can't learn anything else. My brain is full!" Well, don't give up so easily—your brain has more room than you think. Scientists believe that memories are stored in the part of the brain called the cerebrum. If you were to store ten bits of information each second of your life, by your one hundredth birthday, your memory-storage area would be only half full. So the next time you feel your brain is about to short circuit, take a break and then come back to those books knowing you've got plenty of room in your head for more learning.

_____ 7. In America you are primarily valued not for your good deeds or your good character. You are valued for the money you command. The more money you have, the better you are treated by everyone from your local cop to your congressman. If you doubt this, go to any store or

(Continues on next page)

social agency. Go, for example, to any urban clinic and see what it is like to be old, sick, and poor. There is a living hell. You get neither kindness nor respect nor service. To voluntarily take a step toward that condition you have to be either blind or mad. For as your ability to command money decreases, so too does your stature as a human being. To doctors, you are less important than the forms they must process to get money for their services. To landlords, you are a barrier to higher rents. Small wonder that retirees band together in colonies, in clubs, homes, and hospitals. They want to belong, and they can do so only with their own kind. Everywhere else, their money will be taken, but they will be shut out.

_____ 8. So you're supposed to be on a diet and you've just had a hot-fudge sundae? Not to worry—there are plenty of ways you can work off those extra calories. You could sit around with your friends complaining about society's hangup with thinness. After eight hours and thirty-three minutes of that, your hot fudge will be history. Of course, if you sat around over coffee and donuts, you'll have to keep it up for another two hours and eight minutes (unless you had cream in your coffee; in that case keep going a total of three hours, fourteen mintues). You could even stand in line for a second sundae. Every fourteen minutes you spend in line will earn you another bite.

_____ 9. The barber's red and white spiral-striped pole has its origins in blood-letting. Bloodletting involves removal of small amounts of blood from the body. During the Middle Ages it was considered a remedy for many ailments. Barbers took up bloodletting as a result of their regular trips to monasteries. Besides having the crowns of their heads shaved, medieval monks were required to undergo periodic bloodletting. Barbers simply combined the two services. In villages, barbers placed outside their doors white cloths reddened with blood to indicate the times thought best for bleeding (April, May, and September). Today's barber pole reflects this early form of advertising.

_____ 10. The printed word cannot compete with the movies on their ground, and should not. You can describe beautiful faces, car chases, or valleys full of Indians on horseback until you run out of words, and you will not approach the movies' spectacle. Novels written with film contracts in mind have a faint but unmistakable, and ruinous, odor. I cannot name what, in the text, alerts the reader to suspect the writer of mixed motives; I cannot specify which sentences, in several books, have caused me to read on with increasing dismay, and finally close the books because I smelled a rat. Such books seem uneasy being books; they seem eager to fling off their disguises and jump onto screens.

PURPOSE AND TONE: Test 2

A. In the space provided, indicate whether the primary purpose of each passage is to inform **(I)**, to persuade **(P)**, or to entertain **(E)**.

_____ 1. The real problem with exercise for most people is not a failure to realize that it's good for them but an unwillingness to work it into their daily lives, the most common excuse being "I don't have time." My answer to such people is (if you'll pardon the pun) "That's a lame excuse." People have always managed to find time for the things they really want to do. Finding time for exercise, then, starts with a realization of its importance and a decision—a commitment—to make it a regular part of your life. Just as you brush your teeth every day, eat every day, and sleep every day, you can exercise every day. After a while, you may find, as I did, with regular moderate exercise you get more rest from less sleep and you work so much more efficiently that you actually have more time now that you've given up some time to exercise.

_____ 2. Early birds are an odd breed. It's bad enough to face an alarm clock at dawn, but at least you can throw a clock across the room. It's not so easy to throw an early bird, especially if it happens to be your roommate or wife. These birds are actually energetic in the morning, getting things done and speaking in full sentences. Surely, if the good Lord had expected people to function so early, he wouldn't have created party animals and late night TV. Obviously, mornings are for the birds.

_____ 3. The cheetah, one of the big cats of Africa, is the fastest animal on Earth. Cheetahs have been clocked running seventy miles an hour; forty miles per hour is the top speed achieved by their closest competitor, the horse. The cheetah's speed is made possible by its extremely flexible back, which allows it to bring its hind legs far ahead of its front ones with each stride. But it can hold its greater speed only for short distances. If pursued by a fast attacker with more stamina—a man on horseback or a car, for example—the cheetah will simply lie down in exhaustion soon into the race.

(Continues on next page)

B. Each of the following passages illustrates one of the tones identified in the box below. In each space provided, put the letter of the tone that applies to the passage.

a. ambivalent	c. playful	e. grim
b. inspiring	d. sarcastic	f. vengeful

_____ 4. Only his head and neck stuck out from the wooden enclosure in which he was cruelly locked. The lower lid of his right eye was yanked forward and the test cosmetic was dropped in. He struggled to brush the chemical from his eye, but the enclosure stopped him. Then he started to scream with pain. Before he stopped screaming, the eye was blind. Even then, he was unable to cry. Rabbits can't cry—their helpless eyes produce no tears.

_____ 5. You are not an object to which bad things just happen, a passive nonentity hoping, like a garden slug, to avoid being stepped on. You are the culmination of millions of years of evolution of our species, of your parents' dreams, of God's image. You are a unique individual who, as an active actor in life's drama, can make things happen. You can change the direction of your entire life any time you choose to do so. With confidence in yourself, obstacles turn into challenges and challenges into accomplishments. Shyness then recedes, because, instead of always preparing for and worrying about how you will live your life, you forget yourself as you become absorbed in the living of it.

PURPOSE AND TONE: Test 3

A. Eight italicized quotations in the story below are preceded by a blank space. Identify the tone of each italicized quotation by writing in the letter of one of these tones. (Two tone choices will be left over.)

a. inviting	d. forgiving	g. disbelief	i. sarcastic
b. outraged	e. optimistic	h. pessimistic	j. apologetic
c. malicious	f. matter-of-fact		

The family reunion was in full swing when Laura and her boyfriend, Brian, pulled up at the house. Laura looked at the street lined with cars and sighed.

_____ 1.   Brian smiled. *"Don't worry, Laura. The family that produced you has got to be great. It's going to be fun meeting them all, even crazy Uncle Erwin."*

_____ 2.   "That's Uncle Edwin, and I didn't say he was crazy. I said he was vicious," said Laura. *"You'll probably leave this reunion saying you want nothing to do with someone from such a crazy family."*

_____ 3.   Just then the front door swung open and a voice called out, *"It's Laura! Hi, honey. I'm so glad to see you. Come on in, you two."*

_____ 4.   The couple entered a noisy room packed with people. A woman lying on a couch drawled, *"Laura, so incredibly good of you to make an appearance here. I was convinced I was going to have to die before you'd come. You would attend my funeral, wouldn't you? Not that I'd expect you if you had anything more interesting to do."*

_____ 5.   "Hello, Mother," Laura answered. *"I'd like to introduce Brian Miller, my friend from college. Brian, this is my mother."*

_____ 6.   An enormous man then approached Brian and Laura. Glaring down at the couple, he laughed unpleasantly. *"What's the matter, Laura, couldn't you find a full-size boyfriend?"* he sneered. *"I think this one is the littlest shrimp I've seen you with yet!"*

_____ 7.   "Uncle Edwin!" shouted Laura. *"I have warned you before, and I'm not going to put up with your rudeness anymore!"* With those words, Laura picked up a pitcher of lemonade and dashed it in Uncle Edwin's face.

(Continues on next page)

As if on signal, quarrels broke out all over the room. Shouts and then punches began to fly. The sound of breaking windows was heard over the hubbub.

_____ 8. Several hours later, sitting in the quiet of Laura's apartment, Brian was still shaking his head. *"Tell me again that all that wasn't staged just for my benefit?"* Brian asked Laura for the fifth time. *"Is it possible that people honestly act like that in real life?"*

"To tell you the truth," answered Laura, "that was one of the tamest reunions we've had in years."

B. In the space provided, indicate whether the primary purpose of each passage is to inform (**I**), to persuade (**P**), or to entertain (**E**).

9. _____ Tofu is a product gaining popularity as a cholesterol-free meat substitute. Once found only in Oriental markets and health-food stores, tofu is now sold in many supermarket produce sections. The white cheeselike substance, made from the thickened milk of soybeans, has qualities that appeal to many health-conscious consumers. It is very high in protein and low in sodium and fat. Tofu has a texture that bothers some people and little flavor of its own, but fans feel it mixes well into stir-fry combinations, sauces and soups.

10. _____ A young man visiting this country from Asia became fascinated with our expressions and tried to master some. One day when he was out bicycling with several American friends, his rear tire went flat. He got off his bike, gave the tire a hard kick and exclaimed, "You stone of a peach!" One friend looked at him with confusion and asked, "Is that what you say at home when you are mad at something?" The young man replied, "No, that is what you say in this country. I have heard it many times." Just then two more friends rode up. One saw the flat tire and swore out loud. The young Asian smiled and said triumphantly, "There, you see? Stone of a peach!"

PURPOSE AND TONE: Test 4

A. Eight quotations in the story below are preceded by a blank space. Identify the tone of each italicized quotation by writing in the letter of one of these tones. (Two tone choices will be left over.)

a. apologetic	d. scolding	g. horrified	i. critical
b. joyful	e. admiring	h. threatening	j. downhearted
c. joking	f. comforting		

Elena and Dan walked away from the movie theater discussing their reactions to the film they had just seen.

_e_ 1. *"Didn't you think the acting was great? I just think the whole cast did a great job,"* Elena said.

_l_ 2. *"The movie was short on plot, though. It really had no story at all,"* Dan said.

Before heading down the steps into the subway, Elena reached into her purse for her wallet.

_g_ 3. *"Oh no!"* she cried. *"My wallet's gone!"*

_f_ 4. *"Now, take it easy. You're probably just not spotting it,"* Dan said soothingly. *"Let's take a better look under the street light."*

"No, it's gone," Elena said after searching. "It must have fallen out when I put my purse down at our seats. We have to hurry back!"

When Elena and Dan arrived back at the theater, only the staff remained. "I've lost my wallet," Elena told an usher. "Please let us into the auditorium. We need to look for it at our seats."

The usher agreed.

_a_ 5. *"I'm sorry about this, Dan,"* Elena said with some embarrassment as they searched.

"Hey, it could happen to anybody."

_j_ 6. After searching without success, Elena said, *"I've lost thirty dollars and all my I.D. cards. What's most depressing is that somebody took my wallet—not just the money, but everything else too."*

Just then the usher approached them. "Would you describe your wallet for me?" she asked Elena.

"It was denim," Elena answered. "Blue denim with tan trim."

(Continues on next page)

"Then here you are," the usher said with a grin, handing Elena her wallet.

___β___ 7.   *"That's it! Thank goodness!"* said Elena, beaming.

___C___ 8.   "Someone turned it in right after the movie." Then the usher giggled. *"I guess you're lucky the movie was* Act of Kindness. *That must have inspired the right emotion."*

B. This activity will give you practice in recognizing purpose and tone. Read the paragraphs below. Then carefully consider the questions that follow and circle the best responses.

Television is also a source of nutritional information for youngsters. A barrage of ads invite the child to dietary and dental disaster, pushing color and sweetness over real food value, with an endless succession of sugar-ridden candies, cereals, pies, cakes, ice creams, soft drinks, and fast foods. Children of low-income families are the worst hit by the junk-food blitz, being especially dependent on television for information and entertainment, while often denied access to regular dental and health care. The food commercials depict children as hyped-up little gluttons who devour Twinkies, Hostess Cupcakes, Sugar Frosties, and M&M candies with a greedy enthusiasm seldom displayed for regular meals, all under the approving gaze of Mother, a junk-food pusher who knows how to keep her little ones happy.

9. The primary purpose of this paragraph is
   a. to inform readers that TV is a source of nutritional information for children.
   b. to persuade readers that TV is a poor source of nutritional information for children.
   c. to entertain readers with colorful images of TV as a source of nutritional information for children.

10. The tone of this paragraph can be described as
    a. annoyed but optimistic.
    b. outspoken and critical.
    c. hesitant and ambivalent.
    d. formal and unemotional.

PURPOSE AND TONE: Test 5

This activity will give you practice in recognizing purpose and tone. Read each of the paragraphs below. Then carefully consider the questions that follow and circle the letters of the best responses.

A.   In most cases, little birds lay little eggs. The kiwi is an amazing exception to this rule—it is a smallish bird that lays a big egg. The kiwi, a non-flying bird found in New Zealand, weighs about four pounds, and its egg weighs, believe it or not, about one pound. That is one-fourth of the bird's body weight! If an ostrich laid an egg that was in the same proportion to the ostrich as the kiwi egg is to the kiwi, an ostrich egg would weigh a whopping seventy-five pounds, instead of the usual three pounds.

   1. The primary purpose of this paragraph is
      a. to inform.
      b. to persuade.
      c. to entertain.

   2. The paragraph includes a tone of
      a. joy.
      b. optimism.
      c. astonishment.
      d. regret.

B.   Our justice system has taken a turnaround for the worse. Criminals today have more rights than an honest citizen ever dreamed were contained in our Constitution. Murderers, robbers, rapists and drug dealers walk out of court, free on legal technicalities. And while that scum is back to business (finding more victims), their victims are ignored by the system. Until we start giving some real consideration to those of us who do not commit crimes, instead of to those who do, things are going to get nothing but worse.

   3. The primary purpose of this passage is
      a. to inform.
      b. to persuade.
      c. to entertain.

   4. The tone of this paragraph can be described as
      a. objective.
      b. indignant.
      c. optimistic.
      d. chatty.

(Continues on next page)

C. During our daily bouts of pessimism, we can see its constructive role in our lives. In these mild forms, pessimism serves the purpose of pulling us back a bit from the risky exaggerations of our optimism, making us think twice, keeping us from making rash, foolhardy gestures. The optimistic moments of our lives contain the great plans, the dreams, and the hopes. Reality is gently distorted to give the dreams room to flourish. Without these times we would never accomplish anything difficult and intimidating, we would never even attempt the just barely possible. Mount Everest would remain unscaled, the four-minute mile unrun; the jet plane and the computer would be blueprints sitting in some financial vice-president's wastebasket.

5. The primary purpose of this paragraph is
   a. to inform readers of the advantages and disadvantages of pessimism and optimism.
   b. to persuade readers of the usefulness of both pessimism and optimism.
   c. to entertain readers with inspiring achievements.

6. The author's tone can be described as
   a. critical but concerned.
   b. light-hearted and amused.
   c. cynical and disbelieving.
   d. serious and enthusiastic.

D. With controlled television viewing, the job of bringing up your children the way you desire is enormously simplified. You will be the one to formulate what is really important to you and to your children. . . .
   With less television your children will be the benefactor of a richer life through books, art, and creative play. They will be the source of their own entertainment, and they will discover their own resources. They will learn from the whole range of human experience and be able to choose their own pathway more intelligently.

7. The primary purpose of this passage is
   a. to inform readers of study results on the benefits of controlled television viewing.
   b. to persuade readers that controlled television viewing is beneficial.
   c. to entertain readers with dramatic images about children.

8. The tone of this passage can be described as
   a. critical and pessimistic.
   b. impassioned and optimistic.
   c. sympathetic and forgiving.
   d. playful and cheerful.

PURPOSE AND TONE: Test 6

This activity will give you practice in recognizing purpose and tone. Read each of the paragraphs below. Then carefully consider the questions that follow and circle the letters of the best responses.

A. The running of the bulls in Pamplona, Spain, is an annual event made famous by author Ernest Hemingway in his novel *The Sun Also Rises*. Every July, at the peak of a week's festivities, a group of bulls is released to charge through the city's streets. Ahead, behind and all around them are thousands of men and women seeking the thrill of running with the bulls and living to tell about it. Each participant is allowed to carry only a rolled-up newspaper with which to discourage an attacking animal. Every year a few people are trampled or gored by the bulls, and deaths are not uncommon.

1. The purpose of this passage is
   a. to inform.
   b. to persuade.
   c. to entertain.

2. The tone of the passage can be described as
   a. outraged
   b. admiring.
   c. matter-of-fact.
   d. apologetic.

B. During the earliest weeks of life infants do not distinguish between themselves and their surroundings, between what's inside and what's outside the body. Their primary task at this stage of normal autism, according to Mahler, is the reduction of tension, which they accomplish by eating, eliminating, being covered when they get cold, and being diapered when they're soiled. Since the mother is the agent of so much reduction of tension, infants come to associate her with such reduction. If babies are unable to begin to distinguish what they themselves do (like crying to signal their needs) from what the mother does (like pick them up), they are at risk, says Mahler, for developing infantile autism, an extreme disturbance characterized by an almost total inability to relate to other people.

3. The primary purpose of this passage is
   a. to inform readers of the nature of normal and abnormal autism in infants.
   b. to persuade readers to have their children tested for autism.
   c. to entertain readers with interesting baby stories.

4. The general tone of this passage is
   a. disappointed.
   b. objective.
   c. angry.
   d. encouraging.

(Continues on next page)

C.   Our clients were punctual to their appointment, for the clock had just struck ten
when Dr. Mortimer was shown up, followed by the young baronet. The latter was a
small, alert, dark-eyed man about thirty years of age, very sturdily built, with thick
black eyebrows. . . .

"This is Sir Henry Baskerville," said Dr. Mortimer.

"Why, yes," said he, "and the strange thing is, Mr. Sherlock Holmes, that if my
friend here had not proposed coming round to you this morning I should have come
on my own account. I understand that you think out little puzzles, and I've had one
this morning which wants more thinking out than I am able to give it."

5. The primary purpose of this paragraph is
    a. to inform.
    b. to persuade.
    c. to entertain.

6. The tone of this paragraph can be described as
    a. grim.
    b. straightforward.
    c. ironic.
    d. compassionate.

D.   In Africa's southernmost Lake Malawi swarm millions of shimmering fish in a
rainbow of fluorescent colors that make them popular picks for aquariums. Similar
to perch, they belong to a family of fish called cichlids, of great interest to scientists
because of the unusual variety of behavior they have developed in order to survive.
One brown and white species, for example, drops to the lake bottom, covers itself
with sand, and plays dead. When other fish come to scavenge, it leaps up and
gobbles them. The "upside down" species has reversed its coloration—light on top,
dark on the bottom—so it can flip over and conceal itself from predators above or
below. And the sand dwellers are accomplished transvestites—cleverly
masquerading as the opposite sex so they can steal eggs from other nests or sow
wild oats on the sly.

7. The primary purpose of this paragraph is
    a. to inform.
    b. to persuade.
    c. to entertain.

8. The tone of this paragraph can be described as
    a. concerned and sympathetic.
    b. mainly objective with a touch of wonder.
    c. mainly optimistic, with a touch of fear.
    d. formal but unimpressed.

ARGUMENT: Test 1

A. In each of the following groups of statements, one statement is the point, and the other statement or statements are support for the point. Identify each point with a **P**, and identify each statement of support with an **S**.

Group 1

1. _____ My parents are constantly nagging me about coming in late at night.
2. _____ My mother questions some of the boys who call me on the phone.
3. _____ I think it's time for me to look for my own apartment.
4. _____ My parents want me to start paying rent for living at home.

Group 2

5. _____ Clearly, the ancient Egyptians honored cats.
6. _____ Archaeologists have uncovered entire cemeteries in Egypt devoted to mummified cats.
7. _____ Historians know that ancient Egyptian law protected cats from harm.

Group 3

8. _____ The neighbors are threatening to call the police.
9. _____ You might stumble into the cactus plants or fall against the thorny rose bushes.
10. _____ You'll get sunburned in sensitive spots.
11. _____ You really should stop dancing nude on the front lawn.

B. Each of the three points below is followed by six items, three of which logically support the point and three of which do not. In the spaces provided, write the letters of the three items that logically support each point.

Point: The economy is in a slump.
      a. At present, unemployment is especially high.
      b. Business courses are very popular right now.
      c. There is a federal tax on luxury items.
      d. Construction of new houses is down dramatically.
      e. There are big differences in the rates of all the credit cards in this country.
      f. Many businesses have been dying.

12–14. Items that logically support the point: _____ _____ _____

(Continues on next page)

Point: Ingrid is a good friend.
  a. When one of her friends is sick, Ingrid offers to help out by doing any necessary grocery shopping.
  b. She has been known to return to a store the day after buying something to return the excess change the clerk mistakenly gave her.
  c. Ingrid remembers her friends' birthdays and often arranges some sort of celebration.
  d. Although she makes a modest salary, Ingrid donates generously to various charities.
  e. She listens to her friends' troubles with patience and understanding.
  f. Nobody can make a double chocolate cake like Ingrid.

15–17. Items that logically support the point: _____ _____ _____

Point: Cats and dogs benefit from being neutered.
  a. Cats and dogs should be taken to a veterinarian at least once a year for a check-up and vaccinations.
  b. Neutering reduces the likelihood that a cat or dog will develop certain common forms of cancer.
  c. Neutering can change the personality of an animal.
  d. Neutered cats and dogs tend to be more content to stay at home, where they're safest.
  e. On average, neutered cats and dogs live longer than unneutered ones.
  f. Purebred cats and dogs are more likely than mixed breeds to suffer from inherited disorders.

18–20. Items that logically support the point: _____ _____ _____

ARGUMENT: Test 2

A. In each of the following groups of statements, one statement is the point, and the other statement or statements are support for the point. Identify each point with a **P**, and identify each statement of support with an **S**.

Group 1

1. _____ Lately when I call my girlfriend for a date, she says she's either busy or not feeling good.
2. _____ She wrote "return to sender" on the card I mailed to her.
3. _____ My girlfriend is having second thoughts about our relationship.
4. _____ I saw her engrossed in a magazine article on "saying goodbye to the man in your life."

Group 2

5. _____ Car phones provide an efficient way for drivers to conduct personal and professional business.
6. _____ Car phones can be an asset or a liability.
7. _____ Car phones can distract the driver's attention from the road, causing an accident.

Group 3

8. _____ The biggest female stars make less than the most famous male stars.
9. _____ Very few good roles are written for older women.
10. _____ The film industry tends to treat women as second-class citizens.
11. _____ Only a handful of women have been allowed to direct major motion pictures.

B. Each of the three points on the next page is followed by six items, three of which logically support the point and three of which do not. In the spaces provided, write the letters of the three items that logically support each point.

(Continues on next page)

Point: Our town library building needs to be expanded.

    a. The book aisles are so cramped that people often have to squeeze past each other.

    b. No one is permitted to check out reference books.

    c. The library's check-out system is not computerized.

    d. The library has a bulletin board where people post ads and notices.

    e. The magazine reading room has only eight chairs, and even they crowd the room.

    f. There's not enough room to put all the library's children's collection on shelves.

12–14. Items that logically support the point: _____ _____ _____

Point: A "healthy-looking suntan" may not be so healthy or good looking in the long run.

    a. People should strive to improve their inner beauty.

    b. The ultraviolet rays of the sun can cause skin cancer, particularly in fair-skinned people.

    c. Some people are more likely to burn in the sun than to tan.

    d. Up to 90 percent of all wrinkles are caused by the sun.

    e. Heavy smoking is also thought to be a major cause of wrinkles.

    f. While people are out in the sun getting tan, their skin is losing much of its natural moisture, causing the skin to look dry.

15–17. Items that logically support the point: _____ _____ _____

Point: When naming a baby, parents should consider the effect a name may have on their child.

    a. Michael, Christopher, Jessica, and Jennifer are among the most popular children's names today.

    b. Unusual or out-of-date names such as Zipperath and Ubaldus may make a child a perfect target for teasing by classmates.

    c. Children's initials have been known to have a negative impact on them. Patricia Irene Graham and Anthony Steven Smith are fine names, but when their friends latch on to their initials, they may never hear the end of it.

    d. Samuel Clemens used the name Mark Twain as a pen name.

    e. Names like Buffy and Missy may be perfect for a baby, but they may not inspire confidence in the same person when she or he later runs for Congress or does heart surgery.

    f. The most common family name in the world is the Chinese name Chang, shared by at least 104 million people.

18–20. Items that logically support the point: _____ _____ _____

ARGUMENT: Test 3

A. Circle the letter of the sentence in each paragraph that does *not* support the point of the argument. The point (main idea) is set off in **boldface** type.

1. [1]**Animals can be be useful in promoting mental health**. [2]By forming close relationships with animals, we can demonstrate the kinship of all living things. [3]Experiments in prisons have shown that convicts who are allowed pets become less violent. [4]Also, patients in nursing homes show greater responsiveness and a more positive attitude when they have an opportunity to share affection with dogs and cats. [5]When some autistic children were given the opportunity to interact with dolphins, they made great strides, including speaking for the first time in their lives.

   Which statement changes the subject of the author's argument that animals can be useful in promoting mental health?

   a. Sentence 2
   b. Sentence 3
   c. Sentence 4
   d. Sentence 5

2. [1]**The company I work for is obviously sexist**. [2]This is no surprise from a company that has a history of racial discrimination. [3]Although many of the company's female employees have shown outstanding ability, few have risen to top positions. [4]In general, the company's female employees receive lower pay than male employees who do the same or similar work. [5]The company's publications use language that denies women equal consideration. [6]For example, business people as a group are always referred to as "businessmen."

   Which of the following changes the subject of the author's argument that his or her company is sexist?

   a. Sentence 2
   b. Sentence 3
   c. Sentence 4
   d. Sentence 6

(Continues on next page)

B. Check the conclusion that is best supported by the evidence in each group below.

Group 1

- At Western University last year, seven students were expelled for stealing the answer key to the final biology exam.
- Many teachers report that when they leave the room during a test, students began to compare answers.
- At some schools, students tape the answers for tests to their forearms and the palms of their hands.

3. Which of the following is best supported by the evidence above?

____ a. Kids today can't be trusted—they'll cheat every chance they get.

____ b. Cheating on exams is the number-one problem in American schools today.

____ c. High school students are more likely to cheat than college students.

____ d. Cheating has been a problem at some schools.

Group 2

- In France, no house is given the number 13, and in Italy, the national lottery omits the number 13.
- Friday the 13th is often considered the unluckiest of days; some believe it to be the day that Eve tempted Adam with the apple, the day the Great Flood began, and the day Jesus died.
- In America, many modern skyscrapers, condos, coops, and apartments skip the number 13; the floor above level 12 is numbered 14.

4. Which of the following is best supported by the evidence above?

____ a. Thirteen is an unlucky number, and if you use it, you are just asking for trouble.

____ b. Everyone is superstitious about something.

____ c. Many people throughout the world are superstitious about the number 13.

____ d. Cain probably killed Abel on a Friday the 13th.

C. Circle the letter of the fallacy contained in the argument below.

5. Ms. Rogers opposes hunting in public parks. Apparently, she doesn't think that people have the right to enjoy sports on public property.

a. Personal attack *(the argument shifts to irrelevant personal criticism)*

b. Circular reasoning *(a statement repeats itself rather than providing a real supporting reason to back up an argument)*

c. Straw man *(an argument is made by claiming an opponent holds an extreme position and then opposing that extreme position)*

ARGUMENT: Test 4

A. Circle the letter of the sentence in each paragraph that does *not* support the point of the argument. The point (main idea) is set off in **boldface** type.

1. **[1]Age at marriage is an important predictor of a marriage's success.** [2]Teenagers have high divorce rates for various reasons. [3]Early marriage may lock a couple into a relationship neither one is mature enough to handle, restricting both partners' potential for growth. [4]This in turn makes the young husband and wife less able to deal successfully with the challenges all marriages face. [5]An early marriage and parenthood may also make it difficult for a young person to pursue the education and career he or she otherwise would. [6]Studies show that people who wait until their late twenties or later to marry have the highest chances of success at marriage.

   Which of the following statements changes the subject of the author's argument that age at marriage is an important predictor of a marriage's success?

   a. Sentence 2
   b. Sentence 4
   c. Sentence 5
   d. Sentence 6

2. **[1]The U.S. Commission on Civil Rights has correctly determined that lack of child care and inadequate child care place women at a disadvantage in the workplace.** [2]First of all, women are sometimes prevented from taking paid positions when good child care is unavailable. [3]Participation in many social activities is also difficult for these same women. [4]In addition, child care problems force women to stay in part-time jobs with lower pay, little career mobility, and no fringe benefits. [5]Finally, the child care dilemma discourages women from putting in the time necessary to seek and accept job promotions. [6]Women with child care responsibilities thus often have no choice but to remain in jobs for which they are overqualified.

   Which of the following changes the subject of the author's argument that problems with child care put women at a disadvantage in the workplace?

   a. Sentence 2
   b. Sentence 3
   c. Sentence 4
   d. Sentence 5

(Continues on next page)

B. Check the conclusion that is best supported by the evidence in each group below.

Group 1

- A lambswool duster quickly grips dust by static attraction.
- A lightweight extension handle which attaches to a number of tools helps reach high and low places.
- A large squeegee beats paper towels for speedy window washing.

3. Which of the following is best supported by the evidence above?

____ a. Cleaning can be fun.

____ b. Good tools can make cleaning chores easier and faster.

____ c. Hardware stores are the best places to buy cleaning equipment.

____ d. A clean environment is an essential part of a productive life.

Group 2

- "Ring Around a Rosy" was originally sung about the rose-colored rash that was a symptom of the deadly Great Plague; "they all fall down" meant they died.
- In "Three Blind Mice," the farmer's wife cut off the mice's tails with a carving knife.
- In "Ladybug, Ladybug," the ladybug is told to fly away home because "your house is on fire, and your children—they will burn."

4. Which of the following is best supported by the evidence above?

____ a. Violence on TV can't be so bad for kids.

____ b. All nursery rhymes are morbid and depressing.

____ c. Some traditional children's verses are gruesome.

____ d. Violent criminals are created in early childhood.

C. Circle the letter of the fallacy contained in the argument below.

5. I wouldn't make an appointment with that new doctor if I were you—I felt perfectly fine until the day after my appointment with her.

a. False cause *(the argument assumes that the order of events alone shows cause and effect)*

b. False comparison *(the argument assumes that two things being compared are more alike than they really are)*

c. Either-or *(the argument assumes that there are only two sides to a question)*

ARGUMENT: Test 5

A. Circle the letter of the sentence in each paragraph that does *not* support the point of the argument. The point (main idea) is set off in **boldface** type.

1. [1]**The steel-jaw leghold trap, used to trap animals for their fur, causes great suffering.** [2]In snapping shut on an animal's leg, the trap tears muscle and shatters bone. [3]Commonly, animals caught in leghold traps die slowly and painfully—from exposure, starvation, or lack of water. [4]Those who manage to break free, by chewing off part of their leg, are likely to die from infection. [5]Those still trapped and alive when the trapper returns are strangled or clubbed to death. [6]In any case, with the warmth of modern fabrics, it's absolutely unnecessary to make any fur coats at all.

    Which of the following changes the subject of the author's argument that the steel-jaw leghold trap causes great suffering to animals?

    a. Sentence 2
    b. Sentence 3
    c. Sentence 4
    d. Sentence 6

2. [1]**Our townhouse complex is built in a way that is particularly unwelcoming to people in wheelchairs.** [2]All of the homes have tall, narrow, and winding stairs leading from the living room to the top floor. [3]The doorways of most rooms are too narrow for a wheelchair to pass through. [4]A number of steep steps lead up to the front stoop. [5]The manager of the complex discourages potential renters who are handicapped in any way. [6]In effect, townhouses built as ours are exclude people in wheelchairs from being either residents or visitors.

    Which of the following statements changes the subject of the author's argument that the townhouse complex is built in a way that is unwelcoming to people in wheelchairs?

    a. Sentence 2
    b. Sentence 3
    c. Sentence 4
    d. Sentence 5

(Continues on next page)

B. Check the letter of the conclusion that is best supported by the evidence in each group below.

Group 1

- *Unexpected Visitor* is just one of the many science fiction movies my ten-year-old sister has enjoyed.
- My grandmother thought the movie was silly and boring.
- My grandmother isn't familiar with much science fiction.

3. Which of the following conclusions is best supported by the evidence above?

____ a. All science fiction fans will enjoy *Unexpected Visitor*.

____ b. Science fiction doesn't appeal to the elderly.

____ c. *Unexpected Visitor* is aimed at an audience of children.

____ d. The speaker's sister and grandmother differ in their taste in movies.

Group 2

- My health insurance policy allows me to pay only $10 for a routine visit to my doctor.
- My health insurance policy is cheaper than my husband's.
- For only a small extra charge, my health insurance includes dental coverage.

4. Which of the following conclusions is best supported by the evidence above?

____ a. Men pay more than women for health insurance.

____ b. The speaker's health insurance policy is the least expensive in the country.

____ c. The speaker's health insurance policy has some good features.

____ d. Everyone can find affordable health insurance.

C. Circle the letter of the fallacy contained in the argument below.

5. Students should take a word processing course in school because it's important that everyone learn word processing.

a. Circular reasoning *(a statement repeats itself rather than providing a real supporting reason to back up an argument)*

b. Personal attack *(the argument shifts to irrelevant personal criticism)*

c. Straw man *(an argument is made by claiming an opponent holds an extreme position and then opposing that extreme position)*

ARGUMENT: Test 6

A. Circle the letter of the sentence in each paragraph that does *not* support the point of the argument. The point (main idea) is set off in **boldface** type.

1. [1]**We need better police protection on campus.** [2]So far this year, a dozen dorm rooms have been broken into; in each instance, valuables were stolen. [3]Within the past two months, several students have been mugged when they returned to their cars in campus parking lots. [4]If there were more plentiful parking near the center of campus, students wouldn't have to park in the more isolated lots at the outskirts of campus. [5]While walking back to their dorms from evening classes, several other students have been raped. [6]When I walk across the campus at night, I usually fail to see a single police officer or security guard. [7]There may be plenty of security guards protecting the equipment inside the college's buildings, but people are more important than property.

   Which of the following statements does *not* support the author's conclusion that better police protection is needed on campus?

   a. Sentence 2
   b. Sentence 3
   c. Sentence 4
   d. Sentence 5

2. [1]**The outdoor rock concert held in our city's park was a nightmare for residents.** [2]The music was so loud that it kept babies crying and dogs barking late into the night. [3]What's more, the rude, poorly dressed musicians set a bad example for American youth. [4]Hours before and after the concert, traffic was so jammed that even ambulances had trouble getting through. [5]A group of people who attended the concert started a fight that resulted in one resident being seriously injured. [6]The concert cost the city thousands of dollars to clean up all the beer cans, soda bottles, and other trash that was left behind.

   Which of the following statements changes the subject of the author's argument that the outdoor rock concert was a nightmare for residents?

   a. Sentence 3
   b. Sentence 4
   c. Sentence 5
   d. Sentence 6

B. Check the letter of the conclusion that is best supported by the evidence in each group. *(Continues on next page)*

Group 1

- Twenty-nine Beatles' songs reached the top-ten list in the 1960s—more than any other group.
- The Beatles had the highest number of records to reach number one during the 1960s. They had seventeen, compared with the second-place Supremes, who had twelve.
- In one year, 1964, the Beatles released thirty-one songs that hit the charts.

3. Which of the following conclusions is best supported by the evidence above?

_____ a. No other group will ever be as popular as the Beatles.

_____ b. During the 1960s, the Beatles were enormously popular.

_____ c. The Beatles shouldn't have split up.

_____ d. The Beatles sold more records than all of the other rock groups of the 1960s put together.

Group 2

- In 1927, Charles Lindbergh flew from New York to Paris, France, in 33 hours, 29 minutes; in 1978, the Concorde supersonic airliner made the same trip in 3 hours, 30 minutes.
- In 1825, an early steam-engine train, Locomotion I, pulled 48 tons at a speed of 15 miles per hour; in 1988, West Germany's Intercity Experimental train attained the fastest speed for a train carrying passengers—252 miles per hour.
- The first gasoline-driven car, built by Karl-Friedrich Benz in 1885, was a three-wheeler that reached 8–10 miles per hour; in 1983, Richard Noble drove his jet-engined car at a speed of over 633 miles per hour.

4. Which of the following conclusions is best supported by the evidence above?

_____ a. Someday soon, trains will go faster than airplanes.

_____ b. The American cars of the future will run on jet engines.

_____ c. Transportation speeds have greatly increased over the past two centuries.

_____ d. No airliner will ever fly faster than the Concorde.

C. Circle the letter of the fallacy contained in the argument below.

5. "When I was your age, calling boys gave them the wrong idea," Sharon's grandmother told her. "That's not a respectable way for you to get dates."

a. False cause (*the argument assumes that the order of events alone shows cause and effect*)

b. False comparison (*the argument assumes that two things being compared are more alike than they really are*)

c. Either-or (*the argument assumes that there are only two sides to a question*)

COMBINED SKILLS: Test 1

After reading the passage, circle the letter of the best answer to each question.

[1]Exact figures on the number of poor are difficult to determine. [2]For one thing, the amount of money needed for subsistence varies by locality. [3]For example, the money needed for rent in New York City is much greater than the money needed in rural Arkansas. [4]Another difficulty is that those most likely to be missed by the U.S. census are the poor. [5]People most likely to be missed in the census live in ghettos (where several families may be crowded into one apartment) or in rural areas, where some homes are inaccessible and where some workers follow the harvest from place to place and therefore have no permanent home. [6]Transients of any kind are sometimes missed by the census. [7]The conclusion is inescapable that the proportion of the poor in the United States is underestimated because the poor tend to be invisible, even to the government.

1. The word *subsistence* in sentence 2 means
   a. food.
   b. basic needs.
   c. moving.
   d. work needs.

2. According to the author, census workers are likely to miss
   a. people in the suburbs.
   b. farm workers who follow harvests.
   c. residents of New York City and of rural Arkansas.
   d. all of the above.

3. The relationship of sentence 3 to sentence 2 is one of
   a. illustration.
   b. time.
   c. contrast.
   d. cause and effect.

4. The main pattern of organization of the passage is
   a. a series of events.
   b. a list of reasons.
   c. a comparison and contrast.
   d. steps in a process.

5. One can conclude from this passage that
   a. there are probably fewer poor people in the U.S. than the number reported in the U.S. census.
   b. poor people deliberately avoid being counted by census workers.
   c. there are fewer poor people in New York City than in Arkansas.
   d. more poor people live in the U.S. than the government census indicates.

(Continues on next page)

6. The author feels that the U.S. census is likely to miss many poor people because
   a. two or more poor families live in what are considered one-family dwellings.
   b. the poor live in areas where homes are inaccessible to census workers.
   c. many poor are inaccessible because they have no permanent home.
   d. of all of the above.

7. You might infer that the author feels people should be classified as poor
   a. according to their income only.
   b. according to income and cost of living.
   c. only according to their state.
   d. according to their income and whether they live in urban or rural areas.

8. TRUE OR FALSE? _____ The author uses mostly opinions to support the main idea of the passage.

9. Which sentence best expresses the main idea of the passage?
   a. The amount of money needed for food and shelter varies greatly from place to place in the United States.
   b. The census is likely to underestimate the numbers of transients in the country.
   c. Because it is difficult to determine the exact number of poor people in the U.S., the proportion of poor is underestimated.
   d. There are various reasons for poverty throughout our country.

10. Which outline best organizes the material in the passage?
    a. There are two reasons why we greatly underestimate the exact number of poor in our country.
       1. It can be unclear who is poor because the income needed to live above poverty varies from place to place.
       2. The U.S. census is likely to greatly undercount the poor.
    b. There are reasons for poverty throughout our country.
       1. More reasons can be found in New York City than in rural Arkansas.
       2. Poverty is sustained by various lifestyles, including rural life and following the harvest from place to place.
    c. Food and shelter needed to avoid poverty
       1. New York City
       2. Arkansas
       3. Ghettos
       4. Rural areas
       5. Transients

COMBINED SKILLS: Test 2

After reading the passage, circle the letter of the best answer to each question.

> [1]Each of us will spend some twenty-five years of life in a strange state of semi-consciousness called sleep. [2]Contrary to popular belief, humans are not totally unresponsive during sleep. [3]Studies show that you are more likely to awaken if your own name is spoken, instead of another. [4]Likewise, a sleeping mother may ignore a jet thundering overhead, but wake at the slightest whimper of her child. [5]Some people can even do simple tasks while asleep. [6]In one experiment, subjects learned to avoid an electric shock by touching a switch each time a tone sounded. [7]Eventually, they could do it without waking. [8](This is much like the basic survival skill of turning off your alarm clock without waking.) [9]Of course, sleep does impose limitations. [10]There is no evidence, for instance, that a person can learn math, a foreign language, or other complex skills while asleep—especially when the snooze takes place during class.

1. The word *whimper* in "a sleeping mother may . . . wake at the slightest whimper of her child" means
   a. scream.
   b. dream.
   c. low, distressed cry.
   d. argument.

2. Sleep is described in this article as
   a. a state of semi-consciousness.
   b. basically unnecessary for human survival.
   c. a state of heightened learning.
   d. a state in which humans are left completely defenseless.

3. TRUE OR FALSE? _____ It has been proven scientifically that people can learn by "listening" to a lecture while sleeping.

4. This passage is mainly made up of
   a. facts.
   b. opinions.

5. From the paragraph, we can infer that during sleep, humans
   a. can ignore sounds which they know do not signal danger.
   b. can identify the names of close friends.
   c. can hear only constant, very loud noises.
   d. can learn simple arithmetic problems.

(Continues on next page)

6. We can infer that the first few times the subjects were shocked,
   a. they never felt the shock.
   b. they woke up.
   c. they became irritable.
   d. they were physically harmed.

7. TRUE OR FALSE? _____ Sentence 10 implies that people have tried to learn certain complex skills while asleep.

8. The author concludes this passage in a tone of
   a. distress.
   b. surprise.
   c. amusement.
   d. optimism.

9. An appropriate title for this paragraph would be
   a. Sleep
   b. The Responsiveness of Humans While Asleep
   c. How Sleeping Subjects Avoided an Electric Shock
   d. Sleep: Twenty-Five Years of a Person's Life

10. Which sentence best expresses the main idea of this paragraph?
    a. People can be taught to touch a switch while sleeping in order to avoid an electric shock.
    b. We are surprisingly responsive during sleep, but there are limits to what we can do when asleep.
    c. Humans spend about twenty-five years of their lives in the state of semi-consciousness called sleep.
    d. Studies reveal surprising things about human behavior.

COMBINED SKILLS: Test 3

After reading the passage, circle the letter of the best answer to each question.

[1]About 85 percent of college students agree that memory is like a storage chest. [2]As a recent ad in *Psychology Today* magazine put it, "Science has proven the accumulated experience of a lifetime is preserved perfectly in your mind." [3]Actually, psychological research has very nearly proven the opposite. [4]Many memories are not copies of our past experience that remain on deposit in a memory bank. [5]Rather, memories often are constructed at the time of withdrawal. [6]Like a paleontologist inferring the appearance of a dinosaur from bone fragments, we may reconstruct our distant past from fragments of information. [7]Thus we can easily (though unconsciously) revise our memories to suit our current knowledge. [8]When one of my sons complained that "The June issue of *Cricket* magazine never came" and was shown where it was, he delightedly responded, "Oh good, I knew I'd gotten it."

1. The word *paleontologist* in sentence 6 means
   a. psychologist specializing in ancient behaviors.
   b. educational philosopher.
   c. scientist specializing in ancient animal life.
   d. physician specializing in bones.

2. The relationship of sentence 5 to sentence 4 is one of
   a. time.
   b. contrast.
   c. addition.
   d. cause and effect.

3. Sentence 6 expresses a relationship of
   a. time.
   b. addition.
   c. contrast.
   d. comparison.

4. The statement that "memory is like a storage chest" suggests that memories are stored
   a. unchanged.
   b. quickly.
   c. and treasured.
   d. and then hidden.

(Continues on next page)

5. The passage indicates that our memories
   a. are always preserved changelessly.
   b. always vanish quickly.
   c. often change according to new knowledge.
   d. change only under extraordinary circumstances.

6. From the passage, one could conclude that the author's son
   a. deliberately lied when he claimed his issue of *Cricket* had not arrived.
   b. reconstructed his past after seeing the magazine.
   c. accurately remembered not having received the June issue of *Cricket*.
   d. could not distinguish fact from fiction.

7. The passage suggests that our memories of a friend who has recently betrayed us
   a. will never change.
   b. may change for the worse.
   c. are probably going to improve in time.
   d. are likely to be limited to the good times.

8. The author's primary purpose is
   a. to inform readers about a current scientific view of memory.
   b. to recommend ways for students to remember better.
   c. to raise questions about scientific research on memory.
   d. to analyze the various tricks people use to remember.

9. Which is an appropriate title for this selection?
   a. Improve Your Memory
   b. Memory Myths
   c. Memory Serves Various Purposes
   d. New Knowledge Influences Memories

10. Which sentence best expresses the main idea of the passage?
    a. College students agree that memory is like a storage chest.
    b. Our memories are often unconsciously revised to suit our current knowledge.
    c. None of our memories are copies of our past experience.
    d. Our memories are usually much more accurate than we realize.

COMBINED SKILLS: Test 4

After reading the passage, circle the letter of the best answer to each question.

[1]Humans generally spend more time working than do other creatures, but there is greater variability in industriousness from one human culture to the next than is seen in subgroups of any other species. [2]For instance, the average French worker toils for 1,646 hours a year; the average American for 1,957 hours; and the average Japanese for 2,088.

[3]One reason for human diligence is that people, unlike animals, can often override the impulses they may feel to slow down. [4]They can drink coffee when they might prefer a nap or flick on the air-conditioning when the heat might otherwise demand torpor. [5]Many humans are driven to work hard by a singular desire to gather resources far beyond what is required for survival. [6]Squirrels may collect what they need to make it through one winter, but only humans worry about college bills, retirement or replacing their old record albums with compact discs.

[7]"In other primates, if you don't need to travel around to get food for that day, you sit down and relax," said Dr. Frans de Waal of Emory University in Atlanta. [8]"It's typically human to try to accumulate wealth and get more and more."

[9]Much of the acquisitiveness is likely to be the result of cultural training. [10]Anthropologists have found that most hunter-gatherer groups, who live day to day on the resources they can kill or forage and who stash very little away for the future, generally work only three to five hours daily.

[11]Indeed, an inborn temptation to slack off may lurk beneath even the most work-obsessed people, which could explain why sloth ranks with lust and gluttony as one of the seven deadly sins.

1. The word *torpor* in sentence 4 means
   a. increased activity.
   b. extreme heat.
   c. industriousness.
   d. inactivity.

2. The word *acquisitiveness* in sentence 9 means
   a. dislike of staying in one place.
   b. desire for possessions.
   c. inability to provide for oneself.
   d. poverty.

(Continues on next page)

3. The relationship of sentence 2 to sentence 1 is one of
   a. time.
   b. illustration.
   c. contrast.
   d. cause and effect.

4. According to the author, humans are so industrious because
   a. they are stronger and better protected than animals.
   b. they can overcome impulses to slow down, and they work for gains beyond survival.
   c. they have an inborn temptation to gather resources far beyond what is required for survival.
   d. they need much more than animals need in order to survive.

5. Sentence 9 expresses a relationship of
   a. time.
   b. addition.
   c. comparison.
   d. cause and effect.

6. The pattern of organization of the passage is a combination of contrast and
   a. cause and effect.
   b. steps in a process.
   c. definition and example.
   d. a series of events.

7. Sentence 2 is a statement of
   a. fact.
   b. opinion.
   c. fact and opinion.

8. The author implies that most hunter-gatherer groups
   a. have not been culturally conditioned to desire many possessions.
   b. often go hungry.
   c. would be happier if they worked more hours each day.
   d. are more industrious than many French people.

9. The tone of this passage is
   a. critical and anxious.
   b. disbelieving and excited.
   c. straightforward and analytical.
   d. ambivalent yet optimistic.

10. Which is an appropriate title for this selection?
    a. Sloth: One of the Seven Deadly Sins
    b. Work Among Humans and Animals
    c. The Accumulation of Wealth
    d. Cultural Training

COMBINED SKILLS: Test 5

After reading the passage, circle the letter of the best answer to each question.

[1]Researchers have observed the process by which behavioral innovations spread from individual to individual and become part of a troop's culture independently of genetic transmission. [2]Consider the case of Imo, a 2-year old female macaque. [3]Imo and her troop of free-ranging monkeys live on the small Japanese island of Koshima, a high, wooded mountain with a surrounding beach. [4]Researchers enticed Imo and a number of other younger monkeys out of the forest by leaving sweet potatoes on a stretch of open beach. [5]In due course Imo began doing something that no other monkey had done. [6]She would carry her sweet potatoes to a fresh-water pool, dip them in the water with one hand, and brush the sand off with the other. [7]Soon her companions began copying her. [8]The behavior spread to the playmates' siblings and mothers. [9]However, adult males, who rarely participated in the group's behavior, did not acquire the habit. [10]When the young females who engaged in potato-washing matured and had offspring of their own, all of the offspring learned to wash potatoes from their mothers. [11]Then Imo undertook another new behavior. [12]She took the potatoes that she had cleaned in the fresh water and washed them anew in the sea. [13]Imo apparently liked the flavor of the salt water. [14]Within ten years, the practice of washing sweet potatoes in the sea had spread to two-thirds of the monkeys.

1. In sentence 1, *behavioral innovations* means
   a. noisy behaviors.
   b. old behaviors.
   c. new behaviors.
   d. genetic behaviors.

2. Imo's practice of washing her potatoes in fresh water was first copied by
   a. fathers of the group.
   b. Imo's children.
   c. mothers of the group.
   d. Imo's companions.

3. What is the relationship of sentence 9 to sentence 8?
   a. Addition
   b. Contrast
   c. Illustration
   d. Time

4. Sentence 10 is a statement of
   a. fact.
   b. opinion.
   c. fact and opinion.

(Continues on next page)

5. From this passage, you could infer that
   a. male macaques do not participate much in teaching their offspring.
   b. most macaques dislike the taste of salt.
   c. Imo was a monkey of average intelligence.
   d. macaques are solitary animals by nature.

6. The passage implies that before the researchers left sweet potatoes on the beach, the young macaques tended to
   a. dislike sweet potatoes.
   b. avoid water.
   c. avoid each other.
   d. stay in the forest.

7. The purpose of this passage is mainly
   a. to inform.
   b. to entertain.
   c. to persuade.
   d. to predict.

8. The tone of the passage can be described as
   a. hesitant.
   b. passionate.
   c. straightforward.
   d. ironic.

9. Which of the following is the most appropriate title for this selection?
   a. Genetic Influences on Animal Cultures
   b. A Diet for Macaques: Sweet Potatoes
   c. How a Young Macaque Changed Her Troop's Culture
   d. Animal Researchers and Subjects in Native Environments

10. Which of the following best outlines the passage?
    a. Scientists observed behaviors among members of a macaque troop in Japan.
       1. Young and female macaques copied a young female macaque's ideas in preparing sweet potatoes for eating—washing the potatoes in fresh water and then in salt water.
       2. Adult male macaques did not copy the new behaviors, presumably because they rarely participated in the group's behaviors.
    b. Macaque innovative behavior
       1. Japanese island of Koshima
          a) a high, wooded mountain
          b) a surrounding beach
       2. Imo and her troop of free-ranging monkeys
    c. New behaviors have been observed to spread from individual to individual and became part of a group's culture.
       1. Imo's washing of sweet potatoes in fresh water became a common behavior in her macaque troop.
       2. Imo's practice of washing sweet potatoes a second time in salt water also spread throughout much of the troop.

COMBINED SKILLS: Test 6

After reading the passage, circle the letter of the best answer to each question.

[1]Most of the current excitement over vitamins is being caused by a group of vitamins—C, E and beta carotene, the "parent" of vitamin A—that are known as antioxidants. [2]These nutrients appear to be able to defuse the toxic molecules, known as oxygen-free radicals, that result from normal cell activity. [3]These molecules are also created in the body by exposure to sunlight, X-rays, ozone, smoke, car exhaust and other pollutants.

[4]Free radicals are cellular rebels. [5]They damage DNA, alter biochemical compounds, corrode cell membranes, and kill cells outright. [6]Such molecular damage, scientists increasingly believe, plays a major role in the development of ailments like cancer, heart or lung disease, and cataracts. [7]Many researchers are convinced that the cumulative effects of free radicals also underlie the gradual deterioration that accompanies aging in all individuals, healthy as well as sick. [8]Antioxidants, studies suggest, might help stop the damage by neutralizing free radicals. [9]In effect, they perform as cellular sheriffs, catching the radicals and hauling them away.

1. The word *defuse* in sentence 2 means
   a. to avoid.
   b. to enlarge in size.
   c. to make less dangerous.
   d. to cause to increase in number.

2. The word *cumulative* in sentence 7 means
   a. harmless.
   b. gradually increasing.
   c. sudden and severe.
   d. beneficial.

3. According to many researchers, free radicals
   a. help stem the damage of aging.
   b. damage cells.
   c. gradually deteriorate.
   d. catch "cellular rebels."

4. Antioxidants
   a. may slow the deterioration that accompanies aging.
   b. are more effective in halting cataracts than in halting cancer.
   c. are hard to get.
   d. cannot be harmful in large amounts.

(Continues on next page)

5. The images of free radicals as "cellular rebels" and of antioxidants as "cellular sheriffs" were used to communicate the fact that
   a. free radicals and antioxidants are similar.
   b. free radicals and antioxidants are unrelated.
   c. free radicals can be harmful and antioxidants counter that harm.
   d. free radicals work on the cellular level and antioxidants do not.

6. The pattern of organization of the passage can be described as
   a. a narration of a sequence of events in the lives of researchers.
   b. a list of vitamins and each of their effects.
   c. a discussion of the similarities between free radicals and antioxidants.
   d. a discussion of causes and effects of free radicals and antioxidants.

7. The passage indicates that vitamin A
   a. alters DNA.
   b. is derived from beta carotene.
   c. is created by exposure to sunlight.
   d. corrodes cell membranes.

8. On the basis of this passage, one could conclude that
   a. a diet rich in vitamins C, E, and A may prevent serious health problems.
   b. more health problems are caused by pollution than by any other single source.
   c. free radicals are the only agents capable of killing cells outright.
   d. free radicals are apparently a major cause of childhood illnesses.

9. The author's purpose is
   a. to present the evidence for varying points of view on antioxidants and free radicals.
   b. to present the evidence for the view that antioxidants are beneficial because of their effects on free radicals, harmful molecules in the body.
   c. to explain a current view held by many researchers on the harmful effects of free radicals and the benefits of antioxidants.
   d. to question the currently popular view among researchers on the benefits of antioxidants.

10. Which is an appropriate title for this selection?
    a. Bodily Damages of Aging
    b. Vitamins and Their Effects
    c. How Pollutants Lead to Damaged Health
    d. Vitamins May Counteract Free Radicals

Part III

TEN READING SELECTIONS

1

Writing Effectively in Business
Constance Courtney Staley and Robert Stephens Staley II

Preview

As you climb up a business career ladder, chances are you will need to do writing on the job. Your writing skills can greatly affect your career success, say the authors of the following excerpt from the textbook *Communicating in Business and the Professions* (Wadsworth, 1992). They offer a practical three-stage process to help you become a more effective business writer. Their suggestions will be helpful even for non-business needs, including writing essays for school or personal letters.

Words to Watch

> *generated* (4): produced
> *peers* (4): those with equal standing
> *subordinates* (4): those under one's authority
> *liberating* (13): freeing
> *tyranny* (14): oppression
> *valet* (15): manservant
> *provocation* (24): something that brings about some action or feeling

No one disputes the importance of language skills—of writing and speaking effectively—in organizations. But although we admit its importance, skill in using the English language is not as widespread as you'd think in many organizations. Why not? Because while we agree we should be better writers and speakers, often we don't know

371

how—or, even worse, the "how" we know just doesn't work.

Many high school and college courses teach "scholarly" writing techniques that are 2 crucial in completing a history or political science assignment. But while useful in your education, these are not the practical skills you'll use in organizations throughout your life. Letters, memos, reports, instructions, sales presentations, interviews, and contracts—*these* are the means by which we exchange and record ideas, plans, needs, and disagreements—in short, the information that keeps the organization alive. And often these are the tools of growth, the means we use to come up with new ideas and more effective methods of doing business. These are the new "assignments" you'll encounter on the job.

WHY YOUR LANGUAGE ABILITIES COUNT

Chief executives and personnel officers across the country agree: Those who write 3 and speak well are valuable to the organization. Those who don't, aren't. If these leaders had their way, college graduates would learn to write and speak more effectively than most do. From these experts' comments, you might fairly draw this conclusion: If you learn to write and speak well, you'll stand out in a field of inept (or at best mediocre) communicators.

Who'll read your writing? Much of the writing generated° within an organization 4 stays there, and most of your conversations may be "local." On any given day, you'll write a memo to your peers°, talk over a project with a coworker, prepare a report for your supervisor, send a letter to your subordinates°, and perhaps even take notes or prepare documents for your own future use. Such *internal writing and speaking* is absolutely necessary in any organization with more than a few people.

You'll also aim a good deal of your communication outside the organization. Letters 5 to customers, associates, competitors, suppliers, lawyers, and even government agencies all produce far-reaching results that affect your organization—for good and for ill. Your *external writing* not only affects your organization's public image but also its competitive success.

Why do we say *your* writing? Because your language skills are peculiar to *you*, not 6 the organization. Corporations don't communicate—*you* do. Your words not only contribute to the organization's success but also help you succeed within the organization.

But this is not to say that individuals in organizations write in isolation. Far from 7 it. Organizational writing often is a team effort. Colleagues collaborate on projects, contribute sections to a report, edit one another's work, and even check one another's spelling. To be an effective part of that collaborative undertaking, your own skills must be sharp.

Clear, concise writing also is important to the organization's "bottom line." From 8 annual surveys conducted by the Dartnell Institute of Business Research, we estimate that in the next few years the average cost of producing one business letter—writing, dictating, revising, typing, processing, mailing, filing, and ultimately reading—will climb to more than $11. Altogether, letters alone cost U.S. companies more than $100 billion each year.

We agree, then, that language skills are important in the organization, and that you 9 want to be an effective writer. The next question we must answer is "How?" How do *you* become more effective in using the English language?

THE WRITING PROCESS

Writing doesn't just happen—at least not often. More often than not, the writer 10 works through a three-stage process of prewriting, writing, and rewriting.

Prewriting

Even on a particular project, the process of writing starts well before pen touches 11 page or fingers hit keys. Writing begins in thought, in observation, in searching, and perhaps even in worrying. You usually have some idea of what you want to say before you begin to speak, even though you may not be sure exactly what words will surface in the act of speaking. And the same thing happens in writing. So realize that even though you've nothing on paper yet, some of the work, some of the writing process—what we call *prewriting*—already has been accomplished.

To begin, think about your task. Ask questions about your audience and your 12 purpose: "Who am I writing to, and what do I want them to know or do?" You also may ask what facts and opinions you'll need, and where you'll find them. To find them, you may read, interview, discuss, observe, brainstorm, and reflect. Unless you have a perfect memory or a very simple writing task, you'll probably also take notes. And as your research progresses, you'll find yourself forming an opinion, favoring a particular point of view or a certain way of seeing your task. You also may discover a useful way to organize what you find.

Notice that you're probably already doing some writing in this prewriting stage. If 13 you've taken notes or written questions, opinions, or phrasings, you're helping yourself begin the writing process. These notes do *not* have to be grammatically correct or in any sense final or finished. Rather, they're only pieces of your work in progress. They're raw material for later use. And that attitude, that realization, is liberating°. Hold onto it even into the writing stage. Nothing has to be perfect, nothing is permanent, as you put together your thoughts. That's for later.

Writing

Have you ever had the frustrating experience of sitting down to write a paper and 14 finding that you just didn't know how to start? This common problem sometimes is called "writer's block" or "the tyranny° of the blank page." But whatever you call it, you'll be relieved to know there are ways around it.

Some professional writers resort to strange, almost ritualistic strategies to get going. 15 Victor Hugo supposedly wrote at the same time every day in his study—without clothes on! His valet° was ordered to lock away all Hugo's clothes until each day's writing was done. Apparently, the method worked—witness *Les Miserables*. But we're sure this technique would not be received well in most organizations.

A simpler way of starting is simply to start. Just write freely on whatever comes into 16 your head, whether it gets right to the point or not. For example, imagine that your boss wants a report by tomorrow morning on your division's morale. You've already prewritten this report: You've asked her what specifically she is looking for, you've interviewed some of your coworkers, and you've done some reading and taken some notes on previous morale problems (and their solutions) in your organization. Having done this much, you might begin by writing what's on your mind:

I'm having trouble starting this report because there's a lot at stake. Our morale problems seem to result from an overactive rumor mill—overactive because we don't get enough accurate information quickly enough from the top. . . .

Now stop and look at what you've written. If you take away the first sentence and the doubtful "seem to," you'll discover a useful beginning for a first draft: 17

Our morale problems result from an overactive rumor mill—overactive because we don't get enough accurate information quickly enough from the top.

Another starting technique is to begin with the words, "The purpose of this letter [or 'report' or 'briefing' or 'study'] is. . . ." As in the preceding example, you'll find yourself with plenty to say if you've already done your prewriting. And because you know you can get rid of these starter words later *and* change what follows, you're on your way to a useful first draft.   18

Another technique is to work step by step from an outline toward a finished product. Take the facts and ideas you collected during the prewriting stage and organize them in whatever way makes sense for now. It doesn't have to be perfect; in fact, you'll be better off if you expect your outline to change as you proceed. Once you have an outline, write a beginning statement that expresses your opinion, your argument, or in some way summarizes what all this prewriting boils down to. Place that thesis statement at the top of the outline. Then write a sentence (or several) to summarize each major section of your outline. Follow each statement with the items of support or information you've found, and build each into a paragraph one by one. You'll end up with a collection of paragraphs that, when tied together with transitions, will prove a serviceable rough draft.   19

Rewriting

This last stage is concerned with both form and content. Here you'll make the wording changes that provide your reader with the clearest, most powerful product possible. Here you'll ensure that grammar, punctuation, and spelling are correct and that your document looks good. But beyond such necessary technical considerations, you'll also take a fresh look at what you've said.   20

Rewriting often is called *revision*, and we think the term is a powerful one. It can mean not merely changing, but literally reseeing or *reenvisioning* your work. To help you see your work as others will see it, set it aside for a time before rewriting. "How long is 'a time'?" you ask. We can only answer, "As long as you can comfortably afford." The Roman writer Horace advised his students to put their work aside for seven years before revising. In most modern organizations, seven *hours* may be too long! But if you can plan ahead and give yourself an hour, a day, or a week before revising, you will have distanced yourself from your work enough to see its true weaknesses and to correct them.   21

As you reexamine your writing, ask whether it makes sense. Is it clear? Could it be better expressed in any part? Is the organization easy to follow? Does it accomplish what you set out to accomplish?   22

One effective way to discover how your writing will affect others is by simply asking them. Show someone your draft or revision. Ask someone whose judgment you trust to give you feedback on your work, in part or in whole. As we stated earlier, much of the writing in organizations results from collaboration between colleagues. So share your   23 writing *before* it becomes final.

One more tip. Throughout these three stages, be prepared to move fluidly from one to the other at the slightest provocation°. In the middle of your *rewriting*, if you come across some *prewriting* information—new information that would prove useful—copy it down and fit it in. In the *prewriting* stage, if you think of *writing* a good argument or a phrase that strikes you as powerful, then write it down.   24

Finally, realize the importance of polishing, proofing, and presenting the final document in perfect form. Be positive you've no spelling errors and be proud of the document's final appearance—paper clean, type dark and crisp, margins consistent, headings useful, names and addresses correct. If everything else is done perfectly, but you misspell your reader's name, then you lose.   25

BASIC SKILL QUESTIONS

Vocabulary in Context

1. The word *inept* in "If you learn to write and speak well, you'll stand out in a field of inept (or at best mediocre) communicators" (paragraph 3) means
    a. wise.
    b. qualified.
    c. unskilled.
    d. unpopular.

2. The word *collaborate* in "Organizational writing is often a team effort. Colleagues collaborate on projects" (paragraph 7) means
    a. compete.
    b. argue.
    c. separate.
    d. work together.

Central Point and Main Ideas

3. Which sentence best expresses the central point of this selection?
    a. The "scholarly" writing taught in high schools and colleges differs from the type of writing needed in business organizations.
    b. Language skills are important in business, where effective writing can be achieved through a three-stage process.
    c. Language skills are important in various walks of life, from business organizations to academic institutions.
    d. While working through the three stages of writing, be prepared to move easily from one stage to the other whenever useful.

4. The main idea of paragraph 8 is best expressed in its
    a. first sentence.
    b. second sentence.
    c. third sentence.

5. Which sentence best expresses the main idea of paragraph 19?
   a. Expect an outline to change as you proceed.
   b. A workable writing technique is to work from an outline toward a finished product.
   c. There is more than one way to write a rough draft.
   d. At the top of an outline write your thesis statement, which should express what all your prewriting boils down to.

Supporting Details

6. Prewriting is
   a. an unimportant part of writing.
   b. done only on paper.
   c. grammatically correct.
   d. collecting, thinking about, and focusing the information you will be using.

7. The object of the writing stage is to
   a. get everything in perfect order.
   b. stay with the original outline.
   c. create a useful first draft.
   d. get all your thoughts into one paragraph.

Transitions

8. The relationship of the second sentence below to the first is one of
   a. addition.
   b. illustration.
   c. contrast.
   d. comparison.

   Many high school and college courses teach "scholarly" writing techniques that are crucial in completing a history or political science assignment. But . . . these are not the practical skills you'll use in organizations throughout your life. (Paragraph 2)

9. The relationship between the two sentences below could be emphasized by inserting in the blank:
   a. Furthermore.
   b. Then.
   c. For example.
   d. However.

   Some professional writers resort to strange, almost ritualistic strategies to get going. _____, Victor Hugo supposedly wrote at the same time every day in his study—without clothes on! (Paragraph 15)

Patterns of Organization

10. The overall pattern of organization of paragraphs 11–25 is
    a. time order.
    b. list of items.
    c. cause and effect.
    d. definition and example.

ADVANCED SKILL QUESTIONS

Summarizing and Outlining

11. Which sentence best summarizes paragraphs 3–8?
    a. Business communication skills are important within one's company and with outsiders, both individually and as a team member.
    b. Much of the communication in business is aimed at peers, supervisors and subordinates within one's company.
    c. External communication—with customers, associates, competitors, suppliers, lawyers, and government agencies—influences a company's public image and success.
    d. One reason concise writing is important is that, according to the Dartnell Institute of Business Research, letters are becoming very expensive.

12. Which sentence best summarizes paragraphs 11–13?
    a. Writing begins even before one begins to write—it begins in the mind.
    b. Asking questions about your audience and your purposes will help you begin to think about your writing task.
    c. Prewriting includes thinking about your writing task, finding any necessary information, and writing useful notes.
    d. Notes written during prewriting do not have to be grammatically correct or final in any sense; they are only raw material for use during the writing process.

Fact and Opinion

13. The final sentence of paragraph 8 is
    a. a fact.
    b. an opinion.
    c. both fact and opinion.

Inferences

14. We can conclude from the selection that good speakers and writers
    a. have a better chance of getting and keeping a job and advancing at work.
    b. are not very common in the workplace.
    c. are valuable to a business organization in various ways.
    d. all of the above.

15. The authors imply that good writing
  a. is easy.
  b. takes years and years to learn.
  c. usually requires an organized approach.
  d. can be taught only in the classroom.

16. _____ TRUE OR FALSE? The author implies that very often a rough draft will require little or no revision.

Purpose and Tone

17. _____ TRUE OR FALSE? The authors' purposes are to inform and to persuade.

18. The tone of the selection can best be described as
  a. serious and distressed.
  b. compassionate and sympathetic.
  c. tolerant and forgiving.
  d. straightforward and encouraging.

Argument

19. Label the point of the following argument, based on the reading, with a **P** and the two statements of support with an **S**. Note that one statement should be left unlabeled—it is neither the point nor the support of the argument.

  _____ Numerous letters and memos must be written by people in business.

  _____ Many schools teach "scholarly" writing techniques that are not the practical skills needed in business organizations.

  _____ Good writing skills are useful in a business organization.

  _____ The public image of a company is affected by the written communications it produces.

20. Which fallacy is illustrated by the statement below?
  a. Changing the subject *(the evidence sounds good but has nothing to do with the argument)*
  b. False cause *(the argument assumes that the order of events alone shows cause and effect)*
  c. False comparison *(the argument assumes that two things being compared are more alike than they really are)*
  d. Either-or *(the argument assumes that there are only two sides to a question)*

  If you don't write well, you'll never succeed in business.

OUTLINING

The following outline based on "Writing Effectively in Business" is missing five items. Complete the outline by filling in the missing supporting details, which are listed after the outline.

Central Point: Language abilities count in business organizations, where effective writing can be achieved through a three-stage process.

I.   Language abilities count in business organizations.

    A. In business one has to communicate often.

        1. _____

        _____

        2. There's a frequent need for business writing that goes outside the organization.

    B. Much organizational writing is a team effort which requires sharp skills.

    C. Since letters cost so much, clear, concise writing is especially desirable.

II.   _____

        _____

    A. In prewriting, raw material is created for later use.

    B. During writing, a serviceable rough draft is written, which may require using any of several techniques that overcome writer's block.

        1. Some professional writers resort to strange, almost ritualistic strategies to overcome writer's block.

        2. A simple way of getting started is to write freely on whatever comes into your head.

        3. Another starting technique is to begin with the words "The purpose of this letter" (or of whatever is being written).

        4. _____

        _____

    C. _____

        _____

        1. _____

        _____

        2. Double-check your writing by showing it to someone whose judgment you trust for feedback.

Items Missing from the Outline:

- After putting writing aside for as long as possible, reread and revise it.
- There's a frequent need for writing within one's company.
- Another technique for writing a rough draft is to work step by step from an outline toward a finished product.
- During rewriting, make improvements in content and form, including such technical aspects as punctuation, spelling, and appearance.
- Effective writing in business can be achieved through a three-stage process.

DISCUSSION QUESTIONS

1. The article suggests a three-part process to writing. Do you make use of such a process as you do your own writing? Have you found another system that you believe works as well?

2. The authors refer to "writer's block" or "the tyranny of the blank page" that prevents many people from getting their first thoughts down on paper. Are you acquainted with the problem of writer's block—for example, when you're faced with a school writing assignment? Have you, like Victor Hugo, invented any means of dealing with it?

3. One purpose of the rewriting stage, according to the authors, is to ensure "that your document looks good." If the document is well-written, why do you think it matters how good it looks?

4. Are you in the habit of setting your writing aside for a time before coming back to revise it? Do you find this a useful practice? Does your work look different to you immediately after you write it than it does a day later?

Check Your Performance	WRITING EFFECTIVELY IN BUSINESS		
Skill	*Number Right*	*Points*	*Total*
BASIC SKILL QUESTIONS			
Vocabulary in Context (2 items)	_____	x 4 =	_____
Central Point and Main Ideas (3 items)	_____	x 4 =	_____
Supporting Details (2 items)	_____	x 4 =	_____
Transitions (2 items)	_____	x 4 =	_____
Patterns of Organization (1 item)	_____	x 4 =	_____
ADVANCED SKILL QUESTIONS			
Summarizing and Outlining (2 items)	_____	x 4 =	_____
Fact and Opinion (1 item)	_____	x 4 =	_____
Inferences (3 items)	_____	x 4 =	_____
Purpose and Tone (2 items)	_____	x 4 =	_____
Argument (2 items)	_____	x 4 =	_____
OUTLINING (5 items)	_____	x 4 =	_____

FINAL SCORE (OF POSSIBLE 100)   _____%

Enter your final score into the reading performance chart on the inside back cover.

2

Considering the Alternatives
Richard Lacayo

Preview

Our overcrowded prisons are a national problem that has inspired some imaginative solutions. In the following article, which originally appeared in *Time*, Richard Lacayo describes some of these alternatives to imprisonment and speculates about their effectiveness in crime prevention.

Words to Watch

contend (3): cope
bedlam (3): confused scene
beleaguered (5): overwhelmed
bracing (5): reinforcing
extramural (6): occurring beyond the walls (of a city, school, prison, etc.)
trappings (13): outward characteristics
contrition (14): regret
dispiriting (16): depressing
tentative (16): uncertain
recidivism (16): a return to criminal behavior

Jim Guerra sells cars today in Dallas. He used to sell cocaine in Miami. But last year, after being robbed and even kidnapped by competitors, he decided it was time for a career change. He gave up drugs—and the drug trade—and headed out to Texas for a new law-abiding life. The old life caught up with him anyway. In December federal agents arrested him on charges connected to his Florida coke dealing. After pleading guilty in the spring, Guerra faced fifteen years in prison.

He never went. These days Guerra, 32, is putting in time instead of doing it, by 2 logging four hundred hours over two and a half years as a fund raiser and volunteer for Arts for People, a nonprofit group that provides artists and entertainers for the critically ill at Dallas-area hospitals and institutions. His sentence, which also includes a $15,000 fine, means that a prison system full to bursting need not make room for one more. He sees a benefit to the community too. "I just love the job," he says. "I'll probably continue it after the sentence is up."

The work may be admirable, but is a stint of public service the just deserts of crime? 3 Many people would say no, but they may not be the same ones who must contend° with the bedlam° of American prisons. In recent years a get-tough trend toward longer sentences and more of them has had a predictable consequence. Even as crime rates generally declined during the first half of the 1980s, inmate numbers increased by nearly 60 percent. The nation's prison population now stands at a record 529,000, a total that grows by 1,000 each week; new cells are not being built in matching numbers. While virtually everyone convicted is a candidate for prison, many experts believe perhaps half the inmate population need not be incarcerated at all.

The dismal result is evident almost everywhere. Throughout the country, convicts 4 have been crammed into existing facilities until their numbers have pressed against the outer limits of constitutional tolerance. Currently in thirty-eight states the courts have stepped in to insist on, at the least, more acceptable levels of overcrowding. In Guerra's new home state of Texas, a federal judge earlier this month gave officials until March 31 to improve inmates' living conditions or risk fines of up to $800,000 a day. The despairing Texas solution has been to close its prison doors briefly whenever it reaches the court-mandated limit. At least Guerra did not go scot-free.

So "alternatives" to incarceration, which once inspired social workers and prison 5 reformers, have become the new best hope of many beleaguered° judges—and jailers too. In courts across the nation, people convicted of nonviolent crimes, from drunken driving and mail fraud to car theft and burglary, are being told in effect to go to their rooms. Judges are sentencing them to confinement at home or in dormitory halfway houses, with permission to go to and from work but often no more—not even a stop on the way home for milk. The sentences may also include stiff fines, community service and a brief, bracing° taste of prison.

Some supporters of alternative schemes look to the day when prison cells will be 6 reserved exclusively for career criminals and the violent, with extramural° penalties held out for the wayward of every other variety. "We're all against crime," says Herbert Hoelter, director of the National Center on Institutions and Alternatives, a nonprofit group that designed Guerra's package of penalties and persuaded the judge in his case to accept them. "But we need to convince people that there are other ways to get justice."

Anyway, who can afford to keep all offenders behind bars? Depending on the 7 prison, it can cost from $7,000 to more than $30,000 to keep a criminal in a cell for a year. Most alternative programs, their backers argue, allow lawbreakers to live at home, saving tax dollars while keeping families intact and off welfare. Since the detainees can get or keep jobs, part of their salaries can be paid out as fines or as compensation to victims. And alternatives give judges a sentencing option halfway between locking up offenders and turning them loose.

It remains to be seen, however, whether the new programs will have much appeal 8 for a crime-wary public and law-enforcement establishment. That prison time can be harrowing is to some minds its first merit. The living-room sofa is by comparison a painless instrument of remorse. "Until the alternatives are seen by the public as tough, there won't be support for them," says Thomas Reppetto of the Citizens Crime Commission in New York City. The problem is even plainer when the offenders are well heeled. Will justice be served if crooked stock traders are confined to their penthouses?

Most such misgivings will remain unsettled while officials try out the range of possibilities before them. In September, suburban Nassau County, near New York City, began testing one of the most talked-about new approaches, electronic house arrest. Probationers selected for the program are required to be housebound when not at work. To make sure they comply, each wears a kind of futuristic ball and chain: a four-ounce radio transmitter that is attached to the ankle with tamperproof plastic straps. The device broadcasts a signal to a receiver hooked up to the wearer's home phone, which in turn relays it to a computer at the probation department. If the wearer strays more than a hundred feet, the computer spits out a note for the probation officer. 9

"They can't leave home without us," quips Donald Richberg, coordinator of the program. Following an initial outlay of $100,000, the project has cost the county only about $10 a day per probationer. The anklets have been tried in at least eight states since New Mexico introduced electronic monitoring in 1983. The cost accounting looks favorable, but technical gremlins have been showing up too, resulting in reports of false disappearances or failures to report real ones. 10

Until the high-tech methods are perfected, more conventional alternatives remain the most popular. About thirty states have funded "intensive probation supervision," in which participants are typically required to work, keep a curfew, pay victims restitution and, if necessary, receive alcohol or drug counseling. Instead of the usual caseload—the nationwide average is 150—a probation officer in such experiments oversees just twenty-five people. Even with the added staff expense, the programs still cost less than incarceration. 11

The experience of Ron Rusich, 29, a house painter in Mobile, was typical. In 1984 he received a fifteen-year sentence for burglary. But an intensive probation scheme used in his state since 1982 eventually sent him back outside, and back to work, under strict supervision. A 10 p.m.-to-6 a.m. curfew was enforced during the first three months after release by at least one surprise visit each week from the corrections officer. There were three other weekly meetings, with restrictions eased as his time in the program increased. Living at home, as he was required to do for two and a half years, Rusich cost the state $8.72 a day, less than a third of the expense of keeping him in prison. The experience was a "lifesaver," says Rusich, who is now on parole. 12

Alabama and a number of other states also have a similar but more restrictive option: the work-release center, a sort of halfway house where offenders must live out their sentences. The system allows them to work, often at jobs found by the local government, but maintains more of the trappings° of confinement, such as dormitory life and security checks. In Indiana, where there are ten such centers, offenders do prison time first, with the hope of work release as a carrot for good behavior. That method lets the state consider, through observation and psychological testing, which inmates are likely to succeed in the program. "We want to see how they'll perform," says Vaughn Overstreet of the Department of Corrections. 13

A few localities have resorted to the most low-tech deterrent of all: shame. Sarasota County, Florida, is trying the "scarlet letter" approach, by requiring motorists convicted of drunk driving to paste bumper stickers on their cars announcing the fact. In Lincoln County, Oregon, a few felons have even been given a choice between prison and 14 publishing written apologies, accompanied by their photographs, in local newspapers. Roger Smith, 29, paid $294.12 to announce his contrition° in two papers after a guilty plea growing out of a theft charge. A published apology "takes the anonymity out of crime," insists Ulys Stapleton, Lincoln County district attorney. "People can't blend back into the woodwork."

Do alternatives work? That depends on what they are asked to accomplish. If the goal is cost efficiency, the answer is a qualified yes. They often seem cheap enough, but there are concerns that they may actually add to the bill for corrections because judges will use them as a halfway measure to keep a rein on people who would otherwise go free in plea bargains. James K. Stewart, director of a Justice Department research institute, contends that the cost to society of crimes committed by those not imprisoned must be factored in as well. For certain offenders, Stewart concludes, "prison can be a real, real cheap alternative."   15

If the goal is a society with fewer criminals, then firm judgments are even harder to draw. Criminology is a dispiriting° science. Its practitioners commonly caution that no criminal sanction, no matter how strict, no matter how lenient, seems to have much impact on the crime rate. But prison does at least keep criminals off the street. Home confinement cannot guarantee that security. Some data, tentative° and incomplete, do suggest, however, that felons placed on intensive probation are less likely to commit crimes again than those placed on traditional probation or sent to prison. Joan Petersilia, a Rand Corporation researcher, says the recidivism° rate of such offenders is impressively low, "usually less than 20 percent." And many keep their jobs, she adds. "That's the real glimmer of hope—that in the long run these people will become functioning members of the community."   16

The benefits of alternatives will remain mostly theoretical unless more judges can be persuaded to use them. That may require changes in some mechanisms of government. For instance, fines are a crucial part of many alternative sentencing packages. But they frequently go unpaid. Courts and prosecutors are not good at collecting them, says Michael Tonry of the nonprofit Castine Research Corporation, which specializes in law-enforcement issues. He proposes that banks and credit companies be deputized to fetch delinquent fines, with a percentage of the take as their payment. "To make fines work as a sentencing alternative," he says, "they must be both equitable, based on a person's ability to pay, and collectible."   17

One essential for getting courts to consider alternative sentencing, says University of Chicago Law professor Norval Morris, is to develop a publicly understood "exchange rate" between prison time and other forms of punishment, a table of penalties that judges can use for guidance on how to sentence offenders. "We should be able to say that for this crime by this criminal, either x months in prison, or a $50,000 fine plus home detention for a year plus x number of hours of community service," Morris contends.   18

A similar table is already in use in Minnesota, where alternative sentencing has become well established since the 1978 passage of a law that limits new sentences to ensure that prison capacity is not exceeded by the total number of inmates. The crime rate has not increased, supporters boast. Other states remain far more hesitant. Still, the present pressures may yet bring a day when the correctional possibilities will be so varied and so widely used that prison will seem the "alternative" form of punishment.   19

BASIC SKILL QUESTIONS

Vocabulary in Context

1. The word *restitution* in "About thirty states have funded 'intensive probation supervision,' in which participants are typically required to work, keep a curfew, pay victims restitution and, if necessary, receive alcohol or drug counseling" (paragraph 11) means
   a. annual salaries.
   b. apologies.
   c. repayment for loss or injury.
   d. bills.

2. The word *sanction* in "[Criminologists] commonly caution that no criminal sanction, no matter how strict, no matter how lenient, seems to have much impact on the crime rate" (paragraph 16) means
   a. reward.
   b. punishment.
   c. offender.
   d. trial.

Central Point and Main Ideas

3. Which sentence best expresses the central point of the selection?
   a. Jim Guerra never went to prison for his crimes.
   b. Overcrowded prisons are encouraging the use of alternative punishments.
   c. Keeping people in prisons costs too much money.
   d. The problem of crime has become more complicated in America.

4. Which sentence best expresses the main idea of paragraph 4?
   a. U.S. prisons are overcrowded.
   b. U.S. prisons are so full that courts are insisting on limits to overcrowding.
   c. A federal judge ordered Texas to improve living conditions in its prisons or risk heavy fines.
   d. Texas prisons are closing their doors when they get too full.

Supporting Details

5. One of the possible advantages of alternative punishments is that
   a. fewer probation officers are needed.
   b. they may cost less than imprisonment.
   c. judges must use them.
   d. fines are always paid.

6. Alternatives to imprisonment include
   a. public service.
   b. confinement at home.
   c. confinement in halfway houses.
   d. all of the above.

7. _____ TRUE OR FALSE? According to a Rand Corporation researcher, criminals who are given prison sentences are more likely to become law-abiding citizens than criminals who receive alternative sentences.

Transitions

8. The sentence below expresses a relationship of
   a. time.
   b. contrast.
   c. cause and effect.
   d. illustration.

   . . . there are concerns that [alternatives] may actually add to the bill for corrections because judges will use them as a halfway measure to keep a rein on people who would otherwise go free in plea bargains. (Paragraph 15)

Patterns of Organization

9. The pattern of organization of paragraph 1 is
   a. time order.
   b. list of items.
   c. comparison.
   d. definition and example.

10. Paragraph 4
    a. provides a definition and an example of "constitutional tolerance."
    b. compares and contrasts prison sentences.
    c. lists some effects of increasing numbers of inmates.
    d. discusses the causes of increasing number of inmates.

ADVANCED SKILL QUESTIONS

Summarizing and Outlining

11. Which of the following best summarizes paragraph 14?
    a. Sarasota County, Florida, uses an alternative sentence for drunk drivers requiring them to paste on their cars bumper stickers that announce their crime.
    b. Some localities use the alternative punishment of shame: one requires drunk drivers to confess their crime on bumper stickers; another lets felons choose between prison or apologizing in local papers.
    c. A published apology "takes the anonymity out of crime," according to Ulys Stapletone, Lincoln County district attorney. "People can't blend back into the woodwork."
    d. Some localities are using the most low-tech deterrent of all to crime. Those localities include Sarasota County, Florida, and Lincoln County, Oregon.

12. Which ending best completes the following partial summary of paragraphs 17–19?

    Alternative sentences will become more workable once . . .
    a. banks and credit companies are deputized to fetch delinquent fines, with a percentage of the take as their payment.
    b. all judges have a table of alternate penalties corresponding to prison time, which they can use for guidance on how to sentence offenders.
    c. fine collection is improved and judges have a table of penalties as a guide to sentencing.
    d. all states follow the lead of Minnesota, where alternative sentencing has been well established since 1978.

Fact and Opinion

13. Which of the following is a statement of opinion?
    a. "Jim Guerra sells cars today in Dallas."
    b. "Depending on the prison, it can cost from $7,000 to more than $30,000 to keep a criminal in a cell for a year."
    c. "In Lincoln County, Oregon, a few felons have even been given a choice between prison and publishing written apologies, accompanied by their photographs, in local newspapers."
    d. "Criminology is a dispiriting science."

14. Paragraph 1 is made up of
    a. facts.
    b. opinions.
    c. both facts and opinions.

Inferences

15. In the first two sentences of paragraph 3, the author implies that the people who work in the criminal justice system are more likely than others to

_____

Purpose and Tone

16. The main purpose of this article is
    a. to inform readers about alternative sentences.
    b. to persuade readers that alternative sentences are more effective than jail sentences.
    c. to entertain readers with anecdotes about the criminal justice system.

17. The tone of this article can be described as mainly
    a. angry.
    b. objective.
    c. pessimistic.
    d. cheerful.

Argument

18. Which of the following illustrates the fallacy of hasty conclusion?
    a. Alternative sentencing is unworkable because it won't work.
    b. Michael Tonry probably favors paying companies for collecting fines because he plans on owning a credit company himself.
    c. Either we put criminals in jail, or we flood our cities with violent criminals.
    d. Only jail can teach criminals not to lead a life of crime.

19. Label the point of the following argument, based on the reading, with a **P** and the two statements of support with an **S**.

    _____ Imprisoning offenders is expensive.

    _____ We shouldn't keep all criminal offenders behind bars.

    _____ If all offenders were jailed, our prisons would be unconstitutionally crowded.

20. The point below is followed by four statements, three of which logically support the point. Which of the statements changes the subject of the argument?

    Point: Alternative sentencing can be beneficial.
    a. Public-service work benefits the public.
    b. Alternative sentences are less expensive than imprisonment.
    c. There is evidence that those serving alternative sentences are less likely to commit another crime.
    d. If we were more successful fighting our drug problem, there wouldn't be so many criminals to deal with.

OUTLINING

Complete the following outline based on "Considering the Alternatives."

Central Point: There is growing interest in alternative sentencing.

    A. The main reasons for the growing interest in alternate sentencing are

    _____ and the high cost of imprisonment.

    B. There are several types of alternate sentences that have been used so far.

        1. _____

        _____

        2. Intensive probation supervision typically requires participants to work, keep a curfew, pay restitution and perhaps receive counseling.

3. _____

   _____

4. Some localities use shame to punish those convicted of certain crimes.

C. So far, there are conflicting opinions about the benefits of alternate sentences.
   1. There are disagreements about their expense.
      a. Some feel alternate sentencing is inexpensive.
      b. Others fear it may increase costs because judges will use them on people who would otherwise have gone free on plea bargaining.
   2. There are disagreements on whether or not they deter crime.
      a. Some say punishments of any kind do not deter crime.

      b. _____

   _____

DISCUSSION QUESTIONS

1. Many people consider charity work to be a fulfilling and satisfying experience. Knowing this, do you think justice was served in the case of Jim Guerra, the ex-drug dealer who was sentenced to do charity work rather than to serve fifteen years in prison?

2. What are some of the positive and negative aspects of home confinement? Consider such things as safety, impact on the family, and financial obligations. Do you believe justice is served with this type of sentence?

3. Which alternative to imprisonment seems better to you, supervision or shame? Would one or the other be better for particular types of crimes?

4. In paragraph 18 of the selection, Lacayo refers to a law professor's suggestion "to develop a publicly understood 'exchange rate' between prison time and other forms of punishment." What types and amounts of alternate sentencing do you think would equal, for example, a year in prison?

Check Your Performance   CONSIDERING THE ALTERNATIVES

Skill	Number Right	Points	Total
BASIC SKILL QUESTIONS			
Vocabulary in Context (2 items)	_____	x 4 =	_____
Central Point and Main Ideas (2 items)	_____	x 4 =	_____
Supporting Details (3 items)	_____	x 4 =	_____
Transitions (1 item)	_____	x 4 =	_____
Patterns of Organization (2 items)	_____	x 4 =	_____
ADVANCED SKILL QUESTIONS			
Summarizing and Outlining (2 items)	_____	x 4 =	_____
Fact and Opinion (2 items)	_____	x 4 =	_____
Inferences (1 item)	_____	x 4 =	_____
Purpose and Tone (2 items)	_____	x 4 =	_____
Argument (3 items)	_____	x 4 =	_____
OUTLINING (4 items)	_____	x 5 =	_____

FINAL SCORE (OF POSSIBLE 100)   _____%

Enter your final score into the reading performance chart on the inside back cover.

3

Preview, Read, Write, Recite
Gayle Edwards

Preview

Do you sometimes wonder if others know something about studying that you don't? Do they seem to have a successful system that helps them deal with reading assignments? In fact, there are methods of study that can make you a more productive student. If you have never learned one of those methods, this selection is your opportunity to do so.

Words to Watch

randomly (9): in a here-and-there fashion
complacent (11): self-satisfied
stimuli (11): causes of a physiological response
adapt (13): adjust
qualitatively (18): in quality
recounting (19): telling
paraphrasing (23): restating in other words
passive (23): inactive
mull (23): consider thoughtfully
selective (28): careful in selection

Your idea of studying a textbook assignment may be to simply read it once or twice. If so, you may be wondering why you have trouble understanding and remembering what you read. The PRWR system is an excellent way to boost your study power. By using it consistently, you'll become a better reader, you'll remember much more of what you read, and you'll be able to study effectively.

PRWR is an abbreviation of the system's four steps: 2

1. **Preview** the reading.
2. **Read** the material and mark important parts.
3. **Write** notes to help you study the material.
4. **Recite** the ideas in your notes.

You can put this system to work immediately. Each step is explained in detail   3
below, and a textbook selection is included for you to practice on.

STEP 1: PREVIEW THE READING

When you go to a party, you might look the scene over to locate the buffet, check   4
out the music, and see who's there. After getting an overview of what's happening, you'll
be more at home and ready to get down to the business of serious partying. Similarly, a
several-minute preview of a reading gives you a general overview of the selection before
you begin a careful reading. By "breaking the ice" and providing a quick sense of the new
material, the preview will help you get into the reading more easily. There are four parts to
a good preview:

- *Consider the title.* The title is often a tiny summary of the selection. Use it to help   5
  you focus in on the central idea of the material. For instance, a selection titled
  "Theories of Personality" will tell you to expect a list of differing theories of
  personality.

- *Read over the first and last paragraphs of the selection.* The first paragraph or so of   6
  a reading is often written as an introduction. It may thus present the main ideas,
  giving you an overview of what's coming. The last paragraphs may be a summary of
  a reading and thus give you another general view of the main ideas.

- *Note headings and their relationships.* Main headings tell you what sections are   7
  about. They are generally printed in darker and/or larger type; they may be written
  all in capital letters or in a different color. The main headings under the title
  "Theories of Personality," for example, would probably tell you which theories are
  being covered.

    Subheadings fall under main headings and help identify and organize the   8
  material under main heads. Subheads are printed in a way that makes them more
  prominent than the text but less prominent than the main headings. A selection may
  even contain sub-subheadings to label and organize material under the subheads.
  Here is how a series of heads might look:

MAIN HEAD (at the margin in larger type)
   Subhead (indented and in slightly smaller type)
     Sub-subhead (further indented and in even smaller type)

Together, the headings may form a general outline of a selection. Note, for instance,
the main heading and subheads in this article.

- *Sample the text randomly°.* Read a few parts that seem likely to contain especially   9
  significant information—the first sentence of some paragraphs, words set off in

italics or **boldface,** and visuals (pictures, diagrams, and graphs). Also keep an eye out for prominent lists and definitions.

Does all this sound like a waste of time to you? You may wonder if it wouldn't be   10
better just to get on with reading the assignment. Well, don't reject previewing until you've tried it a few times. The few minutes spent on previewing will help you to better understand a selection once you do read it. To see how this works, take about three minutes to preview the following textbook selection.

LISTENING

Listening provides us with data to which we can respond. You may   11
already be aware that in your daily communication you spend more time
listening than you do speaking, reading, or writing. One study of college
student communication habits shows that college students spend 22
percent of their time speaking, 20 percent reading, 8 percent writing, and
50 percent of their time listening. Yet of these four skills, people tend to
be most complacent° about their listening. Although most people have
the physical capabilities of recording audio impulses, many are not good
listeners. Receiving audio stimuli° is hearing; *listening means making
sense out of what we hear*. Research studies have shown that most of us
listen with only 25 to 50 percent efficiency.

Listening Factors

Your listening is a product of many factors; you have only minimal   12
control over some, but others you can change if you want. Let us first
consider two factors in listening that are a function of your heredity and
environment—hearing acuity and vocabulary—and then discuss ways to
improve your listening.

Hearing acuity   Some people have real hearing problems. Nearly 15   13
million Americans suffer some hearing impairment. If you are among
this number, you may now wear a hearing aid or you may have learned
to adapt° to the problem. However, if you are not aware of the problem,
poor hearing alone may limit your listening effectiveness.

If you suspect you may have a hearing problem, have a complete   14
hearing test. Most schools have facilities for testing hearing acuity. It is
painless and is usually provided at minimal, if any, cost to the student.

Vocabulary   Listening and vocabulary are definitely related. If you   15
know the meaning of all the words a person uses, you are likely to have
a better understanding of the material and, as a result, to retain more.
However, if you do not know the meaning of words used in a
conversation or if you are not familiar with the specialized vocabulary
used in a particular field of study, your listening will be affected and you
may not understand. Many "poor students" have average or better

intelligence but may be handicapped by a poor vocabulary. If you have a below-average vocabulary, you may have to work that much harder on listening.

Improving Listening

Assuming that your listening efficiency is about average, what can you do about it? An average listener who is determined can almost double listening efficiency in a few months. In fact, by following a few simple steps, you will note improvement in your listening immediately. A key factor in listening is your own attitude and behavior. Each of the following recommendations can be put into practice *now*.   16

Recognize differences in listening difficulty. Listening is similar to reading in that you should listen differently depending on the purpose and degree of difficulty of the material. Yet many people "listen" about the same, regardless of purpose or material. Listening intensity differs depending on whether you are listening primarily for enjoyment, for understanding, or to evaluate.   17

Much of our listening is for pleasure or enjoyment. Listening to music on the car radio is one example of this kind of listening. We are aware of the "background" sound—we find it soothing, relaxing, and generally pleasant. Much of our listening to conversation is for this purpose. For instance, when Tom and Paul talk about the game they saw on television, their listening is for pleasure and the details of the conversation are likely to be soon forgotten. Unfortunately, many people approach all situations as if they were listening for pleasure. Yet how you listen should change qualitatively° when you listen for understanding or to evaluate.   18

A more difficult challenge is listening to understand. For this kind of listening we need to develop greater intensity. For college students, classroom lectures provide a situation requiring this type of listening. Likewise, such informal situations as listening to directions (how to get to a restaurant), listening to instructions (how to shift into reverse in a foreign car), and listening to explanations (a recounting° of the new dorm rules) also require listening to understand. In this chapter we consider several skills to help you with this kind of listening.   19

By far the most demanding challenge is listening to evaluate. Daily we are flooded with messages designed to influence our behavior. To function best in this context, we have to be able to recognize the facts, weigh them, separate them from emotional appeals, and determine the validity of the conclusions presented. The remainder of the real recommendations are directed toward helping you in your efforts to understand and to evaluate. Later, in the chapter on persuasive speaking, we will discuss tests of evidence and reasoning that are as important in listening to arguments as they are in constructing them.   20

Get ready to listen. Listening efficiency increases when the listener follows the apparently elementary practice of really being ready to listen. "Getting ready" involves both mental and physical application. Mentally you need to stop thinking about any of the thousands of random ideas that constantly pass through your mind; all your attention should be directed to what a person is saying. In effect, anyone who is talking with you is in competition with all the miscellaneous thoughts and feelings you are having. Some of them may be more pleasant to tune into than what people are saying to you. Anticipation of an exciting evening; thoughts about a game, a test, or what is for dinner; or recreating in your memory scenes from a memorable movie or television show may offer more attractive pleasures than listening to the words of another person, yet attention paid to such competing thoughts and feelings is one of the leading causes of poor listening.

21

You need to stand or sit in a way that will help you listen. Since physical alertness often encourages mental alertness, you may find that how you stand or how you sit affects how you receive messages. You may also find it helpful to look people in the eye when they talk with you. A visual bond between those conversing helps form a mental bond that assists listening effectiveness.

22

Listen actively. Instead of letting your mind wander or preparing what you are going to say when you have a chance, you can practice and use "active listening" skills. Active listening includes questioning and paraphrasing°. Active listening involves you in the process of determining meaning. Too often people think of the listening experience as a passive° activity in which what they remember is largely a matter of chance. In reality, good listening is hard work that requires concentration and willingness to mull° over and, at times, verbalize what is said. Good listening requires using mental energy. If you really listen to an entire 50-minute lecture, when the lecture is over you will feel tired because you will have put as much energy into listening as the lecturer put into talking.

23

If you have previewed the above selection carefully, you already know a bit about it—without even having really read much. To confirm this to yourself, answer these questions:

24

- What is the selection about?
- Which are two factors in listening?
- How many ways are presented to improve listening?

STEP 2: READ THE MATERIAL AND MARK IMPORTANT PARTS

After previewing a selection, take the time to read it through from start to finish. Keep reading even if you run into some parts you don't understand. You can always come back to those parts. By reading straight through, you'll be in a better position to understand the difficult parts later.

25

As you read, mark points you feel are especially significant. This will make it easy 26 for you to find them later when you take study notes. The goal is to mark the most important ideas of a selection. They include:

- Definitions
- Helpful examples
- Major lists of items
- Points that receive the most space, development, and attention.

Because you noted some of these ideas during the preview, identifying them as you read will be easier.

Ways to Mark

Here are some ways to mark off important ideas: 27

- Underline definitions and identify them by writing *DEF* in the margin.
- Identify helpful examples by writing *EX* in the margin.
- Number 1, 2, 3, etc. the items in lists.
- Underline obviously important ideas. You can further set off important points by writing *IMP* in the margin. If important material is several lines long, do not underline it all, or you will end up with a page crowded with lines. Instead, draw a vertical line alongside the material, and perhaps underline a sentence or a few key words. If you're not yet sure if material merits marking, simply put a check by it; you can make your final decision later.

As you mark a selection, remember to be selective°. Your markings should help you 28 highlight the most significant parts of the reading; if everything is marked, you won't have separated out the most important ideas. Usually you won't know what the most important ideas are in a paragraph or a section until you've read all of it. So it's good to develop a habit of reading a bit and then going back to do the marking.

STEP 3: WRITE STUDY NOTES

After reading and marking a selection, you are ready to take study notes. *Notetaking* 29 *is the key to successful learning.* In the very act of deciding what is important enough to write down and of then writing it down, you begin to learn and master the material.

Here are some guidelines to use in writing study notes: 30

1. After you have previewed, read, and marked the selection, reread it. Then write out the important information on 8½-by-11-inch sheets of paper. Write on only one side of each page.

2. Write clearly. Then you won't waste valuable study time trying to decipher your handwriting.

3. Use a combination of the author's words and your own words. Using your own words at times forces you to think about and work at understanding the material.

4. Organize your notes into a rough outline that will show relationships between ideas. Do this as follows:

   a. Write the title of the selection at the top of the first sheet of notes.
   b. Write main headings at the margin of your notes. Indent subheads about half an inch away from the margin. Indent sub-subheads even more.
   c. Number items in a list, just as you did when marking important items in a list in the text. Be sure each list has a heading in your notes.

Try preparing a sheet of study notes for the material on listening. Here is a start for   31
such a sheet of study notes:

Listening

We spend 50% of our time listening, but with only a 25% to 50% efficiency.
Listening factors:
   1. Hearing acuity
   2. Vocabulary
Improving listening. . . .

The activity of taking notes will help you see how useful it is to write out the important information in a selection.

STEP 4: RECITE THE IDEAS IN YOUR NOTES

After writing your study notes, go through them and write key words in the margin   32
of your notes. The words will help you study the material. For example, here are the key words you might write in the margin of notes taken on the material about listening:

Listening efficiency
2 factors in listening
3 ways to improve listening
3 kinds of listening

To study the material, turn the words in the margin into questions. First ask yourself,   33
"What is listening efficiency?" Then recite the answer until you can say it without looking at your notes. Then ask yourself, "What are two factors in listening?" Then recite that answer until you can say it without looking at your notes.

Then—and this is a key point—go back and review your answer to the first   34
question. Test yourself—see if you can say the answer without looking at it. Then test yourself on the second answer. *As you learn each new bit of information, go back and test yourself on the previous information.* Such repeated self-testing is the real key to effective learning.

In summary, then, this article describes a simple but extremely helpful study system   35
that you can use to learn textbook material. On a regular basis, you should preview, read, write, and recite your college reading assignments. By doing so, and by reciting and learning your classroom notes as well, you will be well prepared to deal with college exams.

BASIC SKILL QUESTIONS

Vocabulary in Context

1. The word *merits* in "If you're not yet sure if material merits marking, simply put a check by it; you can make your final decision later" (paragraph 27) means
   a. forbids.
   b. deserves.
   c. illustrates.
   d. provides.

2. The word *decipher* in "Write clearly. Then you won't waste valuable study time trying to decipher your handwriting" (paragraph 30) means
   a. create.
   b. make out.
   c. defend.
   d. misunderstand.

Central Point and Main Ideas

3. Which sentence best expresses the central point of the selection?
   a. Some people have trouble understanding their textbooks.
   b. PRWR is a four-step system that improves textbook study skills.
   c. There are systems that can improve study skills.
   d. The PRWR system begins with previewing the reading.

4. The main idea of paragraph 27 is best expressed in its
   a. first line.
   b. second line.
   c. third line.
   d. last sentence.

Supporting Details

5. When previewing a selection, you should *not*
   a. look at the title.
   b. read the first and last paragraphs.
   c. read every word.
   d. check the headings and their relationships.

6. _____ TRUE OR FALSE? As you read through a selection for the first time, you should stop to reread parts you don't understand.

7. Study notes
   a. focus your attention on the important parts of a reading.
   b. should be written on both side of the paper.
   c. should always be taken word for word from the text.
   d. should be written before the selection is marked.

Transitions

8. The relationship of the second sentence below to the first is one of
   a. time.
   b. addition.
   c. comparison.
   d. contrast.

   > After getting an overview of what's happening, you'll be more at home and ready to get down to the business of serious partying. Similarly, a several-minute preview of a reading gives you a general overview of the selection before you get down to a careful reading. (Paragraph 4)

Patterns of Organization

9. The main pattern of organization of paragraph 30 is
   a. definition and example.
   b. cause and effect.
   c. list of items.
   d. comparison.

10. The main pattern of organization of the PRWR system (and thus of the selection) is
    a. time order.
    b. comparison.
    c. cause and effect.
    d. contrast.

ADVANCED SKILL QUESTIONS

Summarizing and Outlining

11. Write a one-sentence summary of paragraphs 5–9 in which you state the main idea (given at the end of paragraph 4) and then briefly list the major details.

    _____

    _____

    _____

    _____

12. Which ending best completes the following partial summary of paragraphs 32–34?

    After writing your study notes, write key words in the margin. Then . . .
    a. turn the key words into questions, and answer them until you can do so without your notes; then repeatedly self-test yourself on the material.
    b. without referring to your notes, study the original material until you can recite it all.

c. turn those key words into questions. For example, if the key words are "definition of listening efficiency," you would ask yourself, "What is listening efficiency?"

d. use those key words to write key definitions.

Fact and Opinion

13. The statement below is a(n)
    a. fact.
    b. opinion.
    c. both fact and opinion.

    Each step [of PRWR] is explained in detail below, and a textbook selection is included for you to practice on. (Paragraph 3)

Inferences

14. _____ TRUE OR FALSE? The author implies that the PRWR method will help you make the most of your study time.

15. _____ TRUE OR FALSE? From the first paragraph of this selection, we can conclude that for study purposes, one or two readings are not enough.

16. From the selection, we can conclude that the PRWR system
    a. is used by all good students.
    b. is too difficult for some students.
    c. is a relatively new approach to study.
    d. may help you improve your grades.

Purpose and Tone

17. The purpose of this selection is
    a. both to inform and to persuade.
    b. both to persuade and to entertain.
    c. only to persuade.

18. The author's tone can be described as
    a. ironic and ambivalent.
    b. distressed but informal.
    c. encouraging and optimistic.
    d. sympathetic and light-hearted.

Argument

19. Label the point of the following argument, based on the reading, with a **P** and the two statements of support with an **S**. Note that one statement should be left unlabeled—it is neither the point nor the support of the argument.

    _____ The PRWR system is not difficult to understand.

    _____ Marking a reading forces you to read carefully enough to make sense of the important parts.

    _____ The PRWR system can help you to understand and remember material.

_____ The repetition involved in reciting your notes fixes ideas in your memory.

20. The argument below (suggested by the reading) would be an example of what fallacy?

a. Hasty conclusion *(the argument comes to a conclusion based on insufficient evidence)*

b. False cause *(the argument assumes that the order of events alone shows cause and effect)*

c. False comparison *(the argument assumes that two things being compared are more alike than they really are)*

d. Either-or *(the argument assumes that there are only two sides to a question)*

If students don't use the PRWR system, they will never do well in school.

OUTLINING

Complete the following outline of "Preview, Read, Write, Recite." You will find headings and lists in the selection helpful. Note that the outline excludes the reading on listening.

Central Point: PRWR, a helpful textbook study system, involves four steps.

A. *Step 1:* Preview the Reading

1. _____

2. Read over the first and last paragraphs of the selection.

3. Note headings and their relationships.

4. _____

B. *Step 2:* Read the Material and Mark Important Parts

1. Read the selection from start to finish.

2. Mark significant parts.

3. Use various ways of marking.

C. *Step 3:* Write Study Notes

1. Reread selection and write out important information.

2. _____

3. Use a combination of the author's and your own words.

4. _____

_____

D. *Step 4:* Recite the Ideas in Your Notes

1. Write key words in the margins of your notes.

2. Turn key words into questions, and recite the answers.

3. _____

DISCUSSION QUESTIONS

1. What study system or approach to study do you use? How does it compare or contrast with the PRWR approach?

2. Do you plan to use all or part of the PRWR system? (Be honest.) Why or why not?

3. In what ways has Edwards organized her article so that it can be studied with the PRWR system?

4. Why does Edwards write that "notetaking is the key to successful learning"? Why isn't merely reading and marking a selection enough?

Check Your Performance	PREVIEW, READ, WRITE, RECITE		
Skill	*Number Right*	*Points*	*Total*
BASIC SKILL QUESTIONS			
Vocabulary in Context (2 items)	_____	x 4 =	_____
Central Point and Main Ideas (2 items)	_____	x 4 =	_____
Supporting Details (3 items)	_____	x 4 =	_____
Transitions (1 item)	_____	x 4 =	_____
Patterns of Organization (2 items)	_____	x 4 =	_____
ADVANCED SKILL QUESTIONS			
Summarizing and Outlining (2 items)	_____	x 4 =	_____
Fact and Opinion (1 item)	_____	x 4 =	_____
Inferences (3 items)	_____	x 4 =	_____
Purpose and Tone (2 items)	_____	x 4 =	_____
Argument (2 items)	_____	x 4 =	_____
OUTLINING (5 items)	_____	x 4 =	_____

FINAL SCORE (OF POSSIBLE 100)   _____ %

Enter your final score into the reading performance chart on the inside back cover.

4

Motivation and Needs
Virginia Quinn

Preview

If you had to choose between friendship and achievement, which would you pick? And how much security would you give up in order to avoid boredom? According to psychologist Abraham Maslow, we all would answer these questions in more or less the same way—because we all share the same basic human needs. In this selection from her textbook *Applying Psychology* (McGraw-Hill), Virginia Quinn explains Maslow's view of human motivation and needs.

Words to Watch

hierarchy (2): a group arranged in order of rank
apathetic (7): having little interest
dispirited (7): discouraged
novelty (10): something new
fluctuate (10): alternate
affiliation (13): social connection
superficial (13): shallow
implications (15): inferences
refraining from (15): not using
capitalize on (18): take advantage of
spontaneous (31): behaving freely

W hether their motivation is conscious or unconscious, people have a broad range   1
of needs. Some needs are shared by everyone. For example, everyone is motivated to stay alive and survive. Food, rest, oxygen, and other necessities for life are common to all people. Other needs vary from one person to the next. For example, some people need to

drive a fancy sports car and wear designer clothes. Others may need to travel to far-off lands and live among different cultures. Undoubtedly, you have heard of individuals who had a need to climb high mountains or do missionary work in underdeveloped countries. Strangely, some people even feel a need to write psychological books!

Trying to sort and organize every possible need seems like a monstrous task. Yet Abraham Maslow, one of the most important contributors to the field of motivation, managed to classify human needs or motivations into a pyramid-like hierarchy°. In order to progress upward to the top of the pyramid, you need to satisfy each need along the way.   2

At the base of his pyramid, Maslow placed everyday physiological needs required for survival—needs for food, drink, rest, elimination, etc. On the next level, Maslow put need for stimulation and escape from boredom. The need to explore and satisfy curiosity would be included on this second level. Safety and security needs follow. As you continue up his pyramid, you develop a need for love and a sense of belonging. At this fourth level, friendships become important. As you move to the upper levels of the hierarchy, you need to feel respected by others. The final level is reached by very few people. It involves carrying out one's total potential. Maslow labeled the top step of his hierarchy "self-actualization."   3

Maslow felt that people move up and down this pyramid throughout their lives. Indeed, people can move to different steps or needs on the pyramid within a single day. His pyramid is like a ladder you climb throughout your life. You must step on each rung to reach the next. But suppose a person is on a high rung. For example, a woman may have progressed to the point where she is looking for approval and self-esteem. Suddenly, a man points a gun in her back. She will abruptly descend the hierarchy to satisfy her need for safety and security. Whenever a rung in the hierarchy "breaks," the person must return down to that level to satisfy the need. However, usually their progress back up to the higher level will occur rapidly.   4

In the next sections, you will focus on what specifically is encountered at each step of Maslow's hierarchy of needs.   5

SURVIVAL NEEDS

Most Americans experience only a mild form of survival need. Survival needs are biological necessities required to continue living. You may have believed yourself starving or dying of thirst. But chances are your needs were minimal when compared with people who had beyond doubt been without water or food for days.   6

During World War II, Keys *et al.* studied men who had been fed just enough to stay alive. They found that the men became preoccupied with food thoughts and fantasies. The men delighted in reading cookbooks and exchanging favorite recipes. They forgot about wives, girlfriends, and sex. They became apathetic°, dispirited°, and irritable.   7

There has been considerable evidence that thirst needs are even stronger than hunger needs. When any physiological needs are not satisfied, personality changes generally result. Persons who have been without sleep for extended periods have been known to become anxious and hallucinate. Have you ever been in steady, persistent pain for a prolonged time? You probably noticed your own personality change. In all likelihood, you were easily irked and had difficulty concentrating. Your interest and motivation were concentrated on how to relieve yourself of some pain and become more comfortable.   8

Newborn infants are motivated on this lowest level of Maslow's hierarchy. Initially   9 their concerns are biological. If provided with food, drink, and comfortable, restful surroundings where they are free from pain, the newborn infant's motivational needs will be satisfied. But not for long! Once this step is met, the infant quickly progresses to the next level, stimulation needs.

STIMULATION NEEDS

Just as the infant who is fed, rested, and comfortable begins to look for something of 10 interest, all children and adults also seek ways to escape boredom. However, as you might have suspected, the rattles and mobiles that satisfy the infant's need for novelty° and stimulation rarely, if ever, excite interest in adults. As you grow older, your interests and stimulation needs change and fluctuate°. Maslow would consider that sexual interest, curiosity, and pleasure were stimulation needs. Although sexual activity is biological or physiological in nature, it is not essential for survival. Consequently, the need for sex is on the second step of Maslow's hierarchy and is classified as a stimulation or psychological need.

SAFETY AND SECURITY NEEDS

Chances are you take many precautions to be certain you are safe and secure. You 11 live in some type of shelter, whether it be an apartment, a house, a teepee, or a barn. This shelter protects you from rain, snow, and other unfavorable elements. But undoubtedly, your motivations and concerns for safety and security extend well beyond your need for shelter. Do you have locks on your doors and windows? How about flashlights and hurricane lanterns? If you keep a spare tire in your car and maintain health and auto insurance, you are responding to your motivation to satisfy safety and security needs. Our country supports a national military force; towns and cities have police and fire departments. These men in uniform all attest to our needs for safety and security.

LOVE AND BELONGINGNESS NEEDS

The first three levels of Maslow's hierarchy may have seemed selfish to you. 12 Indeed, the needs described are basic, self-centered, and narrow. Physiological, curiosity, and security needs may be satisfied without calling on other people. However, these basic needs must be met before the need for other individuals can be recognized and accepted.

The needs for love and belongingness are sometimes called "affiliation° needs." If 13 you have ever felt lonely or isolated, you have experienced a need to affiliate. Affiliation is not limited to romantic or parental love. You also need friends who accept you. There are immense differences in affiliation needs. Some people are satisfied with one or two close, deep friendships. Others crave superficial° relationships with large groups. Some fluctuate between group and individual friendships. Selection of friends usually changes with development.

At this level of the hierarchy, people look for ways to please others and win their 14 approval. Most are selective, seeking acceptance from only certain friends and associates. It would clearly be impossible to win everyone's approval!

Clubs such as Alcoholics Anonymous and Weight Watchers are designed to motivate 15 people through their need for affiliation and social approval. Many individuals drink or eat because they feel unwanted or lonely. Although eating and drinking are physiological needs, they are often also associated with affiliation. Whether enjoying a formal dinner party or a few beers with some friends, the purpose is not solely satisfying hunger and thirst needs. Alcoholics Anonymous and Weight Watchers recognize the social implications° of eating and drinking. The groups were formed to approve refraining from° alcohol and excessive food. To win acceptance from the groups, you must keep sober and thin.

Just as there are differences in the type and number of friends needed, there are also 16 wide variations in the intensity and strength of the need to belong and be accepted by others. Crowne and Marlowe developed a test to measure the need for social approval. They then used subjects who had either extremely high or extremely low scores on their tests. Next, the high and low scorers were asked to do a chore. They were told to put twelve spools in a box, lifting only one at a time. When the box was full, they had to empty it and repeat placing each spool back in the box. Sound like fun? Interestingly, the subjects who had high scores on the need-for-approval test claimed they enjoyed the task. They were also far more enthusiastic about the scientific usefulness of the experiment than were the low scorers. High scorers even stated they had learned something from the experiment. Evidently the low scorers had less need to be approved and could recognize a dull chore!

High needs for approval and affiliation can also be identified through clothes. 17 Sorority and fraternity pins, team or club windbreakers and dressing alike are ways of demonstrating a need to belong. Adolescents often show remarkable conformity in their dress. Men and women who frequent singles bars or attend every mixer and dance usually have strong affiliation needs.

Advertisers capitalize on° the need for love and belongingness. Many ads begin with 18 a negative appeal. Jim is lonely and disapproved of by everyone. He has either dandruff, messy hair, bald spots, bad breath, a bad odor, or ill-fitting underwear. However, after using the advertised product, his problem is solved and he gains popularity. The advertisers are appealing to your need for approval. They hope you will believe their product will gain you the same popularity as Jim. Check magazines, newspapers, and your television for this type of ad.

ESTEEM AND SELF-ESTEEM NEEDS

Once you feel approved of and accepted by others, you are prepared to progress to 19 the next step in the hierarchy, esteem and self-esteem. At this level you seek what both Rodney Dangerfield and Charlie Brown never get, namely, "respect." To satisfy the need for esteem, you need more than acceptance and belonging. You have to be held in high regard and have some status in your group.

How can you convince others that you are worthy of their respect? Usually an 20 outstanding achievement will win some praise and prestige. If you score a goal in a soccer game, win a beauty contest, create an outstanding mural, or produce a perfect exam paper, you will usually win the esteem of others. Achievements also improve your own self-esteem. When you convince others that you deserve respect, you also convince yourself.

The need to achieve. Clearly, esteem and self-esteem needs are related to each other. 21 And achievements are a key way to satisfy the need for both. Achievements can be any accomplishment, from getting an office with a view or a personal secretary to maintaining the clearest complexion on campus. An achievement is a demonstration of success. Think of some achievements that you felt gave you status among others. Did you ever receive the highest grade on an exam or earn enough money for a car or an unusual vacation? Perhaps you have won a contest!

Some contests require an accomplishment while others are based strictly on luck. 22 Often people feel a sense of achievement in winning contests based more on chance than on actual accomplishments. Bingo and sweepstake addicts delight in the possibility of winning huge sums of money easily. Studies have shown that only rarely are these individuals strong achievers at work. Strong achievers usually want to feel personally responsible for their own success.

Games of chance do not require individual efforts. According to McClelland, people 23 with strong needs for achievement like to use their own skills and want to improve themselves. They prefer tasks that require some effort but are not impossible. If they have control of their jobs and set their own goals, they feel more satisfied with themselves. A high achiever would prefer a game of chess to a game of poker.

Achievers usually set goals for themselves that everyone else will believe is a symbol 24 or sign of success. They want to do well and enjoy getting positive feedback from others. Men and women with strong needs for achievement like to get pats on the back. Feedback from others is more important than money. Adams and Stone reported that high achievers will even spend their leisure time in activities that will reflect achievement.

Why do some people have strong needs for achievement? McClelland found that the 25 need for achievement is related to parent attitudes. Parents who are high achievers themselves usually demand independence from their children. The children must become self-reliant at a relatively early age. As a result, the children develop a sense of confidence and find enjoyment in their own achievements.

On the other hand, parents who have low needs for achievement are more protective 26 of their children. They help their children perform everyday tasks such as dressing and feeding far more than necessary. Their children have less freedom and usually have low achievement needs.

Fear of success. What about people who are afraid to achieve? Psychologists believe the 27 fear of success is usually related to a lower need, the need for love and belongingness. They are afraid they will lose valued friendships and affection if they become successful.

Horner was a pioneer in the study of fear of success in women. She gave college 28 students one sentence and asked them to complete an essay. Male students were given the sentence: "After first-term finals, John finds himself at the top of his medical school class." Female students were given the same sentence, with the name "Ann" substituted for "John." The men had a positive attitude toward "John." Only about 10 percent of the male students had any negative comments. Interestingly, almost two-thirds of the women had a negative attitude toward "Ann." They described her as either unpopular and rejected, or a guilty cheat, or a hoax.

Recent studies by Maccoby and Jacklin and Monahan and Shaver have supported 29 Horner's findings. In our society, fear of success is common among women. Successful competitive women are often not socially acceptable. Although more prevalent in women, fear of success has also been found to occur in men. Many men feel insecure about achieving and losing the friendship of their coworkers and their acquaintances in their own economic group. Again, from Maslow's point of view, unless the need for love and belonging is met fully, achievement will not be possible.

SELF-ACTUALIZATION

At last to the top of the pyramid! But only when every imaginable need has been 30 met is a person ready for the maximum growth through self-actualization. Maslow himself had difficulty finding a precise definition for self-actualization. He felt that all people have some inner talents or abilities that they want to use or actualize. If all lower needs are met, people can grow and develop by using these abilities. This growth is a continuous process that allows individuals to find self-fulfillment and realize their full potential.

In his attempt to identify some characteristics of people who have reached the level 31 of self-actualization, Maslow studied the lives of forty-nine people that he believed to be self-actualizers. Among those studied were Albert Einstein, Eleanor Roosevelt, Abraham Lincoln, Thomas Jefferson, William James, and Jane Addams. Among the common characteristics of self-actualizers were:

Honesty	They have an ability to be objective and do not show selfish interest.
Creativity	They are spontaneous° and natural and enjoy trying new approaches.
Acceptance	They have total acceptance of themselves and are willing to accept others for what they are.
Appreciation	They possess an ability to become fully absorbed, enjoying even simple and basic experiences.
Sense of humor	They can recognize cleverness and whimsy and will laugh easily.
Sensitivity	They experience a deep feeling of sympathy for other people.

According to Maslow, self-actualization is extremely rare. He screened about three 32 thousnd students and found only one self-actualized person. Although self-actualization is slightly more likely among older individuals, it is far from common. Most people never move above the level of esteem. They never reach self-actualization and fully develop their potential.

Slightly more common than self-actualization are what Maslow called "peak 33 experiences." A peak experience is an extremely brief, momentary sense of total happiness or fulfillment. For a few seconds or perhaps a minute, you have a sense of self-actualization. This feeling could come from such experiences as watching a spectacular sunset, holding a baby, running a marathon, creating a sculpture, or greeting a returned love. Peak experiences give the same feeling of aliveness and wholeness that self-actualizers encounter. However, the feeling ends abruptly.

BASIC SKILL QUESTIONS

Vocabulary in Context

1. The word *irked* in "Have you ever been in steady, persistent pain for a prolonged time? . . . In all likelihood, you were easily irked and had difficulty concentrating" (paragraph 8) means
   a. pleased.
   b. informed.
   c. annoyed.
   d. entertained.

2. The words *attest to* in "towns and cities have police and fire departments. These men in uniform all attest to our needs for safety and security" (paragraph 10) mean
   a. are evidence of.
   b. remain ignorant.
   c. become silent.
   d. make complaints.

Central Point and Main Ideas

3. Which sentence best expresses the central point of the selection?
   a. Everyone has various needs to satisfy.
   b. Motivation can be conscious or unconscious.
   c. Maslow classified human motivations into six levels through which people progress.
   d. The most fundamental needs, according to Maslow, are physiological survival needs.

4. The main idea of paragraph 18 is stated in its
   a. first sentence.
   b. second sentence.
   c. third sentence.
   d. last sentence.

Supporting Details

5. The first three levels of Maslow's hierarchy
   a. depend on other people.
   b. are self-centered.
   c. are always fully met.
   d. result in "peak experiences."

6. _____ TRUE OR FALSE? According to Maslow, most people never reach the level of self-actualization.

Transitions

7. The transition beginning paragraph 26 signals
   a. addition.
   b. time.
   c. contrast.
   d. cause and effect.

8. The relationship of the second sentence at the top of the next page to the first is one of
   a. addition.
   b. time.
   c. contrast.
   d. illustration.

Peak experiences give the same feeling of aliveness and wholeness that self-actualizers encounter. However, the feeling ends abruptly. (Paragraph 33)

Patterns of Organization

9. The pattern of organization of paragraph 31 is
   a. a series of events.
   b. steps in a process.
   c. list of items.
   d. cause and effect.

10. The term being defined in paragraph 33 is "_____."

    The paragraph provides *(how many?)* _____ examples of that term.

ADVANCED SKILL QUESTIONS

Summarizing and Outlining

11. Which sentence best summarizes paragraph 11?
    a. To be certain we are safe and secure, most people live in some type of shelter, whether it be an apartment, a house, or a barn.
    b. Security is a basic need, which is evident in how, through personal and civic means, we protect ourselves from the weather, criminals, and accidents.
    c. Entire professions have been developed because of the human needs for safety and security.
    d. Our homes and cars are equipped in ways that help us achieve safety and security. For example, we put locks on our doors and windows and keep spare tires in our cars.

12. Complete the following summary of paragraphs 25–26 by briefly explaining the major details.

    According to McClelland, people's need for achievement is related to their

    parents' attitudes. _____

    _____

    _____

    _____

Fact and Opinion

13. The author's statement that Abraham Maslow is "one of the most important contributors to the field of motivation" (paragraph 2) is a statement of
    a. fact.
    b. opinion.

14. _____ TRUE OR FALSE? The statement below is an opinion.

    Some contests . . . are based strictly on luck. (Paragraph 22)

Inferences

15. We can infer that Maslow's hierarchy is considered to be like a ladder because
    a. ladders come in different heights.
    b. Maslow was influenced by housebuilding techniques.
    c. one can begin with the top need and work downwards.
    d. one must "climb" from the lower needs to the higher ones.

16. From the reading we can conclude that
    a. people's needs for esteem can be met in different ways.
    b. upbringing greatly influences how people meet their needs for esteem.
    c. people who have not met all their esteem needs may still enjoy peak experiences at times.
    d. all of the above.

17. _____ TRUE OR FALSE? From paragraphs 27–29, we might conclude that children who gain a strong sense of being loved and belonging are more likely than other children to seek success as adults.

Purpose and Tone

18. The main purpose of this selection is
    a. to inform.
    b. to persuade.
    c. to entertain.

19. The tone of this selection is
    a. critical and uncaring.
    b. lighthearted.
    c. straightforward and somewhat informal.
    d. solemn.

Argument

20. Label the point of the following argument based on the reading with a **P** and the two statements of support with an **S**. Note that one statement should be unlabeled—it is neither the point nor the support of the argument.

    _____ Sexual interest and curiousity help fulfill adult stimulation needs.

    _____ Sexual activity is not essential for survival.

    _____ Well-fed, comfortable babies may meet their stimulation needs with rattles and mobiles.

    _____ Our stimulation needs change throughout our lives.

MAPPING

Using the headings and other boldfaced words in the selection, complete the map below.

Central point: According to Abraham Maslow, there are six levels of human needs.

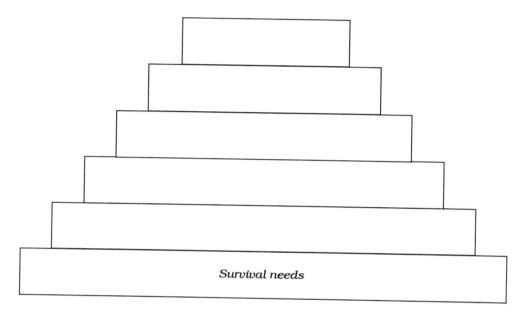

Survival needs

DISCUSSION QUESTIONS

1. What ads have you seen recently that appeal to our need for approval? Which ones begin with "a negative appeal," as Quinn describes it in paragraph 18?

2. According to the reading, "achievements are a key way to satisfy the need" for esteem and self-esteem. What achievements of yours have most strengthened your esteem and self-esteem? What achievement goals do you have for the future?

3. Based on your own experience, why might some people fear success? And what reasons can you see for the fear of success being much more common among women than among men?

4. Do you know a workaholic, a compulsive gambler, a television addict, or a joiner? Which of Maslow's needs do you think each of these people is trying to meet?

Check Your Performance   MOTIVATION AND NEEDS

Skill	Number Right	Points	Total
BASIC SKILL QUESTIONS			
Vocabulary in Context (2 items)	_____	x 4 =	_____
Central Point and Main Ideas (2 items)	_____	x 4 =	_____
Supporting Details (2 items)	_____	x 4 =	_____
Transitions (2 items)	_____	x 4 =	_____
Patterns of Organization (2 items)	_____	x 4 =	_____
ADVANCED SKILL QUESTIONS			
Summarizing and Outlining (2 items)	_____	x 4 =	_____
Fact and Opinion (2 items)	_____	x 4 =	_____
Inferences (3 items)	_____	x 4 =	_____
Purpose and Tone (2 items)	_____	x 4 =	_____
Argument (1 item)	_____	x 4 =	_____
MAPPING (5 items)	_____	x 4 =	_____

FINAL SCORE (OF POSSIBLE 100)   _____ %

Enter your final score into the reading performance chart on the inside back cover.

5

A & P
John Updike

Preview

Have you ever witnessed someone being publicly embarrassed? How did you react? Was your response affected by how you felt about the victims of the unfairness? In this story written in 1962 by John Updike, one of America's best-known authors, a young man is confronted by such a situation. His reaction is surprising, perhaps even to himself.

Words to Watch

prima-donna (2): of a vain or arrogant person
fuselage (8): main body of an airplane (on which military pilots would record the number of enemy airplanes they had downed)
haggling (13): arguing over price
scuttle (13): run hurriedly
tony (14): high-toned
ticked (14): went lazily
saunter (31): walk leisurely

In walks these three girls in nothing but bathing suits. I'm in the third checkout slot, with my back to the door, so I don't see them until they're over by the bread. The one that caught my eye first was the one in the plaid green two-piece. She was a chunky kid, with a good tan and a sweet broad soft-looking can with those two crescents of white just under it, where the sun never seems to hit, at the top of the backs of her legs. I stood there with my hand on a box of HiHo crackers trying to remember if I rang it up or not. I ring it up again and the customer starts giving me hell. She's one of these cash-register-watchers, a witch about fifty with rouge on her cheekbones and no eyebrows, and I know it made her day to trip me up. She'd been watching cash registers for fifty years and probably never seen a mistake before.

1

By the time I got her feathers smoothed and her goodies into a bag—she gives me a little snort in passing, if she'd been born at the right time they would have burned her over in Salem—by the time I get her on her way the girls had circled around the bread and were coming back, without a pushcart, back my way along the counters, in the aisle between the checkouts and the Special bins. They didn't even have shoes on. There was this chunky one, with the two-piece—it was bright green and the seams on the bra were still sharp and her belly was still pretty pale so I guessed she just got it (the suit)—there was this one, with one of those chubby berry-faces, the lips all bunched together under her nose, this one, and a tall one, with black hair that hadn't quite frizzed right, and one of these sunburns right across under the eyes, and a chin that was too long—you know, the kind of girl other girls think is very "striking" and "attractive" but never quite makes it, as they very well know, which is why they like her so much—and then the third one, that wasn't quite so tall. She was the queen. She kind of led them, the other two peeking around and making their shoulders round. She didn't look around, not this queen, she just walked straight on slowly, on these long white prima-donna° legs. She came down a little hard on her heels, as if she didn't walk in her bare feet that much, putting down her heels and then letting the weight move along to her toes as if she was testing the floor with every step, putting a little deliberate extra action into it. You never know for sure how girls' minds work (do you really think it's a mind in there or just a little buzz like a bee in a glass jar?) but you got the idea she had talked the other two into coming in here with her, and now she was showing them how to do it, walk slow and hold yourself straight.

She had on a kind of dirty-pink—beige maybe, I don't know—bathing suit with a little nubble all over it and, what got me, the straps were down. They were off her shoulders looped loose around the cool tops of her arms, and I guess as a result the suit had slipped a little on her, so all around the top of the cloth there was this shining rim. If it hadn't been there you wouldn't have known there could have been anything whiter than those shoulders. With the straps pushed off, there was nothing between the top of the suit and the top of her head except just her, this clean bare plane of the top of her chest down from the shoulder bones like a dented sheet of metal tilted in the light. I mean, it was more than pretty.

She had sort of oaky hair that the sun and salt had bleached, done up in a bun that was unravelling, and a kind of prim face. Walking into the A & P with your straps down, I suppose it's the only kind of face you can have. She held her head so high her neck, coming up out of those white shoulders, looked kind of stretched, but I didn't mind. The longer her neck was, the more of her there was.

She must have felt in the corner of her eye me and over my shoulder Stokesie in the second slot watching, but she didn't tip. Not this queen. She kept her eyes moving across the racks, and stopped, and turned so slow it made my stomach rub the inside of my apron, and buzzed to the other two, who kind of huddled against her for relief, and then they all three of them went up the cat-and-dog-food-breakfast-cereal-macaroni-rice-raisins-seasonings-spreads-spaghetti-soft-drinks-crackers-and-cookies aisle. From the third slot I look straight up this aisle to the meat counter, and I watched them all the way. The fat one with the tan sort of fumbled with the cookies, but on second thought she put the package back. The sheep pushing their carts down the aisle—the girls were walking against the usual traffic (not that we have one-way signs or anything)—were pretty hilarious. You could see them, when Queenie's white shoulders dawned on them, kind of jerk, or hop, or hiccup, but their eyes snapped back to their own baskets and on they pushed. I bet you could set off dynamite in an A & P and the people would by and large keep reaching and checking oatmeal off their lists and muttering "Let me see, there was a third thing, began with A, asparagus, no, ah, yes, applesauce!" or whatever it is they do mutter. But there was no doubt, this jiggled them. A few houseslaves in pin curlers even looked around after pushing their carts past to make sure what they had seen was correct.

You know, it's one thing to have a girl in a bathing suit down on the beach, where   6
what with the glare nobody can look at each other much anyway, and another thing in the cool of the A & P, under the fluorescent lights, against all those stacked packages, with her feet paddling along naked over our checkerboard green-and-cream rubber-tile floor.

"Oh Daddy," Stokesie said beside me, "I feel so faint."   7

"Darling," I said. "Hold me tight." Stokesie's married, with two babies chalked up   8
on his fuselage° already, but as far as I can tell that's the only difference. He's twenty-two, and I was nineteen this April.

"Is it done?" he asks, the responsible married man finding his voice. I forgot to say   9
he thinks he's going to be manager some sunny day, maybe in 1990 when it's called the Great Alexandrov and Petrooshki Tea Company or something.

What he meant was, our town is five miles from a beach, with a big summer colony   10
out on the Point, but we're right in the middle of town, and the women generally put on a shirt or shorts or something before they get out of the car into the street. And anyway these are usually women with six children and varicose veins mapping their legs and nobody, including them, could care less. As I say, we're right in the middle of town, and if you stand at our front doors you can see two banks and the Congregational church and the newspaper store and three real-estate offices and about twenty-seven old freeloaders tearing up Central Street because the sewer broke again. It's not as if we're on the Cape; we're north of Boston and there's people in this town who haven't seen the ocean for twenty years.

The girls had reached the meat counter and were asking McMahon something. He   11
pointed, they pointed, and they shuffled out of sight behind a pyramid of Diet Delight peaches. All that was left for us to see was old McMahon patting his mouth and looking after them sizing up their joints. Poor kids, I began to feel sorry for them, they couldn't help it.

Now here comes the sad part of the story, at least my family says it's sad, but I don't   12
think it's so sad myself. The store's pretty empty, it being Thursday afternoon, so there was nothing much to do except lean on the register and wait for the girls to show up again. The whole store was like a pinball machine and I didn't know which tunnel they'd come out of. After a while they come around out of the far aisle, around the light bulbs, records at discount of the Caribbean Six or Tony Martin Sings or some such gunk you wonder they waste the wax on, sixpacks of candy bars, and plastic toys done up in cellophane that fall apart when a kid looks at them anyway. Around they come, Queenie still leading the way, and holding a little gray jar in her hand. Slots Three through Seven are unmanned and I could see her wondering between Stokes and me, but Stokesie with his usual luck draws an old party in baggy gray pants who stumbles up with four giant cans of pineapple juice (what do these bums *do* with all that pineapple juice? I've often asked myself) so the girls come to me. Queenie puts down the jar and I take it into my fingers icy cold. Kingfish Fancy Herring Snacks in Pure Sour Cream: 49 cents. Now her hands are empty, not a ring or a bracelet, bare as God made them, and I wonder where the money's coming from. Still

with that prim look she lifts a folded dollar bill out of the hollow at the center of her nubbled pink top. The jar went heavy in my hand. Really, I thought that was so cute.

Then everybody's luck begins to run out. Lengel comes in from haggling° with a 13 truck full of cabbages on the lot and is about to scuttle° into the door marked MANAGER behind which he hides all day when the girls touch his eye. Lengel's pretty dreary, teaches Sunday school and the rest, but he doesn't miss that much. He comes over and says, "Girls, this isn't the beach."

Queenie blushes, though maybe it's just a brush of sunburn I was noticing for the 14 first time, now that she was so close. "My mother asked me to pick up a jar of herring snacks." Her voice kind of startled me, the way voices do when you see the people first, coming out so flat and dumb yet kind of tony°, too, the way it ticked° over "pick up" and "snacks." All of a sudden I slid right down her voice into her living room. Her father and the other men were standing around in ice-cream coats and bow ties and the women were in sandals picking up herring snacks on toothpicks off a big glass plate and they were all holding drinks the color of water with olives and sprigs of mint in them. When my parents have somebody over they get lemonade and if it's a real racy affair Schlitz in tall glasses with "They'll Do It Every Time" cartoons stencilled on.

"That's all right," Lengel said. "But this isn't the beach." His repeating this struck 15 me as funny, as if it had just occurred to him, and he had been thinking all these years the A & P was a great big dune and he was the head lifeguard. He didn't like my smiling—as I say he doesn't miss much—but he concentrates on giving the girls that sad Sunday-school-superintendent stare.

Queenie's blush is no sunburn now, and the plump one in plaid, that I liked better 16 from the back—a really sweet can—pipes up, "We weren't doing any shopping. We just came in for the one thing."

"That makes no difference," Lengel tells her, and I could see from the way his eyes 17 went that he hadn't noticed she was wearing a two-piece before. "We want you decently dressed when you come in here."

"We *are* decent," Queenie says suddenly, her lower lip pushing, getting sore now 18 that she remembers her place, a place from which the crowd that runs the A & P must look pretty crummy. Fancy Herring Snacks flashed in her very blue eyes.

"Girls, I don't want to argue with you. After this come in here with your shoulders 19 covered. It's our policy." He turns his back. That's policy for you. Policy is what the kingpins want. What the others want is juvenile delinquency.

All this while, the customers had been showing up with their carts but, you know, 20 sheep, seeing a scene, they had all bunched up on Stokesie, who shook open a paper bag as gently as peeling a peach, not wanting to miss a word. I could feel in the silence everybody getting nervous, most of all Lengel, who asks me, "Sammy, have you rung up their purchase?"

I thought and said "No" but it wasn't about that I was thinking. I go through the 21 punches, 4, 9, GROC, TOT—it's more complicated than you think, and after you do it often enough, it begins to make a little song, that you hear words to, in my case "Hello (*bing*) there, you (*gung*) happy *pee*-pul (*splat*)!"—the *splat* being the drawer flying out. I uncrease the bill, tenderly as you may imagine, it just having come from between the two smoothest scoops of vanilla I had ever known were there, and pass a half and a penny into her narrow pink palm, and nestle the herrings in a bag and twist its neck and hand it over, all the time thinking.

The girls, and who'd blame them, are in a hurry to get out, so I say "I quit" to 22 Lengel quick enough for them to hear, hoping they'll stop and watch me, their unsuspected hero. They keep right on going, into the electric eye; the door flies open and they flicker across the lot to their car, Queenie and Plaid and Big Tall Goony-Goony (not that as raw material she was so bad), leaving me with Lengel and a kink in his eyebrow.

"Did you say something, Sammy?"   23

"I said I quit."   24

"I thought you did."   25

"You didn't have to embarrass them."   26

"It was they who were embarrassing us."   27

I started to say something that came out "Fiddle-de-doo." It's a saying of my 28 grandmother's, and I know she would have been pleased.

"I don't think you know what you're saying," Lengel said.   29

"I know you don't," I said. "But I do." I pull the bow at the back of my apron and 30 start shrugging it off my shoulders. A couple customers that had been heading for my slot begin to knock against each other, like scared pigs in a chute.

Lengel sighs and begins to look very patient and old and gray. He's been a friend of 31 my parents for years. "Sammy, you don't want to do this to your Mom and Dad," he tells me. It's true, I don't. But it seems to me that once you begin a gesture it's fatal not to go through with it. I fold the apron, "Sammy" stitched in red on the pocket, and put it on the counter, and drop the bow tie on top of it. The bow tie is theirs, if you've ever wondered. "You'll feel this for the rest of your life," Lengel says, and I know that's true, too, but remembering how he made that pretty girl blush makes me so scrunchy inside I punch the No Sale tab and the machine whirs "pee-pul" and the drawer splats out. One advantage to this scene taking place in summer, I can follow this up with a clean exit, there's no fumbling around getting your coat and galoshes, I just saunter° into the electric eye in my white shirt that my mother ironed the night before, and the door heaves itself open, and outside the sunshine is skating around on the asphalt.

I look around for my girls, but they're gone, of course. There wasn't anybody but 32 some young married screaming with her children about some candy they didn't get by the door of a powder-blue Falcon station wagon. Looking back in the big windows, over the bags of peat moss and aluminum lawn furniture stacked on the pavement, I could see Lengel in my place in the slot, checking the sheep through. His face was dark gray and his back stiff, as if he'd just had an injection of iron, and my stomach kind of fell as I felt how hard the world was going to be to me hereafter.

BASIC SKILL QUESTIONS

Vocabulary in Context

1. The word *jiggled* in "The sheep pushing their carts down the aisle . . . were pretty hilarious. You could see them, when Queenie's white shoulders dawned on them, kind of jerk, or hop, or hiccup, but their eyes snapped back to their own baskets and on they pushed . . . But there was no doubt, this jiggled them" (paragraph 5) means
   a. delighted.
   b. rolled off.
   c. unsteadied.
   d. scared.

Central Point and Main Ideas

2. Which sentence best expresses a central point of the selection?
   a. Sammy is destined to be a loser all of his life.
   b. People should be dressed properly in public places.
   c. Places like supermarkets have special problems in keeping their employees.
   d. There are often no easy decisions to make in everyday life.

3. Which sentence best expresses the main idea of paragraph 6?
   a. The beach is warmer and has more glare than the A & P.
   b. Because of the glare, nobody at the beach can look at each other much.
   c. A barefoot girl in a bathing suit might be ignored at the beach, but not in the A & P.
   d. The A & P has fluorescent lights and a checkerboard green-and-cream rubber-tile floor.

Supporting Details

4. The customers in the A & P
   a. didn't even notice the girls in bathing suits.
   b. were surprised when they saw the girls.
   c. were numerous.
   d. had probably also gone to the nearby beach.

5. _____ TRUE OR FALSE? Even though the girls may be wealthier than Sammy and show no interest in him, he feels both sympathy and admiration for them.

6. _____ TRUE OR FALSE? Lengel gives Sammy an opportunity to change his mind about quitting.

7. From Lengel's conversation with Sammy, the reader knows that Lengel
   a. despises Sammy and has been looking for a way to get him fired.
   b. doesn't really know Sammy and, therefore, has no feelings about him.
   c. is a friend of Sammy's family and doesn't want Sammy to do anything he'll regret.
   d. is happy to see Sammy quit so that he can give Stokesie more hours.

Transitions

8. The relationship of the last part of the sentence below to the first two parts is one of
   a. addition.
   b. time.
   c. comparison.
   d. contrast.

   Now here comes the sad part of the story, at least my family says it's sad, but I don't think it's so sad myself. (Paragraph 12)

Patterns of Organization

9. The overall pattern of organization of the story is
   a. time order.
   b. list of items.
   c. comparison.
   d. definition and example.

10. The pattern of organization of paragraph 6 is
    a. time order.
    b. list of items.
    c. contrast.
    d. definition and example.

ADVANCED SKILL QUESTIONS

Summarizing and Outlining

11. Which of the following best summarizes paragraph 31?
    a. Lengel, an old friend of Sammy's parents, told Sammy he'd regret quitting. Sammy knew that was true, but having said he would quit, he felt he had to follow through. Also, he was still annoyed at how Lengel had embarrased Queenie, so Sammy quit and sauntered out of the store.
    b. Sammy was glad that it was summer because then he didn't have to fumble around with getting his coat and galoshes. So he just took off his apron and bow tie, walked leisurely past the electric eye, through the open doorway, and outside into the sunshine.
    c. Lengel, who had been a friend of Sammy's parents for years, advised Sammy not to quit. "Sammy, you don't want to do this to your Mom and

Dad," he said. Then he added, "You'll feel this for the rest of your life."
Sammy knew that Lengel was right.

Fact and Opinion

12. Which of the following reveals one of Sammy's opinions?
    a. "I stood there with my hand on a box of HiHo crackers trying to remember if I rang it up or not."
    b. "She was the queen."
    c. "He's twenty-two, and I was nineteen this April."
    d. "He's been a friend of my parents for years. 'Sammy, you don't want to do this to your Mom and Dad,' he tells me."

Inferences

13. In paragraph 5, Sammy calls the customers "sheep" because
    a. it is a term of affection; he believes they are friendly and gentle.
    b. they wear heavy clothing even in the summer.
    c. they passively follow the rules, including unwritten ones such as traveling one way in a grocery aisle.
    d. all the workers in the store also call them by that name.

14. _____ TRUE OR FALSE? One of the reasons that Sammy admired Queenie was that, by wearing her bathing suit into the store, she distinguished herself from the "sheep."

15. Sammy may have quit his job for several reasons. The part of the story below suggests that Sammy quit
    a. because he thought the girls would be impressed.
    b. because he felt that he needed to stand up for his beliefs.
    c. both of the above.
    d. neither of the above.

    "The girls, and who'd blame them, are in a hurry to get out, so I say 'I quit' to Lengel quick enough for them to hear, hoping they'll stop and watch me, their unsuspected hero." (Paragraph 22)

16. The part of the story below suggests that Sammy quit
    a. because he thought the girls would be impressed.
    b. because he felt that he needed to stand up for his beliefs.
    c. both of the above.
    d. neither of the above.

    "'You'll feel this for the rest of your life,' Lengel says, and I know that's true, too, but remembering how he made that pretty girl blush makes me so scrunchy inside. . . . I looked around for my girls, but they're gone, of course . . . and my stomach kind of fell as I felt how hard the world was going to be to me hereafter." (Paragraphs 31–32)

Purpose and Tone

17. _____ TRUE OR FALSE? The purpose of this story is to entertain and engage the reader and also to provoke thought.

18. In general, the tone of the story might be described as
    a. straightforward and objective.
    b. desperate and grim.
    c. informal and colorful.
    d. bitter and angry.

Argument

19. Label the point of the following argument with a **P** and the two statements of support with an **S**.

    _____ Although Stokesie might also have resented the way Lengel treated the girls in the bathing suits, he had more to lose by defending them.

    _____ Stokesie is married and has two children.

    _____ Stokesie's goal is to become manager of the A & P.

20. Label the point of the following argument with a **P** and the two statements of support with an **S**.

    _____ Sammy agrees with Lengel when Lengel tells him, "You'll feel this for the rest of your life."

    _____ Sammy states that he knows the world is going to be harder for him now.

    _____ Even though Sammy believes he has important reasons for quitting his job, he knows there will also be painful consequences to this action.

SUMMARIZING

Complete the following brief summary of "A & P."

Sammy, a cashier at the A & P, watches three girls enter the A & P and walk around the store. They get a lot of attention because _____

_____

Greatly attracted by the girls, Sammy closely observes them, especially the one he calls "Queenie." He is passionately moved by her sexy appearance and high-class manners. After Queenie hands a jar of herring to Sammy and gives him a dollar bill, _____

_____

In reaction, Sammy says he quits, hoping to impress the girls as a hero; but they pay no attention and leave the store. Nevertheless, despite Lengel's advice to stay on and his own realization that he'll regret quitting, Sammy—still annoyed at how Lengel embarrassed Queenie and reluctant to go back on his word—stubbornly quits.

DISCUSSION QUESTIONS

1. The tone of this story is distinctive. Updike uses conversational, even sloppy language ("sort of," "kind of," "gunk") that alternates between the present and past tenses ("In walks these three girls"; "She was a chunky kid"). Why has he chosen to use this style for his story? What is the effect?

2. How would you describe Sammy's feelings for the three girls in the store, particularly the one he calls Queenie? Why is he so indignant at the store manager's treatment of them? And how do you reconcile his support for the girls with his view of girls' minds, as expressed in paragraph 2?

3. What is your opinion about Sammy's decision? Is it a foolish and useless one, or is it in some way admirable—or is it a bit of both? Provide supporting reasons from the story to back up your opinion.

4. Have you ever found yourself taking sides between youth and adulthood, adventure and law and order, spontaneous behavior and "policy"? Which side have you chosen, and why? Did you later regret your decision?

Check Your Performance

A & P

Skill	Number Right	Points	Total
BASIC SKILL QUESTIONS			
Vocabulary in Context (1 item)	_____	x 4 =	_____
Central Point and Main Ideas (2 items)	_____	x 4 =	_____
Supporting Details (4 items)	_____	x 4 =	_____
Transitions (1 item)	_____	x 4 =	_____
Patterns of Organization (2 items)	_____	x 4 =	_____
ADVANCED SKILL QUESTIONS			
Summarizing and Outlining (1 item)	_____	x 4 =	_____
Fact and Opinion (1 item)	_____	x 4 =	_____
Inferences (4 items)	_____	x 4 =	_____
Purpose and Tone (2 items)	_____	x 4 =	_____
Argument (2 items)	_____	x 4 =	_____
SUMMARIZING (2 items)	_____	x 10 =	_____

FINAL SCORE (OF POSSIBLE 100) _____%

Enter your final score into the reading performance chart on the inside back cover.

6

Propaganda Techniques in Today's Advertising
Ann McClintock

Preview

Did you buy that car—or shampoo or pair of athletic shoes—after evaluating your options carefully? Or did a persuasive ad convince you? We all know ads represent a biased view,   but many of us are probably not aware of just how far advertisers go to gain our support. And the less alert we are to their techniques, the more likely we are to fall for them. This article can help you avoid those pitfalls of advertising.

Words to Watch

bombardment (1): attack
alluring (1): tempting
buzzwords (6): words or phrases that are common clichés within certain groups
aura (10): atmosphere
slew (12): group
suppressing (17): withholding
waffling (17): being indecisive

We Americans, adults and children alike, are being seduced. We are being brainwashed. And few of us protest. Why? Because the seducers and the brainwashers are the advertisers we willingly invite into our homes. We are victims, seemingly content—even eager—to be victimized. One study reports that each of us, during an average day, is exposed to over *five hundred* advertising claims of various types. This bombardment° may even increase in the future since current trends include ads on movie screens, shopping carts, video cassettes, even public television. We read advertisers' messages in newspapers and magazines; we watch their alluring° images on television. We absorb their messages into our subconscious.

1

Advertisers lean heavily on propaganda to sell their products, whether the 2 "products" are a brand of toothpaste, a candidate for office, or a political viewpoint. *Propaganda* is a systematic effort to influence people's opinions, to win them over to a certain view or side. Propaganda is not necessarily concerned with what is true or false, good or bad. Propagandists simply want people to believe the messages being sent. Advertisers often use subtle deceptions to sway people's opinions; they may even use what amount to outright lies.

What kind of propaganda techniques do advertisers use? There are seven common 3 types:

1. Name Calling Name calling is a propaganda tactic in which a competitor is 4 referred to with negatively charged names or comments. By using such negative associations, propagandists try to arouse feelings of mistrust, fear, and even hate in their audiences. For example, a political advertisement may label an opposing candidate a "loser," "fencesitter," or "warmonger." Depending on the advertiser's target market, labels such as "a friend of big business" or "a dues-paying member of the party in power" can be the epithets that damage an opponent. Ads for products also often use name calling. An American manufacturer may refer in its commercial, for instance, to a "foreign car"—not an "imported one." The label of foreignness will have unpleasant connotations in many people's minds. Another example is the MasterCard ad that shows a man trying unsuccessfully to get some cash with his American Express card. A childhood rhyme claims that "names can never hurt me," but name calling is an effective way to damage the opposition, whether it is another credit card company or a congressional candidate.

2. Glittering Generalities A glittering generality is an important-sounding but 5 general claim for which no explanation or proof is offered. Advertisers who use glittering generalities surround their products with attractive—and slippery—words and phrases. They use vague terms that are difficult to define and that may have different meanings to different people, such as *great, progress, beautiful,* and *super.* This kind of language stirs positive feelings in people, feelings that may spill over to the product or idea being pitched. As with name calling, the emotional response may overwhelm logic. Target audiences accept the product without thinking very much about what the glittering generalities really mean.

The ads for politicians and political causes often use glittering generalities because 6 such buzzwords° can influence votes. Election slogans include high-sounding but basically empty phrases like the following:

"He cares about people." (That's nice, but is he a better candidate than his opponent?)

"Vote for progress." (Progress by *whose* standards?)

"They'll make this country great again." (Does "great" mean the same thing to the candidate as it does to me?)

"Vote for the future." (What kind of future?)

Promotions for consumer goods are also sprinkled with glittering generalities. 7 Product names, for instance, are often designed to evoke good feelings: *Luvs* diapers, *Joy* liquid detergent, and *Loving Care* hair color. Product slogans lean heavily on vague but comforting phrases: General Electric "brings good things to life," Dow Chemical "lets you do great things," and Coke is "the real thing."

3. Transfer   In transfer, advertisers try to improve the image of a product by   8
associating it with a symbol or image most people respect and admire, like the American
flag or Uncle Sam. The advertisers hope that the trust and prestige attached to the symbol
or image will carry over to the product. Many companies use transfer devices to identify
their products: Lincoln Insurance shows a profile of the president; Continental Insurance
portrays a Revolutionary War Minuteman; Amtrak's logo is red, white, and blue; Liberty
Mutual's corporate symbol is the Statue of Liberty; Allstate's name is cradled by a pair of
protective, fatherly hands.

Corporations also use the transfer technique when they sponsor prestigious shows on   9
radio and television. These shows function as symbols of dignity and class. Kraft
Corporation, for instance, sponsored a "Leonard Bernstein Conducts Beethoven" concert,
while Gulf Oil is the sponsor of *National Geographic* specials and Mobil supports public
television's *Masterpiece Theater*. In this way, corporations reach an educated, influential
audience and improve their public image by associating themselves with quality
programming.

Political candidates, of course, practically wrap themselves in the flag. Ads for a   10
candidate often show either the Washington Monument, a Fourth of July parade, the Stars
and Stripes, or a bald eagle soaring over the mountains. The national anthem or "America
the Beautiful" may play softly in the background. Such appeals to Americans' love of
country surround the candidate with an aura° of patriotism and integrity.

4. Testimonial   The testimonial is one of advertisers' most-used propaganda   11
techniques. Similar to the transfer device, the testimonial capitalizes on the admiration
people have for a celebrity—even though the celebrity is not an expert on the product
being sold.

Print and television ads offer a nonstop parade of testimonials: here's Cher for   12
Holiday Spas; here's basketball star Michael Jordan eating Wheaties; Michael Jackson
sings about Pepsi; American Express features a slew° of well-known people who assure us
that they never go anywhere without their American Express card.

Political candidates, as well as their ad agencies, know the value of testimonials.   13
Barbra Streisand lent her star appeal to the presidential campaign of Bill Clinton, while
Arnold Schwarzenegger endorsed George Bush.

As illogical as testimonials sometimes are (Pepsi's Michael Jackson, for instance, is   14
a health-food adherent who does not drink soft drinks), they are effective propaganda. We
like the *person* so much that we like the *product* too.

5. Plain Folks   The plain folks approach says, in effect, "Buy me or vote for me.   15
I'm just like you." Regular folks will surely like Bob Evans' Down on the Farm Country
Sausage or good old-fashioned Country Time lemonade. Some ads emphasize the idea that
"we're all in the same boat." We see people making long-distance calls for just the reasons
we do—to put the baby on the phone to Grandma or to tell Mom we love her. And how do
these folksy, warmhearted scenes affect us? They're supposed to make us feel that
AT&T—the multinational corporate giant—has the same values we do. Similarly, we are
introduced to the little people at Ford, the ordinary folks who work on the assembly line,
not to bigwigs in their executive offices. What's the purpose of such an approach? To
encourage us to buy a car built by these honest, hardworking "everyday Joes" who care
about quality as much as we do.

Political advertisements make almost as much use of the "plain folks" appeal as they   16
do of transfer devices. Candidates wear hard hats, farmers' caps, and assemblyline

coveralls. They jog around the block and carry their own luggage through the airport. The idea is to convince voters that the candidates are at heart average people with the same values, goals and needs as you and I have.

6. Card Stacking   When people say that "the cards were stacked against me," they   17
mean that they were never given a fair chance. Applied to propaganda, card stacking means telling half-truths—misrepresenting the facts by suppressing° relevant evidence. Card stacking is a difficult form of propaganda both to detect and to combat. When a candidate claims that an opponent has "changed his mind three times on this important issue," we tend to accept the claim without investigating whether the candidate had good reasons for changing his mind. Many people are simply swayed by the implication that the candidate is "waffling°" on the issue.

Advertisers also use a card stacking trick when they make an unfinished claim. For   18
example, they will say that their product has "twice as much pain reliever." We are left with a favorable impression. We don't usually ask, "Twice as much pain reliever as what?" When Ford claimed that its LTD model was "400 percent quieter," many people assumed that the LTD must be quieter than all other cars. When taken to court, however, Ford admitted that the phrase referred to the difference between the noise level inside and outside the LTD.

7. Bandwagon   In the bandwagon technique, advertisers urge, "Everyone's doing   19
it. Why don't you?" This kind of propaganda appeals to people's deep desire not to be different. Political ads tell us to vote for the "winning candidate." The advertisers know we tend to feel comfortable doing what others do; we want to be on the winning team. Or ads show a series of people proclaiming, "I'm voting for the senator. I don't know why anyone wouldn't." Again, the audience feels under pressure to conform.

The bandwagon approach is also a staple of consumer ads. They tell us, for example,   20
that "nobody doesn't like Sara Lee" (the message is that you must be weird if you don't). They tell us that "most people prefer Brand X two to one over other leading brands" (to be like the majority, we should buy Brand X). If we don't drink Pepsi, we're left out of "the Pepsi generation." To take part in "America's favorite health kick," the National Dairy Council urges us to drink milk. And a Ford ad urges us to choose from the "Best-Selling Cars and Trucks Four Years Running."

Why do these propaganda techniques work? Why do so many of us buy the   21
products, viewpoints, and candidates urged on us by propaganda messages? They work because they appeal to our emotions, not to our minds. Clear thinking requires hard work: analyzing a claim, researching the facts, examining both sides of an issue, using logic to see the flaws in an argument. And the propagandists are happy to do our thinking for us.

Because propaganda is so effective, it is important to detect it and understand how it   22
is used. We may conclude, after close examination, that some propaganda sends a truthful, worthwhile message. Some advertising, for instance, urges us not to drive drunk, to become volunteers, to contribute to charity. We may even agree that a particular soap or soda is "super." Even so, we must be aware that propaganda is being used. Otherwise, we will have consented to handing over to others our independence of thought and action.

BASIC SKILL QUESTIONS

Vocabulary in Context

1. The word *epithets* in "labels such as 'a friend of big business' or 'a dues-paying member of the party in power' can be the epithets that damage an opponent" (paragraph 4) means
   a. flattery.
   b. descriptive phrases.
   c. dues.
   d. delays.

2. The words *capitalizes on* in "the testimonial capitalizes on the admiration people have for a celebrity" (paragraph 11) mean
   a. reports about.
   b. ignores.
   c. cuts back on.
   d. takes advantage of.

Central Point and Main Ideas

3. Which sentence best expresses the central point of this essay?
   a. According to one study, Americans are exposed daily to over five hundred advertising claims of some sort.
   b. Name calling is a propaganda technique in which competitors are referred to in negative ways.
   c. People should be on guard against seven common propaganda techniques, which appeal to the emotions rather than to logic.
   d. Our daily bombardment of ads may intensify in the future since current trends include advertising in untraditional places, such as on movie screens and shopping carts, and even public television.

4. Which sentence best expresses the main idea of paragraphs 8, 9, and 10?
   a. The first sentence of paragraph 8
   b. The first sentence of paragraph 9
   c. The last sentence of paragraph 9
   d. The first sentence of paragraph 10

Supporting Details

5. The technique in which important-sounding but unsupported claims are made with attractive but vague words is called
   a. glittering generalities.
   b. transfer.
   c. testimonials.
   d. bandwagon.

6. The technique in which evidence is withheld or distorted is called
   a. glittering generalities.
   b. bandwagon.
   c. plain folks.
   d. card stacking.

7. The technique that takes advantage of people's admiration for celebrities is called
   a. glittering generalities.
   b. plain folks.
   c. testimonial.
   d. card stacking.

8. A way to avoid being taken in by propaganda is to use
   a. our emotions.
   b. name calling.
   c. clear thinking.
   d. our subconscious.

Transitions

9. The relationship of paragraph 7 to paragraph 6 is one of
   a. time.
   b. addition.
   c. cause and effect.
   d. illustration.

Patterns of Organization

10. The pattern of organization of most of the essay can be described as a
    a. combination of time order and list of items.
    b. list of definitions and examples.
    c. comparison of effects.
    d. combination of time order and definition-example.

ADVANCED SKILL QUESTIONS

Summarizing and Outlining

11. Which statement best summarizes paragraphs 1–2?
    a. Americans are bombarded with numerous ads every day.
    b. The numerous ads we see daily make great use of propaganda, the systematic attempt to influence our opinions.
    c. We are bombarded daily by hundreds of ads for products such as toothpaste, political views, or political candidates.
    d. Propagandists are concerned with convincing people.

12. Which statement best summarizes paragraphs 3–20?
    a. Name calling and glittering generalities are common types of propaganda techniques.
    b. There are seven common types of propaganda technique, all of which are aimed at persuading the public to do or buy something.
    c. The most unfair type of propaganda technique is card stacking, which means telling half-truths—that is, suppressing or distorting information and oversimplifying the facts.
    d. Advertising, a form of propaganda, ought to be more closely regulated.

Fact and Opinion

13. The first paragraph of the essay is made up
    a. only of facts.
    b. only of opinions.
    c. of both fact and opinion.

Inferences

14. The author implies in paragraph 2 that propagandists don't care about
    a. money.
    b. presenting both sides of a question.
    c. their products.
    d. the political candidates they promote.

15. From the conclusion of the essay (paragraphs 21–22), we can deduce that the author feels
    a. we are unlikely to analyze advertising logically unless we recognize it as propaganda.
    b. propaganda should not be allowed.
    c. if we don't want to hand over to others our independence, we should ignore all propaganda.
    d. we should not support any of the "products, viewpoints, and candidates urged on us by propaganda messages."

16. When candidates pose with a baby in their arms, they are using the technique of
    a. name calling.
    b. testimonial.
    c. plain folks.
    d. bandwagon.

17. The ad described below uses the technique of
    a. transfer.
    b. plain folks.
    c. the testimonial.
    d. bandwagon.

    An ad for Superslims cigarettes features a glamourous super-slim and sexy woman relaxing with a Superslim cigarette.

Purpose and Tone

18. _____ TRUE OR FALSE? This essay has two purposes—both to inform and to persuade.

19. The tone of this essay can be described as
    a. fearful and desperate.
    b. amused and light-hearted.
    c. outspoken and impassioned.
    d. ambivalent and thus hesitant.

Argument

20. Which fallacy best describes the logical weakness of the testimonial (which implies that we should buy or do something because a celebrity does)?
    a. Changing the subject *(the evidence sounds good but has nothing to do with the argument)*
    b. False cause *(the argument assumes the order of events alone shows cause and effect)*
    c. Circular reasoning *(a statement repeats itself rather than providing a real supporting reason to back up an argument)*
    d. Either-or *(the argument assumes that there are only two sides to a question)*

OUTLINING

Complete the following outline of the essay by filling in notes on the missing points. (An outline such as this one is a very helpful form in which to prepare review notes on material you need to study.)

Central Point: Propaganda, a systematic attempt to influence opinions by appealing more to emotion than logic, includes the use of seven common techniques.

  A. Seven common propaganda techniques
    1. Name calling
      a. *Definition:* using negatively charged names or comments in reference to a competitor
      b. *Purpose:* to arouse feelings of mistrust, fear, and hate
      c. *Examples:* damaging labels such as "friend of big business"; Master-Card ad shows disadvantage of American Express card

2. Glittering generalities
   a. *Definition:* important-sounding general claims for which no explanation or proof is offered
   b. *Purpose:* to stir positive feelings that may spill over to product or idea
   c. *Examples:* _____

3. Transfer

   a. _____

   _____

   b. _____

   c. _____

   _____

4. Testimonial
   a. *Definition:* a statement on behalf of a product by an admired celebrity with no product expertise
   b. *Purpose:* to transfer some of admiration for celebrity to product
   c. *Examples:* Michael Jackson on Pepsi ads; stars associated with political candidates

5. Plain folks
   a. *Definition:* association of a product with—or portrayal of a candidate as—regular folks
   b. *Purpose:* to convince target audience that company or person has the same values, goals, and needs as they do
   c. *Examples:* plain-folks wording (Country Time lemonade); plain-folks images—assembly line workers at Ford; political candidates shown wearing coveralls or jogging

6. Card stacking
   a. *Definition:* misrepresenting the facts by suppressing relevant evidence
   b. *Purpose:* to leave deceptively favorable impression
   c. *Examples:* omission of reasons—candidate changing "mind five times"; unfinished claims—"400 percent quieter"

7. Bandwagon
   a. *Definition:* telling an audience that "Everyone's doing it and so should you"

   b. _____
   c. *Examples:* "nobody doesn't like Sara Lee"; "America's favorite health kick"

B. Since propaganda is so effective at appealing to our emotions, we can gain independence from them only through clear thinking—analyzing claims, researching facts, examining both sides of issue, using logic.

DISCUSSION QUESTIONS

1. As the essay points out, advertising is present everywhere in our society. Which of the seven techniques that McClintock describes have you seen recently? Cite examples from your own experiences of the techniques.

2. McClintock writes that the number of ads in our lives may increase "since current trends include ads on movie screens, shopping carts, video cassettes, even public television." What are some of the stranger places where you've seen ads?

3. Have you ever found that a consumer or political ad was misleading—either when you saw or read the ad or later, after you bought the product or learned more about the politician? Explain.

4. To what extent are you aware of how ads influence you? Do you buy many products or vote for many candidates as a result of their ads? Do you think this article will change how ads affect you in the future?

Check Your Performance	PROPAGANDA TECHNIQUES		
Skill	*Number Right*	*Points*	*Total*
BASIC SKILL QUESTIONS			
Vocabulary in Context (2 items)	_____	x 4 =	_____
Central Point and Main Ideas (2 items)	_____	x 4 =	_____
Supporting Details (4 items)	_____	x 4 =	_____
Transitions (1 item)	_____	x 4 =	_____
Patterns of Organization (1 item)	_____	x 4 =	_____
ADVANCED SKILL QUESTIONS			
Summarizing and Outlining (2 items)	_____	x 4 =	_____
Fact and Opinion (1 item)	_____	x 4 =	_____
Inferences (4 items)	_____	x 4 =	_____
Purpose and Tone (2 items)	_____	x 4 =	_____
Argument (1 item)	_____	x 4 =	_____
OUTLINING (5 items)	_____	x 4 =	_____

FINAL SCORE (OF POSSIBLE 100)   _____ %

Enter your final score into the reading performance chart on the inside back cover.

7

The Older Family
Rodney Stark

Preview

What images come to mind when you think of older Americans? A vibrant older couple retiring to days of tennis and golf? A financially struggling, depressed single person living out the loneliest years of life? Both images have a basis in truth, but you may be surprised to learn some of the facts about older Americans presented in the following textbook excerpt from *Sociology*, Third Edition (Wadsworth, 1989). If you think people are more likely to be happiest when they are young, this selection will change your view of life's stages.

Words to Watch

nuclear families (1): social units composed of parents and their children
plight (9): troubled situation
assessment (9): evaluation
vulnerability (21): weak spot
cohort (22): group

Until modern times most human beings never got old—they didn't live that long. Even at the beginning of this century, the average life expectancy of people born in the United States was only 47 years, 46.3 for men and 48.3 for women; among black Americans, the figures were 32.5 and 33.5, respectively. Today, nearly ninety years later, life expectancy in America is 74.7 years—71.1 for men and 78.3 for women (67.3 for black men and 75.2 for black women). As a result, the proportion of Americans over age 65 has nearly tripled over the past ninety years. This fact, combined with an overwhelming preference for nuclear families°, means that not only are there more older individuals but there are also a lot more older families.

Our images of older families are contradictory. The media stress the poverty that so 2
often accompanies the "graying" of the family. Yet one gains a very different image by
traveling the highways of the nation, an image of the older family on an endless vacation
in the passing streams of recreational vehicles and trailers. Or nonstop Congressional
hearings on problems of senior citizens produce endless testimony on the need for
improved retirement and social security benefits, but polls show that younger people, not
those over 65, think the government spends too little on social security. Or in one section
of the newspaper we can read of the serious health problems of the elderly, while in
another section we can read about how active most older Americans remain.

Which of these images is true? Probably *all* of them. The older American family is 3
as varied as are younger families. Some older couples live on yachts, some live in shacks;
some run in marathons, some are bedridden. Nevertheless, comparisons between older and
younger families can reveal interesting contrasts. This section will inspect some of these
comparisons based on national survey data. I think you will find many surprises here.

HAPPINESS

I must admit that Table ST4-1 really surprised me. Older Americans are the happiest 4
Americans. People over 65 are significantly more likely than younger people to say they
are "very happy." Moreover, the big difference is between those over 65 and everyone
else—a pattern that held up in comparison after comparison. So we need not examine the
full set of age categories in the remainder of this analysis, but can simply compare groups
over and under 65.

Table ST4-1: Age and happiness.

Age:	18–29	30–39	40–49	50–65	Over 65
Percent who are "very happy"	29.4%	29.1%	31.5%	32.7%	38.8%

Source: Prepared by the author from National Opinion Research Center, General Social Survey,
combined samples for 1986 and 1987.

These data on happiness call up the image of the older American family rolling 5
down the highway in a Winnebago looking for adventures. Of course, many over 65 did
not say they were very happy. Moreover, while men and women age 65 and under were
equally likely to say they were happy, among those over 65, men were significantly more
likely than were women to say they were very happy.

MARRIAGE

Look at Table ST4-2. Here men and women over 65 have been further separated 6
into those who are or are not currently married. It isn't that older women are less happy
than older men; it is that married people are much more likely than unmarried people to be
happy.

Table ST4-2: Marriage and happiness for people over 65.

	Married		Unmarried	
	Men	Women	Men	Women
Percent who are "very happy"	50.9%	53.8%	29.4%	29.2%

Source: Prepared by the author from National Opinion Research Center, General Social Survey, combined samples for 1986 and 1987.

What the gender difference in happiness reveals is perhaps the single most important [7] thing about the older family: Frequently, it includes only *one* member. And because of longer female life expectancy, combined with the tendency of wives to be younger than their husbands, the one-member family is very disproportionately female. In 1984, of the nearly 11 million American men over 65, 78 percent were currently married. But of the more than 15 million American women over 65, only 40 percent were currently married. This marriage gap continues to grow with age. Of people 75 and older, 70 percent of the men still have wives, but only 24 percent of the women still have husbands.

Another way to look at this is through sex ratios. In 1910, among persons over 65, [8] there were 101 men for every 100 women. In 1984 there were only 67.5 men. The average older American wife faces the burden of a lengthy widowhood—which is precisely what these findings on greater male happiness reflect. Now, let's look at a second aspect of happiness.

FINANCES

In light of what we know about the financial plight° of many older Americans, Table ST4-3 offers another surprise. People over 65 are almost twice as likely as younger people to be "pretty satisfied" with their present financial situation. Undoubtedly, some of this greater satisfaction stems from older people no longer having to strive for future occupational status. If many find the work world a "rat race," for most older Americans that race is ended. Hence their assessment° of their present financial situation sums up how they did, and a lot of them think they did pretty well. But here again there is a sex difference; and again we see that this is largely a

Table ST4-3: Satisfaction with finances. [9]

So far as you and your family are concerned, would you say that you are pretty well satisfied with your present financial situation, more or less satisfied, or not satisfied at all?	Percent Who Are "Pretty Satisfied"
65 and under	26.5%
Over 65	46.1%
Married men over 65	57.9%
Married women over 65	60.0%
Unmarried men over 65	45.6%
Unmarried women over 65	33.6%

Source: Prepared by the author from National Opinion Research Center, General Social Survey, combined samples for 1986 and 1987.

function of marriage. Married men and women are much more likely than the unmarried to be pretty satisfied, and the only significant sex difference is the one among the unmarried. Table ST4-4 lets us see why.

People over 65 are much more likely than younger people to report a family income [10] of less than $10,000 a year; more than four out of ten have incomes this low. However, only about one in five among married older Americans have incomes below $10,000. In contrast, over one-third of unmarried men and two-thirds of unmarried women have low incomes. So if unmarried women are less likely to be satisfied than are married people or unmarried men, they have less to be satisfied about.

The unmarried are in greater [11] risk of poverty because even in retirement, married people often constitute two-earner households. Unmarried women run a greater risk of poverty than do unmarried men because they are much less likely to have been employed outside the home and therefore they are less likely to be qualified for social security (except for widow's benefits from their husband's social security) or to have an independent pension.

Table ST4-4: Low incomes.

65 and under	16.5%
Over 65	44.4%
Married men over 65	19.6%
Married women over 65	23.2%
Unmarried men over 65	39.7%
Unmarried women over 65	67.7%

Source: Prepared by the author from National Opinion Research Center, General Social Survey, combined samples for 1986 and 1987.

FAMILY TIES

The image of the older American family as isolated from children and kin [12] undoubtedly fits some people, but in fact most older Americans frequently see their children (Shanas, 1973), and Table ST4-5 shows that people over 65 see relatives as often as younger Americans do. The second item in the table also may come as a surprise. Older Americans overwhelmingly reject the idea of sharing a home with their grown children. In contrast, younger people are much more inclined to see that as a good idea.

Table ST4-5: Family ties.

	65 and Under	Over 65
Percent who spend a social evening with relatives once or twice a week	36.8%	34.3%
Percent who think it is a *good idea* for older people to share a home with their grown children	43.8%	23.8%

Source: Prepared by the author from National Opinion Research Center, General Social Survey, 1986.

LEISURE

So what do older Americans do with their time? Do older and younger people tend 13
to spend their leisure time differently? Table ST4-6 offers some answers.

Table ST4-6: Social and leisure activities.

	65 and Under	Over 65
Percent who read a newspaper every day	50.4%	67.9%
Percent who can name their congressional representative	35.4%	43.5%
Percent who watch TV more than 2 hours a day	49.4%	60.8%
Percent who spend a social evening with a neighbor once or twice a week	26.3%	35.5%
Percent who attend church weekly	33.3%	50.2%
Percent who contribute more than $300 a year to a church	27.7%	38.5%
Percent who go to a bar or tavern at least once a month	29.2%	6.0%
Percent who drink alcoholic beverages	72.2%	46.4%
Percent who have attended an X-rated movie in the past year	29.4%	3.0%
Percent who find life "exciting"	45.0%	42.3%

Source: Prepared by the author from National Opinion Research Center, General Social Survey,
1986.

Older people are more apt to read a newspaper every day. However, this is not 14
because they have more time. Americans now over 65 were more apt to read newspapers
when they were 30 than are people that age today. Consequently, newspaper circulation
has been declining, relative to population size, for decades. For example, in 1950, per
capita newspaper circulation was .35. Today it is only .26.

Perhaps as a result of their newspaper reading, older Americans are more apt to 15
know the name of their local representative in Congress.

Older people are also more likely to watch TV for more than two hours a day than 16
are younger people. That undoubtedly does reflect their greater amount of free time, as
may the fact that older people are more apt to spend frequent social evenings with
neighbors than are younger people.

Younger people are less likely than those over 65 to attend church weekly—even 17
though for many older people transportation can be a problem. More available time would
not seem to be the relevant factor because, despite having lower incomes, people over 65
are substantially more likely to contribute more than $300 a year to a church.

Indeed, despite having more spare time, older people are extremely unlikely to 18
spend any of it in a bar or tavern; only 6 percent do this as often as once a month,
compared with about 30 percent of those under 65. Older people are much more likely to
drink at home (46.4 percent) than to drink out, but are not as likely to do so as younger

Americans, 72.2 percent of whom drink. Older people are not inclined to go out to X-rated movies either. But older people are as likely as those 65 and under to say that they find life to be "exciting."

HEALTH AND MORTALITY

Table ST4-7 shows that older Americans are less likely than those under 65 to rate   19
their health as excellent, but the difference seems smaller than one might expect. In fact, only 11 percent of those over 65 rated their health as poor, as did 4 percent of the younger group. More than half of those over 65 report having been hospitalized during the past five years, but so have more than one-third of those younger.

Table ST4-7: Health and mortality.

	65 and Under	Over 65
Percent who rate their health as excellent	36.8%	19.8%
Percent who have been hospitalized in the past 5 years	35.9%	53.4%
Percent who have had a spouse die	7.6%	51.7%
Percent who have had a brother or sister die in the past 5 years	11.2%	37.7%
Percent who have had a child die in the past 5 years	1.8%	9.6%
Percent who have had another close relative die in the past 5 years	31.5%	59.3%

Source: Prepared by the author from National Opinion Research Center, General Social Survey, 1987.

However, older Americans are much more likely to experience the death of loved   20
ones. Half of those over 65 have lost a spouse, compared with only 7.6 percent of those 65 and under. More than one-third have lost a brother or sister within the past five years, compared with 11.2 percent of those under 65. Indeed, one in ten have lost a child during the past five years—a grown child, not an infant. Finally, about 60 percent have lost another close relative during the past five years, as have one-third of younger Americans.

One major lesson to be learned from these data is that the older American family has   21
high levels of contentment and satisfaction. But there is a second, and darker, lesson to be learned here as well. The older family is, of course, a couple's household—although high levels of contact are maintained, the children and grandchildren live elsewhere. And herein lies a major vulnerability° of the older family. Eventually, the couple becomes a one-person household, and the loss of what was the survivor's most intimate relationship too often also is accompanied by a very substantial decline in income. When discussions of poverty among older Americans arise, they are primarily discussions of the poverty of widows.

This aspect of what some have called the "feminization of poverty" may be only   22 temporary. Because of the rapid expansion of the proportion of females in the labor force, younger women are much less likely to have spent their married years as full-time homemakers. Hence, as each new age cohort° of women reaches retirement age, each year a larger proportion of older women have been employed outside the home for a substantial number of years. These women qualify for social security benefits in their own right, and many have earned other pension benefits. As a result, they are not nearly so vulnerable to financial distress if their spouse dies. The emotional distress of widowhood may prove much more intractable.

BASIC SKILL QUESTIONS

Vocabulary in Context

1. The word *intractable* in "These women qualify for social security benefits in their own right. . . . As a result, they are not nearly so vulnerable to financial distress if their spouse dies. The emotional distress of widowhood may prove much more intractable" (paragraph 22) means
   a. easy to solve.
   b. difficult to manage.
   c. unimportant.
   d. pleasant.

Central Point and Main Ideas

2. Which sentence best expresses the central point of the selection?
   a. People are living longer than ever before.
   b. Comparative research reveals much about the happiness and well-being of older Americans.
   c. The government should be spending more money on the elderly.
   d. With the increase in numbers of working women, the tendency toward poverty among older widows is likely to be reversed.

3. The main idea of paragraph 20 is best expressed in its
   a. first sentence.
   b. second sentence.
   c. third sentence.
   d. last sentence.

Supporting Details

4. Men over 65 are more likely to say they are happy than women over 65 because they are more likely to be
   a. married.
   b. unmarried.

5. _____ TRUE OR FALSE? Most older Americans are eager to share a home with their grown children.

6. _____ TRUE OR FALSE? Surprisingly, younger Americans are more likely than those over 65 to experience the death of loved ones.

Transitions

7. The relationship of the second sentence below to the first is one of
   a. addition.
   b. time.
   c. comparison.
   d. cause-effect.

   > Today, nearly ninety years later, life expectancy in America is 74.7 years—71.1 for men and 78.3 for women (67.3 for black men and 75.2 for black women). As a result, the proportion of Americans over age 65 has nearly tripled over the past ninety years. (Paragraph 1)

8. The relationship of the second half of the sentence below to the first half is one of
   a. addition.
   b. illustration.
   c. contrast.
   d. cause-effect.

   > Younger people are less likely than those over 65 to attend church weekly—even though for many older people transportation can be a problem. (Paragraph 17)

Patterns of Organization

9. The pattern of organization of paragraph 20 is one of
   a. list of items and time order.
   b. contrast and list of items.
   c. definition-example and cause-effect.
   d. time order and cause-effect.

10. The pattern of organization of the reading can be described as a combination of
    a. list of items and time order.
    b. comparison-contrast and list of items.
    c. definition-example and cause-effect.
    d. time order and cause-effect.

ADVANCED SKILL QUESTIONS

Summarizing and Outlining

11. Which sentence best summarizes paragraphs 13–18?
    a. Older people tend to spend their leisure time differently than younger people do.

  b. Older people are—and always have been—more likely than today's younger Americans to read a newspaper.

  c. Older people are more likely to watch TV than are younger people.

  d. Older people are less likely than younger people to drink at a bar or tavern.

12. Which of the following best outlines paragraphs 19–20?

  a. Health and mortality of Americans over 65, compared to younger people
    1. Health not much worse among those over 65
    2. Those over 65 more likely to experience death of loved one

  b. Health and mortality
    1. Men over 65
    2. Men under 65

  c. Health and mortality of Americans over 65
    1. Men over 65
    2. Women over 65

Fact and Opinion

13. This selection is mainly made up of
  a. facts.
  b. opinions.

Inferences

14. The author implies that many older Americans
  a. wish they were young again.
  b. have problems with alcoholism.
  c. do not altogether fit the media image of them.
  d. watch too much television.

15. _____ TRUE OR FALSE? We can conclude that the term "older family" in the essay refers to family units made up either of couples or single people over 65.

16. We can conclude that the single elderly might benefit from
  a. remarriage.
  b. nearby social activities.
  c. increased income.
  d. all of the above.

Purpose and Tone

17. The main purpose of the selection is
  a. to inform.
  b. to persuade.
  c. to entertain.

18. The tone of the article can be described as
    a. mainly distressed.
    b. concerned and shocked.
    c. largely objective, but caring and somewhat surprised.
    d. questioning and interested, but basically light-hearted.

Argument

19. Check the one item that does not support the following point:

    Point: The average life expectancy of people born in the United States has increased considerably since the beginning of this century.

    _____ a. The average life expectancy in the U.S. at the beginning of the century was 47 years; today it is 74.7 years.

    _____ b. In 1910, there were 101 men over 65 for every 100 women over 65; today the ratio is 67.5 men for every 100 women.

    _____ c. The proportion of Americans over age 65 has nearly tripled over the past ninety years.

20. The conclusion that older families are unhappier than younger ones can be said to be based on the fallacy of
    a. changing the subject *(the evidence sounds good but has nothing to do with the argument).*
    b. circular reasoning *(a statement repeats itself rather than providing a real supporting reason to back up an argument).*
    c. hasty conclusion *(the argument comes to a conclusion based on insufficient evidence).*
    d. false comparison *(the argument assumes that two things being compared are more alike than they really are).*

OUTLINING

Complete the following outline of "The Older Family" by filling in the missing items, which are listed below the outline.

Central Point: _____

_____

A. _____

1. In general, Americans over 65 are the happiest, but men are more likely to say they are happy than women.
2. Since the married elderly are happiest and the elderly single tend to be women, most of the unhappy elderly are women.
3. Since the married elderly are more likely than singles to be satisfied with their finances, women over 65 are more likely than men over 65 to be dissatisfied with their finances.

B. Family ties

   1. Most older Americans have close family ties.

   2. _____

     _____

C. Leisure

   1. Americans over 65 are—and always have been—more likely to read newspapers.

   2. Older people are more likely to know the name of their Congressional representative.

   3. _____

   4. Older people are more likely to attend church and contribute more than $300 annually to church.

   5. While older people are less likely to in bars and taverns or to go to X-rated movies, they are as likely as younger people to say they find life "exciting."

D. Health and mortality

   1. The health of those over 65 is not much worse than that of those under 65.

   2. People over 65 are much more likely to experience the death of a loved one.

E. Some conclusions

   1. Discussions of poverty among older Americans are generally about the poverty of widows.

   2. _____

     _____

Items Missing from the Outline

- Older people are more likely to watch TV.
- In contrast with younger people, most older Americans reject the idea of sharing a home with grown children.
- Comparisons between Americans over 65 and those 65 and under are revealing.
- Happiness
- The financial situation of older single women is likely to improve, but their unhappy social situation may not.

DISCUSSION QUESTIONS

1. Of his comparisons between older and younger families, Stark writes, "I think you will find many surprises here." Which finding in the essay did you find most surprising? Why?

2. Stark explains that older people are more likely to read newspapers than younger people today. What reasons can you find for this difference?

3. In paragraph 8, Stark presents some figures which he doesn't explain: "In 1910, among persons over 65, there were 101 men for every 100 women. In 1984 there were only 67.5 men [for every 100 women]." What reasons can you think of to explain this change in the ratio of older men to women?

4. Think about some commercials, television shows, and movies you have seen recently. What specific attitudes were advanced about older Americans? How do these attitudes compare to what you have learned from the article? How do they compare to older Americans you know?

Check Your Performance   **THE OLDER FAMILY**

Skill	Number Right	Points	Total
BASIC SKILL QUESTIONS			
Vocabulary in Context (1 item)	_____	x 4 =	_____
Central Point and Main Ideas (2 items)	_____	x 4 =	_____
Supporting Details (3 items)	_____	x 4 =	_____
Transitions (2 items)	_____	x 4 =	_____
Patterns of Organization (2 items)	_____	x 4 =	_____
ADVANCED SKILL QUESTIONS			
Summarizing and Outlining (2 items)	_____	x 4 =	_____
Fact and Opinion (1 item)	_____	x 4 =	_____
Inferences (3 items)	_____	x 4 =	_____
Purpose and Tone (2 items)	_____	x 4 =	_____
Argument (2 items)	_____	x 4 =	_____
OUTLINING (5 items)	_____	x 4 =	_____

FINAL SCORE (OF POSSIBLE 100)   _____%

Enter your final score into the reading performance chart on the inside back cover.

8

Effects of
Childhood Isolation
Ian Robertson

Preview

It is now widely accepted that environment, like heredity, is a major force in our development as human beings. Still, you may be surprised to read in this selection just how important the contribution of environment is to our very humanity. This selection from the textbook *Sociology*, Third Edition (Worth, 1987) presents some disturbing and persuasive evidence.

Words to Watch

speculated (1): thought
inhibitions (1): controls
medieval (1): of the Middle Ages (about 476 A.D. to 1453 A.D.)
folly (1): foolishness
bade (1): commanded
prattle (1): make childish sounds
socialization (2): the process by which someone learns from infancy how to live
                      in society
impaired (2): damaged
allegedly (2): reportedly
ravenously (3): hungrily
autistic (4): having a form of childhood mental illness marked by a withdrawal
                    from reality
psychotics (13): people with certain severe mental disorders
wretched (13): poor

For many centuries people have wondered what human beings would be like if they   1
were raised in isolation from human society. Some speculated° that such children would

be mere brutes, revealing the essence of our real "human nature." Others felt that they would be perfect beings, perhaps speaking the language of Adam and Eve in the Garden of Eden. Today there are obvious ethical considerations that make any experiment involving the deliberate isolation of children impossible, but earlier ages were not always under such moral inhibitions°. In the thirteenth century the emperor Frederick II conducted just such an experiment, recorded by a medieval° historian in these terms:

> His . . . folly° was that he wanted to find out what kind of speech and what manner of speech children would have when they grew up, if they spoke to no one beforehand. So he bade° foster mothers and nurses to suckle the children, to bathe and wash them, but in no way prattle° with them or to speak to them, for he wanted to learn whether they would speak the Hebrew language, which was the oldest, or Greek, or Latin, or Arabic or perhaps the language of their parents, of whom they had been born. But he laboured in vain, because the children all died. For they could not live without the petting and joyful faces and loving words of their foster mothers.

The unhappy fate of the children comes as no surprise to modern social scientists, for it has been proved beyond doubt that children need more than mere physical care if they are to survive and prosper. They need close emotional attachments with at least one other person: without this bond, socialization° is impaired°, and irreversible damage may be done to the personality. Evidence for this view comes from four main sources: reports of so-called feral (untamed) children who were allegedly° raised by wild animals; studies of children who were deliberately reared in isolation by their own families; studies of children in institutions; and experiments that study the effects of isolation. 2

"FERAL" CHILDREN

The evidence relating to "feral" children is highly dramatic but also highly unreliable. Many societies have myths about children being raised by animals. The Romans, for example, believed that the founders of Rome, Romulus and Remus, had been raised by a wolf. In the late nineteenth and early twentieth centuries, however, a few cases of the discovery of children whose behavior seemed more like that of animals than human beings were reported from India, France, and elsewhere (Singh and Zingg, 1942; Malson, 1972; H. Lane, 1976; McLean, 1978; Shattuck, 1980). In every case the children could not speak, reacted with fear or hostility toward other human beings, slouched or walked on all fours; and tore ravenously° at their food. Attempts to socialize the children are said to have met with little success, and all died at a young age. 3

There are two difficulties with these reports. The first is that the subjects were never systematically examined by trained investigators, and the second is that we know nothing about the history of the children before they were discovered. It seems highly improbable that they had been raised by wild animals. It is far more likely that they had been abandoned by their own parents shortly before they were discovered by other people. It is also possible that the children were already mentally disturbed, autistic°, or had been raised in some form of isolation before being abandoned. 4

CHILDREN RAISED IN ISOLATION

Much more convincing evidence comes from studies of children who were 5
deliberately raised in isolation by their own families. Two such instances, both occurring
in the United States, have been reported by Kingsley Davis.

The first child, Anna, was discovered at the age of six. She had been born 6
illegitimate, and her grandfather had insisted that she be hidden from the world in an attic
room. Anna received a bare minimum of physical care and attention and had virtually no
opportunities for social interaction. When she was found she could not talk, walk, keep
herself clean, or feed herself; she was totally apathetic, expressionless, and indifferent to
human beings. In fact, those who worked with her believed at first that she was deaf and
possibly blind as well. David (1948) comments: "Here, then, was a human organism
which had missed nearly six years of socialization. Her condition shows how little her
purely biological resources, when acting alone, could contribute to making her a complete
person."

Attempts to socialize Anna had only limited success. The girl died four and a half 7
years later, but in that time she was able to learn some words and phrases, although she
could never speak sentences. She also learned to use building blocks, to string beads, to
wash her hands and brush her teeth, to follow directions, and to treat a doll with affection.
She learned to walk but could run only clumsily. By the time of her death at almost eleven
she had reached the level of socialization of a child of two or three.

The second child, Isabelle, was discovered about the same time as Anna and was 8
approximately the same age, six-and-a-half. She too was an illegitimate child, and her
grandfather had kept her and her mother—a deaf-mute—in a dark room most of the time.
Isabelle had the advantage, over Anna, of social interaction with her mother, but she had
no chance to develop speech; the two communicated with gestures. When Isabelle was
discovered, her behavior toward other people, especially men, was "almost that of a wild
animal." At first it was thought that she was deaf, for she did not appear to hear the sounds
around her, and her only speech was a strange croaking sound. The specialists who
worked with her pronounced her feebleminded and did not expect that she could ever be
taught to speak.

Unlike Anna, however, Isabelle had the training of a skilled team of doctors and 9
psychologists. After a slow start, she suddenly spurted through the stages of learning that
are usually characteristic of the first six years of childhood, taking every stage in the usual
order but at much greater speed than normal. By the time she was eight-and-a-half years
old she had reached an apparently normal level of intellectual development and was able
to attend school with other children. Her greater success seems to be related to the skills of
her trainers, the fact that her mother was present during her isolation, and the fact that,
unlike Anna, she was able to gain the use of language.

INSTITUTIONALIZED CHILDREN

The socialization of children who are raised in orphanages and similar institutions 10
differs from that of other children in one very important respect. Institutionalized children
rarely have the chance to develop close emotional ties with specific adults, for although
the children may interact with a large number of staff members, the attendants simply do
not have the time to devote much personal attention to any one individual. The standard of
nutrition and other physical care in institutions is sometimes good and comparable to that

in private homes, but relationships between child and adult are usually minimal.

In 1945, the psychologist Rene Spitz published an influential article on the effects   11
that these conditions have on children's personalities. Spitz compared some infants of the
same age who had been placed in the care of an orphanage. The infants living with their
mothers had plenty of opportunity for close social interaction, but those in the institution
received only routine care at mealtimes and when their clothing or bedding was changed.
Spitz found that the infants in the orphanage were physically, socially, and emotionally
retarded compared with the other infants—a difference, moreover, that increased steadily
as the children grew older.

Spitz's report was followed by a large number of studies on the effects of   12
institutionalization on infants and children, most of which have arrived at similar
conclusions. William Goldfarb (1945), for example, compared forty children who had
been placed in foster homes soon after birth with forty children who had spent the first two
years of life in institutions before being transferred to foster homes. He found that the
institutionalized children suffered a number of personality defects that persisted even after
they had left the institutions. They had lower IQ scores, seemed more aggressive and
distractible, showed less initiative, and were more emotionally cold. Many other studies
have reported similar depressing effects on physical, cognitive, emotional, and social
development, and have confirmed that such disabilities suffered in early childhood tend to
persist or even to grow worse in later years.

MONKEYS RAISED IN ISOLATION

Harry Harlow and his associates at the University of Wisconsin have conducted a   13
series of important experiments on the effects of isolation on rhesus monkeys. Harlow's
work has shown that even in monkeys, social behavior is learned, not inherited. The
monkeys raised in isolation in his labs behave in a way similar to that of human
psychotics°. They are fearful of or hostile to other monkeys, make no attempt to interact
with them, and are generally withdrawn and apathetic. Monkeys reared in isolation do not
know how to mate with other monkeys and usually cannot be taught how to do so. If
female monkeys who have been isolated since birth are artificially impregnated, they
become unloving and abusive mothers, making little or no attempt to take care of their
offspring. In one experiment Harlow provided isolated monkey infants with two substitute
mothers—one made of wire and containing a feeding bottle and one covered with soft
cloth but without a bottle. The infant monkeys preferred the soft, cuddly "mother" to the
one that fed them. This wretched° substitute for affection seemed more important to them
even than food.

Like all animal studies, Harlow's experiments must be treated with caution when   14
inferences are made for human behavior. After all, we are not monkeys. His studies show,
however, that without socialization, monkeys cannot develop normal social, sexual,
emotional, or maternal behavior. Since we know that human beings rely much more
heavily on learning than monkeys do, it seems fair to conclude that the same would be true
of us.

The evidence from these varied sources, then, points overwhelmingly in the same   15
direction: without socialization, we are almost devoid of personality and are utterly unable
to face even the simplest challenges of life. Lacking the "instincts" that guide the behavior
of other animals, we can become social and thus fully human only by learning through
interaction with other people.

BASIC SKILL QUESTIONS

Vocabulary in Context

1. The word *spurted* in "she suddenly spurted through the stages of learning that are usually characteristic of the first six years of childhood, taking every stage in the usual order but at much greater speed than normal" (paragraph 9) means
   a. avoided.
   b. went quickly.
   c. reversed.
   d. questioned.

2. The words *devoid of* in "without socialization, we are almost devoid of personality" (paragraph 15) mean
   a. capable.
   b. full.
   c. steady.
   d. without.

Central Point and Main Ideas

3. Which sentence best expresses the central point of the selection?
   a. Some children have deliberately been raised in isolation.
   b. To prosper, children need an emotional attachment to another person as well as physical care.
   c. Children raised in orphanages are retarded in comparison to other children.
   d. Many societies have myths about children being raised by animals.

4. The topic sentence(s) of paragraph 7
   a. is only implied.
   b. are the first and last sentences.
   c. is the second sentence.
   d. is the next-to-the-last sentence.

Supporting Details

5. According to the author, stories about children thought to be feral are
   a. unknown.
   b. unreliable.
   c. all from other centuries than our own.
   d. strangely varied.

6. The success in socializing Isabelle seems to be related in part to the fact that she
   a. was illegitimate.
   b. could make sounds.
   c. was kept in a dark room.
   d. was isolated with her mother.

7. Monkeys brought up in isolation
    a. are poor mothers.
    b. do not know how to mate.
    c. are fearful of other monkeys.
    d. all of the above.

Transitions

8. The relationship of the first four words below to the rest of the sentence is one of
    a. addition.
    b. comparison.
    c. contrast.
    d. cause and effect.

> Like all animal studies, Harlow's experiments must be treated with caution when inferences are made for human behavior. (Paragraph 14)

Patterns of Organization

9. The pattern of organization of paragraph 10 is
    a. time order.
    b. list of items.
    c. comparison/contrast.
    d. definition and example.

10. The sentence below points out that the selection is mainly organized according to a
    a. time order.
    b. list of items.
    c. contrast.
    d. definition and example.

> Evidence for this view comes from four main sources: reports of so-called feral (untamed) children who were allegedly raised by wild animals; studies of children who were deliberately reared in isolation by their own families; studies of children in institutions; and experiments that study the effects of isolation on other primates. (Paragraph 2)

ADVANCED SKILL QUESTIONS

Summarizing and Outlining

11. Which of the following best summarizes paragraphs 5–9?
    a. Both Anna and Isabelle were children who had been brought up in isolation until being discovered at the ages of six and six-and-a-half, respectively. Both were illegitimate children, which is undoubtedly why

they were forced to live hidden in one room until being discovered. When discovered, neither could speak; both exhibited animal-like behavior.

b. Like Anna, Isabelle was brought up in a single room, apart from the world. Unlike Anna, Isabelle was isolated with someone—her mother. This gave Isabelle the advantage of social interaction. But because her mother was a deaf-mute, Isabelle had no chance to develop speech—she and her mother communicated with gestures. Thus after Isabelle was discovered, it was at first thought she was deaf.

c. Two girls raised in isolation, Anna and Isabelle, show the importance of close emotional attachments during childhood. Both girls were greatly retarded in both physical and language development. Anna, who had been totally isolated until discovery, made limited progress and died in a few years; Isabelle, who had been isolated with her mother and been given superior training after discovery, became apparently normal in two years.

Fact and Opinion

12. The statement below is
    a. fact.
    b. opinion.
    c. both fact and opinion.

    The girl died four and a half years later, but in that time she was able to learn some words and phrases, although she could never speak sentences. (Paragraph 7)

Inferences

13. _____ TRUE OR FALSE? From the selection, we can conclude that the effects of childhood isolation cannot be reversed.

14. The author clearly implies that humans and monkeys
    a. have nothing in common.
    b. both learn social behavior.
    c. can thrive without affection.
    d. are totally guided by instincts.

15. _____ TRUE OR FALSE? The author implies that isolation can deprive people of the opportunity to become fully human.

16. _____ TRUE OR FALSE? We can conclude from the article that healthy human development involves both heredity and environment.

Purpose and Tone

17. The purpose of this selection is
    a. to inform readers of the proof that raising children in isolation damages their socialization.
    b. to persuade readers to fight isolation.
    c. to entertain readers with odd case histories.

18. The tone of the selection is
    a. serious.
    b. indifferent.
    c. angry.
    d. fearful.

Argument

19. Label the point of the following argument with a **P** and the two statements of support with an **S**.

    _____ We know nothing of the history of the so-called feral children, who may not have been isolated until shortly before their discovery.

    _____ Anecdotes about what were thought to be feral children are unreliable.

    _____ The children thought to be feral were never carefully examined by experts.

20. In stating, "Harlow's experiments must be treated with caution when inferences are made for human behavior. After all, we are not monkeys" (paragraph 14), the author addresses the fallacy of

    a. false comparison *(the argument assumes that two things being compared are more alike than they really are).*
    b. circular reasoning *(a statement repeats itself rather than providing a real supporting reason to back up an argument).*
    c. personal attack *(the argument shifts to irrelevant personal criticism).*
    d. false cause *(the argument assumes that the order of events alone shows cause and effect).*

OUTLINING

Complete the following outline of "Effects of Childhood Isolation."

Central Point: Information on isolation shows that children need close human relationships as well as physical care in order to prosper.

1. Stories of untamed children support the central point but are unreliable.

 a. The subjects were not scientifically examined.

 b. _____
 _____

2. _____
 _____

 a. Anna was raised in total isolation and was never successfully socialized.

 b. _____
 _____
 _____

3. Institutionalized children are generally isolated from close emotional ties, which, as Spitz showed, results in poor infant development.

4. _____
 _____

 a. Such monkeys behave like human psychotics.
 b. They do not know how to mate and are unable to learn.
 c. They crave affection even over food.

DISCUSSION QUESTIONS

1. Based on the article, which do you think would be better for a child: growing up in an orphanage or being raised in a foster home? Why?

2. What implications might this selection have for working parents of infants? For the administration of orphanages?

3. Considering the author's view of the evidence about untamed children, why might he have chosen to include that evidence in support of his central point?

4. The author states in paragraph 14 that "human beings rely much more heavily on learning than monkeys do." What are some examples of ways in which humans seem to rely more on learning than do monkeys?

Check Your Performance   EFFECTS OF CHILDHOOD ISOLATION

Skill	*Number Right*	*Points*	*Total*
BASIC SKILL QUESTIONS			
Vocabulary in Context (2 items)	_____	x 4 =	_____
Central Point and Main Ideas (2 items)	_____	x 4 =	_____
Supporting Details (3 items)	_____	x 4 =	_____
Transitions (1 item)	_____	x 4 =	_____
Patterns of Organization (2 items)	_____	x 4 =	_____
ADVANCED SKILL QUESTIONS			
Summarizing and Outlining (1 item)	_____	x 4 =	_____
Fact and Opinion (1 item)	_____	x 4 =	_____
Inferences (4 items)	_____	x 4 =	_____
Purpose and Tone (2 items)	_____	x 4 =	_____
Argument (2 items)	_____	x 4 =	_____
OUTLINING (4 items)	_____	x 5 =	_____

FINAL SCORE (OF POSSIBLE 100)   _____%

Enter your final score into the reading performance chart on the inside back cover.

9

Lyndon Johnson's War
James Kirby Martin *et al.*

Preview

The military conflict in Vietnam caught up the United States in a bitter conflict with grim effects that continue to this day. The following selection from the textbook *America and Its People* (Scott Foresman, 1989) traces the progression of the U.S. involvement in that conflict. In particular, it describes the role of President Lyndon Johnson.

Words to Watch

deployments (1): troop placements
sorties (1): aircraft combat missions
pretext (4): false reason advanced to hide the true one
commence (4): begin
lunar (4): like the moon
regime (5): government in power
counterinsurgency (6): aimed against guerrillas and rebels
bode well (10): was a good sign
hamlets (10): small villages
futile (12): useless

     Lyndon Johnson liked to personalize things. Once a military aide tried to direct Johnson to the correct helicopter, saying "Mr. President, that's not your helicopter." "Son, they're all my helicopters," Johnson replied. So it was with the Vietnam War. He did not start the war, but once reelected he quickly made it "his war." Over the war he exercised complete control. One authority on the war described Johnson's role:

He made appointments, approved promotions, reviewed troop requests, determined deployments°, selected bombing targets, and restricted aircraft sorties°. Night after night, wearing a dressing gown and carrying a flashlight, he would descend into the White House basement "situation room" to monitor the conduct of the conflict . . . often, too, he would doze by his bedside telephone, waiting to hear the outcome of a mission to rescue one of "my pilots" shot down over Haiphong or Vinh or Thai Nguyen. It was his war.

When he became president it was still a relatively obscure conflict for most Americans. Public opinion polls showed that 70 percent of the American public paid little attention to United States activities in Vietnam. At the end of 1963 only 16,300 United States military personnel were in Vietnam; the number rose to 23,300 by the end of 1964. Most of the soldiers there, however, were volunteers. Only a few people strongly opposed America's involvement. All this would change dramatically during the next four years.   2

With the election behind him, in early 1965 Johnson started to reevaluate the position of the United States. In Saigon crisis followed crisis as one unpopular government gave way to the next. Something had to be done, and Johnson's advisors suggested two courses. The military and most of LBJ's foreign policy experts called for a more aggressive military presence in Vietnam, including bombing raids into North Vietnam and more ground troops. Other advisors, notably Under Secretary of State George Ball, believed the United States was making the same mistakes as France had made. Escalating the war could create serious problems. "Once on the tiger's back," Ball noted, "we cannot be sure of picking the place to dismount."   3

Johnson chose the first course, claiming it would be dishonorable not to come to South Vietnam's aid. In February 1965, Vietcong troops attacked the American base in Pleiku, killing several soldiers. Johnson used the assault as a pretext° to commence° air raids into the North. Code named "Rolling Thunder," the operation was designed to use American technological superiority to defeat North Vietnam. At first, Johnson limited United States air strikes to enemy radar and bridges below the 20th parallel. But as the war dragged on, he ordered "his pilots" to hit metropolitan areas. Between 1965 and 1973, American pilots flew more than 526,000 sorties and dropped 6,162,000 tons of bombs on enemy targets. (As a point of contrast, the total tonnage of explosives dropped in World War II was 2,150,000 tons.) As a result, much of the landscape of North Vietnam took on a lunar° look.   4

However, the bombs did not lead to victory. Ironically, the bombing missions actually strengthened the communist government in North Vietnam. As a United States intelligence report noted, the bombing of North Vietnam "had no significantly harmful effects on popular morale. In fact, the regime° has apparently been able to increase its control of the populace and perhaps even to break through the political apathy and indifference which have characterized the outlook of the average North Vietnamese in recent years."   5

The massive use of air power also undermined United States counterinsurgency° efforts. Colonel John Paul Vann, an American expert on counterinsurgency warfare, noted, "The best weapon 'for this type of war' . . . would be a knife. . . . The worst is an airplane. The next worst is artillery. Barring a knife, the best is a rifle—you know who you're killing." By using bombing raids against the enemy in both the North and South, United States forces inevitably killed large numbers of civilians, the very people they were there to help. For peasants everywhere in Vietnam, United States jets, helicopters, and artillery   6 "meant more bombing, more death, and more suffering."

A larger air war also led to more ground troops. As Johnson informed Ambassador 7
Maxwell Taylor, "I have never felt that this war will be won from the air, and it seems to
me what is much more needed and will be more effective is a larger and stronger use of
rangers and special forces and marines." Between 1965 and 1968 the escalation of
American forces was dramatic. When George Ball warned in 1965 that 500,000 American
troops in Vietnam might not be able to win the war, other members of the Johnson
administration laughed. By 1968 no one was laughing. Ball's prediction was painfully
accurate. Escalation of American troops and deaths went hand and hand. The year-end
totals for the United States between 1965 and 1968 were:

1965: 184,300 troops; 636 killed.
1966: 385,300 troops; 6644 killed.
1967: 485,600 troops; 16,021 killed.
1968: 536,000 troops; 30,610 killed.

But still there was no victory.

TO TET AND BEYOND

Throughout the escalation Johnson was less than candid with the American people. 8
He argued that there had been no real change in American policy and that victory was in
sight. Any reporter who said otherwise, he roundly criticized. Increasingly he demanded
unquestioning loyalty from his close advisors. Such demands led to an administration
"party line." As the war ground on, the "party line" bore less and less similarity to reality.

In late 1967, General William Westmoreland returned to America briefly to assure 9
the public that he could now see the "light at the end of the tunnel." In his annual report
Westmoreland commented, "This year ended with the enemy increasingly resorting to
desperation tactics; . . . and he has experienced only failure in these attempts." At the time,
the American press focused most of its attention on the battle of Khe Sanh, and
Westmoreland assured everyone that victory there was certain.

Then with a suddenness which caught all America by surprise, North Vietnam 10
struck into the very heart of South Vietnam. On the morning of January 30, 1968, North
Vietnam launched the Tet Offensive. "Tet," the Vietnamese holiday which celebrates the
lunar new year, traditionally is supposed to determine family fortunes for the rest of the
year. Certainly the Tet Offensive bode well° for North Vietnam. A Vietcong suicide squad
broke into the United States embassy in Saigon, and Vietnamese communists mounted
offensives against every major target in South Vietnam, including five cities, sixty-four
district capitals, thirty-six provincial capitals, and fifty hamlets°.

For what it was worth, the United States repelled the Tet Offensive. For a month the 11
fighting was ferocious and bloody, as the rivals fought in highly populated cities and
almost evacuated hamlets. In order to retake Hue, the ancient cultural center close to the
border between North and South Vietnam, allied troops had to destroy the city. One
observer recorded that the city was left a "shattered, stinking hulk, its streets choked with
rubble and rotting bodies." In another village, where victory came at a high price, the
liberating American general reported, "We had to destroy the town to save it." Both sides
suffered terribly. But after the allies cleared the cities of enemy troops, General
Westmoreland judged the episode a great allied victory.

If technically the Tet Offensive was a military defeat for North Vietnam, it was also   12
a profound psychological victory. Johnson, his advisors, and his generals had been
proclaiming that the enemy was on the run, almost defeated, tired of war, ready to quit.
Tet demonstrated that the contrary was true. Upset and confused, Walter Cronkite, the
national voice of reason, expressed the attitude on his nightly newscast: "What the hell is
going on? I thought we were winning the war!" The Tet Offensive, more than any other
single event, turned the media against the war and exposed the widening "credibility gap"
between official pronouncements and public beliefs. NBC anchorman Frank McGee
reported that the time had come "when we must decide whether it is futile° to destroy
Vietnam in the effort to save it."

After Tet, Americans stopped thinking about victory and turned toward thoughts of   13
how best to get out of Vietnam. "Lyndon's planes" and "Lyndon's boys" had been unable
to achieve Lyndon's objectives. For Johnson this fact was politically disastrous. In the
polls his popularity plummeted, and in the New Hampshire primary, peace candidate
Eugene McCarthy received surprisingly solid support. Too intelligent a politician not to
realize what was happening, on the night of March 31, LBJ went on television and made
two important announcements. First, he said that the United States would limit its
bombing of North Vietnam and would enter into peace talks any time and at any place.
And second, Johnson surprised the nation by saying, "I shall not seek, and I will not
accept the nomination of my party for another term as your President." A major turning
point had been reached. The gradual escalation of the war was over. The period of
deescalation had started. Even in official government circles, peace had replaced victory
as America's objective in Vietnam.

BASIC SKILL QUESTIONS

Vocabulary in Context

1. The word *obscure* in "when he became president it was still a relatively
   obscure conflict for most Americans. Public opinion polls showed that 70
   percent of the American public paid little attention to United States activities
   in Vietnam" (paragraph 2) means
   a. obvious.
   b. unnoted.
   c. hated.
   d. celebrated.

2. The word *plummeted* in "'Lyndon's planes' and 'Lyndon's boys' had been
   unable to achieve Lyndon's objectives. For Johnson this fact was politically
   disastrous. In the polls his popularity plummeted" (paragraph 13) means
   a. was slightly strengthened.
   b. grew rapidly.
   c. stood still.
   d. dropped quickly.

Central Point and Main Ideas

3. Which sentence best expresses the central point of the selection?
   a. America lost the military conflict in Vietnam.
   b. President Johnson's decisions about the Vietnam War made it a disaster for both sides and lost him his political career.
   c. The massive use of air power in both North and South Vietnam was one of the terrible American mistakes during the war.
   d. At the height of the Vietnam War, America had over half a million troops in Vietnam.

4. Which sentence best expresses the main idea of paragraph 8?
   a. Johnson intensely criticized any reporter who contradicted his statements about the war.
   b. Johnson increasingly demanded loyalty from his close advisers, which led to an administration "party line."
   c. Johnson increasingly kept the truth about the war from the American public.
   d. Throughout his term in office, Johnson was not honest with the American people about any of his policies.

5. Which sentence best expresses the main idea of paragraph 12?
   a. Technically, the Tet Offensive was a military defeat for North Vietnam.
   b. The Tet Offensive upset and confused Walter Cronkite.
   c. Frank McGee raised the question of how useful it was to continue fighting as destructively as we were in Vietnam.
   d. The Tet Offensive turned the media against the war and showed Americans how deceiving the government's reports had been.

Supporting Details

6. _____ TRUE OR FALSE? American planes dropped more explosives on Vietnam between 1965 and 1973 than were dropped during all of World War II.

7. General Westmoreland
   a. gave misleading reports to the public.
   b. did not support the president.
   c. pressured President Johnson to cut back on his commitment to the war.
   d. finally spoke out against the war after the Tet Offensive.

8. As Johnson's term as president ended,
   a. he was more popular than ever.
   b. Americans no longer cared what was done about the war.
   c. the war ended in an American victory.
   d. peace, not victory, became America's objective in Vietnam.

Transitions

9. What kind of transitional signal is used in the sentence below?
   a. Time
   b. Illustration
   c. Comparison
   d. Cause and effect

   Then with a suddenness which caught all America by surprise, North Vietnam struck into the very heart of South Vietnam. (Paragraph 10)

Patterns of Organization

10. Two overall patterns of organization of this reading are
    a. time order and cause-effect.
    b. list of items and definition-example.
    c. comparison-contrast and list of items.
    d. definition-example and cause-effect.

ADVANCED SKILL QUESTIONS

Summarizing and Outlining

11. Which of the following best outlines paragraphs 5–6?
    a. The North Vietnamese communist government was strengthened.
       1. U.S. counterinsurgency efforts were undermined.
       2. According to one expert, bombing had great disadvantages in North Vietnam.
    b. The U.S. would have done better in Vietnam if it had replaced bombs with knives and rifles.
       1. Bombs often killed civilians.
       2. According to one expert, bombing had great disadvantages in North Vietnam.
    c. The bombing of Vietnam did not lead to U.S. victory.
       1. The North Vietnamese communist government was strengthened.
       2. The U.S. counterinsurgency efforts were undermined because of numerous civilian deaths.

12. Which of the following best summarizes paragraphs 10–11?
    a. On January 30, 1968, North Vietnam launched its surprise Tet Offensive against South Vietnamese cities and towns. The Vietnamese holiday Tet celebrates the lunar new year and is traditionally supposed to determine family fortunes for the year. The Tet Offensive was a sign that the fortunes of the North Vietnamese would be good.

b. On January 30, 1968, North Vietnam launched its surprise Tet Offensive against South Vietnamese cities and towns. After a month of fierce fighting from which both sides suffered greatly, the North Vietnamese troops were turned back, and General Westmoreland claimed a great victory.

c. In January of 1968, the North Vietnamese launched a surprise attack called the Tet Offensive. Ferocious and bloody battles took place. For example, in order to retake Hue, an ancient Vietnamese cultural center, the allies had to destroy the city. The same thing happened in the village about which an American general reported, "We had to destroy the town to save it."

Fact and Opinion

13. _____ TRUE OR FALSE? "Lyndon Johnson's War" is almost entirely made up of the author's opinions.

Inferences

14. We can conclude that President Johnson
    a. was extremely cautious about escalating the Vietnam War.
    b. had great respect for George Ball's opinions.
    c. manipulated public opinion.
    d. welcomed opposing points of view.

15. As suggested in paragraph 6, Colonel John Paul Vann felt that the worst weapon for wars like the Vietnam War is an airplane because
    a. knives are cheaper.
    b. dropped bombs kill friends as well as enemies.
    c. rifles are better than knives.
    d. all of the above.

16. _____ TRUE OR FALSE? The author implies that the media greatly influence public opinion.

17. _____ TRUE OR FALSE? We can conclude that the author feels President Johnson should have taken George Ball's advice.

Purpose and Tone

18. The main purpose of the selection is
    a. to inform.
    b. to persuade.
    c. to entertain.

19. The tone of the article can be described as
    a. totally objective and thus without opinions about the war.
    b. nostalgic and sentimental about the 1960s.
    c. straightforward but sympathetic toward Johnson and Westmoreland.
    d. analytical and somewhat critical of Johnson and Westmoreland.

Argument

20. Label the point of the following argument with a **P** and the two statements of support with an **S**. Note that one statement should be left unlabeled—it is neither the point nor the support of the argument.

    _____ Johnson and Westmoreland tried to prevent the American public from learning the truth about the Vietnam War.

    _____ Westmoreland misrepresented the American strength in Vietnam.

    _____ President Johnson discouraged reporters from reporting anything that contradicted his claim that American victory was in sight.

    _____ The results of the Tet Offensive were politically disastrous for Johnson.

SUMMARIZING

Complete the following summary of "Lyndon Johnson's War."

When Lyndon Johnson became president, he enlarged the Vietnam War from a relatively small, obscure war to a major one. He began with increasingly large air bombing raids, which strengthened the North Vietnamese government and indiscriminately killed civilians, the people we were supposed to be helping. He also gradually but significantly increased

_____, leading to _____

_____

Throughout this escalation, Johnson and General Westmoreland led the Americans to believe the U.S. was doing much better in Vietnam than it really was. The truth came out after the North Vietnamese's Tet Offensive.

On January 30, 1968, North Vietnam launched its surprise Tet Offensive against South Vietnamese cities and towns. After a month of fierce fighting from which both sides suffered greatly, the North Vietnamese troops were turned back, and General Westmoreland claimed a great victory. _____

_____

As a result, Johnson's popularity plunged. He soon made two important announcements. First, the U.S. would limit its bombing of North Vietnam and seek peace; second, _____

This was the beginning of America's deescalation of the Vietnam War.

DISCUSSION QUESTIONS

1. The author quotes George Ball as saying, "Once on the Tiger's back . . . we cannot be sure of picking the place to dismount." What do you think Ball meant by "the Tiger's back," and why do you suppose he chose that image? Also, what did he mean by the words "the place to dismount"?

2. The author states that although the Tet Offensive was technically a military defeat for North Vietnam, "it was also a profound psychological victory." In what ways could the offensive be considered a "profound psychological victory" for North Vietnam?

3. What role do you think President Johnson's personality played in how he conducted the Vietnam War?

4. The author claims that President Johnson was "less than candid" with the American public about the conduct of the war and the U.S.'s chances of victory. How do you respond to that? Is it within a President's rights to tell the public less than the entire truth about a situation involving U.S. troops?

Check Your Performance   LYNDON JOHNSON'S WAR

Skill	Number Right	Points	Total
BASIC SKILL QUESTIONS			
Vocabulary in Context (2 items)	_____	x 4 =	_____
Central Point and Main Ideas (3 items)	_____	x 4 =	_____
Supporting Details (3 items)	_____	x 4 =	_____
Transitions (1 item)	_____	x 4 =	_____
Patterns of Organization (1 item)	_____	x 4 =	_____
ADVANCED SKILL QUESTIONS			
Summarizing and Outlining (2 items)	_____	x 4 =	_____
Fact and Opinion (1 item)	_____	x 4 =	_____
Inferences (4 items)	_____	x 4 =	_____
Purpose and Tone (2 items)	_____	x 4 =	_____
Argument (1 item)	_____	x 4 =	_____
SUMMARIZING (4 items)	_____	x 5 =	_____

FINAL SCORE (OF POSSIBLE 100)   _____%

Enter your final score into the reading performance chart on the inside back cover.

10

Busy As a Bee? Then Who's Doing the Work?
Natalie Angier

Preview

The next time people praise you for "working like a beaver" or scold you for being "lazy as a sloth," refer them to this essay, first published in the science section of *The New York Times*. In it, author Natalie Angier challenges the myth about the supposed industriousness of our fellow creatures—and she explains how doing nothing much at all can accomplish a great deal.

Words to Watch

ambling (4): walking leisurely
indolence (7): laziness
adaptive (9): helpful in survival
foraging (11): looking for food
pride's (12): belonging to a group of lions
spate (13): sudden outpouring
dormant (20): inactive
ruminants (29): cud-chewing animals
perimeter (32): outer boundary
herbivores (37): animals that eat only plants
maligned (43): falsely spoken of in a negative way
evocative (43): filled with emotion as well as meaning
loath (43): very unwilling
perverse (44): stubbornly wrong
niche (44): an animal's place in its habitat

During midsummer days, humans who feel the urge to take it easy but remain burdened by a work ethic might do well to consider that laziness is perfectly natural, perfectly sensible, and shared by nearly every other species on the planet.

Contrary to the old fables about the unflagging industriousness of ants, bees, beavers 2 and the like, field biologists engaged in a new specialty known as time budget analysis are discovering that the great majority of creatures spend most of their time doing nothing much at all.

They eat when they must or can. They court and breed when driven by seasonal 3 impulses. Some species build a makeshift shelter now and again, while others fulfill the occasional social obligation, like picking out fleas from a fellow creature's fur.

But more often than not, most creatures engage in any number of inactive activities: 4 sitting, sprawling, dozing, rocking back and forth, ambling° around in purposeless circles.

"If you follow an organism in the field for extended periods of time, and catalogue 5 every type of activity for every moment of the day, you can't help but come to the conclusion, by George, this organism isn't doing much, is it?" said Dr. Joan Herbers, a zoologist at the University of Vermont, who has written comparative reports of laziness in animals. "Being lazy is almost universal."

In fact, compared with other creatures, human beings spend anywhere from two to 6 four times as many hours working, particularly if family, household and social duties are taken into account.

But lest people feel smug about their diligence, evolutionary biologists are 7 discovering that animal inactivity is almost never born of aimless indolence°, but instead serves a broad variety of purposes. Some animals sit around to conserve precious calories, others to improve digestion of the calories they have consumed. Some do it to stay cool, others to keep warm. Predators and prey alike are best camouflaged when they are not fidgeting or fussing. Some creatures linger quietly in their territory to guard it, and others stay home to avoid being cannibalized by their neighbors.

So while there may not be a specific gene for laziness, there is always a good 8 excuse.

"When you just see an animal that looks like it's in repose, you may be looking at 9 any number of very adaptive° features," said Dr. Paul Sherman of Cornell University in Ithaca, N.Y. "You can't say it's simply doing nothing, and you can't always predict from common sense alone what the apparent rest is all about."

So diverse are the possible reasons for laziness that some biologists are beginning to 10 shift the focus of their research. Rather than observing the behavior of animals in action, as field researchers historically have, they are attempting to understand the many factors that lie behind animal inertia. They hope that by learning when and why an animal chooses inactivity, they can better understand key mysteries of ecology, like the distribution of different species in a particular environment and how animals survive harsh settings and lean times.

"In the past, field biologists focused on movement, foraging°, mating behavior," 11 said Dr. Herbers. "Now they're worrying about why animals sit still."

HOW THEY DO IT

A Repertory of Resting

Animals certainly give their researchers much to fret over. Dr. Craig Packer and Dr. 12 Anne Pusey, zoologists with the University of Minnesota in Minneapolis, have studied lions in the Serengeti since the 1970s, and they said nearly all of that time has been spent staring through binoculars at tawny heaps of fur, the pride's° collective immobility broken only by the intermittent twitch of an ear.

"A lion can lie in the same spot, without budging, for twelve hours at a stretch," said 13 Dr. Pusey. "They're active on their feet maybe two or three hours a day." In that brief spate° of effort, they are likely to be either hunting or devouring the booty of that hunt, which is one reason they need so much downtime.

"A lion can eat an enormous amount in one sitting," maybe seventy pounds of meat, 14 said Dr. Pusey. "Their bellies get extremely fat, and they look incredibly uncomfortable and incredibly immobile, lying on their backs and panting in the heat."

Monkeys are commonly thought of as nature's indefatigable acrobats, but many 15 species sit around as much as three-quarters of the day, not to mention the twelve hours of the night they usually spend sleeping.

'Monkeys Were Still Sleeping'

Dr. Frans de Waal, a primatologist at the Yerkes Regional Primate Center in Atlanta 16 and author of *Peacemaking Among Primates*, said that he was amused to discover the lax habits of the woolly spider monkey, which he observed in Brazil with Dr. Karen Stryer. One morning the two researchers awoke before dawn to get out to a distant observation site by 7 A.M., when they assumed the monkeys would begin their day's foraging.

"We were sitting there and sitting there," said Dr. de Waal. "By eleven o'clock, the 17 monkeys were still sleeping, at which point I fell asleep myself."

Hummingbirds are the world's most vigorous and energy-intensive fliers—when 18 they are flying. The birds turn out to spend 80 percent of their day perched motionless on a twig; at night, they sleep.

Beavers are thought to bustle about so singlemindedly that their name is often used 19 as a synonym for work. But beavers emerge from the safe haven of their lodge to gather food or to patch up their dam for only five hours a day, give or take a few intermissions. "Even when they're supposed to be most active, they'll retreat back into the lodge for long periods of time, and rest," said Dr. Gerald E. Svendsen, a zoologist at Ohio University in Athens who studies beavers.

11 Months of Immobility

The spade-foot toad of the southwestern desert burrows three feet underground and 20 refuses to budge for eleven months of the year. In that time it does not eat, drink or excrete waste, all the while conserving energy by turning down its core metabolism to one-fifth of what it is during its single active month. "If you find one of these dormant° toads, you've got it," said Dr. Vaughan H. Shoemaker, a zoologist at the University of California at Riverside. "It's just sitting in the soil like a rock or a potato."

Even the busy bees or worker ants of Aesopian fame dedicate only about 20 percent 21 of the day to doing chores like gathering nectar or tidying up the nest. Otherwise, the insects stay still. "They seem to have run out of work to do," said Dr. Gene E. Robinson, an entomologist at the University of Illinois in Urbana-Champaign. "They really do look lazy."

WHY THEY DO IT

Cost-Benefit Study Shows Rest Is Best

In his view, the myth of the tireless social insect probably arose from observations   22
of entire hives or anthills, which are little galaxies of ceaseless activity. "Human
fascination with the industriousness of social insects probably comes from considering
whole colonies rather than from considering what individuals in those colonies do," he
said. "But since we've been tagging individuals to see what each bee does, we've found
that any individual has a lot of surplus time."

Biologists studying animals at rest turn to sophisticated mathematical models   23
resembling those used by economists, which take into account an animal's energy
demands, fertility rate, the relative abundance and location of food and water, weather
conditions and other factors. They do extensive cost-benefit analyses, asking questions like:
How high is the cost of foraging compared to the potential calories that may be gained?

The Cost of Moving

Such a calculation involves not only a measure of how much more energy an animal   24
burns as it rummages about relative to what it would spend resting, but also a
consideration of, for example, how hot it will become in motion, and how much of its
stored water will then be needed to evaporate away heat to cool the body. Overheating can
be a deadly threat for many animals.

When they complete their computations, biologists usually end up respecting an   25
animal's decision to lie low.

"Let's say a moose spends so much time foraging that its body temperature rises   26
close to the lethal maximum," said Dr. Gary E. Belovsky, associate professor of wildlife
ecology at the University of Michigan in Ann Arbor. "And let's say a wolf comes along
and chases it. Well, that raises the moose's body temperature further, and it's likely to
drop over dead. The moose must stay cool if it is to survive."

Some scientists strenuously object to the use of the term laziness to describe any   27
animal behavior, which they say implies some willful shirking of a task that would
improve the animal's lot in life if it were done.

"Animals are inactive when they have to be," said Dr. Belovsky. "It's not as though   28
they're choosing laziness when they'd be better off doing something productive."

For example, moose are ruminants°, like cattle, and must stay fairly still while   29
digesting food, he said. For every hour of grazing on vegetation, he said, the moose needs
four hours to metabolize its food. "It has no other option but to be at rest," he said.

Flying Is So Draining

Researchers who have looked at hummingbird behavior have also concluded that the   30
tiny birds are perfectly justified in taking frequent breaks. To hover in midair while
sipping from long-tubed flowers, they must beat their wings in elaborate figure-eight
patterns at a rate of sixty times a second.

"The cost of their flight is among the greatest of any type of movement in the animal   31
kingdom," said Dr. Frank B. Gill, curator of ornithology at the Academy of Natural

Sciences of Philadelphia. "They burn more fuel in calories per gram of body weight when flying than anything else ever studied."

Flying is so draining that many hummingbirds and their African relatives, the sunbirds, are better off staying motionless unless the food they can obtain is very rich indeed. To help assure that they can get nectar without having to travel too far for their dinner, sunbirds will choose a territory and stand around on the perimeter°, waiting for the flowers within to become plump with nectar.

HOW THEY BENEFIT

Conserving Water and Heat

For some creatures, immobility carries so many benefits that they become almost Buddha-like in their stillness. The fringe-toed lizard, which lives in the desert of the southwest United States, sits motionless just below the surface of the sand for hours, with nothing sticking up but its eyes. As the lizards sit, the sand warms and invigorates them. "They're ready to lurch out at anything edible that passes by, like a butterfly," said Dr. Philip Brownell, a biologist at Oregon State University in Corvallis.

And should it see a predatory snake approaching, the lizard can further immobilize itself by suppressing its breathing. "The lizard just shuts off its engines," Dr. Brownell said.

What is more, by staying snug in its sandy blanket, the lizard cuts down on water loss, a constant threat to desert creatures.

In a harsh place like the desert, most animals spend most of the time waiting for water and coolness. Spade-foot toads come out only in July, when the annual rains bring insects to feed on. Male and female toads meet and mate the very first night they emerge from their rocklike state, and they then begin eating enough to put on an extra 30 percent in body fat required to make it through their dormant eleven months.

Several hundred species of mammals go into hibernation each winter, cutting down on energy expenditure by dramatically lowering their metabolic rates. In hibernating ground squirrels, for example, the heart rate slows to only one or two beats a minute, and the body temperature goes down to near freezing. For herbivores°, winter hibernation makes sense. "There's nothing for you to eat, the weather's bad, you can't reproduce, and there are still predators trying to eat you," said Dr. Sherman. "The best thing to do is go into suspended animation."

WHEN THEY MOVE

Vigilant Resters Spring to Life

But sometimes a biologist is stumped over apparent indolence that cannot be explained by obvious things like inclement weather. Dr. Sherman has been studying the naked mole rat, a peculiar social mammal that spends its entire life underground. He long wondered why the largest mole rats in a group did the least and seemed to sleep the most, but he found out one day when he introduced a snake into the colony he had set up in his lab.

"The big ones instantly sprang into action, and attacked the snake," he said. "We'd thought they were sleeping, but they were just maintaining quiet vigilance."

Such a need for vigilance may help explain why bees and ants spend so much time resting. Dr. Robinson recently has learned that honeybees have a soldier caste; members do little or nothing around the hive but are the first to act should the hive be disturbed. "They're like a standing army," he said. "They're hanging around the colony, not doing anything in particular, but they can be immediately mobilized." 40

Other bees and ants may be saving their energy for a big job, like the discovery of an abundant new source of food, which requires overtime effort to harvest it, or the intermittent splitting of one hive into two, which suddenly leaves fewer workers to do the same tasks. "A colony has a labor force bigger than it really needs to get through those critical episodes," said Dr. Robinson. 41

New studies show that social insects cannot afford to waste their energy on non-critical activities. It turns out ants and bees are born with a set amount of energy to devote to their colony, which for reasons that remain mysterious seems to have less to do with the amount of food they eat than with an inborn genetic program. "They're like batteries," said Dr. Peter Nonacs, who studies ants with Dr. Edward O. Wilson at Harvard University. "They have a fixed amount of energy in them, which they can use up quickly or slowly. The harder they work, the quicker they die." With that knowledge, Dr. Nonacs says he now has great sympathy when he comes upon an ant in repose. 42

And perhaps biologists who study inactivity can even lend luster to the much-maligned° creature that gave laziness its most evocative° term: the sloth. Found throughout Central and South America, the sloth hangs from trees by its long rubbery limbs, sleeping fifteen hours a day and moving so infrequently that two species of algae grow on its coat and between its claws. A newborn sloth sits atop its mother's belly and is so loath° to move that it freely defecates and urinates onto her fur, which she will only intermittently bother to clean. 43

But lest such sluggishness seem almost perverse°, the sloth is suited to its niche°. By moving so slowly, it stays remarkably inconspicuous to predators. Even its fungal coat serves a camouflaging purpose. With the algae glinting greenish-blue in the sunlight, the sloth resembles the hanging plant it has very nearly become. 44

BASIC SKILL QUESTIONS

Vocabulary in Context

1. The word *repose* in "'when you just see an animal that looks like it's in repose. . . . you can't always predict from common sense alone what the apparent rest is all about" (paragraph 9) means
   a. a state of rest.
   b. a state of being busy.
   c. poor health.
   d. despair.

2. The word *inertia* in "Rather than observing the behavior of animals in action, . . . [researchers] are attempting to understand the many factors that lie behind animal inertia" (paragraph 10) means
   a. frequent working.
   b. aggression.
   c. tendency to be inactive.
   d. great distress.

3. The word *shirking* in "laziness . . . implies some willful shirking of a task that would improve the animal's lot in life if it were done" (paragraph 27) means
   a. welcoming.
   b. recognition.
   c. avoidance.
   d. description.

Central Point and Main Ideas

4. Which sentence best expresses the central point of the selection?
   a. There are various reasons for animal behavior.
   b. Some species build makeshift shelters now and then, while others fulfill the occasional social obligation.
   c. Animals spend most of their time in inactivity, which serves various important purposes.
   d. Some biologists use mathematical models to figure out the factors behind animal inactivity.

5. The main idea of paragraph 37 is stated in its
   a. first sentence.
   b. second sentence.
   c. third sentence.
   d. last sentence.

Supporting Details

6. Some biologists have shifted the focus of their research from
   a. South America to Africa.
   b. lions to bees.
   c. plant eaters to meat eaters.
   d. animal activity to inactivity.

7. _____ TRUE OR FALSE? The main reason most animals are inactive is that they are watching out for enemies.

Transitions

8. The relationship of paragraph 29 to paragraph 28 is one of
   a. time.
   b. addition.
   c. contrast.
   d. illustration.

Patterns of Organization

9. In paragraphs 12–21, the author
   a. narrates a series of events in the order in which they happened.
   b. lists examples.
   c. contrasts animals.
   d. defines and illustrates a term.

10. _____ TRUE OR FALSE? After listing examples of inactivity among animals, the article goes on to discuss causes of that inactivity.

ADVANCED SKILL QUESTIONS

Summarizing and Outlining

11. Which item in the box would best complete the outline below of paragraphs 33–37?

---

a. The fringe-toed lizard
b. To wait for water and coolness
c. To avoid winter's difficulties
d. Herbivores

Reasons for great immobility in some species
1. To survive the hot, dry conditions of deserts

2. _____

12. Which of the following best summarizes paragraphs 38–44?
   a. Biologists have learned that one reason certain creatures are inactive is to maintain vigilance and preserve the energy to fight enemies. For example, the largest naked mole rats in a group are the least active—until an enemy shows up. Honeybees also have their "soldiers," inactive members whose job it is to protect the hive.

   b. Reasons for inactivity besides the weather are the need to guard against and fight enemies, as seen among naked mole rats and honeybees; the energy requirements of occasional big jobs, as with ants and bees; the need to conserve energy to extend individual lives, found in social insects; and the maintenance of camouflage, as with sloths.

   c. Other creatures that are inactive include the naked mole rat, honeybees, bees and ants, and sloths, who it turns out are not so much lazy as trying to be inconspicuous to their predators.

   d. New studies show that social insects cannot afford to waste their energy on non-critical activities.

Fact and Opinion

13. The supporting details of this article are mainly
   a. facts.
   b. opinions.

Inferences

14. The author suggests that scientists have only recently begun to
    a. study social insects.
    b. recognize the importance of animal inactivity.
    c. recognize the importance of animal activity.
    d. observe desert life.

15. We can conclude that animals must conserve their energy
    a. in the morning.
    b. when they are being observed.
    c. for life-sustaining activities.
    d. occasionally.

16. From the selection, we can conclude that animals
    a. are all alike.
    b. have few needs.
    c. should be busier than they are.
    d. tend to behave in ways that benefit their species.

Purpose and Tone

17. The article's main purpose is
    a. to inform.
    b. to persuade.
    c. to entertain.

18. The tone of the article can be described as
    a. very skeptical.
    b. somewhat alarmed.
    c. informal but objective.
    d. somewhat apologetic.

Argument

19. Label the point of the following argument with a **P** and the two statements of support with an **S**. Note that one statement should be left unlabeled—it is neither the point nor the support of the argument.

    _____ The myth of the tireless social insect may have arisen from the ceaseless activity in hives and anthills.

    _____ The sloth's inactivity makes it inconspicuous to predators.

    _____ Inactivity among animals is not laziness.

    _____ To digest its food, the moose must rest for four hours for every hour of grazing.

20. We might say that the myth of the tireless social insect (referred to in paragraphs 2 and 21) was the result of
   a. circular reasoning *(a statement repeats itself rather than providing a real supporting reason to back up an argument).*
   b. a hasty conclusion *(the argument comes to a conclusion based on insufficient evidence).*
   c. a false comparison *(the argument assumes that two things being compared are more alike than they really are).*
   d. changing the subject *(the evidence sounds good but has nothing to do with the argument).*

OUTLINING

Circle the letter of the outline notes that best cover "Busy As a Bee? Then Who's Doing the Work?"

A. Researchers are finding that most animals are inactive much of the time.
   1. Lions, monkeys, hummingbirds, beavers, spade-foot toads, bees and ants
   2. Moose, hummingbirds
   3. Fringe-toed lizards, space-foot toads, hibernating herbivores
   4. Naked mole rat, bees, and ants
   5. Bees and ants, social insects
   6. Sloths

B. Researchers are finding that most animals are inactive much of the time for various reasons.
   1. Much more inactivity among animals than previously realized
      Examples: lions, monkeys, hummingbirds, beavers, spade-foot toads, bees and ants
   2. Benefits of inactivity
      a. Balance energy intake and expenditure
         Examples: moose, hummingbird
      b. Adaptation to weather and its effects
         Examples: fringe-toed lizards, spade-foot toads, hibernating herbivores
      c. Maintenance of vigilance and energy for protection
         Examples: naked mole rat, bees and ants
      d. Energy conservation for future needs and longer life span
         Examples: bees and ants, social insects
      e. Camouflage
         Example: sloths

C. Researchers are finding that animals benefit from inactivity.
1. Balance energy intake and expenditure
Examples: moose, hummingbird
2. Adaptation to weather and its effects
Examples: fringe-toed lizards, spade-foot toads, hibernating herbivores
3. Maintenance of vigilance and energy for protection
Examples: naked mole rat, bees, and ants
4. Energy conservation for future needs and longer life span
Examples: bees and ants, social insects
5. Camouflage
Example: sloths

DISCUSSION QUESTIONS

1. Books, articles, and television shows about animal behavior are often very popular. How would you explain the fascination that animal behavior holds for people?

2. Do you have a pet? If so, how inactive is that animal? What do you think might be the similarities and differences between your pet's needs and the needs of animals living in the wild?

3. The article mentions that some scientists object to the term "laziness" being applied to animals and insects. The concept of laziness may apply only to humans. Can you think of any other human characteristics that are frequently attributed to animals? Do you believe the animals actually have those characteristics?

4. In writing about the animal researchers and their work, the author could have used a formal, scientific tone or a lighter, more informal approach. Which tone did she use, and why do you think she made that choice? Find examples to support your opinion.

Check Your Performance

BUSY AS A BEE?

Skill	Number Right	Points	Total
BASIC SKILL QUESTIONS			
Vocabulary in Context (3 items)	_____	x 4 =	_____
Central Point and Main Ideas (2 items)	_____	x 4 =	_____
Supporting Details (2 items)	_____	x 4 =	_____
Transitions (1 item)	_____	x 4 =	_____
Patterns of Organization (2 items)	_____	x 4 =	_____
ADVANCED SKILL QUESTIONS			
Summarizing and Outlining (2 items)	_____	x 4 =	_____
Fact and Opinion (1 item)	_____	x 4 =	_____
Inferences (3 items)	_____	x 4 =	_____
Purpose and Tone (2 items)	_____	x 4 =	_____
Argument (2 items)	_____	x 4 =	_____
OUTLINING (1 item)	_____	x 20 =	_____

FINAL SCORE (OF POSSIBLE 100)   _____%

Enter your final score into the reading performance chart on the inside back cover.

Limited Answer Key

An Important Note: To strengthen your reading skills, you must do more than simply find out which of your answers are right and which are wrong. You also need to figure out (with the help of this book, the teacher, or other students) *why* you missed the questions you did. By using each of your wrong answers as a learning opportunity, you will strengthen your understanding of the skills. You will also prepare yourself for the review and mastery tests, for which answers are not given here.

ANSWERS TO THE PRACTICES IN PART I

1   Vocabulary in Context

Practice 1

1. Examples: *cutting the police force in half, reducing the pay of all city employees*; b
2. Examples: *spades, hoes, rakes*; a
3. Examples: *wages, transportation allowances*; b
4. Examples: *unknown routes, loneliness*; c
5. Examples: *large crowds, skyscrapers, subways*; c

Practice 2

1. Synonym: *reveal*
2. Synonym: *distract*
3. Synonym: *clear*
4. Synonym: *touching*
5. Synonym: *serious crimes*

Practice 3

1. Antonym: *those who were in agreement*; c
2. Antonym: *genuine*; b
3. Antonym: *scarce*; c
4. Antonym: *harsh*; a
5. Antonym: *useless*; b

Practice 4

1. b
2. b
3. b
4. a
5. c

2   Main Ideas

Practice 1

1. *Topic:* d; *Main idea:* c
2. *Topic:* b; *Main idea:* c
3. *Topic:* c; *Main idea:* a
4. *Topic:* b; *Main idea:* c

Practice 2

Group 1. a. SD
        b. MI
        c. SD
        d. T

Group 2. a. MI
        b. SD
        c. T
        d. SD

Group 3. a. SD
        b. T
        c. SD
        d. MI

Group 4. a. T
        b. SD
        c. SD
        d. MI

Practice 3

A. 2
B. 1
C. 1, 9
D. 5

Practice 4

1. b
2. d
3. c

Practice 5

The implied main ideas may be stated in various ways, including the following:

1. There are several advantages for birds to stay in flocks rather than live separately.
2. Some cities are finding ways to limit traffic.
3. Workers in many developing countries prefer jobs at modern factories or plants, despite risks to their health and safety.

3   Supporting Details

Note: Wording may vary throughout these practices.

Practice 1

A. Main idea: Biologically, men and women are different in various ways.
1. b. Difference in strength
2. Differences in genes
   b. More than thirty hereditary diseases found only in men

B. Missing major details:
Buy sound-reduced versions of products
Use sound-absorbing materials at home
Become less noisy

C. Advantages:
1. Ability to reach a mass audience
2. Combination of sight and sound very effective
Disadvantages:
1. Large number of ads takes away from each ad's impact
2. Ads are very expensive

Practice 2

1. c
2. b
3. a
4. destroyed the once-powerful longshoremen's unions
5. c
6. a
7. b
8. a
9. drainage
10. c

4 Transitions

Answers to some of the items may vary.

Practice 1

1. Another
2. Moreover
3. First of all
4. third
5. Furthermore

Practice 2

1. After
2. until
3. often
4. Previously
5. During

Practice 3

1. However
2. in spite of
3. Even though
4. nevertheless
5. On the other hand

Practice 4

1. like
2. Likewise
3. in the same way
4. Just as
5. similar

Practice 5

1. for instance
2. such as
3. For example
4. including
5. To illustrate

Practice 6

1. Because
2. Consequently
3. Since
4. result in
5. Because

5 Patterns of Organization

Wording will vary throughout these practices.

Practice 1a

Main idea: . . . began with the death of a star.
2. The compressed gas became more and more compact as well as increasingly hot.
4. A small portion of the sun's outer material condensed to form the planets.

Practice 1b

Main idea: When overwhelmed by a heavy work load, there are several steps you can take to gain control.
2. Divide the tasks into three groups.
3. Break each task down into the exact steps you must take to get it done.
4. Do the easiest tasks first and go back to the hard ones later.

Practice 2

1. Number of items: 3
   Type of item: People's names that have become permanent parts of the English language
2. Number of items: 3
   Type of item: Ways to put preventive medicine into practice

Practice 3

A. Comparison; 1. People moving to a foreign country; 2. Newlyweds
B. Contrast; 1. Men; 2. Women

Practice 4

A. 1. *Cause:* the fruit had fermented
      Effect: the butterflies became drunk
   2. *Cause:* increased smoking
      Effect: increased risk of having a heart attack

3. *Cause:* a picture of a movie star on the cover
   Effect: the most magazines sold
4. *Cause:* interaction between biological heritage and learning experiences of a particular culture
   Effect: human behavior

B. 5. A torn ligament: *cause*
   A fractured ankle bone: *cause*
   Raheem could not play: *effect*
6. Cost of raising family: *cause*
   Cost of housing: *cause*
   Two-income families: *effect*
7. Products fail: *effect*
   Poor design: *cause*
   Poor performance: *cause*
8. Soil not blown away: *effect*
   Soil not washed away: *effect*
   Planting bushes and trees: *cause*

C. 9. a. Drops in SAT scores
   b. A "back to basics" movement
   c. A renewed student interest in foreign languages
10. a. Evolution, which gave groups a better chance of survival
   b. High-bridged, narrow noses
   c. The air is moisturized before entering the lungs

Practice 5

A. Definition: 2   Example: 3
B. Definition: 2   Example 1: 5
                   Example 2: 9

Practice 6

1. b   4. c
2. c   5. c
3. b

6   Summarizing and Outlining

Practice 1

1. 1, 3, 6
2. 2, 4, 6
3. 2, 4, 5

Practice 2

1. c
2. b
3. d

Practice 3

1. C
2. B
3. B

7   Fact and Opinion

Practice 1

1. F
2. F+O
3. F
4. F+O
5. F
6. F
7. F+O
8. F+O
9. F
10. F+O

Practice 2

1. F
2. O
3. O
4. F
5. F
6. O
7. F
8. O
9. F
10. O

Practice 3

1. O
2. F+O
3. F
4. F
5. O
6. F+O
7. O
8. F
9. F
10. F+O

Practice 4

1. F
2. F+O
3. F
4. O
5. O

8   Inferences

Practice 1

1. d
2. a
3. c
4. b
5. d

Practice 2

1. b		6. b
2. a		7. a
3. c		8. c
4. c		9. b
5. b		10. c

Practice 3

1. c
2. b
3. b
4. c
5. b

Practice 4

1. b
2. c
3. b
4. a
5. c

9   Purpose and Tone

Practice 1

1. I
2. E
3. P
4. I
5. P
6. E
7. I
8. P
9. I
10. E

Practice 2

1. P
2. E
3. I

Practice 3

A. 1. ironic
2. pessimistic
3. angry
4. enthusiastic
5. self-pitying
B. 6. contented
7. self-mocking
8. arrogant
9. mildly regretful
10. matter-of-fact

Practice 4

1. g
2. h
3. b
4. c
5. d

10 Argument

Practice, page 213

1. S, P, S
2. P, S, S
3. S, S, P, S
4. P, S, S
5. P, S, S, S

Practice, pages 215–216

1. c, e, f
2. b, c, e
3. a, b, e
4. c, d, f

Practice 1

1. b
2. c

Practice 2

2

Practice 3

4

Practice 4

1

Practice 5

Group 1: a
Group 2: b

Practice 6

2

Practice 7

1

Practice 8

4

Acknowledgments

Angier, Natalie. "Busy As a Bee? Then Who's Doing the Work?" Copyright © 1991 by The New York Times Company. Reprinted by permission.

Asimov, Isaac. "What Is Intelligence, Anyway?" Reprinted by permission.

Auth, Tony. Cartoon on page 166. Used with the permission of Tony Auth. From *The Philadelphia Inquirer Sunday Magazine*, May 31, 1992.

Calhoun, James F., and Joan Ross Acocella. "Making Time." From *Psychology of Adjustment*, 3rd ed. Copyright © 1990 by McGraw-Hill, Inc. Reprinted by permission.

Edwards, Gayle. "Preview, Read, Write, Recite." Reprinted by permission of Trend Publications.

Gamble, Michael W., and Teri Kwai Gamble. "The Development of Advertising," from *Introducing Mass Communication*, 2nd ed. Copyright © 1989 by McGraw-Hill, Inc. Reprinted by permission.

Garland, Hamlin. Selection on page 328. Reprinted with permission of Macmillan Publishing Company from *A Son of the Middle Border* by Hamlin Garland. Copyright © 1917 by Hamlin Garland; copyright renewed 1945 by Mary I. Lord and Constance G. Williams.

Gergen, Mary M., *et al.* "Baby Love." From *Psychology*, by Mary M. Gergen, Jerry M. Suls, Ralph L. Rosnow, and Robert E. Lana. Copyright © 1989 by Harcourt Brace Jovanovich, Inc.

Gergen, Mary M., *et al.* "Obedience: Milgram's Controversial Studies." From *Psychology*, by Mary M. Gergen, Jerry M. Suls, Ralph L. Rosnow, and Robert E. Lana. Copyright © 1989 by Harcourt Brace Jovanovich, Inc.

Greenwald, Dr. Harold, and Elizabeth Rich. Selection on page 169 from *The Happy Person*. Copyright © 1984 by Harold Greenwald, Ph.D. and Elizabeth Rich. Published in 1984 by Stein and Day.

Hughes, Langston. "Early Autumn." From *Something in Common* by Langston Hughes. Copyright © 1963 by Langston Hughes. Reprinted by permission of Hill and Wang, a division of Farrar, Straus, and Giroux, Inc.

Kellmayer, John. "He Was First." Reprinted by permission of Trend Publications.

Lacayo, Richard. "Considering the Alternatives." Copyright © 1987 by Time, Inc. Reprinted by permission.

Martin, James Kirby, *et al.* "Housework in Nineteenth-Century America." From *America and Its People* by James Kirby Martin, *et al.* Copyright © 1989 by James Kirby Martin, Randy Roberts, Steven Mintz, Linda O. McMurry, and James H. Jones. Reprinted by permission of HarperCollins Publishers.

Martin, James Kirby, *et al.* "Lyndon Johnson's War." From *America and Its People* by James Kirby Martin, *et al.* Copyright © 1989 by James Kirby Martin, Randy Roberts, Steven Mintz, Linda O. McMurry, and James H. Jones. Reprinted by permission of HarperCollins Publishers.

Mayer, Robert. "The Quiet Hour." Originally appeared as a "My Turn" in *Newsweek*. Adapted and used with permission of the author.

McCarthy, Colman. "Selling the Young on Drinking." Copyright © 1982 by the Washington Post Writers Group. Reprinted by permission.

O'Neill, Charles. Selection on page 326. Copyright © 1977 by Little, Brown, and Company. Originally appeared in Gary Goshgarian, Ed., *Exploring Language*.

Quinn, Virginia. "Motivation and Needs." Adapted from *Applying Psychology*. Copyright © 1984 by McGraw-Hill, Inc. Reprinted by permission.

Robertson, Ian. "Effects of Childhood Isolation." From *Sociology*, 3rd ed., by Ian Robertson. Copyright © 1987 by Worth Publishers. Reprinted by permission.

Sandburg, Carl. "Fog." From *Chicago Poems* by Carl Sandburg. Copyright © 1916 by Holt, Rinehart and Winston, Inc., renewed 1944 by Carl Sandburg. Reprinted by permission of the publisher.

Stark, Rodney. "Personal Relationships in the Not-So-Good Old Days." From *Sociology*, 3rd ed., by Rodney Stark. Copyright © 1989 by Wadsworth Publishing. Reprinted by permission.

Stark, Rodney. "The Older Family." From *Sociology*, 3rd ed., by Rodney Stark. Copyright © 1989 by Wadsworth Publishing. Reprinted by permission.

Stephens, James. "Hate." From *Collected Poems of James Stephens*. Macmillan Publishing Company, 1954.

Updike, John. "A & P." From *Pigeon Feathers and Other Stories* by John Updike. Copyright © 1962 by John Updike. Reprinted by permission of Alfred A. Knopf, Inc. Originally appeared in *The New Yorker*.

Verderber, Rudolph. "Managing Conflicts in Relationships." From *Communicate!* 6th ed., by Rudolph Verderber. Copyright © 1990 by Wadsworth Publishing. Reprinted by permission.

Winn, Marie. Selection on page 325 from *The Plug-In Drug: Television, Children, and Family*. Copyright © 1977 by Marie Winn. Published by Viking-Penguin, Inc.

Index